STRONG MOTHERS, WEAK WIVES

STRONG MOTHERS, WEAK WIVES

The Search for Gender Equality

MIRIAM M. JOHNSON

UNIVERSITY OF CALIFORNIA PRESS
BERKELEY   LOS ANGELES   LONDON

University of California Press
Berkeley and Los Angeles, California

University of California Press, Ltd.
London, England

© 1988 by
The Regents of the University of California

Library of Congress Cataloging-in-Publication Data

Johnson, Miriam M.
    Strong mothers, weak wives : the search for gender
equality / Miriam M. Johnson.
    p.   cm.
    Bibliography: p.
    Includes index.
    ISBN 0-520-06161-6 (alk. paper). ISBN 0-520-06162-4
(pbk. :alk. paper)
    1. Wives—Psychology.   2. Mothers—Psychology.
3. Sex role.   4. Sex differences (Psychology).
5. Dominance (Psychology).   I. Title.
HQ759.J645   1988
305.4'890655—dc19   87-30896
                               CIP

Printed in the United States of America

1   2   3   4   5   6   7   8   9

*For the two Rebekahs: my sister, Rebekah Poller,
and my daughter, Rebekah Johnson*

Contents

Preface

In reading this book, different people will find different implications in it for what could or should be done. I do not recommend specific courses of action. My task is to describe some connections that run so deep they go unnoticed in our everyday lives. Now, as the male-headed nuclear family is losing ground, perhaps this understanding can help us plan for a more egalitarian future.

Although I am addressing feminists, I hope the book will be read by many who do not consider themselves feminists but who are interested in the issues feminists address. The changes that are occurring affect everybody, and dialogues between groups need to be substituted for name-calling. I hope that the book will be used in classes on gender and can add to the understanding of how gender inequality is reproduced and how it might be changed.

Acknowledgments

No book is an island. This book could not have been written had I not read the works of other feminist thinkers both inside and outside the academy. Although I have not met many of them, I am indebted to them for communicating their insights and passions. I am also grateful to those who shared their ideas in the interdisciplinary seminars led by visiting scholars at the Center for the Study of Women in Society at the University of Oregon, Eugene. In addition to the intellectual stimulation provided by Center affiliates, the Center also provided me with secretarial help and with funds to buy released time from several classes in order to write. I gratefully acknowledge this support.

I also owe personal debts of gratitude to many individuals. I especially thank those colleagues who read the entire manuscript at one stage or another. First, there is Marilyn Frye, who was a visiting scholar at the Center when I was writing the first chapters. She not only read these but, after she left, continued to read, and to criticize, the manuscript. I found her clearheaded questions and comments enormously helpful. I also want to thank Jean Stockard, my colleague in the department of sociology and collaborator on an earlier book. She read not only the entire manuscript but sometimes various versions of the same chapter, and always made constructive suggestions. I also thank Marion Goldman, another sociological colleague, for editing suggestions and for helping me to be more accurate on some points. Mary Rothbart, from our psychology department, read an early version of the whole manuscript. I am grateful to her for liking it even though it does not quite fit the ways psychologists do "science."

Many other colleagues read and commented on portions of the manuscript relevant to their interests or provided general intellectual stimulation. I especially thank Aletta Biersack for comments on an earlier paper and a version of the chapter on anthropology. I also thank Joan Acker, Patricia Gwartney-Gibbs, Barbara Pope, and Jack Whalen. The general comments of several visiting scholars were also most helpful: Nancy Armstrong, Haane Haavind, Harriet Holter, and Barrie Thorne.

I also owe a special debt to the students in my classes who used the manuscript as a text at various stages of its development. Their reactions and suggestions were most helpful. I especially thank Judith Barker, Joyce Briggs, Sharon Elise, Mark Nallia-Tone, Kathleen Olson, Mary Lou Parker, and Patricia Raney, who read the manuscript, shared information and thoughts with me and were able to use the mother-wife distinction in their own work. I also thank former students who worked with me as the ideas in this book were developing: Michael Finigan, Sandra Gill, Kay McDade, and Jack Sattel.

I thank Nancy Chodorow and Karen Paige Ericksen for reviewing the manuscript for the press and providing encouragement along with criticism and many useful suggestions and references. I especially thank Sheila Levine and Rose Vekony, my editors at the press, for their steady support and good judgment.

Many people helped with the typing of the manuscript, both from the Center for the Study of Women in Society and from the Sociology Department. They were Leisha Sanders, Marcia DeCaro, Pam Borgman, and Lyn Cogswell from the Center and Vicki van Nortwick, Linda Kelm, and Ronald S. Larsen from the Sociology Department. I thank them all and most especially Lyn Cogswell and Vicki van Nortwick, who were able to transform a very worked-over typescript into perfect copy.

I did not consult my husband, who is also a sociologist, about the basic content of this book, and I thank him for understanding why I did not. He did, however, encourage me to write the book and helped with specific questions. He is my dearest friend and I thank him for being with me and for me. Although I did not consult my children directly about the book either, I have learned from them and grown with them, and what I say about the future fits with their lives.

Chapter One

Introduction

Over a decade ago I was impressed with an article whose author claimed that the Women's Movement was losing ground because it had become just another pressure group lobbying for a bigger slice of the capitalist pie, or just another pressure group within the heavily male-dominated socialist movement. Her lament was over the apparent loss of the original issue that fired the radical women's groups of the late sixties: men and male dominance. It is not enough, the author said, for feminist analyses to blame women's situation on "social forces" or "the family" or "the economy" when the problem comes from fathers and men.[1]

Since this indictment there has been a rich flowering of feminist analyses, but it remains true that, with some notable exceptions,[2] the radical core of feminism keeps getting lost. As analyses become more intellectually sophisticated and bring in more variables and sources of variation based on class, race, and cultural differences, the complexities grow and the focus on male dominance and men themselves is buried in diversity. One trend initiated within feminism in the 1970s that did focus on male dominance, most directly by Nancy Chodorow and Dorothy Dinnerstein, emphasized women's hegemony over early child care.[3] Unintentionally, this had the effect of blaming men's misogyny and male dominance more on women's mothering than on men.

This book is not a diatribe against men either. Not all men are to blame for the persistence of male dominance, nor are all aspects of any man, nor men only. I argue, however, that the reproduction of male dominance is something that men themselves are far more

1

responsible for than women, and I show specifically how this is so—yet need not be. This system of male dominance that defines women from a more typically male point of view and affects the gender development of girls has more to do with male peer groups and men as fathers than it has to do with mothers. The evidence for this connection is not obscure; it is just a matter of allowing ourselves to see it.

Feminism and Social Science

Sociologists Judith Stacey and Barrie Thorne in an article on the state of feminist theory in sociology lament that feminism has failed to radically transform paradigms in sociology. They are especially discouraged about sociology as compared to anthropology, about whose progress they are more optimistic than I. They contend that feminism has been somehow contained or coopted by either functionalist or Marxist traditions within sociology and that feminist thinking has been more successful in changing interpretive rather than positivist traditions.[4]

It is unrealistic to expect feminist approaches to effect anything like a total transformation in the positivist tradition in social science. Perhaps some of the "empirical" analyses we as feminists are so afraid of are "telling it like it is" but interpreting it wrongly. In my view, empiricism can be used in the service of a radical critique of "the way things are." Beyond this, it is essential that feminists also use empiricism to help in understanding why we see things as we do. Feminism itself could not have been "invented" in other times and places.

While Audre Lorde is probably correct to contend that one cannot use the master's tools to dismantle the master's house,[5] the tools of social science do not belong just to the master. A better analogy is that social science tools are knives that can cut both ways. It is neither possible nor necessary to start from scratch and dismantle the edifice. This is not to deny the pervasiveness of male bias in the social sciences, but science itself is not totally a male construction nor has it been impervious to feminist input. I believe feminist scholars (and I include myself here) are emerging from the era of the global critique of "man-made" science and are being more selective in their criticism. We really do not want a women's sociology, or a women's anthropology, or, for that matter, a women's "science."

Feminism's contribution to "social science" could be to encourage a broader focus and to discourage disciplinary parochialism. Feminism itself is interdisciplinary, and we need to make connections between disciplines that will shift and merge paradigms but not totally destroy them. In this book I discuss data from many different disciplines and various feminist perspectives. The feminism that informs my approach is one that applauds women's less hierarchical ways of thinking and women's ability to see connections instead of conflict. I try in this book to demonstrate the value of applying this approach to an examination of women's situation and to feminism itself. I hope that my analysis will help bridge some of the failures of communication between disciplines, between feminists, and between feminists and social scientists.

This is a book not of discovery but of interpretation. Much of what I do is to take an analytical approach to what radical feminists have been saying about heterosexual relations all along. I differ from many radical feminists, however, in my more positive view of "the maternal" and in my belief that inequality is *not* inherent or inevitable in heterosexual relations. I have no particular quarrel with many Marxist-feminist analyses, and my focus on ideological factors and noneconomic structures is done in the spirit not of minimizing material factors but rather of balancing the account.

My goal is to be sensitive to the diversity of women's experience but not to give up on the possibility of making meaningful generalizations by following through on a few simple distinctions. I try to maintain a focus on the problem of male dominance while locating this dominance more specifically in heterosexual interactions rather than in women's mothering.

Structural Points of Reference

Women and men are not just biological creatures; they are social actors who play, indeed live, many roles connected with the differing groups in which they interact and with which they identify. The patterning of relations between women, men, and children is not fixed by biology; rather, it is socially organized by institutions and roles. Every child has two biological parents, but this does not directly dictate the social structuring of the relationship among them nor their relationships with other kin. In spite of enormous cross-cultural variations, however, there are some socially constructed regularities in the patterning of reproductive relationships. These regularities are not directly determined by biology; they result from biological cues interacting with socially constructed patterns. I use these structural regularities as points of reference to analyze the developmental events that are involved in the social generation of male dominance.

One structural regularity is women's early caretaking of both male and female children, which means both male and female children's first attachment and identification figure is likely to be a female. Women's mothering gives women power over children of both genders when they are most malleable and the mother-child relationship constitutes the first step in both female and male children's induction into organized social life. In contrast to Chodorow and Dinnerstein, who in somewhat different ways stress the negative aspects of women's power as mothers and its relationship to male dominance, I point out the positive aspects and focus on other developmental factors that are more directly involved in the production of male dominance.

Another regularity, gender segregation of children's play groups, also seems to characterize all societies. This segregation, among other things, serves to support male gender identity and male feelings of difference from and superiority to females. Feminist thinking has not dealt with this aspect of the development of male dominance, partially, I suspect, because of the distinctly antifeminist uses to which discussions of male peer groups have been put. I am thinking particularly of books such as Lionel Tiger's *Men in Groups* that attempt to explain, and to justify, male dominance on the basis of male bonding. I begin with the argument that males tend to be more concerned than females with preserving gender distinctions and male superiority, and I maintain that these tendencies are more likely to develop in separate male groupings than in any direct early interactions with females.

My focus here, however, is on heterosexual marriage, which is another structural regularity. Marriage makes women into wives and gives adult men (not necessarily the biological or social "fathers" of a woman's child) a measure of control over mothers and children and over women's early primacy in children's lives. I argue that the structure of the husband-wife relationship, considered apart from other contravening sources of power, tends to define wives as lesser partners in any marriage. From an individual psychological standpoint, this can serve as a defense against the power of women as mothers. From a structural standpoint, marriage institutions tend to be controlled by men and serve to control and organize women's mothering.

Although conservative antifeminists and radical feminists might be willing to countenance these generalizations as true, liberals of various sorts might dispute any transhistorical or cross-cultural generalizations. I too am suspicious of "universals," but these cross-cultural regularities of which I speak are empirically established on a general level. Few anthropologists would dispute that heterosexual marriage and the social assignment of early child care to women are generally found to be normative in all societies. The ubiquitousness of gender segregation in childhood is perhaps less clearly established, but recent work tends to suggest that this too is found to characterize all societies. I use these "universals" not to support any argument about the inevitability of male dominance but merely to provide points of orientation for examining historically and culturally specific situations and their implications for gender asymmetry.

Men's "fathering" as a social role is less of a structural constant than women's mothering and is on a different level than the other three structural regularities I described above. Women "mother" but men do not necessarily "father." Indeed, in this culture "to father" a child means to impregnate a woman and implies nothing about the nature of the social relationship between father and child. Moreover, there is no generally understood social relationship of men to children cross-culturally. In this book, I especially analyze men's fathering as it is now constituted within nuclear families.

Wives versus Mothers

Throughout this book I maintain an analytical distinction between "mother" and "wife," viewed as both a role and an idea. I mean by *role* the system of expectations shared to some degree within a given group for the behavior of a person in a particular status. By *idea* I refer to the cultural image attaching to a certain status. Thus we have images of mothers and notions about what mothers' "roles" are, and we also have images of wives and what the "roles" of wives are.[6]

The first step is to distinguish between mother and wife social roles, or between the "maternal" and male-dominant "heterosexual" components of "femininity," with femininity itself being viewed as a cultural construct that emphasizes women's weakness as wives and ignores women's strength as mothers. I argue that it is the wife role and not the mother role that organizes women's secondary status. Although both women's mothering and heterosexual marriage are structural universals, they are best seen as constituting separate systems that may be related to each other and to the wider social system in a variety of ways. Using this distinction may help to reconceptualize how women's and men's relations in the world at large might be.

If one looks at concrete relationships, one may not always find husband dominance, but at an analytical level, holding constant other cross-cutting relationships, husbands are expected to be dominant over wives. Worry in our own society over hen-pecked husbands, battleaxes, and castrating bitches reinforces the point that husband-dominated marriages are the norm that these epithets help enforce. Some may argue that egalitarian marriages are the norm, but language usage tends to belie this. There are expressions suggesting that husbands may abuse their power and that wives may exert power, but the underlying assumption is that a husband should have the edge over his wife. To say a wife "puts in her two cents' worth" is common. We rarely hear this said of husbands, since two cents is not worth very much.

Some mothers are not wives, some wives are not mothers, some women are neither wives nor mothers, often women are both. I make this analytical distinction to show that heterosexual marriage can be viewed as a system separate from women's mothering and that the husband-wife relationship is male-dominated. This is a major theme underlying every chapter in the book.

In my view, male dominance cannot be totally explained by or reduced to material, economic, or demographic factors. By *male dominance* I mean the tendency in societies to assign the highest value to roles played or skills exercised by men. Although the content of the roles assigned to women and men varies considerably from society to society, whatever roles carry the most prestige are felt to be something that only males are able to do, or that males do better than females. Male dominance is also reflected in the tendency for males to hold more positions of overriding authority in a society. Women are not necessarily less *powerful* than men, but men tend to hold the kind of power that is considered legitimate, or by Max Weber's definition, "authority." Male dominance is also expressed in expectations that in a marriage the husband should exercise authority over his wife. Assumptions of male dominance underlie and explain why we perceive the same acts and positions differently depending on whether we are judging wife or husband. For example, the structure of marriage itself helps explain why women in the labor force outside the home do not insist that their husbands take greater responsibility for household work. Acting as a wife and assuming her duties is seen as demeaning for a man, while "wearing the pants" does not demean a woman in the same way. Thus when a husband acts as a housewife, he requires compensation, special appreciation, and praise; otherwise, his superiority is endangered. Against this backdrop the wife prefers to do the extra work herself rather than to be further beholden to her already "superior" husband.[7]

Husband-wife relationships are clearly not the only place male dominance shows up—indeed for some, marriage provides an oasis from this dominance—but, even though marriage provides women a measure of protection from other forms of exploitation by men, the relationship is expected to be male-dominant. Women are constrained to marry to avoid greater problems. Moreover, all males are not dominant over all females. Class and race privilege can overcome gender disadvantage in some instances, but heterosexual marriage is located in every class and race group. Perhaps this is another way of saying that marriage organizes gender relations in ways that are connected to but cannot be deduced from economic or political relations.

In the United States in spite of our lip service to egalitarian marriage, our psychological constructs as well as the organization of work and the male provider role push women to both need and want their husbands to be superior to them. Thus women are constrained to "choose" an asymmetrical relationship, which in fact reinforces the societal expectation that husbands be dominant. Many feminist analyses leave marriage ties unexamined, yet the marriage relationship is a fundamental organizer of gender relations and of women's mothering itself. This unequal marriage situation has implications for any serious analysis of the "equal parenting solution" to male dominance that many feminists advocate. In this society equal parenting will solve nothing; indeed it will reinforce male dominance unless husband and wife are more truly equal.

Fathers versus Mothers

My view differs from those who argue that male misogyny and male dominance are a result of men's absence from early child care. Although the initial impulse behind these arguments was to move us away from Freud's phallocentric vision, the practical result has been to lay the blame for male dominance at the feet of mothers. Making the distinction between mothers and wives avoids this implication and allows us to see that although male dominance is contradicted in the relationship between mothers and sons, it is clearly expressed and even exaggerated in the relationship between fathers and daughters. It is this latter relationship that trains daughters to be wives who are expected to be secondary to their husbands.

My work has been about gender development in the nuclear family (a type of family that is by no means universal), especially the ways that fathers, or children's images of fathers, affect children's personality orientations. In this book I contend that although girls and boys get mothering capacities and their general human orientation from their mothers, girls learn to be wives, to look up to men, from their fathers, especially in a nuclear family. This phenomenon is related to husbands' dominance over wives and to husbands serving as a link between the domestic unit and the "outside world." Boys encounter male dominance in connection with their fathers, whose stance toward their sons is partly that of a caretaker mother and partly that of a representative of the adult male peer group. As representatives of the latter, fathers, not mothers, have been the focus of "sex typing" in the sense of fostering a male-oriented dependence in girls and a male-oriented independence in boys. Chodorow and Dinnerstein and any number of other feminists concerned with the psychological aspects of gender inequality have contended that male misogyny and male dominance might be ended if males contributed equally to childcare.[8] In my view, this "solution" is premature and may prevent us from taking a closer look at male dominance within marriage and how it tends to reproduce orientations conducive to male dominance in children.

Male-defined Sexuality versus Gender

I also argue that in order to understand male and female parenting and the impact of men's fathering, it is necessary to distinguish between gender and sexuality. Our society (and Freud) tends to define men as sexually active and women as sexually passive or as objects of male sexuality. In my view both women and men are sexual creatures, capable of sexual pleasure and of playing an active or a passive role in sexual encounters. I disagree with those who assume that the difference between men and women is one of "sexuality." I use *gender* to remove connotations of superior and inferior, active and passive, more sexual and less sexual from the differences between females and males. These kinds of distinctions reproduce male dominance in a narrowly sexual context, using a paradigm of sexual intercourse in the missionary position to depict the "proper"—or worse, the "true"—relation between "the sexes." The whole arena of sexuality has become permeated with male dominance, thus erasing the active sexuality of women. Empirically, gender difference would seem to rest less on sexual activity, in which both men and women participate, than on gestation and lactation, which are functions of women only. Women's biological connection with childbearing, or any other biological fact, does not in itself, however, explain gender inequality, which in the last analysis is a social and cultural phenomenon, or, under modern conditions, partially a political decision.

Feminists, especially middle-class white liberal feminists, have been far more likely to criticize the mother role than the wife role. I argue, however, that it is not women's mothering but the constraint on women in this society to define themselves in terms of their relationship to men that lies more directly behind male dominance as manifested in this society. By definition, now, women as wives are not of comparable worth to their husbands. This is not necessarily "normal" in heterosexual relationships, but heterosexual relationships have been socially constructed to be this way. "Giving up on men," in my view, offers no large-scale solution for women; however, women are not going to be empowered so long as they are culturally defined and define themselves primarily as wives.

The overarching process in contemporary society is individualism, which has deep ideological roots in America. This individualism is the basis for the feminist claim that a person's gender should not be allowed to limit who and what a person can be. Although this trend is on the whole desirable, in practice it has often worked to the detriment of women as mothers. Rather than arguing that women cannot achieve equality until they give up "mothering" or until child care is shared equally with men, I argue that we should accept the facts that women are going to have babies and that women will tend to be more responsible for early child care than men, and, by deliberate social policy, we should keep these facts from being the impediment to women's equality that they have been made to be in this society.

This book, however, should not be taken as a recommendation for any specific policy or set of policies. Decisions concerning specific political stances involve a myriad of narrowly political and strategic considerations that cannot be dealt with "in general," and my analysis *is* general. My aim in writing this book is political only in the broadest sense; that is, I hope to bring into balance and perspective two concerns within feminism: the desire for greater equality and the desire that values more associated with maternal attitudes should govern the behavior of both women and men.

A Multilevel Approach

One of my aims is to bring social structural levels of analysis and understandings about personality development into better alignment with each other. One should not have to choose between personality explanations and social explanations; rather, we need to explore systematically how the two are related.

My focus is on social structural regularities, their interrelationships with each other, and their consequences for gender differentiated personalities. The regularities I discuss are in the domain of marriage, child rearing, and kinship rather than in the domain of economic or political organization. Because of the sharp distinction we in this culture make between the public realm and the domestic realm, we tend to see family and kin as somehow individual and private or as "given" by biology. In fact, the organization of kinship is fully as structural as the organization of the economy. How the domestic and public domains are related, or if they even are separate domains in the first place, is an empirical question. Nevertheless, even in modern societies, the social organization of gender cannot be deduced simply from economic and political relations.

In assessing the consequences of social structural regularities for gender-differentiated personalities, I adopt an inclusive approach that is compatible with object relations theory within psychoanalytic theory, with cognitive developmental theory and social learning theory within psychology, and with those symbolic interactionist approaches that have developed out of the work of George Herbert Mead within sociology and social psychology. Much of the friction, or noncommunication, between these various schools is unnecessary and might be alleviated by taking a broader view. My approach is inclusive and in this way fits within Talcott Parsons's theory of social action, a theory that attempts to bridge disciplinary distinctions between biology, psychology, psychoanalysis, sociology, and anthropology.

Although Parsons was neither analyzing nor criticizing male dominance and did not succeed in his own efforts to tie a theory of personality "need" structure to nuclear family structure, his overall approach, which attempts to take various levels of analysis into account, seems far more useful than those analyses whose main aim is to discredit the approach taken by another school of discipline.[9]

Parsons's model puts Freudian and Meadian insights together and assumes that self-images develop as a result of acting in a physical environment and, far more importantly, that they develop from interacting in reciprocal role relationships with others. Parsons translates Freud's nascent ideas about the internalization of social objects, an approach far more fully developed by object relations theorists within psychoanalysis, into the language of social roles. Freud sees the personality as made up of precipitates of lost objects, that is, the internalized representations of what a relationship meant emotionally and cognitively to a child at a certain stage of development. Internal representations, or "objects," are neither the real person nor the whole person but rather represent the meaning of a relationship to an individual at a particular time. Parsons uses the language of interaction in roles but understands that these internalized relationships are heavily laden with emotional meaning.

Parsons brings the Meadian, or symbolic interactionist, perspective into an analysis of earliest child development and claims that interaction from the very beginning of life is socially patterned and that an individual internalizes both sides of the interaction; that is, conceptions of self and other are formed simultaneously. Parsons makes links to classical drive-oriented psychoanalytic theory only in recognizing underlying biological propensities, but his concern is with how these vague organismic promptings are socially organized and given "meaning" in social interaction.

Parsons, then, treats the infant's first interactions with its caretaker as genuinely social, with both caretaker and child making adjustments to the other. This interaction is particularly significant for the infant because it is erotic, visceral, and total from the infant's standpoint, because of the diffuse pleasure of body contact and because of the infant's cognitive inexperience. The infant does not see beyond this relationship and its potential for pleasure or pain. But even in these earliest infant-caretaker interactions, social learning is taking place and mutual expectations are being established between "mother" and child.

From this general perspective, I argue that infants of both genders learn to become genuine "social actors," or to become "human," in interaction with a mother figure. This earliest interaction with a maternal figure (regardless of the person's gender) represents the common humanity that both genders share and lays down or consolidates the capacity to love and be loved, to care about as well as to be cared for, in both females and males. To the extent that women retain and elaborate this maternal orientation, they retain and elaborate qualities of caring and human connectedness. To the extent that males are constrained to differentiate "self" from "mother" because they are male, they gain a stake in emphasizing gender difference. This "difference" is reinforced by the idea that males are superior to females. But in so doing, men become less human in the sense that they are constrained to deny human con-

nectedness, and later, in a strange metamorphosis, may deny
women's humanity by making them into "other" and "object" and
representatives of "nature" outside of human culture.

Plan of the Book

This book is conceived in three parts. Chapters 1 to 3 introduce
my general theoretical perspective, show how it fits into feminist
concerns, and introduce some key distinctions and concepts. Specifically in Chapter 2, I describe an ongoing tension within the
feminist movement between a focus on gender similarity and role
assimilation and a focus on gender difference.[10] In connection with
the difference focus, I attempt to clarify thinking concerning women
and the family by introducing the distinction between women as
mothers and women as wives. I argue that women's secondary
status ultimately lies more in the structure of marriage than in
mothering itself. I introduce the idea that women's mothering provides a basis for women's solidarity and power, but women's being
"wives" in the "modern family" separates women from one another
in the pursuit of husbands and isolates women from one another in
nuclear families.

In Chapter 3, I make a parallel distinction between women's orientation toward interdependence and the dependence that women
are often accused of and accuse themselves of. In a rough way I
connect the former tendency with women as mothers and the latter
with women as wives. In preparation for a developmental account
of these orientational differences, I argue that women's tendency to
see themselves in relationship to others should not be viewed as a
complement to some more desirable tendency males might be
thought to have, but is rather the more basic and distinctively human orientation that both genders share but that men later tend to
reject.

In Chapters 4 to 7 I give an account of gender development and
differentiation as it takes place within a cultural framework that assumes male-headed nuclear families as the norm. These chapters
analyze how male dominance is reproduced within this particular
system. In contrast to the earlier feminist focus on the consequences of women's mothering for male dominance, I argue that

the male peer group and some aspects of men's fathering are more directly responsible for reproducing male dominance and the kind of gender differentiation that tends to keep women subordinate.

Chapter 4 gives my own version of the most important feminist work on the developmental consequences for males and females of women's hegemony over early child care. Chapter 5 describes the positive aspects of women's mothering and also how male peer groups affect male development and male self-images and stances toward females. In Chapters 6 and 7 I argue that the developmental consequences of men's fathering are quite different from those of women's mothering and tend to reproduce male dominance. There is another sense, however, in which individual fathers can temper this dominance. To show how fathers affect gender development, in Chapter 6 I use data from experimental and survey research and in Chapter 7 I use Freud's own account. I argue that it is the heterosexual aspects of gender development that fathers affect. In both these chapters on fathers I also discuss how homosexuality might logically be seen as a protest against the male-dominant aspects of the nuclear family system.

Whereas in Chapter 7 I point out those aspects of Freud's account of early gender development that are more or less accurate, in Chapter 8 I question the aspect of his work that conflates gender with male-dominated sexuality. I also begin the task of reconstructing from a perspective that does not assume male dominance our understanding of the bases for gender identity and how conceptions of gender develop. Chapter 9 provides a cross-cultural and historical analysis of women in the "modern family." I discuss matricentered "solutions" to male dominance in simple societies and in class societies and the effect of maternal orientations on modern Western individualistic societies. I then trace briefly the vicissitudes of middle-class women's efforts to gain a foothold in the public sphere in the United States in the nineteenth and twentieth centuries. In Chapter 10, I examine women's present situation in an individualistic society and suggest that gender-blind assumptions are not always in women's best interest. Finally, I suggest that marriage is losing its former centrality in middle-class women's lives as they increasingly partake of the individualism that men in this society take for granted. The decreasing importance of marriage is associated with much dislocation in the present but holds the possibility for constructive changes in the future. These changes must keep the differences that remain between women and men (women are mothers in a way that men are not) from hindering gender equality.

Chapter Two

The Question of Difference

Within the feminism of the nineteenth century that culminated in women's gaining the vote and within the feminism that resurfaced in this century during the 1960s, two contrasting tendencies can be found. On the one hand, there is a tendency to minimize gender difference, with a stress on the degree to which males and females share traits and capacities. On the other hand, there is an emphasis on the need to give value to what is more characteristically female. These contrasting tendencies among feminists have been referred to by various terms. Catherine Stimpson, founding editor of *Signs*, the leading interdisciplinary feminist journal, has called the first tendency "minimalist" and the second tendency "maximalist".[1] Minimalists minimize gender differences, and maximalists presumably maximize them. I prefer not to use these terms, however, because "maximalist" is misleading to the extent that it implies that the alternative to minimizing difference is to overplay, exaggerate, or celebrate difference. Obviously, in an overall sense men and women are basically similar; thus the differences between women and men are minimal. The term "maximalist" applied to those who speak of difference is likely to be used pejoratively to describe those who go "too far" in asserting difference. Of course, logically one might be able to go "too far" in minimizing difference, but as far as I know the minimalist-maximalist distinction has been used only by "minimalists."

Another contrast between these two tendencies is an emphasis on androgyny versus a woman-centered emphasis. Androgyny implies that combining the qualities usually assigned to one gender or the other is good and desirable, whereas a woman-centered emphasis may declare "women are different and women are better" than men. This women-are-different approach served as the organizing principle of Hester Eisenstein's 1983 book, *Contemporary Feminist Thought*.

On another level is the distinction between individualism and its critique.[2] Some feminists have focused on the right of all individuals to develop to their highest potential; others have claimed that this individualistic focus means only that women will become integrated as individuals into a man-made competitive society. These latter feminists would have us focus on a critique of this kind of society instead. The "individualists" focus on common human qualities and equal rights; the others criticize our competitive society and the male paradigm it represents.

I shall refer to the general distinction simply as that between a stress on *similarity* and a stress on *difference*. Similarity-versus-difference does not refer to the question of how different the genders are but rather to whether similarity or difference is emphasized in any given analysis.[3] There are virtues and pitfalls on both sides of the tension and some feminists have shifted their emphases through time in response to changes in women's situation.

The dialectic between similarity and difference is reflected in the contrasting social policies of assimilation and differentiation. The two policies arose in recognizable modern form in response to "the woman question" posed by the advent of industrialization in the 1800s.[4] One solution, the "rationalist" response, involved assimilating women and men, single and married, into industrial production, but this did not last. Instead, the ultimate solution, after much chaos, was the creation of a radical disjunction between home and work and the establishing of women in the former. This "romantic" response eventually won out and was embodied in the doctrine of the separate spheres. This was definitely a difference doctrine: middle-class married women were to hold sway over sweetness and light, intuition, morality, motherhood, and goodness, while men were to take on "the real world" of competition, wage labor, achievement, money-making, and providing.

Many feminist historians in the 1970s tended to view the doctrine of the separate spheres as an unmitigated evil that underlay a decline in women's status in the modern period, because it removed women from any direct role in production. More recently, however, other historians have emphasized the extent to which married women in the nineteenth century used their hegemony over motherhood and morality as a basis for claiming the right to vote, at first locally and then nationally, and to obtain an education, at least through high school. Women also used their "difference" to effect changes in the public sphere relating to child and maternal health and welfare.[5] These historians point out that even though farm wives contributed substantially to production, they were clearly subordinate to their husbands, who headed both the farm and the family, which constituted a single enterprise. The segregation of place of work from place of residence at least gave women some control over one area of life, which they then used as a basis for directly affecting arrangements in the public sphere. By the time women gained the vote in national elections in 1920, however, the emphasis was shifting toward similarity and assimilation.[6]

Similarity, Inclusion, and Assimilation

The most widespread tendency among the women who identified themselves as feminists in the 1960s and early 1970s stressed women's similarity to men, not their differences. The emphasis was on women's rights and not on women's culture or women's difference. The increasing number of women working outside the home coincided with the feminist push for equal rights in employment. The arguments for these rights were squarely based on the grounds that women should be judged by the same criteria that men were supposed to be judged by. Now, although women are by no means paid equally to men, the typical married woman does work outside the home, and in that sense, women have been assimilated to the male-dominated world of jobs.[7]

The younger and more radical feminists of the 1960s were concerned not so much with job assimilation as with sexual assimilation. The "sexual revolution" aimed to legitimate sexuality for women, and feminists stressed in their arguments the similarity between female sexuality and male sexuality. The emphasis was on the clitoris and orgasm and on women's need for sex and sexual freedom. This "revolution" carried much further the trends toward sexual emancipation in the middle class that had begun in the

1920s and virtually demolished the nineteenth-century dichotomy between asexual "good women" and sexual "bad women."

Unfortunately, this assimilation, which freed married women to work outside the home and to be sexual, has proved to be a mixed blessing. Although some women gained, many women are working at low-paying jobs in the public sphere while continuing to be responsible for home and family. Men are not increasing their participation in housework in response to women's working outside, and women are working two jobs instead of one. Women's sexual assimilation has also put pressure on women to be sexually available and may be related to an increase in rape and other kinds of unwanted sexual contact. Partially in response to these recognitions, many feminists who were stressing similarity earlier began to stress difference.

The feminists of the late 1960s and early 1970s, with the exception of lesbian separatists, tended to focus on women's exclusion from the rewards, challenges, power, freedom, and fun of the male-dominated world of work, politics, sexuality, and leisure. Liberals like Betty Friedan pointed out that housewives who are usually just as educated, competent, and energetic as their husbands cannot be expected to live vicariously through their husbands while imprisoned in a suburban wasteland. They needed jobs commensurate with their training. Alice Rossi's "immodest proposal" also emphasized the goal of letting women into the world of work on an equal footing with men. Socialist feminists explained women's problems as relating to the exclusion of women and their work (housework) from the public world of production and exchange. Shulamith Firestone, who constructed her own amalgam of socialist and radical feminism, saw equality explicitly as being attainable if we could but eliminate women's physical childbearing, thus making it possible for women to be fully assimilated into the world of work and sexuality.[8]

In contrast to the predominant tendencies toward assimilation, some radical feminists from the very beginning warned against assimilation to the male world and argued for varying degrees of separatism instead.[9] Ti Grace Atkinson, a nonlesbian separatist, urged women to end their identification with all those heterosexual institutions, especially marriage, that give women a stake in the male world and oppress them at the same time.[10] Although in a sense these feminists were *in fact* stressing difference because they rejected males and a world that they believed males had constructed, they did not want to *stress* women's difference because they felt that this difference was created in oppression. To embrace women's "virtues" seemed dangerous because they were presumed to have developed in the context of oppression.[11] From this standpoint then, both inclusion and difference are suspect. Women should not seek inclusion (except to destroy the oppressive male gender categories), and women should not stress difference (except to create a different person from oppressed women now).

The thrust for inclusion on an equal basis in the public world of work was complemented by research in psychology and sociology by feminist academians that focused on gender similarities rather than differences. When a psychological difference was found between women and men, there was a strong tendency to question the accuracy of the study or to attribute the difference to women's "socialization" (which presumably could be changed so as to eliminate the difference). Maccoby and Jacklin's *Psychology of Sex Differences* reported fewer differences than had usually been attributed to boys and girls; it is a compendium of scientific research documenting similarity. In sociology, Rosabeth Moss Kanter argued that any lack of competitive motivation on the part of women was a result of the dead-end nature of women's jobs. Her research suggests that if women were not excluded from the status ladders to which men have access, their orientation to occupational achievement would be identical to men's.[12]

Ethnomethodologists Suzanne Kessler and Wendy McKenna made a more radical argument that fits with similarity by questioning the fundamental assumption that there *are* two genders. They suggested that gender categories themselves may be arbitrary, or that the characteristics by which gender is "recognized" are arbitrary. By implication, then, assimilation could be effected by simply demolishing the differentiating categories.[13]

These feminists stressed similarity out of an acute awareness that difference had almost always been used against women to imply women's inferiority or incapacity. If a woman admitted to difference from a man, she was immediately in danger of admitting to deficiency or agreeing to give up some possibility. Naomi Weisstein in a classic early article noted that presumably "scientific" tests of characteristics or capacities (designed by men) always have right and wrong answers and that women always seemed to end up being wrong. Even women's presumed virtues were turned into failures, so best to emphasize women's similarities to, not their differences from, the dominant gender. Feminists had every reason to fear difference because difference was used to explain and justify women's secondary status. This fear continues, and, unfortunately, it continues to be justified. Jean Lipman-Blumen, a sociologist, shows how gender differences are used against women in sometimes quite contradictory "male control myths." In psychology, Rhoda K. Unger describes how women scientists for years have been disproving derogatory hypotheses concerning the way in which women differ from men, but as these hypotheses have been disproved and dropped, others have been substituted. Thus the emphasis on similarity, while empirically supported, has tended to have a defensive quality about it.[14]

A related fear of feminists in the 1970s had to do with biology. Most feminists who stress similarity have been extremely leery of any biological perspective on gender differences. If the differences that are used to justify women's disadvantaged position could be shown to be related in any way to biological differences, then it was feared that perhaps they were immutable and women's disadvantage must inevitably continue. It is true that biology has been used and continues to be used to "explain" and justify the status quo. For example, Steven Goldberg argues that because of their "hormonally based" aggressiveness, men try harder and compete more aggressively and therefore win in competition with women.[15] Since males' success is based on hormones, according to Goldberg, he concludes that nature has made male superiority inevitable. One might note that it is quite a conceptual leap from aggression to trying harder and to winning, but Goldberg's approach is characteristic of the simplistic nature of reductionist attempts to explain and enshrine male dominance by recourse to biology.

The stress on similarity was of course not simply negatively motivated by the recognition of the ways in which difference had been used against women. The similarity emphasis was mainly based on the profound truth that males and females are far more similar than different—biologically, psychologically, and even socially. Biologically, men and women have twenty-three chromosomes in common and only one chromosome that is different; both women and men have the same hormones, only in somewhat different proportions. Psychologically, men and women think, reason, possess the same gamut of emotions, and so forth. Most important, on the societal level, the predominant trend in modern society has been toward assimilation. Men and women go to the same schools, take the same IQ tests (tests that, incidentally, were designed to minimize gender difference), attend social functions together, are expected to marry and form a household together, and often have parents who at least believe in equal treatment. The high degree of assimilation in boys' and girls' school curricula made inequities stand out (boys took shop, girls took home economics, girls were cheerleaders, boys played sports). Now this unequal access has been seriously challenged and rectified to some extent.

Feminists in the 1970s helped the process of assimilation along considerably and (in spite of the current talk about backlash) changed the entire tone and level of public talk about women. One simply cannot say the sexist things nor make the sexist jokes that were commonly made by men in the 1960s. The jokes are still made, but not so publicly. Moreover, one cannot refuse to hire a woman on the grounds that she will "just get married and quit anyway." Perhaps of all the movements of the 1960s, feminism has had the most lasting impact. Women have been assimilated to a large extent into the occupational structure outside the home. This does not mean job discrimination has ended—far from it—but sexism has at least been defined and declared illegal and immoral. Women are human and women are individuals. These are the positive gains of minimizing difference.

Difference and the Challenge to
a Male Paradigm

Although there can be no doubt that the stress on similarity is generally correct and is basic to attaining equality, it is also important to be clear about the hazard of not recognizing gender difference. The danger is that those who minimize difference or attempt to eliminate difference in order to gain admission to the public sphere may be unwittingly accepting and thereby implicitly affirming a masculine view of what constitutes value. This includes accepting a masculine analysis of women's deficiencies and why these alleged deficiencies make women's exclusion and secondary status understandable or justifiable. Some emphasis on difference is essential to feminism if women are not to be swallowed up in masculinism. The difference emphasis says that women need to define themselves, to construct themselves, not in the image of men nor in the image of what men say they are but in an image they can call their own. This is not an easy task and simply affirming the extent to which male standards prevail will not do it. A case in point here is the pathbreaking work of Simone de Beauvoir. Even though she brilliantly analyzed the extent to which women are measured by male norms and standards of value, she nevertheless tended in her own life and work to valorize masculine perspectives.[16]

The shift in emphasis toward recognizing difference has emerged among feminists of all stripes and their academic counterparts. Betty Friedan, a representative of liberal feminism, in her book *The Second Stage* strongly affirms women's interest in the family or familial-type relationships that are not to be sacrificed to careerism but somehow combined with it. Friedan states that "we must admit and begin openly to discuss feminist denial of the importance of family, of women's own needs to give and get love and nurture, tenderloving care." Socialist feminists are increasingly questioning whether feminism can ever be totally compatible with Marxism because of the latter's economism and masculinist perspective.[17] Radical feminists have always stressed women's difference, focusing either on the existence and importance of female bonding or on males' sexual oppression of women. Mary Daly has been for a long time engaged explicitly in finding and creating a voice for women, even if the category "woman" must be renamed.[18]

In more strictly academic circles, the difference trend is unmistakable. As early as 1977 Alice Rossi seemed to some to contradict her earlier "immodest proposal," which stresses similarity, by suggesting that women's mothering capacities and needs were greater than men's and were not being met as society is now constituted. The scholarly historical work on women's friendships begun by Carroll Smith-Rosenberg and published in the first issue of *Signs* has continued and burgeoned, showing that women do bond, but in a way that is different from men, and also showing the extent to which twentieth-century women have been prevented from bonding by the increasing privatization of the family. Jessie Bernard in *The Female World* describes the positive aspects of women from a female perspective, not a male perspective. Dorothy Smith in sociology and many others in various disciplines have suggested that women's somewhat different perspectives can inform scientific methodology and help eliminate the male bias that now characterizes science.[19] There is also the work, which I will discuss in detail later, on women's mothering, which sees it as a basis for gender difference and to some extent as a cause of gender difference.[20]

In psychology, the work of Carol Gilligan on the differences between the moral thinking of males and females has won great popularity both within and outside academic circles and has become a focal point for a reintroduction of a positive view of difference. According to Gilligan, women are more likely to think in terms of responsibility and interdependence, whereas men tend to see moral issues in terms of rights and noninterference in the rights of others. Gilligan defines women's approach to moral dilemmas in a way that women can identify with, and at the same time she argues convincingly that the approach more characteristic of females than males is by no means inferior.[21]

Some difference feminists take the idea of difference much too far. Certainly it does a disservice to women and to the facts to posit an essential, unchanging, biologically given female "nature." Such "essentialism" is contradicted by historical and anthropological data on the diversity of human social arrangements and the diversity of cultural definitions of what women and men are and should be like.[22] Most feminists who stress difference, however, do not consider "difference" to be all-encompassing and invariant. Although gender differences exist, they are not absolute or irreducible, rather, they are in large part socially constructed.[23]

It is also dangerous to imply by difference that women are somehow inevitably associated with the private sphere, which often translates to "keeping out of things."[24] In modern times at least, power resides in the public sphere. The difference focus within feminism would be of little use to feminists if the bases of male power in the public sphere remained undisturbed. Women's difference then would need to gain a voice in the public sphere to move women toward more equitable gender arrangements. In the long run, recognizing difference and then bonding on the basis of that difference might allow women to become a positive force for social change that not only lets women into the public sphere but allows them to effect changes for women in the society as a whole, including changing the ideological separation between public and private.

Certainly the solution to women's inequality does not lie in emphasizing difference. For women to make progress, however, we must explore who we are and what we want to become on our own terms so far as possible. Thanks largely to the degree of assimilation women have achieved, we are in a better position to see our problem and to construct our own version of what women share and what women want. Although women's interests as women are cross-cut by class, race, and ethnic differences, all women have some things in common. Some claim women share only oppression, but I disagree. In the next section I suggest a way of thinking about oppressive and nonoppressive aspects of what women share.

Women and the Family

One of the most complex issues in thinking about similarity and difference has to do with women's relationship in the family. Feminists of the nineteenth century rarely questioned the value and importance of the family for women, even though they themselves may have chosen not to marry, but feminists of the 1970s saw the family as being highly problematic for women. Many feminists saw the role of wife and mother (usually spoken of in one breath) as that which was preventing women's inclusion in the public sphere, and more radical feminists saw it as the central locus of oppression. Now, as we have seen, some have reasserted women's desire for and need for relationships similar in some way to familial relationships. Is this reassertion of familial values to be taken as conservative backlash, or is it somehow related to women's reassertion of their right to difference?

In my view the question is unanswerable, or the answer must be "both," so long as we treat the concept of family, or more specifically the mother-wife role, as a single entity. Although in most societies biological mothers are expected to "legitimate" their offspring through marriage, both mother and wife are best viewed as social roles that are analytically separable from each other and from sexuality. By separating the concept of mother from the concept of wife, it is possible to see that women are one thing when seen as wives and quite another when seen as mothers. The mother "role" involves caring for and nurturing dependents, while the wife "role," if unmitigated by other status-giving relationships, involves being dependent on and in varying degrees subordinate to the husband.[25]

In this society, both men and women influenced by a more typically male perspective tend to assume that the main reason women need husbands to protect and support them economically is that they have children. Thus women's mothering is used to justify and explain as necessity women's being dependent on men in marriage.[26] But this is not as inevitable as it may seem. As the anthropologist Karen Sacks has documented in detail, in the vast majority of societies women's childbearing and child-caring has not impeded their heavy involvement in the economic, political, and cultural activities of their societies. The degree of their dependence on men is not determined by women's mothering.[27] The idea that childbearing is debilitating characterizes industrialized cultures, but not all cultures. Certainly the idea that the rearing of her own children could be a full-time occupation for an adult woman is very modern and without precedent, as far as I know, in earlier cultures. Childbearing is unquestionably a serious occupational hindrance for women in this society, but the cause is largely this society's social arrangements. Society could be arranged so that women's mothering would not create economic dependence. It would be difficult but not nearly as difficult as doing away with women's childbearing and child-caring.

The "sexual revolution" of the late 1960s fed into a tendency to see women's mothering capacities as impediments rather than as strengths. This seemed partially to be because the male paradigm defined motherhood as an impediment to sexuality and partially because motherhood was associated with wifehood and confinement to the nuclear family.[28] Now there are a number of feminists who see women's mothering as an important part of who and what women are. These feminists do not romanticize women's mothering as a glorious privilege nor as a sacred "duty," but they recognize women's mothering as central to what difference there is between women and men and see it as one basis for women's self-esteem.

Beyond this, as we shall see in examining the process of socializing children, it is not women's mothering that creates the kinds of differentiation between males and females that put women at a disadvantage, but rather certain aspects of male bonding and of male fathering. I will argue later that, in this society, fathers, not mothers, have been the focus of the type of differentiation between male and female children that can be debilitating for women. In speaking of the unequal status of "wives" relative to "husbands" and of the problematic aspects of male fathering for their female children, I do not leap to the conclusion that a woman would be better off rearing children without a husband. Although many women today are deliberately choosing to rear their children alone, this is unlikely to be a viable solution on a large scale if other institutional arrangements remain unchanged. My purpose in analytically separating mother from wife is to counter the tendency within feminism to blame women's mothering for women's problems. To do so is to buy into a "male paradigm."

Women as Mothers

Several feminists, coming from very different starting points, have depicted women's mothering positively. Mary O'Brien's concept of "reproductive consciousness," Sara Ruddick's "maternal thinking" and Adrienne Rich's "lesbian continuum," all contribute to an understanding of how women's mothering may serve as a basis for female solidarity and power.

O'Brien's Reproductive Consciousness

Mary O'Brien is a Marxist, who, significantly enough, began her career as a midwife and perhaps through this experience was led to focus on the importance of biological maternity to women's lives. O'Brien's project is to create a theory of reproduction to parallel Marx's theory of production.[29] In so doing she hopes to correct the male bias of Marxism. For O'Brien, women's ability to bear children is the "true" basis of gender difference (not sexuality, as Freud would have it) and is the material ground for women's "reproductive consciousness" that is in opposition to men's consciousness—the maternal principle versus the potency principle. O'Brien sees women and their progeny as the central phenomenon in reproduction and men's ability to impregnate as distinctly secondary because it is alienated from the birth process itself. Paternity is thus not a natural relationship to a child but a social right to a child. In order to ameliorate the uncertainty of biological paternity, men have created the institutional forms of the social relations of reproduction that have privatized women's "maternal consciousness." In O'Brien's words, "The historical isolation of women from each other, the whole language of female internality and privacy, the exclusion of women from the creation of a political community: all of these have obscured the cultural cohesiveness of femininity and the universality of maternal consciousness."[30] For O'Brien, "The opposition of public and private is to the social relations of reproduction what the opposition of economic classes is to the social relations of production."[31]

O'Brien sees marriage as fundamentally a contract between men in which they acknowledge each other's right to the issue of specified women's bodies (p. 236). This is similar to the anthropologist Lévi-Strauss's concept of the "exchange of women by men," but Lévi-Strauss stressed male bonding, not women's mothering. Rights in women and their offspring is also a conception lying behind Karen Paige and Jeffery Paige's analysis of public rituals in prestate societies. In these ritual ceremonies, men are, according to these authors, essentially negotiating, affirming, testing, or establishing the legitimacy of their social claims in women and their offspring.[32]

There are a number of points one might quarrel with in O'Brien's analysis. She sees at times, but fails to see at others, that biological facts are always interpreted through a cultural lens; for example, she errs (with Engels and many others) in thinking the discovery of "the facts" of the male role in reproduction is of crucial significance in human history. Actually, children may be claimed or rejected by men for any number of reasons; biological paternity is only one possibility. The biological fact of paternity is just another legitimation for men's social claims to a woman and her child—a legitimation that seems particularly compelling to modern minds since children are no longer "useful workers" in the way they once were. Children's usefulness now lies in representing the ego (or, for the sociobiologists, the genes) of the parent; hence, biological relatedness may seem especially crucial.

One may also quarrel with O'Brien's use of the public-private distinction. Women have played more public roles in other times and places than they do now, and the public-private split itself has been less clear-cut in other societies. Overall, however, it seems sound from both a scientific and a feminist perspective to analyze reproduction using women's capacity to bear and nurse children as the central phenomenon that then necessitates social agreements concerning men's (and women's) rights in women and children. This focus makes particular sense in analyzing premodern societies, as Karen Paige and Jeffery Paige have done, and is an important counter to the more characteristically male view that birth is "the tie which mires women in nature and thus precludes them from historical praxis."[33] This view epitomizes what O'Brien refers to throughout her book as "malestream thought."

According to O'Brien, "a widely based . . . women's movement cannot emerge from the devaluation of the intimate, humane, exasperating, agonizing and proud relations of women and children. The feminism of the pseudo man is passe."[34] In the last analysis, women's weapon, says O'Brien, is not the withholding of sex but the withholding of maternity itself. This sentiment has been echoed by Harriet Holter, a social psychologist from Norway. In her lectures in the United States she recommends, only partially facetiously, that women stage a "birth strike" until more humane ways of child-rearing are devised—ways that do not penalize women with respect to jobs and access to the public sphere and ways that genuinely take into account the best interests of both mother and child.[35] Women's connection with children, in other words, could be a basis for improving the lot of women and children, but as things stand now the male paradigm in contemporary society makes women's connection with children and motherhood into the explanation for women's lack of power. O'Brien is suggesting that women's mothering capacities could be a basis for women obtaining power.

The danger in O'Brien's work is that it could feed into compulsory pronatalist or antichoice arguments. Certainly just because many women and no men bear children does not mean that all women *should* bear children. To have a physical capacity does not make one duty-bound to use it. Neither should women's ability to bear children be used to justify placing the right to life of any fetus over the right of mothers to make their own judgments, which balance any number of maternal concerns about the quality of life in the future for themselves, for the unborn child, and for others.

Ruddick's Maternal Thinking

While O'Brien stresses women's greater biological closeness to reproduction and men's separation from it, Ruddick's work moves us
further away from women's physical childbearing to women's thinking as child-rearers. Starting from the philosophical position that
social practice gives rise to thought, Ruddick considers how maternal practices in response to the demands of children for "preservation, growth and social acceptability" give rise to distinctive ways
of "conceptualizing, ordering, and valuing." According to Ruddick
this maternal thinking, informed by feminism, can become important in reorienting public policy. Ruddick fully understands that
mothers are not necessarily all wonderful, or even good, but out of
maternal practices, mothers do come to develop conceptions of
what a good mother is and beyond this a stance toward life itself. It
is these conceptions and values that Ruddick describes.[36]

According to Ruddick, maternal thought differs from instrumentalism and scientism because in "preserving fragile life" it stresses
"holding" over "acquiring." Maternal thinking involves the practice
of "humility" in response to a recognition of both limits and unpre-
dictability; it also involves "a resilient good humor" or "cheerful-
ness" in the face of the ongoingness of life and the necessity to go on.
In a male-dominant society these capacities may be downgraded,
but such virtues require considerable control and discipline. Mothers not only preserve, they also seek to foster growth; maternal
thought expects change and expects to change with change. Finally, mothers seek to make the child acceptable to others, and it is
here that the child's growth may be stunted. That is, mothers trans-
mit to their children to varying degrees the values of the dominant
culture, a male-dominant culture in which women are subordinate
to men. Because of mothers' tendency to make their children acceptable to society, maternal thought needs to be transformed by
feminist consciousness.

Drawing on the work of Simone Weil and Iris Murdoch, neither
of whom were biological mothers, Ruddick summarizes the content of maternal thinking with the concept of "attentive love"
(p. 86). The capacity for attentive love—the capacity to ask "what
are you going through?"—constitutes the foundation of maternal
thought as well as a basis for subverting the strong pressures to go

against children's needs in order to ensure their acceptability in a male-dominant society. "Attention and love again and again undermine a mother's inauthentic obedience as she perceives and endorses a child's experience though society finds it intolerable" (p. 86). Thus Ruddick separates the idea of making the child acceptable to a male-dominant society from authentic maternal thinking, which would tend to support the child against the system.

Although she offers equal parenting by father and mother as an ultimate goal, Ruddick warns us that "we must not forget that so long as a mother is not effective publicly and self-respecting privately, male presence can be harmful as well as beneficial. It does a woman no good to have the power of the Symbolic Father brought right into the nursery, often despite the deep affectionate egalitarianism of an individual man" (p. 90). Rather than touting equal parenting, which after all can apply only to some parents, Ruddick argues that "we must work to bring a *transformed* maternal thought into the public realm, to make the preservation and growth of all children a work of public conscience and legislation" (p. 90). Beyond this, "the self-conscious inclusion of maternal thought in the dominant culture will be of great intellectual and moral benefit" (p. 88).

Ruddick carries this further in a later article, "Pacifying the Forces: Drafting Women in the Interests of Peace." In this work she relates maternal thinking to the idea of "preservative love" defined as "caring for or treasuring of creatures whose well-being is at risk." This kind of caring is at odds with military destruction, and indeed "the theory of conflict that maternal thinkers develop bears remarkable similarity to that of pacifists" (p. 482). Ruddick wrestles with the question of whether peaceable women might transform the unpeaceable military while reaping some of the power and benefits offered by military service. She concludes that pacifist goals in the public sphere might best be realized not by recruiting women into the military but by recruiting women into peace movements.

Ruddick's work is a model of sensitivity to the issues raised for feminists by the opposing tendencies of similarity and difference. Overall, her position is that maternal thinking has something positive to offer and may indeed save us from destruction, yet her final words warn us that associating women with peacefulness risks reinforcing gender stereotypes.

There is a danger for women in embracing maternal thinking if it means feeling that we must take care of everybody else in the world besides ourselves. O'Brien and Ruddick could be interpreted as calling upon women to mother not only children but also everybody on earth and the earth itself. Surely there is danger here of women becoming careworn with caretaking, while men continue to be cared for. Many women feel overburdened with caretaking already, especially poor women.

But this danger is why *maternal thinking as women's "difference" must be thought of simultaneously with similarity and assimilation*. The similarity stance and the push for inclusion in the public world has helped women to understand that it is legitimate to care for themselves and not "sacrifice" themselves for others. Ideally, women's caring is not an expression of sacrifice, not a giving up of self, but a recognition of interdependence and an expansion of self. The similarity stance also is an important antidote to the idea that maternal thinking is the only kind of thinking women can or should do. To say that women think more maternally than men does not imply that this exhausts the possibilities for women. Maternal thinking is only a tendency that has not been sufficiently valued.

The similarity stance also reminds us that maternal thinking is not something that only women can do. Most men, however, will probably need more training to be able to think maternally. Now many men seem only to value maternal thinking when women do it, and for men's benefit. The next step is for men to prove that they value maternal thinking by learning to do it themselves. This process of inducting men into the maternal virtues took hold in the nineteenth century when husbands were enjoined to listen to their wives and to allow themselves to become civilized by them. The process is still going on, and it is gaining ground.

Some have argued that maternal thinking will keep women mired in the status quo. I believe that this view can be held only by those who do not understand the extent to which maternal thinking has been distorted, submerged, and subverted by its embedment in the isolated, privatized, and male-headed nuclear family. Both O'Brien and Ruddick are well aware of this embedment but do not sufficiently isolate the structures that cause women's oppression. Neither do they stress how women's caretaking of each other might be the ultimate basis of bonding between women.

Rich's Lesbian Continuum

In 1976 Adrienne Rich described from both a personal and a scholarly standpoint the positive power of women's mothering in *Of Woman Born*. In writing this, she was ahead of the trend toward an emphasis on difference, but she was scientifically legitimating and making more popular a body of feminist thought that had appeared earlier. Carefully distinguishing between motherhood as an institution under patriarchy and motherhood as a relationship between a woman and her children, she draws on archeological, anthropological, historical, and other types of evidence to show the power that has been attributed to women's mothering in reality and in fantasy in other eras and even in the present. This power, however, has always tended to be undermined and controlled by patriarchal institutions.

Rich had three boys, and her observations support my view that mothers qua mothers do not respond to their children so much in terms of their gender as in terms of their being young children. Indeed, according to Rich, in loving their sons as human beings, mothers give sons their humanity even as they recognize that later on these sons will have to make choices between this humanity and the inhumane aspects of "the male group" (p. 209). Rich also maintains that it is not overweening mother love but rather the radical repression of dependency and humanity characterizing the male role that causes men to be emotionally dependent on women.

Although she had no daughters, Rich finds the mother-daughter relationship, in spite of its ambivalences and guilts, a basis for a vision of women's togetherness and strength. Even though most daughters in some ways feel that their mothers failed them, daughters nevertheless need their mothers in order to touch their own strength as women. This need becomes "the germ of our desire to create a world in which strong mothers and strong daughters will be a matter of course" (p. 225). Although many others have chronicled mother-daughter ambivalence and the role mothers have played in stifling sexuality,[37] Rich calls on us to separate the mother-daughter relationship from the mother's response to a male-dominant world and to focus on the simple primal cathexis between mother and daughter. In *Of Woman Born*, she says, "before sisterhood, there was the knowledge, transitory, fragmented, perhaps, but original and crucial—of mother-and-daughterhood" (p. 225).

In 1980, Rich wrote her highly influential article "Compulsory Heterosexuality and Lesbian Existence." This article is not a celebration of motherhood but rather of lesbianism and the life-giving powers of sexual expression. In this work, Rich shifts her image of what might form the basis for women's solidarity from the image of the mother to the image of the lesbian. On the face of it, this may seem very strange indeed if only because concretely there are far more mother-identified women in the world than lesbian-identified women. Moreover, lesbians, as Rich herself notes, have been dealt with by heterosexual feminists as either invisible or deviant. When we look at what Rich means by lesbian identity, or by a lesbian continuum, however, we are brought back again to maternal imagery, but to a maternal imagery that has been taken out of its embedment in a system of marital and sexual relations with men. In describing the lesbian continuum, she puts maternalism, sensuality, and caring together:

If we consider the possibility that all women—from the infant suckling her mother's breast, to the grown woman experiencing orgasmic sensations while suckling her own child, perhaps recalling her mother's milk-smell in her own; to two women . . . who share a laboratory; to the woman dying at ninety, touched and handled by women—exist on a lesbian continuum, we can see ourselves as moving in and out of this continuum, whether we identify ourselves as lesbian or not.

(pp. 650–51)

From this Rich goes on to show the continuity between identification experiences with each other that all women have had and the various resistances women, both individually and collectively, have put up against male tyranny throughout the ages.

By using the concept of compulsory heterosexuality, Rich attempts to help heterosexual feminists see the extent to which heterosexuality itself is an institution and an ideology that oppresses women. Far from being a mere choice or lifestyle, heterosexual relations as they are currently structured and have been structured historically constitute "a beachhead of male dominance" (p. 633).

Most heterosexual feminists, because of the emphasis in this society on sex and sexuality, have tended to take women's heterosexuality for granted to an even greater extent than they have women's mothering. Because of most people's unquestioning acceptance of heterosexuality, Rich has an uphill battle to convince women that it is the mechanism by which women are oppressed. She argues that each one of the various types of male power reflecting gender inequality outlined by the anthropologist Kathleen Gough are in fact ways of enforcing heterosexuality. These types include "the power of men to deny women sexuality or to force it upon them, to command or exploit their labor, to control their produce, to control or rob them of their children, to use them as objects in male transactions, to confine them physically" (pp. 638–39). Rich argues that "the issue we have to address as feminists is not simple 'gender inequality,' nor the domination of culture by males, nor mere 'taboos against homosexuality,' but the enforcement of heterosexuality for women as a means of assuring male right of physical, economical, and emotional access" (p. 647). Rich draws on Kathleen Barry and Catharine MacKinnon for many of her concrete examples of the uses and abuses of women by men. Both authors attempt to widen the oppressive implications of heterosexuality by showing the degree to which sex objectification is built into almost all male-female relationships. Making oneself pleasingly subordinate to males permeates most heterosexual interactions wherever they take place.[38]

If one thinks of lesbianism and heterosexuality in their narrowest, clinical sense, it becomes easy to dismiss Rich's argument as saying that all women have to do to end male dominance is start sleeping with women instead of men.[39] If one takes Rich's argument more abstractly, however, one can see that she is concerned less with heterosexuality as a sexual proclivity than as a set of institutionalized practices governing the relations between men and women that are damaging to women and that prevail far beyond strictly sexual activities. The idea of compulsory heterosexuality then locates women's oppression in heterosexual institutions that have controlled and coopted women and their children. In turn, the image of the lesbian, at its most abstract, can stand for women-identified women, women who bond with women, against these institutionalized practices based on the assumption of heterosexuality. Rich invites women to see "the lesbian" in themselves even though they may sleep with men.

Although the idea of a lesbian continuum may make sense in this society, the idea is less meaningful on a cross-cultural basis. All known societies have a concept of marriage as a fundamental element in social structure, but heterosexuality as an orientation may be overlaid by any number of other considerations. This culture's emphasis on sexual orientation is related to marriage nowadays being based on personal, subjective feelings and preference; hence, sexual feelings become especially relevant. Although sexual intercourse is a universal symbol of marriage, the institution of marriage could exist even within a society that was not heterosexist or homophobic. In other words, we live in a society that has made sexuality and sexual orientation of great importance to personal relationships, and marriage is increasingly seen as such a personal relationship. The lesbian continuum implies that heterosexuality is the enemy, when in fact male dominance in heterosexual relations is the enemy. Heterosexual relations have embodied male dominance, but I do not believe that this connection is inevitable or absolute.

Many lesbian and radical feminists disagree with this position because they see heterosexual relations as unequal by definition. For example, Jill Johnston in *Lesbian Nation* notes with some sarcasm that it is difficult to conceive of an equal sexual relationship between two people when one is the biological aggressor. It is, she points out, the man who retains the prime organ of invasion. But just because the penis and sexual intercourse has been symbolized as invasion does not mean it must continue to be. Intercourse could mean destroying the penis in a vaginal vortex, or it could mean mutual pleasuring. The meaning of intercourse does not inhere in the act but in the mind. Ti Grace Atkinson argues that equal heterosexual relations are a contradiction in terms: how can one have equality between master and slave?[40] But, again, the master-slave relationship is not inherent in men and women or in sexual intercourse but is socially constructed and symbolized.

Monique Wittig wants to do away with the term *woman* entirely because for her *woman* means a relationship of servitude to a man. I believe we lose too much by doing away with *woman*, which has connotations of strength. In my terms, what Wittig is saying is that *woman* has become the same as *wife*, and this is true. The lesbian insight is that the heterosexual couple *is* male-dominated and is expected to be male-dominated in spite of the egalitarian gloss we give to the idea of marriage.[41] Wittig suggests we use the term *lesbian* to mean "not being in the service of a dominant male."[42] Perhaps what needs to be done away with instead is the term *wife*, not in the sense of heterosexual partner, but in the sense of underling.

Women as Wives

O'Brien, Ruddick, and Rich all distinctly separate maternal orientations and concerns from their context in a male-dominant society. Rich makes this separation central in her thinking and explicitly suggests that heterosexual institutions, not motherhood, lie at the root of women's oppression. The basic contribution all three have made is to offer a counter to those who do not make such a separation and who in one way or another end up saying that to dispense with male dominance we must dispense with women's mothering. Jeffner Allen, for example, who takes the strongest stance against motherhood in Trebilcot's anthology on mothering, defines a mother as "she who produces for the sake of men."[43] She explicitly states that she is talking about a woman in patriarchy. Thus she says, "If woman, in patriarchy, is she who exists as the womb and wife of man, every woman is by definition a mother" (p. 315) and "motherhood is men's appropriation of women's bodies as a resource to reproduce patriarchy" (p. 317).

It is clear that Allen is aware of the patriarchal control of mothering, but she goes on to argue for the elimination of mothering. What Allen ends up showing she is against is "male sexuality," which "appropriates women's biological possibility in order to reproduce itself" (p. 318), and beyond literal mothering, men also appropriate all of women's "work" for the purpose of regenerating men (p. 325). Allen might find much to agree with in Rich, but she cannot envision mothering or sexuality outside of patriarchy.

On quite another level, some males, including small boys, come to extol motherhood for women precisely because of its male-dominated context. For example, Letty Pogrebin, in exposing the hidden agenda of "sex roles," describes the stereotypes of children: "Boys are Better. Girls are Meant to be Mothers."[44] But are we to take this explanation to mean that being a mother is by definition inferior? As Pogrebin continues her analysis, it becomes clear that there is nothing bad about being a mother per se, but rather that mothers are wives of men. She goes on to discuss "Big Daddy being in charge of the family" and exercising power outside the family: "Girls must be trained to admire and depend upon the men who exercise power and to believe themselves unworthy of controlling their own or others' destinies" (p. 41). Females are "to stay out of the action themselves" in public arenas and

> are themselves to be the incentives that motivate males to strive for power, the sexual and ornamental rewards that the male controls and sometimes marries. . . . As a wife, 'his woman' further rewards him with offspring (she 'gave' him a son) to carry on his name. . . . For this gender arrangement to come into being, girls must learn to see themselves as sexual entities after puberty and be motivated to be mothers after marriage. Only when she is under male control (married) can a woman be exalted in motherhood and her child be officially recognized.
>
> (p. 41)

From these quotes it should be clear that Pogrebin's analysis of the statement, "Boys are Better. Girls are Meant to be Mothers," does not really show that women's mothering accounts for boys being better; rather it shows that being a mother means being a wife to a husband who is seen as, defined as, and expected to be "better" than she.

In different ways both Jeffner Allen and Letty Pogrebin, two very different types of feminists, equate women's mothering with women's lesser status. On another level, however, they both clearly understand that men's control over women's mothering is the problem. The virtue of O'Brien, Ruddick, and Rich is to envision the possibilities for women's mothering outside a male-dominated context.

Feminists who do not separate motherhood from its male-dominated context are likely to interpret a positive evaluation of motherhood as conservative. For example, historian Mary Ryan interprets the "difference" emphasis and the more positive view of women taken by some feminists recently as "timidity" and as seeking the revival of "femininity" and family feeling.[45] Certainly, this could hardly be said of O'Brien, Ruddick, or Rich. They are not conservatives and do not recommend a revival of anything. Moreover, the mothers they depict are hardly timid. The alternative is not to go back to the 1950s, or to any other period for that matter, but rather to become more sensitive to the positive possibilities of women's mothering and to the negative implications of women's mothering in a male-dominant context. None of the authors I have discussed, however, have made a direct comparison between the status of wife and the status of mother.

Wives as "The Lesser" Cross-Culturally

O'Brien, Ruddick, and Rich affirm the idea that mothers qua mothers are neither weak, dependent, nor powerless. None claim that women are powerful as wives, but they do not explicitly make the comparison between mother and wife. Indeed, I know of no work that depicts the wife role as a strong role in itself. Wives may gain power through their husbands, wives may powerfully influence their husbands and through them influence the world, but there is always the underlying assumption that the term *wife* implies husband, and *wife* is the subordinate term in the relationship. A wife through other connections (such as the family she was born into) may have more power than her husband, but if we focus on only the husband-wife relationship, the wife is the lesser.

Among the various kinship roles that adult women play cross-culturally, the role of wife often tends to be least powerful. Although marriage may set up the possibility of other important roles for women—sister-in-law, mother-in-law, and of course mother and grandmother—within the husband-wife relationship, the symbolism of wife is as subordinate to husband. This may be seen in relatively egalitarian societies such as the !Kung, a band society that forages in the Kalahari Desert. Although there is some question about how egalitarian the !Kung are, the greatest gender inequality that exists seems to be associated with the husband's domination of the wife, particularly in the first years of marriage.[46] Among the not-so-egalitarian African Yoruba, women gain some power through their trading activities, yet, as wives, they must feign ignorance and obedience in approaching their husbands and they must kneel to serve them.[47]

In many societies, if a woman is expected either to exercise power or to symbolize power in her own right, she cannot hold the status of wife, because wife vis-à-vis husband implies low status.[48] Although the word *queen* in English most often denotes the wife of a king, it may also refer to a woman who rules in her own right. When *queen* refers to a woman who rules, however, the husband of this woman is not called a king but is a prince or a prince consort. This prevents the ruler from being a "wife" by rendering her spouse a prince (son) consort rather than a husband.

In the last analysis, then, it is not women's being mothers but their being wives that is connected to their secondary status to a greater or lesser degree (depending on any number of kinship or political arrangements) in all cultures. Through marriage mothers become wives, and this basic element of kinship systems places males in control of women. Yet marriage in all cultures is also often mandatory or made strongly preferable to other alternatives. The solution for individual women is ordinarily to choose marriage, but the structure of marriage has undergirded women's inequality as wives.

Wives in the United States

Rich is perhaps more correct than even she knows about the degree to which marriage as a heterosexual institution par excellence reinforces male superiority in our own society. The point is not so much that marriage in this society allows a male to beat or rape his wife, though this is true and deplorable, but rather that marriage itself is predicated upon inequality. The good marriage is seen as one in which the husband is superior to the wife in age, height, strength, judgment, earning capacity, and public status. If the husband is not all of these, then we say that his masculinity is threatened and that she is not "feminine." Female superiority as a wife in virtually all respects runs counter to the implicit rule that adult heterosexual relationships are to be male-dominated.

This view of marriage can be seen most clearly in the middle class in the United States precisely because other kinds of kinship relationships, obligations, and claims have been minimized. The marriage relationship tends to be the core adult solidary relationship and as such makes the very definition of "woman" become that of "wife." The name of the game for a middle-class woman has been to find a man who is better than she and to gain a livelihood and status through him. Until recently in the middle class it was considered extremely important that a woman be married to become a mother. Beyond this, being a mother has been subordinated to being a wife in that children have been viewed as the romantic fulfillment of the couple (having his baby); the couple's relationship takes precedence over the children and the children are not allowed to interfere with it.

Among working-class black women, being a mother has not been as closely connected to being a wife as it has been among middle-class white women. The reason for this in part is that black males are often in no economic position to provide, and therefore the status of wife carries no economic survival benefits for the black mother. Black women, because of their lesser dependence on a husband's financial support, seem more likely to hold their own mothers in higher esteem than white women hold their mothers. Many middle-class white mothers were so financially and psychologically dependent on men that they defined men and marriage to their daughters as not necessarily good but their "only hope."

But as marriages become less stable and as more and more women work outside the home, the inequality of heterosexual interaction continues. So long as women are thought of and think of themselves primarily as attractive facilitators of men's enterprises, as real wives or office wives, there is little hope for equality. The male language itself has made women into cute appendages in roles where they are potentially equal. Women finally got the national vote more readily by being suffragettes rather than suffragists, they joined men as coeds rather than as students, and upon marriage joined the JC-ettes as wives of businessmen. And now, at least in terms of pay, women hold "jobettes." These disabilities are related to women's status as wives or potential wives, not as mothers.

The symbolism of wife is apparently well understood in the United States today. In an article for *Working Woman*, Kathleen Fury reacts to the *New York Times* report of a poll showing that only 6 percent of their respondents checked "being a wife" as one of the two or three most enjoyable things about being a female—well behind both career and motherhood. Fury suggests that women still very much want an equalitarian relationship of friend, lover, and life companion (the equalitarian marriage); being a wife, however, suggests inequality, taking a back seat, economic dependence, being a provider of personal service, and loss of self.

Now marriages are unstable, and a higher proportion of women are unmarried than men.[49] Relatedly, the proportion of women who undertake motherhood without marriage is rapidly rising.[50]

The rising rate of births to unmarried women forces us to reconsider women's mothering and to see it as an important separate component in women's lives. As women examine what is best for them and their children, husbands are no longer automatically seen as the solution. Indeed, in many circumstances, most notably when they are jobless, husbands may be more of a problem than a solution.

Wendy Luttrell, writing in the *Socialist Review*, describes working-class women's attitudes toward mothering as very positive. They do not see themselves as burdened by children and place great value on the mothering experience. Luttrell comments, "As these women talked about the need for ending sexist job classifications so they could survive in the world 'without the backing of a man,' they also talked of expanding their dreams and expectations for themselves and their children."

We do not yet know what the new evolving feminist paradigm will look like, but in my view it will embody an increasingly positive evaluation of women's "maternal thinking." This positive evaluation will not be coupled with pronatalist policies, the banning of abortions, nor a retreat into the home. Rather, maternalism will cease to be defined as the cause of women's oppression (it is too bad you have to stay at home with the kids and be dependent on your husband) but will instead become definitive of values that need to be realized in the public sphere and within heterosexual relationships.

More crucially, to the extent that a female paradigm can gain a power base, the inequality that prevails in cross-gender relationships, not women's childbearing capacity in itself, will increasingly be seen as the cause of women's oppression.

Summary

In this chapter I have argued that feminism as an ideology is not to be identified with either an argument for women's similarity or for their difference from men. Both these perspectives have always been present within feminism. The similarity perspective lies behind a push for the inclusion of women in the public sphere on the basis of their similarity to men. The difference perspective has reminded us that women are not men and that what men "are" is not necessarily desirable. Often the difference perspective has implied that women's traditional association with the family (which has now become private and sharply separated from the public sphere) cannot be all bad. I contend that in speaking of difference, we must analytically separate women's situation in the nuclear family into its two main aspects: wife and mother. Women become one thing when viewed as wives and quite another when viewed as mothers. Male dominance characterizes the heterosexual husband-wife relationship and its extensions in other male-female interactions. This husband-wife relationship, though potentially egalitarian, lies behind women's secondary status within the family at present and adversely affects women economically and politically by making women dependent on men.

In the next chapter I will discuss women's "difference" as it might be seen by women and how it has been interpreted from a male perspective as dependence and inadequacy. The difference women see is more connected to maternal thinking; the difference men see is more related to a perception of women as wives.

Chapter Three

Defining Difference:
Psychological Perspectives

In Chapter 2, I made a distinction between women as mothers and women as wives. In this chapter I want to make a distinction between women's orientation toward interdependence and dependence. Too often in stereotypical thinking the orientations related to women's mothering, which include caring about others and seeing self in relation to others, are merged and fused with images of dependence and passivity. Confusing interdependence and dependence is akin to speaking about mother and wife in the same breath. In this chapter, I will review various attempts to conceptualize how women might differ from men in terms of personality orientations. I begin with Carol Gilligan's work and the further research it has stimulated, and then review other distinctions, going all the way back to Talcott Parsons's expressive-instrumental distinction.

Each of the conceptualizations I discuss can be viewed as attempts to recognize a vital "something else" besides the culturally dominant mode. There is something else besides instrumental action and agentic action to get things done; there is something else besides separate and bounded egos and protecting the individual rights of self and others. This "different" voice can be used as a critique of a culture in which male perspectives predominate. This "difference" attributed to women can also be turned against women, however, and used to discriminate against them.

Generally, though, feminists are coming to see the nondominant mode as more attractive and valuable and as deserving legitimacy.

At the same time, a clearer conception of just what this presumably more typically female mode may be is being developed. Gilligan's "different" moral voice, for example, is not new, but she gives this voice more cultural value and new depth and sophistication. Gilligan's book is a persuasive plea for the worth of this more typically female orientation, even though she offers little empirical evidence of the sort psychologists accept that it does indeed differentiate between men and women.

Beginning in the 1970s and using Parsons's instrumental-expressive distinction as a starting point, my colleagues and I began conducting research on expressiveness. Instrumental action is means-end action aimed at controlling the environment outside the immediate interactive system. Expressive action is directed toward interpersonal relationships and the socioemotional meanings of acts and objects. Because instrumental values are so prominent in our culture, expressive action has been downgraded and has been difficult to define in ways that do not sound pejorative.

In our research we begin to rehabilitate the concept of expressiveness by defining and measuring it in such a way that it cannot be confused (as it has often been) with emotionality, dependence, and incompetence. Our findings suggest that the most consistent difference between women and men across diverse samples occurs with regard to the expressive dimension and that instrumentality, at least as we measured it, does not constitute a unitary dimension nor does it consistently differentiate between women and men. I use these research findings to critique some of the reigning ideas of the 1970s in psychology, including the concept of androgyny, and some of the explanations for women's lack of achievement.

It is important to understand that an orientation toward expressiveness or relationality (I use these terms interchangeably) as such has little bearing on power. Power has been taken from women by the privatization of their more relational orientations by marriage and by the cultural emphasis on the male-dominated heterosexual couple. In the United States, women's expressiveness has been put in the service of individual men in the home. This association accounts for why some women are wary of claiming a more relational orientation for themselves: in this society, expressiveness or relationality has been associated with an individual woman "taking care of" a man and his progeny under his headship. Whereas a woman's relational needs get defined as her "dependency," men may disguise their dependency needs because they are being met every day by women—wives, mistresses, secretaries, and daughters. In fact, women are financially dependent on men, but this dependence must not be confused with psychological dependency. Given a different power situation, women's maternal thinking and greater orientation toward interdependence could be the basis for a more humane society.

A Different Voice

Many of the issues concerning difference and feminists' stances toward difference discussed in the previous chapter resurfaced in response to Carol Gilligan's *In a Different Voice*. Gilligan, a developmental psychologist at the Harvard School of Education, contends that women tend to construct the moral domain differently than men. While men tend to think of morality in terms of individual rights and noninterference with the rights of others, women are more prone to think in terms of interdependence and the balancing of conflicting responsibilities in making moral decisions. Because masculine modes of approach to moral issues prevail in the public world of social power (including the construction of "tests" measuring moral development), they influence both genders, but women often find these approaches deficient. Gilligan argues that what may sometimes appear to be indecisiveness, lack of clarity, or dependence in women's moral reasoning is produced when women's different construction of moral issues comes into conflict with the controlling masculine view. Gilligan's aim is to articulate the moral voice associated with women so we can hear it as strong, viable, and legitimate in its own right.

Gilligan is careful to point out that she is not talking just about the cliché between male "justice" and female "mercy" or (worse yet) male "thinking" and female "feeling" (p. 69). Rather, she is describing two different ways of constructing the moral domain. Women are more likely to think in terms of equality, process, conflict resolution, not hurting, and caring for others. In masculine conceptions, these considerations may appear to be weak-minded or "unprincipled," but to women they may constitute an alternative perspective, not an unprincipled one but one that is difficult to articulate in terms of principles or one that balances a complex variety of "principles." This perspective is not well captured by the questions and scoring procedures used to measure moral development. Even though adult females, especially educated ones, may give the "right" responses by pinpointing the "right" principles, the assumptions embodied in the measurement procedures remain flawed. Gilligan's point is that Kohlberg's scale and the culture's whole approach misses or sidelines another reality. The moral reality women see is by no means totally different, however; it is not "another world" but is very much a part of both men's and women's world, and it needs to become an integral part of our thinking about morality.

Gilligan lets us hear this different female voice by her own lucid analysis of selected quotations from individual girls and women in various contexts. She uses male and female children's responses to Kohlberg's moral dilemmas to argue that his "stages" of moral development are more often stages of *male* moral development because they do not adequately take into account the perspective more typical of females. She also draws on interviews with such diverse groups as college students from a class on moral and political choice, pregnant women considering the pros and cons of abortion, and matched male and female subjects in a study of life-cycle changes. Although her evidence is not of the sort to pass rigorous scientific muster, apparently many people, including feminists, felt intuitively familiar with what she was talking about and hailed her book as a major breakthrough.

Perhaps because her focus was on morality, or perhaps because the timing of her book coincided with a general trend toward an interest in difference, Gilligan's work has received more attention than similar efforts that preceded hers. Not all of this attention has been favorable, however, and negative assessments have become more prominent as those who see the dangers in stressing gender difference react to the positive responses Gilligan's work elicited in the popular feminist press.[1] These criticisms run the gamut from those that claim the differences are not really there to those that claim the differences exist but they exist in response to oppression or they are the very differences that have kept women separate and stigmatized. For example, an interdisciplinary forum on the book, published in *Signs*, begins with a historian's warning that Gilligan's "different moral voice" sounds like and "reifies" the nineteenth-century doctrine of the separate spheres,[2] an argument that is not helped when Gilligan implies that biology may have something to do with this difference. The two psychologists' comments that follow tend to deny any difference (except as stereotype) and complain that Gilligan does not provide any systematic evidence from existing tests that men and women actually do differ.[3] The anthropologist, Carol Stack, concludes that Gilligan's typology is probably culture-bound and seems not to apply to African-American conceptions of morality. Stack suggests that there is an African-American model of moral development that women and men more nearly share and that sounds to me like Gilligan's more typically female (relational) approach.[4]

I am oversimplifying these positions, but I believe they generally miss the point and do not address what Gilligan was trying to do, as I have described it above. In response to these criticisms, Gilligan notes that educated women's ability to display male moral reasoning (in a context where they presume it is expected) "has no bearing on the question of whether they would spontaneously choose to frame moral problems in this way." Her point is that the instruments are not measuring what needs to be measured.[5] It is especially important to understand that "difference" does not mean a denial of the important degree to which men's and women's personalities and goals (and moral thinking) are similar. Overall, similarity and areas of difference need to be taken into account simultaneously; one does not preclude the other. Most differences are only tendencies.

Gilligan deals with the problem of similarity versus difference by recognizing that benefits have accrued to women from their partial assimilation to the masculine emphasis on rights. Women's increased emphasis on their own rights has allowed them to become less dependent on men, and, somewhat paradoxically, less dependent on typically male constructions of the moral domain. As women begin to see assertion of self as less dangerous, Gilligan tells us, they tend to move away from dependence toward a fuller expression of their belief in interdependence, and they also consider it moral to care for themselves as well as others. Thus the emphasis on rights may mitigate whatever tendencies women may have toward self-sacrifice. Put another way, the emphasis on rights

helps women to extricate themselves from the belief characteristic
of an earlier stage in women's moral development to the effect that
goodness means self-sacrifice, that caring for others must necessarily be at the expense of caring for self.[6]

Gilligan's book has already inspired and will undoubtedly continue to inspire others to attend to the female voice in other fields.
For example, the four authors of *Women's Ways of Knowing* apply a
version of Gilligan's description of women's construction of the
moral domain to women's approach to epistemology, or the question of how we know what we know. On the basis of 135 interviews
with students and recent alumnae of colleges and "invisible colleges" (human service agencies supporting parents), these authors
focus on a differentiation between connected knowing and separate
knowing. The authors point out that the procedures used by connected knowers are less well understood than the more culturally
legitimate procedures associated with separate knowing. Their task
is to make connected knowing more legitimate and to describe it in
such a way that it does not simply recapitulate and reaffirm the familiar objective-subjective, impersonal-personal type of dichotomies that have been used against women.[7]

Gilligan's work and the more recent work it has inspired are the
latest in a long line of efforts to delineate broad differences in orientation between the genders in a way that is not pejorative to
women and that does not take these more typically female modes
as deviation from the masculine standard. Although Gilligan's work
concerns differences in typically male and typically female ways of
thinking about morality, the contrasts she makes can be and have
been compared to other qualitative typologies used by psychologists to delineate differences in masculine and feminine orientations. Examples of such typologies include David Gutmann's distinction between allocentric (masculine) and autocentric (feminine)
ego styles, David Bakan's concepts of agency and communion, and
Talcott Parsons's instrumental-expressive distinction, which has
been in the literature somewhat longer.[8] These typologies, especially Parsons's, were ignored or rejected in the 1970s by those feminist scholars concerned with similarity and inclusion.

Gilligan, in answering her critics, denies that she is creating a
different typology and points out that she is simply criticizing
Kohlberg's classification system because it was created using male

subjects and reflects a male point of view. Nevertheless, she has described in some detail what she considers to be an alternative to the male view; in this sense her distinction can be compared to the earlier typologies.

Bakan Revisited

In the early 1970s several feminist psychologists employed distinctions made by David Gutmann and David Bakan to analyze research findings or to design research that could elucidate difference in a way that did not turn out to be pejorative to women. David Gutmann directly attacked the masculine bias in the psychoanalytic concept of "ego strength," arguing that its definition was based on attributes of the male ego only and thereby caused women to appear to lack ego strength. Gutmann attempted to counteract this bias by defining two types of egos. He characterized the masculine ego as allocentric, an ego that tends to objectify others and to experience its own separateness from others. In contrast, the autocentric feminine ego is characterized by more permeable boundaries in which the distinctions between self and others, and between self and environment are less rigid and more merged. Psychologist Rae Carlson found some support for Gutmann's distinctions in an analysis of the words, approaches, and constructs used by college students in written exercises. She concluded, however, that although Gutmann's formulation is clearly the better elaborated in portraying the qualities of masculine and feminine ego functioning, Bakan's formulation using the concepts of "agency" and "communion" is capable of addressing a wider range of phenomena.[9]

For Bakan, agency and communion are dynamic principles operating throughout nature. *Agency* refers to the organism acting as an individual in self-protection, self-assertion, and self-expansion. *Communion* refers to the organism as part of a larger whole and manifests itself in the sense of being at one with other organisms. "Agency manifests itself in isolation, alienation, and aloneness; communion in contact, openness, and union. Agency manifests itself in the urge to master; communion in contractual cooperation."[10] Bakan argues that if societies or individuals are to be viable, "unmitigated agency" must be combined with "communion." Thus, Bakan's formulation, unlike Gutmann's, allows for both masculine and feminine qualities in one individual.

Both Carlson and another psychologist, Jeanne Block, have used Bakan's very broad behavioral distinction to characterize aspects of masculinity and femininity. Carlson reviewed two samples of one hundred abstracts each of research on sex differences from Eleanor Maccoby's *Development of Sex Differences* and finds agency and communion to be applicable to almost all of those studies that found significant gender differences.[11] Carlson's own empirical work also supports the thesis that males express slightly more agentic themes than females in reporting significant emotional experiences. Moreover, she found that females combine agentic and communal orientations more often than males.[12] This fact will become important to my later discussion. Jeanne Block used Bakan's agency and communion to describe gender role changes over the life cycle because it allowed one principle to be tempered with the other. Block predicts that, as their emotional maturity increases during adulthood, both men and women may eventually arrive at an integration of both orientations, although males will specialize in agency and females in communion.[13]

Bakan's distinction is important in defining overall orientations, but it is also confusing. The concepts are so all-inclusive that their specific meaning is difficult to pin down. For example, the term *agentic* describes highly disciplined, self-oriented striving in the occupational world as well as the impulse-ridden self-assertion and self-extension of the infant. Such a remarkable equation may obfuscate more than clarify. If the referents of the concepts are carefully specified and not overgeneralized, however, they can be of use in producing a different and more complex picture of male and female differences and similarities.

Michael Finigan defined Bakan's concepts quite specifically and applied them in an observational study of the interaction in male-predominant and female-predominant groups, using groups of professionals in six social work agencies. In the interaction of these groups Finigan measures what Bakan calls "unmitigated agency" as "holding the floor for sixty seconds or more, interrupting, establishing the floor and reestablishing the floor." As one might guess, he found that males in both male-predominant and female-predominant groups were much more likely than females to engage in unmitigated agentic behaviors such as "floor holding."[14]

Finigan found, however, that although males were more likely to engage in "unmitigated agency," both males and females engaged much more equally in other agentic behaviors such as giving opinions and stating positions and in initiating ideas or solutions. Finigan also found that groups in which females predominated exhibited much more communal behavior—that is, they were more supportive of each other—than the groups in which males predominated. In male-predominant groups, although an individual might have an ally or so, an atmosphere of group supportiveness was absent. It is important to note that female professionals were supportive of each other. The giving of support was not something they did just for men, at least not in that setting. Finigan's work is important in showing that women do act agentically but in ways that are less likely to threaten the group's cohesion.

Expressiveness Revisited

Also in the early 1970s, I, along with several colleagues at the University of Oregon, attempted to use Parsons's more sociological and less global instrumental-expressive distinction as a basis for research on orientational similarities and differences between college men and women. Following Parsons, we defined expressiveness as a concern with the relations among the individuals within a social system, especially the attitudes and feelings of group members toward the self and each other. Instrumentality we defined as an orientation to goals outside the relational system itself. In Parsons's functionalist terms, instrumental action relates system to environment, and expressive action relates units within the system; both types of action are essential for the survival of any given social system. Both actions are goal-oriented, but the goal of instrumental action is external to the relational system and the goal of expressive action is internal to the system.

By the mid-1970s, Parsons's instrumental-expressive distinction had received much criticism from feminists. At the same time, however, the terms had been adopted by academic psychologists and were being used in "androgyny" research. Because the terms are still used, we decided to attempt to rehabilitate the concept of expressiveness by defining it carefully and by removing it from the context of Parsons's functionalism.[15] We wanted to show that the pejorative connotations that had been attributed to the concept are not a part of its definition.

One major line of criticism of the terms *instrumental* and *expressive* had to do with Parsons's use of them in his functionalist description of the family. Taking the nuclear family as the relevant social system, Parsons maintains that the adult male role is specialized in the instrumental direction and the adult female role is specialized in the expressive direction. Parsons views this specialization as functional for marital solidarity because it eliminates competition between husband and wife. Many feminists at the time took this view to be a prime case of Parsons's attempt to justify or legitimate the middle-class mentality of the 1950s, when married women did not work outside the home or worked at minor jobs. In other words, the instrumental-expressive distinction was interpreted as a legitimation for the male provider role and the stay-at-home-wife role.

Actually, however, Parsons's argument has nothing to do with justifying housewifery, which he saw as a shrinking and unsatisfying role for middle-class women. His argument is that the male role is anchored in the predominantly instrumental occupational sphere, and the female role is anchored in the more expressive kinship sphere. Thus, if one takes Parsons's statement about role specialization in the nuclear family as description rather than prescription, the statement is an accurate general characterization of the division of labor that tends to prevail in husband-wife families. Husbands do tend to be the primary breadwinners (they certainly make more money), and wives do continue to be primarily responsible for "taking care of the relationship." Parsons's error is not in his description but in his failure to emphasize the differential power that accrues to the male provider role and the high valuation of instrumental action in this culture.[16]

Our interest in the instrumental-expressive distinction, however, was not in using the terms to describe interaction in social systems but as general descriptors of gender-differentiated personality orientations. Here again, many feminists in the late 1960s and early 1970s rejected "expressiveness" because it had become associated with emotionality, incompetence, and dependence.[17] My associates and I questioned whether these negative connotations formed an inherent part of the definition of expressiveness and tried explicitly to counteract this view of expressive orientations.

Although expressiveness does engage socioemotional skills, it is misleading to view it as simply being emotional or emotionally labile. Expressiveness does not mean simply expressing emotion in an unpatterned way. Women, in this culture at least, are provided with patterned ways of expressing and negotiating socioemotional subtleties in interaction, whereas men are enjoined to be inexpressive or nonexpressive. Because of this inexpressiveness, men (when the inexpressive mask breaks down) are more likely to express raw emotion, spontaneous unpatterned emotion, than women. Women may resonate with, respond to, cope with, and even define emotion for others, but this is hardly the same as being emotional. Expressiveness then is an integrative skill, not unbridled weeping, so to speak. This view of expressiveness is consonant with Arlie Hochschild's description of women's "emotion work." Hochschild makes a clear distinction between being "easily affected by emotion" and the action of managing emotion.[18]

Neither should expressiveness be confused with dependence and passivity. The seeking of interpersonal rewards is not the same thing as being dependent and lacking autonomy. Expressiveness does not mean giving in to other people, although people in an instrumental culture would tend to interpret expressiveness in this way. This instrumental bias leads us all to think in terms of who is getting the best of whom. Expressiveness denies this way of looking at the world and does not see people and interaction as instrumentalities but more as ends in themselves. Thus, we attempted to develop measures that could separate expressive orientations from an autonomy-dependence dimension.

Finally, to lay claim to expressiveness does not mean one cannot also be instrumental. The research I and my colleagues undertook does not assume that instrumental orientations and expressive orientations are at opposite ends of a continuum, so that if one is instrumental, one cannot be expressive, but rather that they may constitute two separate dimensions. Whether the two are related and how should be an empirical question.

On the basis of the theoretical considerations described above, we had judges select adjectives from the Adjective Check List often used by psychologists that seemed to them to represent the three dimensions with which we were concerned: instrumentality, expressiveness, and independence or autonomy.[19] Only adjectives on which there was high agreement among the judges were used.

We presented these adjectives to male and female college students enrolled in introductory sociology courses at the University of Oregon and asked them to rate themselves on each adjective by checking "very true of me," "somewhat true of me," "somewhat untrue of me," and "very untrue of me." Multivariate analyses were applied to determine to what extent these students grouped items together into the three dimensions we had hypothesized.

The major finding from these analyses was that only the adjectives we had selected to represent the positive aspects of expressiveness seemed to form a unified group. Adjectives such as *sympathetic, understanding, pleasant, considerate, good-natured, warm,* and *obliging* clustered together as a distinguishable group.[20] The theoretical dimension we had labeled instrumental broke up into two distinct subgroups represented by *thorough, efficient, industrious,* and *planful* on the one hand, and *analytical, foresighted,* and *rational* on the other. The autonomous dimension contained three separate groups: (1) a stern, forceful, aggressive, outgoing, and assertive cluster, (2) an independent, active cluster, and (3) a daring, adventurous cluster. Thus expressiveness, but not instrumentality, showed up as a distinct dimension.

The largest difference between men and women students shown by the scores on these dimensions was that men saw themselves as less positively expressive than women. The differences on the other dimensions were much smaller. This finding is consonant with the results of Bennett and Cohen's earlier study of self-attribution of traits: "the major difference in the self-concepts of the sexes is that women conceive of themselves as being richer in the positive qualities of social warmth and empathy."[21] These authors go on, however, to say that women secondarily see themselves as more helpless, timid, and fearful than men and suggest that women's kindness may be developed out of fear of attack. That is, they offer the "psychology of the oppressed" explanation for women's greater expressiveness. Our findings based on internal correlations within sex groups, however, were that women tend to relate expressiveness to independence and that men do so much less clearly. Men strongly associated the words *active* and *assertive* with instrumental qualities and much less so with expressive qualities. These associations were not true for women, however. In other words, although these college women included positive expressiveness with positive instrumental qualities and autonomous qualities in their self-pictures, college men could not so easily include expressiveness with instrumental and autonomous qualities.[22]

Ten years later, in 1982, we returned to introductory level sociology courses at the University of Oregon with the same list of adjectives and instructions we had used before. The list was also administered to high school juniors and seniors at a small rural school in Oregon, and a subset of the items was administered to a statewide representative sample of male and female nurses. Using a similar analysis, we again found that a strong positive expressive factor underlay the self-ratings of both females and males in these diverse groups.[23] Indeed the expressiveness factor was even more clearly seen as a single factor by men in 1982 than it had been seen by them in 1972. Moreover, in every group in both years, women not only saw positive expressiveness as a unitary cluster but rated themselves significantly higher on these expressive qualities than men did.

The instrumental items continued to divide into an industrious cluster and an analytic cluster. College women in 1982 (but not in 1972) and women nurses rated themselves higher on industriousness than men. College men in 1972 and 1982 and the male nurses reported significantly higher levels of analytic characteristics (analytic, foresighted, rational). Not all males, however, see themselves as analytic, since among the high school students, women rated themselves as higher on analytic qualities than men. Moreover, the differences we found between adult men and women on the analytic items are much smaller than the difference on positive expressiveness.

With regard to what we call the autonomy dimensions, the factor structures were least consistent from one sample to the next, but two main factors appeared to be those of forcefulness (stern, forceful, aggressive, outgoing, assertive, independent, and active) and, secondly, adventurousness and daring. (The items "independent" and "active," which were separate in 1972, combined in 1982 with other items on the forceful dimension.) Although high school boys and male nurses, unlike college males, rated themselves as more adventurous than their female counterparts, there were no statistically significant gender differences in any of the groups studied on the large group of adjectives forming the forcefulness cluster.

Finding no gender differences in "forcefulness" contradicts the strong stereotype of forcefulness as "male."

The relative complexity and multidimensionality of both the instrumental and autonomy scales and the gender differences on them being small and related to life-cycle stages (high school boys see themselves as daring, and not analytic) strongly suggests that expressiveness is a more basic dimension of gender difference. At least as represented by our fairly diverse samples, males see themselves as having less of a socially desirable characteristic than females. This is quite different from the usual statement that females lack instrumental or autonomous qualities and thus by implication deserve their secondary status.

Our findings support a reconceptualization of gender difference in which it is males, not females, who claim less of certain desirable qualities. This reconceptualization is not a simple turning of the tables in which expressiveness becomes "good," and autonomy "bad." It is not what Alice Echols calls "the new feminism of yin and yang." Neither does it support Parsons's implication that instrumentalness and expressiveness are complements. Rather, our findings suggest a more complex view of difference in which females are able to combine expressive qualities with autonomous qualities in their self-pictures, and males deny expressiveness in theirs.[24] Expressive qualities in women have tended to be defined as the opposite of those forceful-autonomous qualities that men use to explain or justify male dominance. Our research suggests that females see their expressiveness not as the weak opposite of forcefulness but as a desirable and positive set of characteristics that do not necessarily limit their autonomy. Men are more likely than women to see autonomous traits as contradicting expressive traits. This latter finding suggests further that men are more likely to downgrade expressiveness than women, because they are more likely than women to associate expressiveness with dependence.

The Trouble With Androgyny

During the 1970s, feminist psychologists developed the idea of measuring "androgyny" as opposed to difference. In the original masculinity-femininity scales, if one were more masculine, one had to be less feminine. This idea needed to be challenged. Although the idea is not new that masculinity and femininity were multidimensional rather than unidimensional concepts and that they could not be represented by a single bipolar dimension with masculinity on one end and femininity on the other, feminist psychologists were the first to construct "androgyny" scales, which explicitly denied the bipolar assumption concerning masculinity and femininity.[25] The feminist impulse behind these scales was to counteract the negative assessment of women that seemed to result from an emphasis on gender difference by suggesting that the ideal personality might combine both masculine and feminine traits in its self-image. The desirability of androgyny might be tested by demonstrating that people who saw themselves as having both masculine and feminine traits would be more likely to respond appropriately to a greater variety of situations than people who saw themselves as either decidedly masculine or feminine.

Bem's Sex-Role Inventory consists of a mixed list of twenty stereotypically masculine characteristics (such as "self-reliant" and "competitive"), twenty stereotypically feminine characteristics (such as "happy" and "sincere"), and twenty gender-neutral characteristics. Subjects are asked to indicate on a seven-point scale how well each characteristic describes themselves. Subjects who score high in both stereotypically masculine and stereotypically feminine traits are considered androgynous.[26] The Personality Attributes Questionnaire is also based on stereotypes. On this test, subjects are asked to respond on a five-point rating scale ranging from strong denial of the characteristic to strong endorsement, or from one trait to its polar opposite; for example, not at all kind to very kind, very cold in relations with others to very warm in relations with others, and so forth.[27] Both scales are based on the requirement that the items be considered socially valued behaviors.

Matters did not work out well for androgyny, however, for a variety of reasons. Both Bem's Sex Role Inventory (BSRI) and Spence, Stamp, and Helmreich's Personality Attributes Questionnaire (PAQ) were widely used for a few years to measure androgyny before they were overtaken by serious attacks on theoretical, methodological, and philosophical grounds.[28] In my view, the basic problem with androgyny is simply this: Putting two wrongs together does not make a right; that is, combining sexist stereotypes of masculinity and femininity does not lead to a nonsexist solution.[29] The problem with Bem's and with Spence and Helmreich's measure of masculinity and femininity is that the adjectives they use do not accurately represent the concepts of instrumental and expressive, at least as I and my colleagues define them.

Although psychologists have adopted the terms *instrumental* and *expressive*, they have paid relatively little attention to their conceptual definition. Neither the BSRI nor the PAQ items were chosen with the terms in mind, but in summarizing their results, both Bem and Spence and Helmreich equate their masculine items with instrumentalness and their feminine items with expressiveness. Thus Bem considers words such as *childlike, shy,* and *yielding,* which were included on her scale, to be indicative of expressiveness, yet we would not associate these words with expressiveness by our or Parsons's definition. The PAQ includes "emotional" and "does not hide emotions" among its expressive items and includes both "independent" and "active" with its instrumental items. In our view none of these properly belong with expressiveness or instrumentalness. To some extent then, however well-intentioned, these conceptions of androgyny undercut the empowerment of women by reinforcing the stereotype of femininity (and expressiveness) as weakness and emotionality.

In fact, Bem's own early research showed that women who embraced the traits considered feminine-expressive on her scale to the exclusion of others were so passive that they were competent in neither masculine nor feminine spheres.[30] Although it is true that "femininity" is stereotypically associated with passivity and dependence, expressiveness, technically defined as a relational orientation, does not have this implication and did not seem to have this implication for our women subjects and for the women subjects in other studies that isolated this expressive factor.[31]

Another difficulty with the idea of androgyny as embodied in these scales is that it consists of equal parts masculine and feminine. This conceptualization precludes the possibility that expressive qualities are basic to the self-concepts of both genders and constitute the common human matrix from which men deviate in a negative direction. But this possibility is exactly what our research suggests: males see themselves as less expressive or relational than females, but females do not see themselves as less instrumental than males. Obviously, these findings challenge the perspective that tends to equate male with human and female as deviation.[32]

Bem has abandoned the study of androgyny in favor of a developmental focus on how children form "gender schemas" that they use to encode and organize information. She proposes that we try to raise "gender-aschematic children", that is, children who are less gender-conscious and less gender-differentiated. She does not propose (wisely, I think) that we attempt to eliminate recognition of gender difference altogether, but rather suggests that we try to confine the "meaning" of gender to the genital differences themselves.[33] Sensible as it sounds, it is difficult to limit gender to physiological differences, because these are themselves symbols. Physiological markers still leave the door wide open for masculinist interpretations—one has only to think what Freud was able to do with the fact that boys have penises! Physiological features are given social meanings with implications for social roles far beyond physiology. Even the physiological features one chooses to emphasize are telling. Bem tries to keep a strict parallelism (penis and testicles, clitoris and vagina). She ignores the uterus, undoubtedly because she feared it could be used against women. Simply warning children about sexist views as Bem advocates does not get at the male-dominant features of the nuclear family structure itself, where she assumes child-rearing should take place.

Interdependence versus Dependence

The confusing of psychological dependence with expressiveness partially explains why many feminists do not see expressiveness in a positive light. This confusion has also led some feminists into self-blame or a "women are their own worst enemy" position. The logic runs something like this: Women are expressive, which is erroneously assumed to mean dependent. This dependency is then seen as leading to any number of other defects such as blind conformity, passivity, inability to take control of one's life, and inability to achieve or to "get ahead." The next step is to conclude that women are their own worst enemy, which of course is what men have been saying, or suspecting, all along. Women are then exhorted to recognize these deficiencies, get over their dependency, take charge of their lives, quit complaining, and make something of themselves. Colette Dowling's *The Cinderella Complex: Women's Hidden Fear of Independence*, which appeared in 1981, is one example of this approach that became a bestseller. Dowling's main thesis is that "personal psychological dependency—the deep wish to be taken care of by others—is the chief force holding women down today" (p. 21).

I do not deny that women have dependent motivations, but these are brought about by structural factors (not the least of which is women's economic dependency on men) other than those related to women's expressiveness. As our research and women's common sense suggests, expressiveness is not the same as dependency, and many women do not associate it with dependency. Miriam Greenspan, author of *A New Approach to Women and Therapy*, argues, counter to Dowling, that women must not deny their authentic need for "intimate connection" by confusing that need with helpless dependency and then blaming themselves for being dependent.[34] As a therapist, she tries to show her women patients that their relational needs are legitimate.

The tendency to confuse expressiveness with dependency has also plagued studies of "achievement" in psychology. A widely reprinted article written a decade earlier by Judith Bardwick and Elizabeth Douvan provides an example. The article is entitled "Ambivalence: The Socialization of Women," and is itself a model of the authors' own ambivalence, created in part by the initial failure to separate dependency from expressiveness. They begin with a list of traits that they say are ascribed to women. This list includes psychological dependence, passivity, and fragility along with the more desirable traits of interpersonal orientation, nurturance, and supportiveness. They then argue that girls' problem is that they remain dependent on others for feelings of affirmation. When Bardwick and Douvan asked their students, both undergraduate and graduate, what they wanted, they answered, "When I love and am loved; when I contribute to the welfare of others; when I have established a good family life and have happy, normal children; when I know I have created a good, rewarding, stable relationship" (p. 231). While these statements do sound "traditional" in the sense that they imply children and marriage, they also express an active and responsible orientation to the general welfare of others. Bardwick and Douvan take a dim view of these statements, however, and conclude that "up until now very few women have succeeded in traditionally masculine roles, not only because of disparagement and prejudice, but largely because women have not been fundamentally equipped and determined to succeed" (p. 233). What it takes to succeed in these roles, according to Bardwick and Douvan, is "objectivity rather than subjectivity, aggression rather than passivity, the motive to achieve rather than a fear of success, courage rather than conformity, and professional commitment, ambition, and drive" (p. 233).[35]

Although Bardwick and Douvan criticize women for not meeting these standards, their point is that women are ambivalent about them. They point out that "the masculine [is] the yardstick against which everything is measured." They go on to say "since the sexes are different, women are defined as not-men and that means not good, inferior" (p. 234). The ambivalence women feel then is the product of women liking the way they are and at the same time, because both men and women esteem masculine qualities and achievements more, knowing that their own qualities are second rate. The authors then find it "disturbing to review the extent to which women perceive their responsibilities, goals, their very capacities as inferior to males" (p. 234). Although Bardwick and Douvan at this point try to upgrade women's contributions in traditional roles, it is a losing battle, and women end up sounding weak. The traits attributed to women become even more ridiculous when one thinks of women who are not white and upper middle class. Those women who have always worked and who also constantly take on responsibility for others on a reciprocal basis can hardly be called dependent and passive. To paraphrase Sojourner Truth, "aren't they women?"

I do not blame Bardwick and Douvan or other psychologists for their ambivalence concerning women in 1970. Many of us shared this ambivalence because we accepted the more typically masculine definition of what women were. Bardwick and Douvan's article made a positive contribution, however, in pointing out the ambivalence that accepting a male paradigm causes women to feel, and in recognizing the existence of a male paradigm in the first place. The task now is to extricate ourselves from that paradigm more clearly than was possible in 1970.

Increasingly, what seems to be happening is that women are able to attain and achieve in high-level jobs while retaining a sense of self as expressive. Lillian Rubin describes middle-aged middle-class women who, while sitting in their offices surrounded by work and the symbols of work, still answered the question of "who and what they are" by describing themselves as "warm, sensitive, considerate and kind." No one mentioned work.[36] In a sample of college-educated women born in the 1950s, Rosalind Gottfried documents that these women did not maintain that work took primacy in their lives over relationships. Although they did view work as important, these women were most concerned with their connections to other people, and these connections were more basic to their self-concepts. Moreover, these attitudes about connectedness were those of women who were the least passive, most feminist group— those most concerned with directing their own lives.[37]

In 1976 Jean Baker Miller made the point clearly that women are being punished for making affiliations central to their lives and that women can be highly trained, high achievers, and still give great weight to affiliations. To simply dismiss women's need for affiliation as dependency is an error.[38] Finally, if we look at school achievement, it is incorrect to assume that women perform less well than men. With regard to school performance rather than occupational performance, the "problem of female underachievement" ceases to exist. Women achieve beyond their potential as measured by IQ tests to a greater extent than men at every grade level through college.[39]

Men and Dependency

Although the cultural stereotype has it that men are psychologically independent and women are dependent, from a structural standpoint this is hardly the case. The appearance of masculine autonomy outside the home is made possible by wives meeting men's dependency needs in the home, and other supportive females meeting their needs outside the home. Men's dependency needs are not readily apparent to outsiders because they are taken care of by women in the normal course of life. The key to how this operates rests on the males' dominance in relationships in which men are dependent on women.

Middle-class marriages are clearly structured in such a way that husbands' dependency needs are met by wives. Women as wives "take care of things" and continue to do so even when they have full-time jobs outside of the home.[40] In fact, wives sometimes de-

scribe their husbands as "big babies"; the "bigger" in importance
he is, the bigger the baby. Some men may be babies, but men do
not present themselves as babies to their fellow males. Only in circumstances and roles in which they have a firm power base do men
express dependency. Being the husband and male head of household provides such a power base.

Women may also play supportive roles to men at work. The
clearest example here is the secretary—the office "wife." Often a
boss will even admit to his dependency on a woman, but generally
only in the context of his being in the superior position in the relationship. A boss might say of his secretary, "I do not know what I
would do without Jenny here; I depend on her for everything." At
the same time, in one way or another he will also make it clear that
her ministrations to him ultimately testify to his superior judgment—he hired her, he pays her, she works for him under his direction, at his behest.[41]

Whereas men's dependency needs are met by wives (and wife
substitutes), wives' dependency needs often go unmet by husbands. Who soothes wives and binds up their psychological and
physical wounds? Who takes care of things for wives? The poorer
mental and physical health that characterizes married women compared to married men has been attributed to women's role as the
mental and physical caretakers of husbands and children. Wives
are the ones who cannot ever be dependent—to the detriment of
their own physical and mental health.[42] Yet women are called psychologically dependent. In reality, a sense of connectedness with
others is different from and transcends both "taking care of" and
"being taken care of." It involves a generalized stance that can be
egalitarian and mutual. It can be shared by men and be a part of
relationships between women and between women and men.

Women and Aggression

Aggression is often considered in common parlance to be the opposite of dependence, passivity, and failure to make it. This juxta-
position makes it abundantly clear that aggression is at the "good"
end of the pole. In their comprehensive review of psychological
studies on gender differences in children, Eleanor Maccoby and
Carol Jacklin find girls to be less aggressive than boys. Although

Maccoby and Jacklin generally consider there to be fewer gender differences than many other psychologists, they argue that there is a clear-cut difference with respect to aggressiveness. They contend that males are more aggressive than females, both physically and verbally, directly and indirectly, and in a wide variety of settings. Does this mean women are doomed to passivity? Not in the least. Maccoby and Jacklin define aggression as action with the intent to hurt. It is not constructive and it is not the opposite of passivity.[43]

It is true that girls have more anxiety about aggression than boys. Some have interpreted this to mean that girls have aggressive tendencies equal to those of boys but repress them out of fear of punishment or retaliation. Maccoby and Jacklin suggest, however, that if this were so, surely the aggression would come out in some attentuated form. What happens, though, is that boys act out aggressive impulses in play as well as in reality. In addition, boys are more likely than girls to aggress in the presence of weakness in another male. Girls do not respond to weakness in either boys or girls with aggression.

We know that women account for slightly more child abuse than men, but when one takes "opportunity" into account, that is, the time women spend with children compared to the time men spend, this tendency is reversed.[44] A review of the experimental literature on aggression argues that women may act as aggressively as men under certain experimental conditions. These conditions involve a situation where the women do not empathize with the victim and in which they feel the aggression is justified. Over all situations, of all the traits discussed in the review, aggressiveness does appear to be most clearly a generalized trait that characterizes males far more than females.[45]

It is important that readers be aware of their own biases about the value of aggressiveness. In a society governed by a masculine paradigm, aggression is likely to have desirable connotations. In the public mind, it is often associated with competitiveness, single-mindedness, or strong will. But why? Maccoby and Jacklin do not define aggression as a desirable characteristic and argue that it is as likely to interfere with constructive activity as it is to underlie it. Their definition of aggression as the intent to hurt emphasizes its antisocial nature. While our measure of expressiveness was only a tiny aspect of the whole picture, male aggressiveness may be reflected in the lesser amount of positive expressiveness males attributed to themselves in our study.

Like aggression, the term *dominance* tends to have a positive meaning in a society controlled by a masculine paradigm, which tends to define many situations in terms of "dominate or be dominated." A female paradigm, on the other hand, might deny the necessity for either dominance or submission. Resistance to domination would be desirable, but domination would not be. Male aggression could play into dominance-striving, but as Finigan's work suggests, dominance is not at all the same as constructive leadership.

In an article published after their book, Maccoby and Jacklin examine the question of male aggression cross-culturally and conclude that in other societies too, boys between three and six years old are more likely to initiate aggression than girls in the same age range. This initial difference may be either maintained or eliminated or even reversed by subsequent socialization experiences. Maccoby and Jacklin note that one type of socialization experience that has been found to moderate aggressiveness in boys is being assigned to child care. There are forms of aggression in which no gender differences are found, such as self-defense, quarreling over desirable resources, or even effecting a swift, silent kill. Maccoby and Jacklin suggest that future research on aggression will need to pay more attention to the particular interpersonal setting in which aggression takes place and also to differing types of aggression. Much aggression among boys occurs in male-male pairs in noisy contests over dominance. Girls may fight with each other but not in order to establish dominance.[46]

When Maccoby and Jacklin speak of aggression, they clearly distinguish it from both activity and competition. Confusion over this issue has led Sarah Hrdy in her book *The Woman That Never Evolved* to argue against "maternal" feminists because she assumes that they envision women as passive and noncompetitive. Hrdy contends that studies of female primates show them to be highly competitive with each other and that "competition among females is one of the major determinants of primate social organization, and has contributed to the organisms women are today" (p. 189). In part Hrdy's stress on female competitiveness seems merely to be reiterating "the logic" of the sociobiological argument in its crudest form, namely, that whatever exists must have gotten there by having won out in some sort of competitive struggle. In other words, a passive, noncompetitive woman could never have evolved. Hrdy envisions females' mothering as being the basis for their competition with other females. "Throughout millions of years of evolution, mammalian mothers have differed from one another in two important ways: in their capacity to produce and care for offspring and in their ability to enlist the support of males, or at least to forestall them from damaging their infants" (p. 189). In their efforts to secure resources for themselves and their offspring, mammalian mothers engaged in subtle competition with one another, which sometimes involved simply nonconfrontation and keeping out of the way. Hrdy is not saying females behaved as aggressively as males; her concern is to show that females had dominance hierarchies and were not politically insignificant or passive. This does not directly contradict the thesis that females are less likely than males to initiate aggression and make direct dominance attempts.

Indeed, the significance of Hrdy's descriptions of female primate behavior and speculations about early female human behavior is that only among humans do females become clearly subordinated to males. This subordination has to do with human cultural institutions. Hrdy speaks of various means to control women's sexuality, including clitoridectomy and castration of daughters and wives as well as those marital residence rules that separate women from their kin.

This picture of animal mothers that Hrdy draws has been systematically denied by the cultural image of women that defines them not as active mothers but as passive sideliners, cheering on their men. Niles Newton has argued that since the industrial revolution there has been a sharp conflict between what she calls a woman's "cultural femininity" and her "biological femininity." Newton says that although "cultural femininity . . . decrees that women should be passive," actually "the woman in her female biological role must be active, productive, and capable of concerted effort." Newton points out that not only is bearing and nursing a child physically and emotionally demanding, but the care of a child is not a matter of passively providing comfort; it involves active and sometimes aggressive interventions on behalf of the child in the physical and social environment. In sum, there is nothing passive about maternal emotions.[47]

Finally, in addition to distinguishing expressiveness from emotionality, dependence, ineptitude, and inability to aggress, it is also important to emphasize that the term must always be defined at a very general level. Only when expressiveness is thought of as a mode of personality organization or as a generalized stance rather than in terms of specific traits can it make sense to claim that expressiveness can differentiate women from men cross-culturally. Although we used descriptive adjectives defining expressiveness in our research, these are far from ideal measures because they are too narrowly confined to an empathetic dimension and also because they inevitably become intertwined with a very specific cultural and social structural context.

For example, these adjectives may be class or race bound. Consider, for example, the popularity of "interpersonal sensitivity." This term may mean nothing more than a style of interacting in which one listens to others and tries to assess their needs and agendas as a means of selling oneself or selling something else. It may simply be an expressive overlay to instrumental action—a style, not an orientation. "Interpersonal sensitivity" has become something that middle-class whites value highly, and it is a stance that the so-called new man is readily adopting.[48] This is not what I want to convey by the idea that women are more relational, and I do not believe it is what women mean when they say they wish men could be more relational. Relationality is a stance that takes others into account not as "other" but as important in themselves. The forms that a relational orientation could take would vary greatly in terms of class and race or culture.

Some of the most interesting work now on gender similarity and difference focuses on interaction patterns rather than on personality orientations. Thus, for example, Marjorie Goodwin and Charles Goodwin have analyzed the "conversational procedures" used by preadolescent girls and boys in informal arguments. Their main finding was that both boys and girls engage in argumentation and generally in quite similar ways. They found, however, that girls argued in a more complex manner than boys. Girls used what the researchers call a "he-said–she-said" structure unknown among boys. This structure allows for extended and complex debate that nevertheless saves the faces of both accuser and accused by reference to third and fourth parties, thus avoiding direct confrontations of the "I win, you lose" variety. Such a method avoids direct aggression, while still getting the job done.[49]

Summary

In this chapter I have presented empirical support for an assessment of women and men in terms of orientational similarities and differences that is less distorted by male bias. Women see themselves as more relational or interdependent or expressive than men see themselves. Instrumentality, however, does not hold up as a single dimension, and women and men do not differ consistently with respect to its components. Women's greater expressiveness is not to be confused with dependence or lack of autonomy. Men are more likely than women to make a mental connection between relationality and dependence. Moreover, structurally, men in fact have their dependency needs met. I used Maccoby and Jacklin's conclusions concerning greater aggressiveness in a wider range of contexts among males to suggest that this greater aggressiveness may play a part in our male subjects' reluctance to see themselves as being as positively expressive as our female subjects.

The reader may feel that much of the preceding discussion involves a very airy quibble over words and concepts—but words are never neutral. Words carry evaluative and power connotations, and definitions become important because we live in a male-dominant society. Feminist analyses or investigations must be highly self-conscious about terms. But one can only get so far with these large global assessments; the major intervening factor is power.

Expressiveness or relationality as an orientation does not determine power. Instrumentality, as we defined it, does not directly involve power either. Much of the purpose of my detailed discussion of the definition of expressiveness was to make clear that the terms that are obviously relevant to power (or lack of it), such as submissive, yielding, and dependent, do not properly belong in the expressive dimension. Being expressive does not render one powerless or powerful, but the structure of male-dominated marriages make women less powerful. Given a different power situation, women's somewhat greater expressiveness can also be the basis for human bonding.

In Chapter 5, I will discuss how women's mothering and women's greater relationality develop and how they might be connected. Before doing so, however, I will examine the hypothesis that gained popularity among some feminists in the 1970s, namely, that women's mothering contributes to male dominance. There is an element of truth in this argument, but it is a partial truth at best. My emphasis will be on the positive motivation that being mothered produces. I will argue that the mother is the focus of the learning by both genders of common human expressive qualities, although males may later deny these qualities and substitute male dominance. This transformation is not the work of mothers, but of adolescent male peer groups and to some extent fathers.

Chapter Four

Women's Mothering and
Male Misogyny

During the 1970s, feminists using psychoanalytic theory considered women's mothering to be highly problematic. In this chapter I trace the vicissitudes of the hypothesis that women's mothering—that is, being the primary caretakers of children—lies behind male misogyny and male dominance itself.[1] The hypothesis derives from psychoanalytic theory and its extensions and has been discovered and rediscovered, worked over and overworked in various ways by feminists, including myself, since the early days of psychoanalysis. But only in the 1970s was it called upon to bear the burden of explaining the entire system of male dominance. This argument that blames male misogyny on women's mothering has an important element of truth in it, but in my view, it does not hold the key to a viable solution to systems of male dominance; moreover, the argument has become an impediment to seeing the positive aspects of women's mothering, or better, of a maternal stance.

Feminists who use psychoanalytic theory in conjunction with an analysis of social structure suggest that male misogyny is far from superficial and cannot be easily eradicated. Psychoanalytic explanations focus on the generation of motivation that is nonrational and operates outside conscious awareness. These motivational explanations offer an alternative to simplistic "role theory" explanations of male dominance that suggest that to do away with male dominance, all we need to do is to redefine roles or eliminate gender-based role differentiation. Similarly, these explanations at the motivational level seem preferable to those nonpsychoanalytic "psychological" analyses that suggest that male dominance can be eradicated by getting rid of outmoded stereotypes. There is nothing wrong with advocating role and stereotype change, but attempts to effect real change (as opposed to a change in the forms male misogyny takes) may fail unless we recognize unconscious motivational tendencies and their underlying dynamics.

Moreover, psychoanalytic theory offers an alternative to simplistic biological explanations that attempt to account for male dominance by recourse to some presumably immutable genetic or hormonal differences between men and women. Psychoanalytic theory used in conjunction with an analysis of social structure appealed to feminists precisely because it could explain the persistence and seeming intractability of certain attitudes without recourse to biological factors. The structural fact the theorists under consideration use is that women, not men, tend to be responsible for early child care. In later chapters I will be increasingly critical of some important elements in psychoanalytic interpretations of gender, but my concern now is with how psychoanalysis can help explain the generation of sexist motivation in men and women.

Two major themes in psychoanalytic accounts of male personality development relate to the early primacy of women in the lives of male children. One is the idea that infants and children of both genders, but especially males, feel fear and envy toward the mother and develop defenses against these feelings; the other theme is the problems males encounter in establishing a secure sense of masculine gender identity. The first tendency emphasizes infantile dependency needs and the "primary process" thinking in which the mother appears overwhelmingly powerful; the second emphasizes the idea that identity develops from a process of separating the self from the mother, including boys' learning that they are a different gender from mother. Both these strands of gynecentric (i.e., mother-centered) psychoanalytic theory have been used to explain why men are motivated to denigrate and dominate women, whereas women feel few or no comparable motives toward men.

I begin by showing how the earlier themes fit into feminist explanations of male dominance, while also pointing out the limitations of such analyses.[2] I then discuss the work of Evelyn Fox Keller and Jessica Benjamin, who relate males' special problems with separation from the mother to their greater tendency to emphasize difference, hierarchy, and domination in their thinking. Keller's and Benjamin's analyses, which derive from combining psychoanalytic hypotheses with a "critical theory" perspective, differ from earlier analyses and need to be examined separately. ("Critical theory" is the name adopted in the United States by the Frankfurt School of Marxism, which emphasizes cultural and psychological factors.) I find problems with the specific psychoanalytic account Keller and Benjamin use, but the direction they take in emphasizing women's lesser concern with preserving gender difference and lesser tendency to control through domination is progressive. It also fits in with my interest in how fathers, not mothers, are the main focus of the more narrowly "sexual" aspects of gender differentiation.

The Fear and Envy Hypothesis

The fear and envy hypothesis is almost as old as psychoanalysis itself. The early names most associated with the hypothesis are Ernest Jones, Melanie Klein, and Karen Horney. Although their accounts differ substantially, they all have a common thread of opposition to what Jones labels Freud's "phallocentric" views. Each stresses the significance of the preoedipal period and the mother rather than of the oedipal period and the father; all see the penis envy in girls, which Freud took for granted as being primary, as being in fact a secondary response. Although male dominance itself is not problematic for these theorists, their ideas nevertheless can be used to shed light on the motives behind male dominance.

Jones tried to be an arbiter in what came to be called the Freud-Jones controversy, which represents the conflict between phallocentric and gynecentric approaches.[3] Jones draws heavily on the views of both Klein and Horney, both of whom take as their starting point the helplessness of the infant, that is, the infant's almost total physical and emotional dependence on an adult. Klein emphasizes the infant's sadistic aggressive responses to this dependency coupled with anxiety engendered by a fear of the mother's reprisal for aggression. According to Klein, the boy compensates for his feelings of "hate, anxiety, envy and inferiority that spring from his feminine phase by reinforcing his pride in the possession of a penis."[4]

Horney, by contrast, links men's general fear of women to the boy's fear of being rebuffed by the all-important mother and the subsequent loss of self-esteem. This fear of deflation by a woman on whom he was dependent then becomes the prime motivating factor in men's compulsion to prove themselves and their manhood and to seek to possess many women or to attempt to "diminish the self-respect of the woman."[5]

Horney suggests that, in addition to fear, there is in men a strong element of envy and even awe of women's capacity for motherhood. Surely, she says, there must have been a time in the psychic development of boys and girls when neither sex was convinced that women were inferior. She backs this up by describing how in analyzing men "one receives a most surprising impression of the intensity of this envy of pregnancy, childbirth, motherhood as well as the breasts and the act of suckling."[6] Boys, she suggests, defend themselves against this envy by asserting the phallocentric idea that motherhood is in reality a burden and that what women basically want is not a child, but a penis. In Horney's view, Freud's phallocentric idea represents a masculine defense against womb envy.

Margaret Mead, who was influenced considerably in the 1940s by psychoanalytic thinking, has also argued that men envy women's procreative powers. Rather than using clinical experience, she uses the myths that abound in various cultures, including our own, to bolster her interpretations. According to Mead, in the areas of New Guinea she studied, "It is men who spend their ceremonial lives pretending that it was they who had borne the children, that they can 'make men.'"[7] Mead also describes how men in New Guinea tell stories about how their mythical man-making powers were invented by a woman and stolen from her by men. Mead attributes men and women's according higher value to what men do than to what women do (that is, what men do is considered an achievement) to a perception of males' psychological need to compensate for their lack of procreative powers.

Dorothy Dinnerstein's *The Mermaid and the Minotaur* offers the most sustained account to date that attributes male dominance directly to infantile fear and envy of mothers.[8] Dinnerstein states explicitly that she is concerned not with personal male misogyny but with the entire system of male dominance. This system, she says, is created not by men alone but rather is based on a conspiracy by both men and women. This conspiracy consists of substituting male dominance for the far more threatening dominance that mothers held over us as male and female infants.

Although it is not always clear what Dinnerstein thinks the crucial mechanisms are that intervene between male dominance and early child care by women, her central theme is that the power we as infants ascribe to mothers creates a need in us for a more bounded authority. Formal authority is always vested in males because male authority appears to be a refuge from the primitive and seemingly unlimited despotism of the mother as perceived by the infant. Dinnerstein follows Melanie Klein in explaining men's fear and contempt for women and argues that in the child's mind, since the mother does not always meet the infant's needs, she is perceived as "capricious" and "sometimes actively malevolent."[9] But there is also the child's ambivalence, made up of destructive rage when disappointed as well as abounding gratitude when satiated. This ambivalence is then projected onto women in general. Dinnerstein sees men's sexual possessiveness as an attempt to "own" women's life-giving powers, and sex-segregated institutions as being created by men in order to defend themselves from "the temptation to give way to ferocious voracious dependence" on women (p. 67).

In Dinnerstein's analysis, women take on characteristics as unlovely as those she attributes to men. Whereas men may express their vindictive feelings against the mother directly in "arrogance toward everything female," women express those feelings "directly in distrust and disrespect toward other women, and indirectly by offering ourselves up to male vindictiveness" (p. 174). Women have supported men in their evil deeds against Mother Nature because of their own infantile rage, but women then use their powerlessness to absolve themselves from blame and take some pleasure in blaming men. Now, Dinnerstein says, women have come to hate men as much as men have always hated women.

According to Dinnerstein, male dominance must be ended, not so much because it oppresses women as because masculine "achievements" threaten to destroy the world. Dinnerstein sees us as having created a "megamachine" (Lewis Mumford's term) bent on destroying the earth and the vitality of human life. Her main interest, in fact, is to criticize the enterprises in which men are engaged and to which women are acquiescing. In so doing, she breaks with Simone de Beauvoir, whom she generally holds in high esteem. Dinnerstein dislikes de Beauvoir's uncritical acceptance of masculine ways of thinking—for taking "the male world-making enterprise at face value" and for believing that freedom for women can be had by "a simple entering into man's realm" (p. 24).

It is true that Dinnerstein blames women's mothering for the ills of the world, but at the same time she defines what those ills are from a maternal, caring, preserving perspective. But in spite of Dinnerstein's own maternal values (one wonders where she got them), the women in the horror show Dinnerstein depicts are not thinking like mothers; they are thinking like dependent *wives* and girlfriends, supporting men in their madness. Her final message is that women can stop providing support for men's life-threatening enterprises. This is the reading I prefer to give Dinnerstein, but the message that comes across more strongly is that women's mothering, by causing men and women to reject the overwhelmingness of their early experience with female power, is to blame for all this.

Dinnerstein's book is written not from the point of view of an adult mother doing the best she can under the circumstances, but from the perspective of an infant who expects nothing short of perfection.[10] She communicates to the reader through the language of "primary process thinking," that is, thinking in which only infantile needs matter. She does this well, presumably in hopes that we will recognize this thinking in ourselves and also the infant in ourselves. Dinnerstein is saying that infants blame mothers when the world is not right, but she becomes so totally caught up in her own apocalyptic vision that she never stops taking the point of view she attributes to infants.

Dinnerstein does not argue that women do not mother well; rather, she argues that infants are not rational and only gradually learn to take the point of view of the mother instead of looking at the world from the standpoint of their own voracious needs. She sets up the problem as infantile thinking but prescribes that the realistic solution is for fathers to mother. After her description of what men are like (because of their infantile thinking), however, one is inclined to agree with Pauline Bart, who exclaimed in a review of Dinnerstein's book, "I wouldn't even buy a used car from people like that! What kind of generation would they produce?" Moreover, Dinnerstein does not explain how an infant might be persuaded to disperse its apparently unlimited needs and resentments equally between a male and a female parent and thereby presumably cease to be misogynist.

It seems to me that the basic problem here is not so much women's mothering but the nonrational, "unprocessed," or primary process thinking that continues to influence the adult's responses in certain triggering situations. A more effective solution to this kind of thinking than equal parenting would be for all of us to grow up and for women to take the lead in helping us do so. That is, we all need to recognize the nonrational elements in our thinking, the elements that make us expect perfection from mothers and fear abandonment and humiliation by them. Here, of course, I mean not one's own real mother but rather women perceived as mothers. Growing up would mean learning to take others' needs and perspectives into account besides our own and thus putting one's self into a wider perspective. Most of us do grow up, more or less, and women are in a better position than men to take the lead in insisting that men and women take others into account as mothers do, rather than continuing to take the point of view of the egocentric child. Perhaps this is implied in Dinnerstein's idea of equal parenting, but it does not come through.

The devaluation of women (by both men and women) is not an inevitable reaction formation to women's prominence in early child care. It is a choice, helped along by the male dominance institutionalized in political and economic structures and supported in male peer groups. I am convinced that all of us harbor irrational ideas and expectations focused on women because women are so prominent in our early life and that these ideas feed into male rage and male misogyny. Feminists with an awareness of the psychoanalytic tradition naturally focused on these ideas as an explanation of the roots of male misogyny, and these ideas suggest that the roots run very deep. Male fear and envy of mothers cannot stand alone, however, as the explanation of male dominance even on a psychological level, in part because it ignores the positive consequences that being mothered has for both men and women.

The Tenuous Masculine Identity
Hypothesis

Generally, the theorists concerned with the various consequences of a boy's making an initial "feminine identification" have been social scientists who have been influenced by psychoanalytic ideas. Social learning theorists have often readily assumed that because mothers are far more available and primary in the lives of young children than fathers, children of both sexes initially make a "feminine identification." From this perspective, growing up for males means shifting from a feminine identification to a masculine one. Psychoanalysts and social learning theorists alike have assumed that it is important for the son to have a "good" relationship with his father in order to be helped "to identify" with him or to learn by observing him and thus to become "masculine" or to learn "masculinity." Few of these accounts specify what is meant by identification and sometimes the term is used simply as a synonym for modeling or copying the parent of the same gender.

In the 1950s, worry about a boy's problematic identification gave rise to the concept of "compulsive masculinity." For example, Walter Miller argued that lower-class boys who grew up in predominantly female homes that lacked "a consistently present male figure with whom to identify" were likely to become compulsively concerned with toughness and masculinity as a reaction formation against the femininity surrounding them. Miller claimed that father-deprived males were likely to commit delinquent acts to prove their masculinity to the gang.[11] In a similar vein, Rohrer and Edmonson studied a group of black males in New Orleans and argued that the black male joined a gang in a "search for masculinity he cannot find at home." These gangs in turn come to see "the common enemy not as a class, nor even as a sex, but as the 'feminine principle' in society."[12]

Whereas most of the studies in this country on compulsive masculinity were on the "lower class" and particularly blacks, Talcott Parsons applied the idea to middle-class children. He pointed out that in highly industrialized societies the place of work is separated from the place of residence and fathers leave home to work. In the middle class this work is time-consuming and often incomprehensible to a child. Thus there is a kind of "father absence" in the middle class that causes children to interact chiefly with their mothers and other women. Women, not men, become the rule givers and represent the demand to "be good." This situation tends to produce what Parsons called "the bad boy pattern" and the "tenderness taboo," whereby males in attempting to be masculine without a clear masculine model express masculinity in largely negative ways by being "bad" and "tough." In trying not to be feminine, the boy unconsciously identifies "goodness" with femininity, and being a "bad boy" becomes a positive goal.[13] Leslie Fiedler has described this "bad boy pattern" as a pervasive theme in U.S. fiction. From Mark Twain's stories to Ken Kesey's *One Flew Over the Cuckoo's Nest* are numerous sagas in which men (or boys) seek to escape a world that they perceive to be dominated by female morality.[14]

The idea of boys making an initial "feminine identification" was also used by anthropologists in the 1950s in interpreting other behavior patterns found in a given society. These anthropologists reported that societies in which fathers were absent or virtually absent during a boy's infancy were more likely than others to have compensating rituals later on that symbolically broke the mother-son bond and affirmed the boy's masculinity.[15] In a different but related vein, an analysis of forty-eight societies reported that the frequency of crime in these societies was associated with situations in which the opportunity for the young boy to form an identification with his father was limited.[16] More recently, Beatrice Whiting reported that in her and her associates' study of children from six different cultures there was greater adult violence in the two societies where infants saw their fathers infrequently. She specifically assumed the "status envy" hypothesis that young children would identify with the person who seems most important to them, the person who is seen as controlling the resources that they want. In the earliest years when this person is almost exclusively the mother, boys would be expected to make a feminine identification. Whiting then used the idea of compulsive masculinity to explain the violence that erupted in later years when the boys had to break this feminine identification.[17]

Whiting points out that in the six cultures study described above and in the studies by other anthropologists, the phenomenon of sex-identity conflict occurs only when a great deal of gender segregation and male dominance exists in the adult society. This finding suggests that in more egalitarian societies, where femininity is not so devalued, one of the motives for males' compulsive resistance to femininity (both within and outside themselves) is lost.

At the time it was published, the research I have been describing was used to bolster the argument that fathers were vital to the well-being of children. It played into a persistent worry about father absence and the fear that males would be made "effeminate" by their mothers. Fathers were needed, it was claimed, to show boys what masculinity was and to prevent them from being made into sissies by their mothers or from overdoing masculinity as a defense against feminization.

The idea of "compulsive masculinity," or exaggerated masculinity, became something of a bridge to a feminist use of the idea that maleness was a less secure identity than femaleness and that this insecure identity provided a motive for male misogyny. Ruth Hartley moved in this direction in 1959. Writing at a time when male dominance was seldom subjected to criticism, she noted that males generally learn what they must *not* be in order to be masculine, before they learn what they can be. Because adult males are rarely closely involved with boys, many boys define masculinity as simply "not being feminine." Hartley argued that males compensate themselves for the pains involved in breaking away from the world of women by viewing females in very negative ways. The eight- to eleven-year-old boys she studied described adult women as weak, afraid, easily tired, in need of help, squeamish, inadequate in emergencies, making an undue fuss over things, not very intelligent, and demanding and jealous of their husbands![18] (Significantly, this description is clearly more congruous with definitions of women as wives than of women as mothers.) Boys, at least middle-class white boys in the United States, seem to force themselves into masculinity to avoid being such a pitiful specimen as a stereotypical wife. Hartley's article was reprinted in a widely used text on the "male sex role" that popularized the idea that one of the cornerstones of "masculinity" was its "antifeminine" element—whatever else one does, at all costs, do not be like a female.[19]

In 1974, in "Family Structure and Feminine Personality," Chodorow stated the above premise from a more psychoanalytic perspective and took its implications much further, suggesting that the male tendency to define masculinity as "that which is not feminine or involved with women . . . explains the psychological dynamics of the universal social and cultural devaluation and subordination of women." The boy denies his attachment and deep personal identification with his mother "by repressing whatever he takes to be feminine inside himself, and, importantly, by denigrating and devaluing whatever he considers to be feminine in the outside world." Beyond this, Chodorow suggests that as a member of society, "he also appropriates to himself and defines as superior particular social activities and cultural spheres—possibly, in fact, 'society' . . . and 'culture' . . . themselves" (p. 50). Thus Chodorow uses the search for masculinity as an explanation for the male view that society and culture are male products.[20] In 1979, Jean Stockard and I suggested that the greater rewards and power of masculinity act as an inducement to boys to break with femaleness. Women, in contrast, do not have a psychological need for "greater glory" as an inducement to be mothers.[21]

Nowadays when feminists and, increasingly, modern psychologists speak of masculine gender identity, they usually do not mean the degree of masculinity as measured by ordinary psychological tests or the degree of conformity to a stereotyped "male role." Since the early 1970s, the idea of gender identity has referred not to the extent to which one is masculine, feminine, or even androgynous but rather to the simple emotional, cognitive, and bodily grounded conviction of being male or female and to being able to take this conviction for granted as a comfortable and desirable reality.[22] The tenuous gender identity hypothesis then claims that this secure sense of gender is considerably less problematic for women than it is for men.

Robert Stoller's studies of transsexuals provide empirical support for the tenuous masculine identity hypothesis at this deeper level. On the basis of his research, Stoller concludes that masculinity is not a "core-gender identity" for males in the same way that femininity is for females. Rather, masculinity is achieved by males only after they have separated themselves from the "femininity" of the mother.[23]

Stoller thinks that female transsexualism has quite different origins than transsexualism in males. He considers female transsexuals to be a type of homosexual and male transsexuals to be different from either homosexuals or transvestites. Their "femininity" goes much deeper; psychically (but not physically) they *are* women. Stoller sees this phenomenon as the result of a too-close and too-gratifying mother-infant "symbiosis." This symbiosis occurs before the child has enough of an ego structure to actually "identify with" the mother. It is something even more primitive. It is *"being the same as* mother, which would be the destruction of masculinity" (p. 353).

Stoller's most significant argument is that every male must overcome and resist the excessive merging with the mother that happens with the transsexual. As Stoller sees it, every male infant experiences some degree of oneness with the mother; transsexuals are simply those at the far end of a continuum. Thus Stoller considers males making a feminine identification not a "defense" of one sort or another but rather the primary state. This view takes the idea of the primacy of the feminine in its maternal aspects in the male ego farther than most other psychoanalysts have done. Stoller's emphasis on the fundamentality of the maternal identification and his association of it with femininity implies that masculinity represents a deviation from femininity in its maternal aspects. Stoller does not relate his idea of primitive symbiosis with the mother to male misogyny, much less to male dominance. He also sees a sharp difference between his theory and the fear and envy hypothesis; his emphasis on idyllic symbiosis causes him to deny that there is early ambivalence and conflict in the mother-child relationship. Chodorow uses Stoller's work to bolster the argument that if fathers also mothered, it would not eliminate gender identity altogether but it would help the child feel that he is a male and that males can nurture too, and that it is not necessary to denigrate women to convince oneself that one really is a male.

Linking the Two Hypotheses in Gynecentric Thought

The fear and envy hypothesis and the tenuous masculine identity hypothesis are quite different from a psychoanalytic standpoint and seem to rest on different assumptions about the nature of the earliest infant-mother relationship. They may be viewed as essentially compatible, however, if they are seen as representing differing phases of the mother-infant relationship. Stoller is probably correct in assuming that the overriding emotion in the earliest mother-child relationship is love. Yet it is also possible to imagine how something akin to both fear and envy might accompany the infant's developing capacities for autonomy. As Melanie Klein suggests, infants fear that this person on whom they are so dependent might turn against them, and, as Horney suggests, they envy her capacities. Those who stress the fear and envy hypothesis, then, seem essentially to be saying that men's motive to segregate and dominate women comes not so much from the necessity to break their identification with the mother but rather from a fear of the consequences of their dependency on a woman whose powers they do not possess.

These same hypotheses can be couched in language more compatible with developmental theory and more relevant to development beyond earliest infancy. The tenuous gender identity hypothesis holds that since male figures tend to be conspicuously absent in early childhood, the boy, in trying to compensate for his lack of clarity about what it means to be masculine, is constrained to devalue and degrade female-typed activities and to stress the superiority of males over females and of male roles over female roles. The fear and envy hypothesis (which is likely to strike cognitively oriented developmentalists and role theorists as embarrassing and exaggerated) can be translated to refer to boys' efforts to cope with their recognition of relative powerlessness and the concomitant recognition that dependency is disparaged in males. Thus, in a sense, males are motivated to dominate females as a means of coping with their dependency needs.

Males, then, face both their dependency and their lack of clear gender identity as they move toward greater autonomy. Girls also experience the dangers of dependency and often struggle with their own mothers to escape it, but girls do not have to form a gender identity different from that of the mother. Males, however, continue throughout their lives to be threatened in different ways and on different levels with an identity problem and with a fear of dependency that is linked to it. The institutional arrangements embodying male dominance and the cultural justification of male dominance serve males well in coping with these threats by assuring them of their gender's superiority. Moreover, institutionalized male dominance gives even greater significance to not being female and in the end exacerbates rather than quells male identity and dependency problems.[24]

Pleck's Critique

Joseph Pleck, in his book *The Myth of Masculinity*, extensively criticizes the kinds of hypotheses and research I have been describing relating mainly to the tenuous gender identity hypothesis. Basically, he argues that empirical support for the hypotheses embodied in what he calls the Masculine Sex Role Identity (MSRI) paradigm is lacking and that from a political standpoint the paradigm has been used to discredit mothers and poor or black males (in the absent-father studies) and to justify traditional male role expectations. In a brief statement toward the end of his book, Pleck exempts Dinnerstein's work and at least part of Chodorow's work from his critique (pp. 156–57). He also speaks favorably of Stoller's ideas concerning transsexuals. Pleck says all of the work he has exempted has been misinterpreted by the general public, however, as supporting the importance of clear-cut sex roles; actually, the implication of these works is that a secure sense of self as male or female may make it easier rather than harder to play nontraditional roles. This is quite correct. Pleck has a general bias against psychodynamic hypotheses, and even against developmental hypotheses, however, and this bias limits his later analysis.[25]

In essence Pleck would have us substitute a normative explanation for problems associated with men for a psychodynamic one. As an alternative to the Masculine Sex Role Identity paradigm, Pleck proposes a Sex Role Strain (SRS) paradigm. This paradigm maintains that it is difficult, if not impossible, for anyone to live up to the normative male role and that this places undue strain on men and women. This strain, Pleck believes, can account for male aggressiveness. Although I have no particular quarrel with the rather bland propositions in Pleck's alternative paradigm, I believe it focuses attention away from the gut-level emotional issues involved in gender attitudes and away from male dominance itself. Pleck asks rhetorically, "Are psychodynamic theories to account for men's attitudes toward women necessary?" My answer is yes, because the emotions that males and females have about themselves and each other are deeply felt and cannot be adequately accounted for by biology or role theory alone. Feminists who use psychoanalytic theory suggest that male dominance is far from superficial, because it gets built into our deepest feelings and understandings about what being masculine or feminine means. Moreover, Pleck's "critique of the male role" approach to gender relations minimizes the pervasiveness of male dominance, male privilege, and male power.

Equal Parenting as Solution?

Nancy Chodorow and Dorothy Dinnerstein argue that the remedy for the male motive to dominate women, which they see as being set in motion by the social assignment of mothering to women, is equal parenting by fathers and mothers. Neither of them suggests that women should not mother but rather that fathers should mother too. One gets the feeling, however, that the solution they propose is a rather distant prospect even in their own minds, and one that they feel cannot bear too-close scrutiny. Chodorow clearly understands that other aspects of social organization will have to change if fathers are to be able to mother, but she does not deal with this in any detail. Then too, these authors completely ignore the many obvious practical problems with precisely what is meant by an "equal division."

Many critics, including Chodorow herself, have pointed out that it is difficult to see why, in terms of her own analysis, men would ever be motivated to mother. According to the analysis, men are presumably made hostile to female activities by virtue of being dominated by a female, so why would they take on this female activity? In addition to the problem of getting men to mother in the first place, there is the danger (suggested by phallocentric versions of psychoanalytic theory that I will discuss later) that men will father in such a way as to reproduce patriarchy instead of gender equality.

The equal parenting "solution" would also strengthen the heterosexual couple relationship by making mothering a joint activity. Certainly lesbian coparents and heterosexual single mothers would hardly be served by this solution, which would work against any kind of female bonding, sexual or otherwise, and further emphasize the male-dominated couple relationship. A more effective way of reducing male resentments of women may be to diffuse mothering in this society not equally between a mother and a father but between mothers and other caretakers, male and female, with mothers retaining primary responsibility. This in fact seems to be the direction in which this society and other industrialized Western societies are moving in their childcare arrangements.

Difference and Dominance

I agree with those who say the most significant psychological difference between the thought tendencies of men and women is that men tend to emphasize and focus on gender difference more than women. That is, men seem to have a greater psychological investment in seeing and emphasizing gender difference than women do.[26] My own work on fathers has long been concerned with this phenomenon.[27] The difference as men see it is likely to be expressed in terms of hierarchy—strong-weak, dominant-submissive, independent-dependent, subject-object, penetrator-penetrated, and so forth. The tendency can easily lead men (and women) to define relational virtues, such as openness to the perspectives and needs of others, as "weakness."[28]

Both Evelyn Fox Keller and Jessica Benjamin relate the male emphasis on preserving a rigid distinction between self and other to a need to objectify and control the other, in short, to dominate the other. Their accounts bear some resemblance to those I reviewed above, especially that of Dinnerstein, that attempt to explain the devaluation of women and male dominance as a system by the fact that women mother. Keller's and Benjamin's focus, however, is less on male attitudes toward women as a group than on general masculine ways of thinking, which have come to characterize Western science and Western eroticism. Keller and Benjamin are both essentially critics of capitalist culture, but in their criticism they link the "critical theory" of the Frankfurt School of Marxism, with its focus on domination, to masculinity by making domination a male propensity. In a sense they turn that school's "critique of domination" into a "critique of masculinity." As Hester Eisenstein points out, the critique of Western culture that connects it with men and their orientations became a basis for woman-centered analysis that sees "maleness and masculinity as a deformation of the human, and a source of ultimate danger to the continuity of life."[29] Keller's and Benjamin's analyses differ considerably from one another both in terms of the substantive problems they address and in terms of the implications for action that they suggest. Specifically, Keller is concerned with domination in Western science and Benjamin is primarily concerned with "erotic domination."[30]

Both Benjamin and Keller rely on a complex account of the infantile roots of the more typically masculine impulse toward domination. Following the work of the object relations theorist D. W. Winnicott, they propose that in making the transition from "symbiotic union" with the mother to a recognition of the autonomy of self and others, the infant develops unconscious ideation to the effect that the subject (the self) has actually destroyed the object (the other person) in the process of becoming separate. To believe the other has been destroyed is highly anxiety-producing because if the object does not exist, how is the subject to maintain any relatedness? The child is thus not only afraid of having destroyed the other in becoming a self but also afraid of losing its own self if the other survives. The child then seeks to defend against both possibilities by seeking mastery over the other. At a later point, in the oedipal stage, this innocent mastery (in which presumably both genders partake) can become converted into mastery over and against the other. This latter mastery for various reasons (including the assumptions that males must not be females and must "disidentify" from the mother) becomes associated with masculinity at both the individual and the cultural level.

Also, in contrast to Dinnerstein and Chodorow, neither Benjamin nor Keller focuses on equal parenting as a primary solution to male dominance, probably because they see masculine ways of thinking as highly problematic. Benjamin, especially, is concerned about the oedipal, authoritarian father, whom both see as enforcing gender polarity and representing authority.[31]

Science and Domination

Keller suggests that the cultural identification of science and objectivity with masculinity is connected to the developmental process of separating self from mother. The boy, who must not only become a separate self but also a separate gender from the mother, is likely to defend himself both from "reengulfment" by the mother and from femaleness by assuming a more objective and distanced stance. The culture helps the process by associating both objectivity and masculinity with science, by making scientific thinking a model for all thinking, and by defining as "scientific" only that which is objective and distanced. Thus science itself has become genderized and has lost much in the process.[32]

But Western science is not only objective and distanced; it also places great emphasis on power and control. Keller suggests that the impulse to dominate is a natural concomitant of "defensive separateness" (p. 596). The impulse feeds into and is fed by the cultural construct of masculinity in which, for example, nature is seen as the mother who must be conquered and subdued. Keller is concerned not with reiterating this familiar connection and its variants but with purveying an alternative view of science. According to Keller, science is not intrinsically dominating; but it may also involve "conversing with," rather than controlling, nature and becoming part of the system under consideration rather than viewing the system from above.

Keller illustrates this with Barbara McClintock's work on DNA, which long went unrecognized, in part because her vision was difficult to grasp if one used a control model of science. McClintock challenged the prevailing view that "the DNA encodes and transmits all instructions for the unfolding of a living cell" with "a view of the DNA in delicate interaction with the cellular environment" so that "the program encoded by the DNA is itself subject to change. No longer is a master control to be found in a single component of the cell; rather control resides in the complex interactions of the entire system" (p. 601). Keller does not claim that only women approach science in this manner. Rather, her argument is that this method of approach can and has been chosen and needs more emphasis. The value of consciousness is that we are able to make choices as individuals and as scientists. Both women and men seek competence, mastery, and rational understanding. Science is a human endeavor. The contribution feminism can make is to "refine that effort" and to show that domination and control are not necessarily intrinsic to science.

Love and Domination

Jessica Benjamin uses the sadomasochistic, master-slave relationship described in Pauline Reage's *The Story of O* as her prototype of erotic domination, or what she calls "rational violence." She contends that the fantasy involved flows underneath "all sexual imagery" and "normal" adult love relationships and sees this fantasy as being ultimately caused by what she calls "false differentiation." In such differentiation, the solution to the fear of aloneness brought about by separation becomes one of preserving the other individual not as a separate being (which would be true differentiation) but by controlling and dominating the other person and denying him or her autonomy. This domination contains the threat of violence against the other and thereby becomes associated with male identity.[33] But the violence must be "rational" for the strategy to succeed. In rational violence the perpetrator controls the victim in such a way as to obtain "recognition" from the victim while at the same time negating the victim's autonomy. In *The Story of O*, the female, O, is constantly recognizing her torturer-lover by her statements of "consent," and he is constantly negating her and testing her boundaries with more and more humiliating requests to which she must consciously and explicitly acquiesce.

It is less clear from Benjamin's account what the masochistic victim, O, gets out of her humiliation. Presumably, she gets recognition and avoids being alone, because she is needed by her lover in the sense that he needs her submission and her need for him. Benjamin also suggests that O identifies with her lover's rational control and thus protects herself from her own loss of control, which is equated with loss of self. In the last analysis, the explanation for O goes back to the differing positions of males and females in the infantile situation. "The male posture, whether assumed by all men or not, prepares for the role of master. The male is disposed to objectify the other, to instrumentalize and calculate his relation to her in order to deny his dependency. The female posture disposes the woman to accept objectification and control in order to flee separation. He asserts individual selfhood while she relinquishes it."[34]

In rational violence, the victim matters to the violator; in nonrational violence, the victim's responses do not matter to the violator. In both cases, the violator is very likely to be male. Benjamin's final statement argues against a politics that "tries to sanitize or rationalize the erotic, fantastic components of human life," because "it will not defeat domination but only play into it" (p. 171). Benjamin says that Andrea Dworkin mistakes *The Story of O* for an affirmation of female degradation (n.4, p. 171). It is hard not to take the novel this way, however. The acquiescence of the woman in the story and her appreciation of the male's "rational control" fits nicely into the convenient male belief that women are in reality masochists and want to be dominated. As a book that sells this idea, I believe *The Story of O* is pornographic and as such should be resisted. This is not to say that domination will end if we ban its description, but certainly it seems useful to point out the sense in which it is degrading to women. I do not say this to counter Benjamin's general argument, but I wish that "cool culturalists" such as Benjamin could find a place in their analyses to condemn the uses to which fantasy may be put.

Benjamin goes on to argue that erotic domination is closely connected to male domination in the culture as a whole. Here she means not direct male dominance over females but rather the cultural hegemony of the male stance; thus our culture is an "instrumental culture" of rational calculation in which nurturance becomes privatized and the maternal world dwindles.[35]

Keller and Benjamin as Culture Critics

Keller's and Benjamin's analyses are valuable in showing how dominant cultural trends are related to masculinity on a variety of levels; however, we must guard against overgeneralizing about the defects of modern culture. In this respect I found Keller's analysis exemplary and Benjamin's analysis problematic. Whereas Keller makes rationality a human propensity par excellence, Benjamin tends to see rationality, instrumentalism, and individualism as "bad." But the orientations she criticizes are the very ones that fueled the women's movement in the 1960s and 1970s. Women who had been restricted to the domains of wife and mother wanted to participate in the rational, instrumental world of work outside the home. In my view the feminist critique of modern culture needs to recognize the positive benefits that have accrued to women from the degree of integration and assimilation we have achieved in the society that we are now in a position to criticize.

In facing the question of change, Keller drops her analysis of infantile dilemmas and says we can change because consciousness makes choice possible. Benjamin tries to stay within the limits set by the underlying assumptions of her analysis and becomes pessimistic. In terms of the particular psychoanalytic premises she uses, the alternative to the development she describes is remaining "merged" with the mother and therefore being a nonself, or all of the world, that is, undifferentiated. In her terms, rational individualism is "a defense against helplessness and the ambivalence of differentiation." If we give that up, we would have to resort to "more primitive defenses (pathological narcissism) or to considering the possibility of a more terrifying state than we have yet been able to endure."[36] Fortunately, this terrible state of being a nonself may be more a male fantasy and fear in an individualistic world than an infantile state. At times Benjamin seems to understand that this fear of "merging" is more characteristic of males' ideation, but because of her use of a theory that assumes an initial total lack of differentiation, she seems to get caught up in it herself and become stymied by her own theory.

One cannot help suspecting that Keller's and Benjamin's speculations about infantile fantasies are adult projections onto infants of adult preoccupations with the typically Western cultural issues of freedom versus nurturance, autonomy versus belonging and (within the culture of the Frankfurt School) recognition versus negation. In my view Keller's and Benjamin's writings should be taken as insightful cultural analyses, but ones that remain at the cultural level. Even when Benjamin discusses fathers and the Oedipus complex, she is discussing the symbolic interpretation adults give to fathers, not necessarily the meaning that fathers have for children themselves at various stages of their development.

Infantile Ideation and Psychoanalysis

The issues discussed in this chapter, and perhaps especially Keller's and Benjamin's reliance on Winnicott's theories, are all relevant to a long-standing debate concerning the nature of infantile thought processes. Many psychoanalysts have been critical of a tendency among some of their colleagues to project adult ideation onto children. Emanuel Peterfreund has called this tendency "the adultomorphization of infancy" and suggests that those who study infants, especially those with a strong biological orientation, find little evidence to corroborate the speculations.[37] To say that psychoanalytic approaches can provide a useful framework for thinking about development is not the same as giving equal weight to every psychoanalytic idea that comes along in this highly speculative field. It is one thing to believe that deeply held emotional reactions are formed early and quite another to buy into an elaborate theory concerning infantile ideation that would be virtually impossible to verify empirically.

While some psychoanalytic theorists, such as Margaret Mahler, posit an initial stage of autism, others, such as Winnicott and Robert Stoller, posit, albeit in different ways, a primary state of symbiosis or nondifferentiation between infant and mother. In this latter state, it is assumed that the infant is merged or fused with the mother and does not differentiate self from mother.

Daniel Stern, who is both a developmental psychologist and a psychoanalyst, contends that there is little reason to believe that a symbiotic state ever exists for the child. On the basis of detailed observations of infant-caretaker interactions as well as his analytic experience with adults, Stern maintains that there never is any confusion between self and other, no merger, no symbiosis in the mind of the infant.[38] Stern suggests that fantasies about "merging" are possible only after the development of a capacity to symbolize. He does not reject psychoanalytic accounts, however, but implies that explanations such as Winnicott's could not apply until a later phase of development beyond infancy has been reached, that is, until after the acquisition of language (p. 11).

Stern also suggests that issues such as autonomy versus dependence (or perhaps interdependence, in my terms) should be thought of as occurring not at one developmental stage or another but rather in different forms at various stages. Freud and Erikson placed the emergence of autonomy at the anal phase and related it to toilet training. Spitz located it at around fifteen months, when children begin to say no. Mahler thought the critical period for autonomy was learning to walk. Stern suggests that the development of autonomy can be seen in very young infants as they learn to control visual engagements with the caretaker. I believe Stern is correct to say that there is no decisive event; dilemmas related to autonomy occur and reoccur and are transformed at various stages in the development of the sense of self (p. 22).

Stern places the self as structure and process in the center of developmental theory, and thus new senses of the self become the organizing principles of developmental stages. Stern sees this as a four-stage process beginning with an emergent sense of self as a physical entity. The second stage is a sense of a "core" self, which includes a sense of self and other as not only separate physical entities but separate entities of action, affect, and continuity. In the third stage the infant begins to become aware of the intentions and affects that guide behavior. This stage represents a quantum leap from the previous stage because it opens up the possibility of intersubjectivity, that is, communication in which we can understand the subjective states of others and communicate our subjective states to them. In Parsons's terms this would be the stage in which the infant learns that physical acts of care "mean" that the mother "cares about" the infant. During this period there might well be a pervasive sense of well-being, of being-at-one with the other, but Stern would not call this a primary state of symbiosis, because the infant is always an active participant.

Finally there is a sense of verbal self on which the capacity to be self-reflective depends. This sense is what G. H. Mead described as "the reflexive self," the capacity to take oneself as an object, to represent the self and the other to the self. This capacity to symbolize to oneself that which one wants to communicate to the other is the key to the phenomenon of intersubjectivity.

Stern's ideas about developmental stages of the self fit well with other developmental and sociological perspectives that view the self as being formed in and through social interaction.[39] The sense of self develops simultaneously with the sense of other. There is much we do not know about the specifics of the process at different levels of understanding and maturity. The points for now are that gender differentiation is involved with more general processes of self-definition and that parsimony is advisable in describing this process in terms of infant ideation. Both the fear and envy hypotheses and the tenuous masculine identity hypotheses can have validity without "adultomorphizing" infant ideation.

Although Stern does not mention gender differentiation in his description of the stages of self-awareness, one might argue that the sense of self, or conceptions about the self in relation to others, may vary as a consequence of the social definition of self as male or female. Does one see the self as separate from others and defending the boundaries of the self while still preserving contact by controlling others, or does one see the self and others as separate but interdependent and without the necessity for control?[40]

Summary and Discussion

The idea that men are more likely to think in terms of difference than women and to see the nature of gender difference in terms of superiority-inferiority could be the critical insight to bring together feminists who deemphasize gender difference with those who focus on and analyze the nature of the difference from a feminist perspective. Feminists who deemphasize gender difference are actually "woman-centered" in the sense that they see that an important virtue of women is that they are less likely to emphasize difference than men. Feminists who emphasize difference accept this larger truth that gender difference should not be as salient as it now is in male-female interaction but nevertheless want to examine the nature of the difference in order to create a woman-centered definition. In short, the insight that one key difference is that men emphasize difference can help integrate diverse positions with feminism.

In this chapter I give my own interpretation of the work of Dorothy Dinnerstein and some earlier work of Nancy Chodorow in connection with the hypothesis that women's early monopoly on child care accounts for male misogyny and male dominance itself. The arguments concerning the production of misogynist attitudes are as old as psychoanalysis, but generalizing these arguments to systems of male dominance is new. I interpret the fear and envy hypotheses as stressing how infantile dependency needs contribute to the primitive perception that women have great power to produce total bliss or total devastation. The more recent hypotheses concerning tenuous masculine identity stress boys' difficulties in "disidentifying" with the femaleness of mothers in order to identify as a male. Psychoanalytic explanations are useful because they take the unconscious and nonrational into account and thus can explain the relative intractability of certain attitudes without claiming that these attitudes are biologically rooted and cannot be changed.

Evelyn Fox Keller and Jessica Benjamin are less concerned with using psychoanalytic ideas to explain male dominance as a system than with using them to explain the development of the attitude of domination itself. This fits in with critical theorists' concern with domination and attaches it to masculine propensities. Both Benjamin and Keller soft-pedal equal parenting as a viable cure for the infantile dilemmas they envision. This downplaying probably results from their fear that males would carry their dominating tendencies into mothering and reproduce the very system we seek to destroy. I share this fear and will develop the reasons for it in the chapters to follow.

The implications of all of these analyses at a psychological level is that we all need to become aware of the nonrational and unconscious bases of our behavior in order to "grow up." In one way or another all of the authors discussed imply that instead of sweeping male misogyny and propensities for domination under the table, we need to examine them not only to see that they run deep but also to hold them up to the light of criticism. I agree. Moreover, men and women are capable of taking thought and changing their own consciousness. It can happen, but it is important not just to give up old ways of seeing but to invent new ones, not out of whole cloth, but out of women's own intuitions. The new emphasis on interdependence and self in relationship seems headed in the right direction. This emphasis keeps the issue from being that of autonomy versus dependence, self-assertion versus passivity, domination versus submission, and so forth.

Consciousness also depends on and creates social structural arrangements. At another level all of the analyses I have been discussing are limited to the psychological consequences of women's being responsible for early child care. If analysis goes no further than the mother-child relationship, we are left with the impression that women's mothering is the problem. This is hardly the case.

Chapter Five

Mothers versus the Male Peer Group

Chodorow to some extent and Benjamin and Keller to a much greater extent can be viewed as beginning a subtle movement away from blaming mothers for male dominance and toward recognizing the virtues of women's less hierarchical, less dualistic, and less "sex-typed" (in this sense, more androgynous) way of thinking. This type of thinking characterizes women as mothers more so than it characterizes women as wives. I will take this direction further and argue that it is mothers who account for our non-gender-differentiated humanness and that male misogyny is fostered in the male peer group, not in the mother-son relationship.

In this chapter I continue to develop a more positive view of women's mothering and women's more relational orientation. I discuss how the two might be developmentally connected. I begin by examining how feminists' various stances on women's mothering are related to their views on why women mother. I will examine the central argument in Chodorow's book, *The Reproduction of Mothering*. Her argument here focuses not on the reproduction of male dominance but on the reproduction in women of a positive desire to mother. I follow this with a discussion of what women's mothering does for infants of both genders and how that gets undermined in males in the course of interactions with their peers. Men's aggression, their distancing, and their sex objectification of women are later phenomena reinforced by males, not by mothers.

Multiple Pressures on Women to Mother

For most people it seems odd to even ask why women mother, because in all known human societies women, not men, have been the primary caretakers of young children.[1] Many factors coalesce to make women's mothering one of the most overdetermined phenomena in human societies. Simply that only women are biologically capable of bearing and nursing children would surely predispose both women and men to assume that early child care would and should be primarily in the hands of women. Hormonal changes during pregnancy and lactation may also make it easier for women to learn to mother infants. There are also the eliciting qualities of infants, who demand mothering of the person with whom they are in contact, and societies regularly organize production so that women are in contact with children the most. Although production has been organized in a variety of ways in different societies, the assumption has generally been made that women will mother. This is clearly true in our own society now, where men's outside earnings are markedly higher than women's.

Certainly too, women have been "expected" by men to mother; men have never assigned the job to themselves. Even in the early days of the kibbutz movement, which self-consciously sought to bring about gender equality and collectivized child care to this end, men were not assigned to early child care and did not take it on.[2] Moreover, the negative sanctions for women's "failure" to mother have been heavy. Women who do not have children and women who abuse children are considered unnatural or sick. Thus women may nurture because of the negative responses they get for not doing so. Finally, beyond all these social factors creating what Judith Blake has called "coercive pronatalism," Chodorow argues that women are motivated to mother and that they get gratification out of the experience of mothering not just because of the way production is organized or because they are expected to or because they are capable of doing it but because they themselves, within themselves, want to.[3] To list all these factors is not to say that the association of women with mothering cannot be changed, but it would be extraordinarily difficult to do so and in my view would not be necessary for women's emancipation. A more useful alter-

native would be to reassess women's mothering in a more positive
light and, at the same time, to emphasize that "mothering" does
not mean that all women should bear or care for children or that
mothering need be central in the lives of the women who do.

Evaluating Biological Influences

Feminists, such as Alice Rossi, who maintain that women's mothering does not have to be a threat to women's equality, urge other
feminists to recognize that there may be biological influences on
women's mothering.[4] Rossi argues quite correctly that equality is
ultimately a political and moral decision that does not have to be
based on some premise of identity between women and men to be
realized. In her zeal to convince feminists and social scientists to
admit biological factors into their analyses, Rossi at times seems to
overstate her case and implies inevitable connections between hormones and behavior where none exist. I believe, however, that it is
an error to call her a biological essentialist.[5] Rossi is much too much
of a sociologist to claim that biology determines social structure;
rather, she claims that biological factors make some learning easier
for one gender than the other and that this difference needs to be
taken into account in any program of action, such as involving men
more in child care.[6]

Generally, feminists who see women's mothering as lying at the
root of women's inequality have often been at great pains to deny
any biological influences. Especially in the past, much feminist energy has gone into arguing against antifeminists who tried to justify
the status quo by using biological arguments. Now feminists who
are knowledgeable about biology have made more sophisticated
critiques of biological determinism that do not totally deny the influence of biology and that spell out in detail the complex ways in
which biological factors interact with individual life history and social structural factors.[7] Overall, the more one knows about biology,
the less one is likely to claim (or to fear) that biological factors constitute a categorical threat to change. It seems to me unnecessary
for feminists to reject the possibility of biological influences on psychological gender differences. To do so renders biological influences more important and potentially devastating to feminist arguments than they need be. As a sociologist and a feminist, I am not

primarily concerned with understanding how biological influences operate, but I am concerned with the symbolic interpretation of biologically related facts. These are separate but related issues and need to be approached from both sides.

Other feminists who see women's mothering as oppressive have not so much denied biological factors as ignored them, pointing instead to social factors that lead to women's mothering and men's nonmothering. Marxist feminists usually consider these factors to be related to the organization of production. Some radical feminists who see women's mothering as especially oppressive have also ignored biology (except to say that it makes women's childbearing possible) and have argued that women are forced to mother by a variety of causes outside themselves. In this latter scenario, women are conceived of as beings who have been duped and coerced, ultimately by men, into taking on this unrewarding and frustrating role. These feminists argue that taking women's mothering for granted is an error and propose that women should refuse to mother.[8]

Shulamith Firestone gives the biological fact of women's childbearing more than its due and ends up blaming women's physical childbearing directly and indirectly for women's oppression. She assumes that if women physically bear children they are by definition at a disadvantage; therefore, her "solution" is for women to no longer physically bear children. She advocates developing the technology whereby children could be created in test tubes, thereby saving women from an experience that she likens to "shitting a pumpkin" and that she sees as setting up women's oppression.[9] Firestone seems to believe that one can prevent women from being child-*rearers* only by preventing them from being child-*bearers*. This connection, of course, is not inevitable. If one could justify a technology for eliminating women's childbearing, surely one could also justify disassociating women from child-rearing without needing to eliminate women's physical childbearing. Firestone ends up being a kind of technological determinist.

Biology influences women's mothering, as does the organization of production, and certainly men have exercised control over women's mothering and have at times foisted mothering onto women. But in my view women's own motivation also lies behind women's mothering. Although this desire is conditioned by other factors, it is desire nevertheless. In saying this I put myself in danger of adding yet another voice to the pronatalist chorus. This is not my aim. I do not urge women to bear children, nor should women feel guilty about not mothering at all. My point is that many women do seem to want to mother in spite of mothering in this society having become an impediment to sexual love and full participation in the public sphere.[10] Children no longer do work, they no longer bring status, they are economic and social liabilities, and mothers tend to be blamed if their children don't turn out right or don't fit in. Some feminists have made all these points and have concluded women's mothering is clearly a burden and that it should be eliminated.

But in spite of all of the disadvantages attached to mothering, women do want to mother, even in the modern era. That women choose to mother under modern circumstances can be taken as evidence of a desire to mother, ambivalent though it may be. Women who are voluntarily childless are more than made up for by women who were involuntarily childless but who now, because of better health and better medical knowledge, can and do have children. There is no evidence that we are moving toward a small class of child-rearers and a large class of "child-free" women.[11] If feminists were to call for a "birth strike," in my view it should be not in order to end women's mothering but to end the penalties that this society exacts from women *for* mothering.

Chodorow on the Motive to Mother

The most sophisticated and sustained attempt to grapple seriously with the question of why women would want to mother is Nancy Chodorow's book on the subject, *The Reproduction of Mothering*. In order to explain the replication in each generation of women's motive to mother and the relative lack of this motive in men, Chodorow uses psychoanalytic theory, especially as interpreted by the object relations school.[12] Chodorow compares her analysis of the reproduction of mothering within the nuclear family to Talcott Parsons's analysis of the relationship between middle-class family structure and children's achievement motivation, and to Max Horkheimer's analysis of the German authoritarian family and compliance motivation.[13] Whereas these theorists were largely concerned with male motivation, Chodorow is concerned primarily with the internalization of gender differentiation and especially the motivation of women.

Chodorow disagrees with social learning theorists who claim in effect that girls are made into mothers by parents who give them dolls instead of trucks and expect them to help with child care, by texts that depict women mainly as mothers, and by schools that teach girls home economics instead of shop. Although agreeing that reinforcement and modeling do play a part, Chodorow feels that only psychoanalysis that focuses on motivation more than behavior and more on early learning than late can explain so basic and pervasive a phenomenon as women's propensity to mother.

Chodorow's central idea is to link women's mothering to women's more relational personality. She argues that the feminine personality includes a fundamental tendency to define self in terms of relationship and that the masculine personality defines self in terms of denial of relationship. This meshes precisely with the conclusions from our research based on self-report described in Chapter 3. Rather than defining women as those who are lacking (according to Freud, the central fact about women was that they lack a penis *and* principles), Chodorow implies that it is men who lack. Women mother and are relational; men do not mother and are less relational. Chodorow offers an explanation.

Although some feminists argue that women are not more relational than men, it is much harder to argue that women do not mother more than men. Chodorow's closely connecting the two strengthens the argument for women's greater relational orientation by making it as universal as women's mothering. Clearly, there is some circularity here, because Chodorow proceeds to explain women's mothering by women's greater relational orientation. She seeks to avoid circularity, however, by positing a specific mechanism by which women's more relational personality is produced. According to Chodorow, gender-differentiated personalities are reproduced because mothers themselves experience, and hence, respond to girls differently from boys, even in earliest infancy. Although mothers have a sense of oneness and continuity with both genders, Chodorow contends that this sense of relatedness is stronger and lasts longer with daughters than with sons because of the mother's own female gender identity. The mother projects her own sense of self onto her female infants and tends to experience them as less separate from herself. Chodorow also brings in a presumption of the mother's heterosexuality into her argument about why mothers bond more closely with their daughters than their sons. She argues that mothers respond to male infants as male "opposites" and begin to sexualize the relationship. These processes then serve to separate the son from her and to bind the daughter to her. Along with other psychoanalytically oriented writers, Chodorow tends to link heterosexuality with gender identity. I question this connection.

To support her argument empirically, Chodorow relies largely on clinical accounts of pathological mothers who presumably manifest normal tendencies in exaggerated form. Because more cases are reported of pathological mothers who deny separateness to their daughters and refuse to allow them to individuate than are reported of mothers who do the same with sons, Chodorow concludes that all mothers tend to deny separateness to their daughters more than to their sons. Furthermore, she finds that, even though clinicians may not point it out, the cases involving sons indicate that the mother reacts to the son as a sexual other rather than as an extension of herself.

Thus, Chodorow feels that it is *women's* differential feelings for and treatment of infants that cause females to have greater feelings of primary identification and primary love, to maintain less clear boundaries between self and other, to experience themselves in relationship to others, and to be more concerned with relational issues than are men. Although she also argues that it is easier for the boy to differentiate himself from the mother because he sooner or later recognizes his anatomical difference from the mother, Chodorow's emphasis is on the mother's own attitude and her own response to physical difference, not on the child's response. Chodorow does not take a strong version of the merging-with-the-mother position discussed in the last chapter. Her analysis is considerably more parsimonious in this respect than Benjamin's or Keller's.

According to Chodorow, girls' tendencies to be attached to their mother do not basically change in the oedipal period, when sexual preference is thought to be established. Even as girls turn to the father (for aid in the process of differentiating self from mother) and finally become, as Chodorow puts it, "genitally heterosexual," they do not give up their primary attachment to the mother. Chodorow agrees with Freud's contention that girls retain their involvement with both parents, whereas boys escape more completely from the mother by identifying with the father.[14]

Assessing Chodorow's Analysis

It is not clear why Chodorow feels she has to assume that the mother is heterosexual for her account to make sense. Bringing heterosexuality into a discussion of early gender formation may well be an unexamined legacy from psychoanalytic theory itself. Could one not just as well contend that mothers bond more closely with their daughters because they are also female and will also be capable of bearing children? Simply that the mother knows that the son cannot bear children could be sufficient to make her feel less close to him. By introducing heterosexuality into the argument, does Chodorow imply that lesbians are not gender-identified as females and thus would not feel a oneness with a female child? This certainly does not seem to be the case with lesbian feminists. Or is she saying that lesbians would be sexually attracted to their daughters and hence because of this would not bond closely with them? Chodorow admits to hedging of the issue of the mother's sexual orientation. If she had spelled out the implications of her assumptions about the mother's heterosexuality, she might have seen the degree to which psychoanalysis does confound gender and sexual orientation in ways that may be far more persuasive to males than to females. In my view, females are less likely to relate gender to heterosexuality than males.[15] Certainly more and more theorists, including Chodorow, argue that gender identity and sexual orientations are not one and the same, but Chodorow in her own analysis does not focus directly on how they might and might not be related.

Even in her more recent writings, Chodorow still insists that the mechanism that produces a more relational orientation in females than males is that mothers bind their daughters to them more closely than sons, that mothers perhaps unconsciously identify more with their daughters than their sons.[16] This view sometimes seems to blame individual mothers by implying that mothers somehow do not allow their daughters to individuate or that mothers impede their daughters' individuation.[17] Chodorow's description of women as less individuated than men obscures the distinction I have tried to maintain between relationality and dependency. Her description implies that mothers' treatment of daughters makes them both more dependent and more relational than males. I believe that both genders seek growth and move away from a relationship of dependency. In this movement toward greater autonomy the girl retains her relational tie to the mother while decreasing her dependency. The relational orientation that the girl gets from her mother should not be confused with the dependency on males that she may adopt first in relation to the father. Fathers may serve as a lever to help boys and girls extricate themselves from infantile dependency, but, as I will argue later, they do so at the price of encouraging dependency on themselves in their daughters.

Is a specific mechanism for explaining women's relational propensities, such as the close-bindingness of the mother, really necessary? In spite of the problem of circularity, it may be better from an empirical and theoretical standpoint to maintain simply that women's more relational orientation is transmitted through women's mothering. The specific mechanism Chodorow posits may be only one of many factors, all of which contribute to this outcome. The other specific factor that she brings in, the mother's heterosexuality, may be important for psychoanalytic theorists, but it seems unnecessary.[18]

In the beginning of her book, Chodorow argues at some length that biological factors, such as differences in hormonal balance between males and females, are neither necessary nor sufficient to explain women's mothering. She argues specifically against Alice Rossi, who points out that women are hormonally *predisposed* (this is not the same as saying inevitably *disposed*) to mother.[19] To deny biological factors affecting gender is out of line with mainstream psychoanalytic thought, and as Janet Sayers points out, psychoanalytically oriented researchers have argued that the biological processes of pregnancy often "serve to revive in women their feelings about their relationships with their own mothers, feelings which subsequently link up with the way they relate to their own children."[20] Chodorow could have used such arguments to back up her case that a mother's relationship with her daughter is the crucial variable in reproducing gender-differentiated personalities, but she did not.

Since the publication of her book, Chodorow has changed her mind a bit regarding biology; she now says that she has been convinced by Rossi that she and other feminists "must be open to the investigation of biological variables and that those who argued or implied that such investigation is illegitimate were wrong." She goes on to say, however, that so far, it has not been shown that biology itself produces a personality type that wants to mother.[21] I agree; biology never acts alone.

I believe that one reason for Chodorow's overly energetic rejection of biological factors had to do with her earlier arguments that linked male misogyny to women's mothering. In 1978, she, along with most feminists, especially nonbiologists, tended to equate "biological" with "immutable" and felt that if one were to seek change, one had to deny biology. Her own account suggests, however, that women's mothering may be just as immutable for psychocultural reasons as it might have been thought to be for biological ones. Even if one has eliminated biology, it becomes difficult to argue for change, because of the universality of women's mothering. Chodorow has been accused of not being historically specific, but her answer is that women's mothering is not historically specific. It is universal in the sense that women, not men, have always been primarily responsible for the care of young children in all societies. Although the organization of parenting, and even the concept of parenting, including the role of fathers, has undergone innumerable historical changes and has been greatly affected by economic and political arrangements, women's mothering has stayed the same in a fundamental way.

Most of Chodorow's book, *The Reproduction of Mothering*, is devoted to just this: how women's mothering is reproduced. Toward the end of her book, however, Chodorow shifts her argument from how women's mothering orientations are developed and turns to the question of gender inequality. At this point she returns to her argument in earlier works (discussed in Chapter 4), having to do with men's tendency to free themselves from making a female identification by devaluing women and overvaluing what men do.[22] This then becomes the reason she recommends a change in mothering arrangements. Chodorow also makes the argument that women's mothering is related to male dominance because it tends to perpetuate women's association with the domestic sphere and men's association with the public sphere, which in turn gives males greater authority.

I am not convinced that women's mothering in itself associates

women with the domestic sphere. In hunting and gathering societies, women with children traveled widely and were not dependent on their husbands for food. What association there was between women and domesticity in these societies had more to do
with women as wives (keepers of their husband's hearth) than with
women as mothers.[23] Chodorow, however, seems to picture the
public-domestic distinction as a direct result of women's more relational orientation.

Chodorow depicts the public and domestic spheres as operating
hierarchically; therefore, she comes close at times to collapsing the
categories of gender differentiation and male domination.[24] She
states, however, that "kinship rules organize claims of men on domestic units and men dominate kinship."[25] This formulation leaves
room for arguing, as I do, that it is not women's mothering but marriage that places women, sometimes directly, sometimes indirectly,
in domestic units. Chodorow does not say this, however, perhaps
because she cannot quite bring herself to separate women's mothering from heterosexual marriage. If one does make this separation, it
becomes clearer that marriage, not mothering per se, puts women in
the domestic sphere—at least in modern Western cultures.

In my view the contribution of Chodorow's book does not lie in
her last-minute reliance on male mothering as a "solution" to male
dominance, but in her sustained development of an argument
about gender differentiation in the preoedipal period. Chodorow's
focus on this period coincides with my interest in separating the
maternal from the heterosexual aspects of being a woman. Her
analysis reinforces an emphasis on the maternal aspects, even
though she seems to need to assume the mother's heterosexuality.
Although Chodorow at times seems to blame mothers for making
daughters dependent on them, her work begins to move toward a
more positive view of women's relationality and women's mothering. Chodorow's analysis is, in this sense, woman-centered and
contributes to the development of a more positive view of women
as mothers, as opposed to an image of women as essentially appendages of men.

Moreover, I do not believe that Chodorow's suggestion that
mothers tie girls more closely to them than boys should mean that
mothers by their own actions create gender difference. Rather, the
greater insight here is that the mother-daughter relationship forms

a basis for positive female bonding. For sons, breaking away from the mother forms the basis for male bonding. In the remainder of this chapter I will take this argument further and broaden it to include more than a narrowly psychoanalytic perspective. I will show also how associations among male peers are the developmental precursors of male dominance and indirectly of males' sex objectification of women.

Mothers and Becoming Human

Talcott Parsons once defined identification as the internalization not of a total personality or of personality traits but of a reciprocal role relationship that is operating at a particular period in the child's development. Thus in Parsons's view, rather than saying an infant "identifies" with its mother, it is more accurate to say that the infant "learns to play a social role *in interaction* with her; his behavior—hence his motivation—is organized according to a generalized pattern of norms which define shared and internalized meanings of the acts occurring on both sides."[26] By *role* Parsons refers to the system or set of expectations that come to characterize a particular interaction. Thus the earliest interactions between infants and others quickly become meaningful interactions in which expectations are established on both sides. Early caretakers define the infant to itself and interpret its actions as carrying certain meanings. Just what these meanings are becomes established in and through the interaction itself. The infant learns to become sensitive to the responses of others and to some extent to elicit the responses it wants.

In Meadian terms the infant internalizes both the other's attitude toward herself or himself and (indirectly) others, as well as responding as "self" to that attitude. In this way the infant learns to "love" and be caring as well as to feel cared for and cared about. Thus social learning, modeling, and cognitive development take place through interacting in complementary or reciprocal roles. Through this interaction a system of shared meaning and values is negotiated and sustained. In this first relationship the caretaker has great power because of the infant's physical dependency and the caretaker's far wider experience and resources, including cultural resources.

This early "role" learning takes place in an erotic context and gets power from an erotic base. For Parsons the primary significance of the infantile eroticism that Freud so stressed is that it serves as a bridge between organismic needs and the more generalized social need to be loved. In Parsons's view the mother-infant relationship is indeed an erotic one, and the generalized eroticism that characterizes the relationship serves as the bridge across which the infant travels from being a biological organism to being a genuinely caring and cared about human being. Parsons is less concerned with Freud's theories about stages of oral, anal, and phallic eroticism than he is with the idea that eroticism itself is first experienced as diffuse, or total. It provides a base upon which more differentiated role learning takes place, learning that is not based on eroticism to the same extent.[27]

Infants need to be cared for in the most general sense, and this care involves body contact, and a nurturant as well as a nurtured self is internalized by children of both genders. The essence of this interaction is not sexual or heterosexual or bisexual in the adult understanding of these terms, although it is certainly erotic and sensual from the standpoint of both caretaker and child. In my view the maternal identification (regardless of who this maternal figure actually is) represents the common humanity that both genders share and lays down the capacity for nurturance in both females and males. To the extent that women retain and elaborate this maternal orientation, they retain and elaborate qualities of caring and human connectedness. To the extent that males are constrained to differentiate "self" from "mother," they gain a stake in emphasizing gender difference, and this difference is reinforced by the idea that males are superior to females. But in reality, males are constrained to deny this human connectedness, and later, in a strange metamorphosis, they deny women's humanness by making them into objects.

While there is a sense in which Chodorow is correct to say that mothers differentiate between their male and female children by feeling more like or akin to their female offspring, the larger truth is that mothers compared to fathers do not make much of a differentiation in the erotic pleasure they receive from their children or in the amount of nurturance they provide their children. For example, mothers breast-feed children of both genders, and the sensuous pleasures mothers get from this activity does not appear to differ significantly in terms of the biological gender of the child. In interviews conducted in connection with my research on the management of sexuality within the family, many women spoke about the sensuousness of children themselves and of the sensual pleasures children brought. Several women spontaneously mentioned feeling sexually stimulated by nursing, but this was not related to the gender of the child. A mother might comment on the difference between the way a boy nurses and the way a girl nurses, but it was the breast stimulation that was pleasurable. Mothers also talked about the pleasure they got out of cuddling and stroking the smooth bodies of very young children regardless of their gender. Presumably also in cultures that permit mothers to stimulate the genitals of children of both genders, mothers' pleasure in this activity does not depend on whether the child is a male or a female.[28] From the mother's standpoint, eroticism is not necessarily heterosexual eroticism. To a mother, a baby is a baby, a child is a child. The gender of the child is likely to be of greater importance to the father, who is more likely than the mother to think of gender in terms of "sex."

Maccoby and Jacklin report that the degree of early attachment to the mother appears to be remarkably the same for both genders. They report that the bulk of studies show no differences on the part of mothers in the amount of affectionate contact between mother and male and female infants.[29] Their evidence is at least consonant with the idea that males begin like females with expressiveness or feelings of connectedness and that mothers do not differentiate appreciably between males and females in the amount of nurturance they provide.

There is every reason to believe that this process of becoming human is far more clearly linked to women's mothering than to men's fathering. I say this not to argue that women must therefore keep on mothering or that men cannot foster "humanness" but rather to point out that mothering is associated with the establishment of positively valued behaviors and orientations in both females and males. Overall, one of the most consistently replicated findings in child-rearing studies (though these studies have methodological shortcomings) is the positive association between ratings of maternal warmth and ratings of conscience in children of both genders, and this disposition to cooperate based on maternal warmth does not appear to be differentiated by gender.[30]

Chodorow claims that women's attitudes toward their sons cause sons to be more distanced and to emphasize difference. Dinnerstein claims that infantile attitudes toward mothers' apparent power lead to male dominance. Both analyses blame women's mothering and prescribe that men should also mother. My position is that in order to promote an end to male dominance, we need to look first at male tendencies to differentiate and dominate, not at female tendencies to mother. The tendency to differentiate and dominate is only indirectly related to women's mothering. It is not what mothers teach or convey; it is established in the company of other males and reinforced by other males in interaction within peer groups.

Childhood Gender Segregation

Child care has universally been far more the province of women than of men. In this sense one can say that women's mothering is universal. Girls and boys self-segregate themselves on the basis of gender as children. In this sense male and female peer groups are universal. In a review of research in this area, Eleanor Maccoby and Carol Jacklin report that gender segregation in childhood is a widespread, cross-cultural phenomenon, having been found in every situation where there are enough children of similar age so that children have a choice of playmates.[31] Adults can manipulate this preference and thereby temporarily decrease gender segregation, but when adults do not interfere, children's own preferences are for segregation.

Maccoby and Jacklin emphasize that this tendency to segregate by gender is not a result of central tendencies in individual differences (e.g., it is not true that more aggressive boys are more likely to segregate than less aggressive boys); rather, there is very little variation within each gender group in the tendency to play with one's own gender. Gender segregation is a genuine group phenomenon rather than a reflection of the different dispositions of individual children. It is also more stable than individual toy or play preferences.

The mechanisms that produce gender segregation are by no means clear, but since it is more stable than individual disposi-

tions, Maccoby and Jacklin tend to believe that cognitive awareness of gender is the key; that is, "knowing" one's own gender sets
gender segregation in motion. But the cognitive knowledge explanation does not preclude other explanations concerning why children seem to want to play separately once they know who belongs
to what gender. There is some evidence that segregation is initiated by girls because they do not like the way boys interact. Maccoby and Jacklin cite a number of studies, even of young infants,
that suggest that "avoidance of dominance" motivates girls to withdraw from boys. Girls begin to direct their affiliative behaviors toward other girls by twenty-eight months, while boys begin orient-
ing to boys more exclusively somewhat later. Girls may withdraw
from boys because they find them to be unsatisfactory playmates,
whereas boys withdraw from girls because of a greater need to con-
solidate a new gender identity, which in turn is shored up by denigrating girls. This is not an absolute distinction, because young
girls tend to disdain boys too, but putting down the other gender
operates more strongly with boys.

Recent research on children's cognitive knowledge of gender
and its influence on children's behavior lends support to the idea
that for boys, at least, an awareness of gender sets in motion the
process of distancing from "feminine things." In a study of very
young children (twenty to thirty months old) who had differing degrees of understanding of gender labeling, Beverly Fagot found
that understanding gender labels did not affect the amount of time
girls spent with male-typical and female-typical toys, but such
understanding did affect the time boys spent. Boys who understood gender cut down on female-typical activities. Thus, boys
without gender labels or gender identity played with dolls as much
as girls, but doll play was virtually nonexistent in boys who showed
some knowledge of gender labels.[32] This clearly suggests that there
is nothing built into males that makes doll play unacceptable to
them. Rather, it suggests that they do indeed internalize a nurtur-
ing-nurtured self image but that they move away from it when gender becomes relevant to them.

The research findings concerning the composition and functioning of boys' versus girls' groups may be summarized as follows.
Boys play in somewhat larger groups than girls. They play in more
public places and more away from adults. They play more roughly

with more body contact and more fighting than girls, and interaction is more oriented to issues of dominance and the formation of a hierarchy. Girls, by contrast, are more likely to take turns, with more participation by all in making decisions. Girls' friendships are more intense and diffuse, and male friendships more oriented around specific activities.[33]

Janet Lever, writing in the mid-1970s, described the differences between the organization and orientation of boys' and girls' games and concluded that boys' games and play styles prepare them for the adult world of impersonal competition better than girls' games and play styles. From Lever's standpoint, girls would be better off "training" with the boys and adopting their games.[34] In the 1980s this assumption of the superiority of male games sounds "sexist." As we examine interaction in informal play groups, we are now able to see the greater complexities and subtleties of the female style and to appreciate its egalitarian features, which can well be used in the public sphere.

These differing structures of male and female peer groups seem to perpetuate themselves "in the doing of gender," as ethnomethodologists put it, through speech patterns. Girls' speech seems to be used to create and maintain close and equal relationships, to control without domination, and to interpret the speech of other girls. Boys' speech is used to attract and maintain an audience, to assert dominance, and to assert one's self when others have the floor.[35] This description of boys' speech seems similar to Finigan's operational definition of "unmitigated agency," which he found in his male-predominant adult occupational groups (see Chapter 3).

Marjorie Goodwin, an ethnomethodologist, provides interesting documentation for this contrast in a detailed study of the differing speech patterns of girls at play and boys at play. She found that boys use more directive forms of speech such as "Gimme this" and "Get out of my way," whereas girls are more likely to use forms of speech that include the group as a whole, such as "Let's do this or that." Whereas boys differentiate speaker and hearer, girls include both speaker and hearer in the action under discussion. Goodwin's findings support the argument about the male propensity for difference and dominance and also suggest that this propensity is constructed in and through male interaction with other males. Goodwin makes it clear that girls are quite capable of using direct commands too when acting in the role of mother or teacher, but they rarely use such commands among female status equals.[36]

Male Peer Group Conformity

Girls have been accused of being conformists because they stay closer to adults, but studies of very young children conducted in naturalistic settings suggest that males may conform fully as much as females—but more often to their own male age mates than to adults. For example, in a study of twenty- to twenty-five-month-old children who entered a play group of similarly aged and somewhat older children, Fagot found that teacher and female peer reactions do not significantly affect boys' continuation of a particular behavior, but that boys definitely respond to reinforcements from other boys. Girls' behavior is affected by both female peers and teachers, but not by male peers. Interestingly enough, girls give other girls positive reinforcements regardless of the type of behavior (male-typical, female-typical, or neutral), whereas the reinforcements teachers give depend on the type of behavior (female-typical or neutral), not the gender of the child. Boys give more positive responses to boys for male-typical behaviors. Fagot does not deny that reinforcements operate but notes that they are most effective where they have been cognitively processed in terms of gender.[37]

Research also indicates that these boys give two kinds of feedback: "stay away from certain behaviors" and "play with others like you." Girls' peer groups also give the message "play with others like you," but girls' groups do not limit play behavior in the same way boys do. Fagot and Leinbach say, "We see that the male peer group starts defining what is *not male* very early, and that the behaviors that are defined as not male drop out of the boys' repertoire. It is also this not-male category that responds most to negative feedback of a kind that carries a great deal of informational value."[38] The information of what is not male is often based on what is perceived as being distinctively female, such as doll play.

Aggression is also reinforced by boys. In a study of assertive-aggressive acts in toddlers, Fagot and Hagan report that boys responded more to the aggressive acts of other boys than to those of girls, whereas girls were much more egalitarian in their responses to aggression.[39] Since ignoring aggression turns out to be an effective terminator of such behavior, one can conclude that boys reinforce aggression in one another. Also, boys do not spend as much time near teachers, and aggressive acts are more likely to occur away from teachers' presence.

The content of what being male is varies to some extent with age. At first it is important not to associate with girls and not to act or be like what girls are said to act and be. Already some dichotomies are in place. It is important to be strong; girls are seen as weak. Boys associate doll play with being a baby, not with caring for a baby. For this reason girls are constrained to deny their interest in doll play, too. In the school described by Raphaela Best, playing rough was important for boys, and obtaining scars a mark of distinction. Best describes the negative canons of masculinity under the rubrics of "don't associate with a sissy, don't play with a crybaby, don't do housework or cook, do not show affection."[40]

Girls and Boys at School

Many studies indicate that teachers are concerned with teaching children how to be "good students." This parallels my argument that mothers are concerned with teaching children how to be "good human beings." Peer groups, however, as the authors of a study on peers as socializers put it, "ignored student identities and instead stressed gender and age identities."[41] There is considerable research literature that attests to the enforcement of gender norms by peers in school and the tendency to view infringements by boys more negatively than infringements by girls.

Bruce Carter and Laura McCloskey interviewed children in kindergarten, second, fourth, and sixth grades about their reactions to hypothetical infringements of gender norms and found older children to be more negative to infringements than younger children. Superficially, this would seem to conflict with those cognitive developmental studies that suggest that children become more rather than less flexible about gender "rules" as they become more mature and experienced. But the authors suggest that what is involved here is an increasing personal distaste for "deviance," even though older children understand cognitively that this deviance is neither unthinkable (impossible), immoral, nor illegal. Older chil-

dren view gender deviant behavior as "weird," that is, deeply un-
conventional, instead and as such it is unacceptable to them personally. Significantly enough, in terms of later arguments, by the
sixth grade some children are beginning to use words connected
with homosexuality, such as "queer," "fag," and "lezzy," to punish
any form of gender deviance.[42] As we shall see, homosexuality
comes to be seen as the major metaphor for gender role deviance in
adults.

Although both boys and girls partake in the overall school culture, the separate subcultures of boys and girls are clearly asym-
metrically arranged. In examining what she calls "borderwork,"
that is, cross-gender interactions that reaffirm boundaries between
boys' and girls' groups, Barrie Thorne notes that boys control more
space than girls and invade all-female games and scenes of play
more often than girls invade those of boys.[43] Moreover, boys consider being kissed by a girl "polluting," and they refer to those boys
whom they have placed at the bottom of the male hierarchy as
"girls." At the same time, boys will admit a few girls into the honor-
ary status of "boy." One might speculate that boys' mock fears of
"pollution" represent a fear of a loss of dominance or capacity if
girls are allowed to get too close. In part, childhood gender segregation may help to minimize gender insecurities for boys and
allows girls to grow and develop outside the confines of male dominance. Boys use "borderwork" between the groups, however, to
act out and display asymmetry between male groups and female
groups.

An important area of study that needs to be explored further is
cross-gender interaction outside the context of female and male
peer groups—the kinds of interactions that might take place between friends or acquaintances. There is some preliminary evidence that when boys and girls interact together informally outside a ritualized game context, the interactions are remarkably
symmetrical.

Ethnomethodologists Jack Whalen and Marilyn Whalen have
launched a research program designed to find out whether informal "conversations" between girls and boys display the same patterns of dominance that adult cross-gender conversations have
been shown to display. Specifically, they ask, do preadolescent
males violate the "rules" of conversational turn-taking and inter-

rupt females at the same rate that adult males do? Or does one see in children the pattern found in adult couples in which females do the "work" of keeping a conversation going by reinforcing the male's talking? And, finally, if these patterns are not found in children, at what age do they begin?[44]

The only previous study relevant to these questions reported that in cross-gender dyadic play between three- and four-year-olds, boys interrupted girls at a rate of two to one. The author interpreted this as indicating that girls are socialized to submission early.[45] Whalen and Whalen, however, fail to find this pattern. Their research indicates that informal interactions among older children are symmetrical. These researchers used a hidden camera to videotape spontaneous conversations between cross-gender pairs of eight- to thirteen-year-olds who found themselves waiting together for an interview. In these interactions, girls interrupted boys fully as much as boys interrupted girls, and there was also no evidence that girls were performing "support work" for boys. Whalen and Whalen also found symmetrical patterns when they analyzed videotapes of children playing house together in a living room. Although the play activities themselves clearly reinforced traditional middle-class role differentiation (e.g., boys were daddies who made the money and girls were mommies who made the lunch), the patterns of interaction were not male-dominant and were equally directed by girls and boys.

Whalen and Whalen note that their findings fit with Marjorie Goodwin's observations that preadolescent girls were quite skilled in verbal aggression in cross-gender arguments. In a more recent report (cited in Chapter 3), Marjorie Goodwin and Charles Goodwin stress that girls are as eager as boys to "display character within oppositional interaction." Goodwin and Goodwin, in other words, do not find female deference in the cross-gender interactions of preadolescents.[46]

As we will see in Chapter 8, preadolescent girls do not accede to the idea of "male dominance" either. Instead, they express resentment at boys' intrusions and self-aggrandizing behaviors and attitudes.[47] It would be highly unlikely then that girls would be motivated to put up with interruptions or to do interaction work for boys on any grand scale. Instead, preadolescent girls avoid boys and assert themselves when the occasion seems to call for it. These occasions are when they are assuming the role of teacher or mother or when directly confronting boys.[48]

There may be other occasions when girls and boys act out versions of adult male-dominated heterosexual relationships in childhood. After all, they witness such adult interactions, to some extent at least. I suspect, however, that it is only later when girls become oriented to catching a boyfriend, or, in my term, to being wives, that they seem to accede to male dominance in cross-gender relationships.

The Male Peer Group and Heterosexuality

As noted earlier in this chapter, young boys in most societies tend to play in larger groups than girls, and within these groups they compete for position within the hierarchy. Girls, by contrast, tend to play in smaller groups that are more egalitarian. There are then two aspects of the male experience with other males: dominance striving, or competition, and solidarity that seems based on being a male—not a sissy, not a girl. Both of these aspects help explain the male tendency to think of women as sex objects. Sooner or later the male peer group faces female sexuality, and the sexual meaning that boys in groups place on girls tends to confirm male identity as heterosexual and dominant and to disconfirm the humanity of females. Girls become, instead, objects of male sexual pursuit and possession. In the male peer group, after a homoerotic phase, heterosexuality gets intimately tied to male dominance. Girls usually become "interested" in boys before boys become "interested" in girls, but the meaning of the interest is not the same.

Making Women into Sex Objects

In early adolescence, masturbation often becomes an occasion for exhibition and comparison among boys. Sixty percent of the preadolescent boys interviewed in the Kinsey survey had engaged in sexual exhibition with other boys. Kinsey comments that this behavior in the young boy "is fostered by his socially encouraged disdain for girls' ways, by his admiration for masculine prowess, and by his desire to emulate older boys." Kinsey goes on to say that "the anatomy and functional capacities of male genitalia interest the younger boy to a degree that is not appreciated by older males who have become heterosexually conditioned."[49] This fascination with the penis has little or nothing to do with love or liking for females (or males, for that matter) but symbolizes masculinity and power and, possibly, hostility. David Finkelhor in his study of incest finds that sexual activity between siblings is quite common and that there is almost as much brother-brother sexual involvement as brother-sister. According to Finkelhor, many of these encounters are not "innocent childhood sexual games" but often involve older brothers and younger siblings with some amount of coercion, including whipping and other forms of torture.[50]

Later on, at adolescence or earlier, depending on class and race, male peer groups are likely to purvey the view that having intercourse with a female is a confirmation of masculinity. These first encounters usually do not involve the idea of loving a woman, far from it; the focus instead tends to be on "getting it from" or "doing it to" girls, with the reactions of the latter being of little concern. To have "fucked" a girl becomes a rite of passage into the group who can call themselves "real males."

If males are constrained to differentiate themselves from the mother, what better way to effect that differentiation than to define women (other than one's own mother) as objects of conquest. The ultimate strategy is to define women as objects whose only purpose is to gratify men sexually. If a woman is a "cunt," a "piece," a "skirt," or if one looks at women as assemblages of "asses," "tits," and "beavers," then males need not fear their judgment; they are merely objects that have a specific use. The pursuit of women thus defined becomes a game that knits together rather than divides the males who pursue it. Thus one may hear middle-aged males reminiscing with one another about their college days, when they (to hear them tell it) were chasing skirts and getting it all. Males who refuse to join in with their peers in sex-objectifying women are likely to be severely punished. Consider the man whose human empathy renders him impotent in a gang rape of a woman; he may be punished for his impotence by being raped himself by his peers.[51]

That the peer group's pressure to be heterosexual occurs in a context in which women are sex-objectified may well have the consequence of making it difficult for males to become sexually aroused in a relationship in which they do not feel dominant over the fe-

male. If one first learns about sexuality in the context of being rewarded by other males for "scoring," for "getting pussy" or just
"getting *it*," then this does not augur well for egalitarian sex. In
some groups a boy who gets too serious with a girl, especially an
outspoken, "uppity" one, is warned by his fellows that he is in danger of letting her get the upper hand, of being "pussy whipped."

Thus heterosexuality becomes associated in the male peer group
with dominating and controlling women, and this makes one into a
real man. This sex objectification, which gives men a sense of control over women, is the sexualized version of the male tendency to
differentiate and dominate, and it is constructed in interaction in
the male peer group. Although this characterization is not typical
of all males nor of all of the thinking about women of even some
males, this kind of thinking is "understood" at some level by most
males. This is not maternal thinking; it is male-peer-group thinking, and it is most evident when women are not around to counteract it, or when women are in a situation of maximum dependency
on a male. The ultimate expression of this tendency is rape.

The Dynamics of Rape

The motivational dynamics behind rape can best be understood in
relation to the male-peer-group mentality. Susan Brownmiller has
argued that the motives of rapists primarily involve male violence
and male bonding.[52] I agree with this, but I disagree if she is saying
rape is not sexual. It seems more correct to say that sexual excitement in males can be fostered and reinforced by male bonding and
dominance motives. The clearest examples of the Brownmiller thesis are rapes that occur during wars. Men show solidarity against
enemy males by raping the enemy's women, their sexual property.
Even though women are the victims, they represent the enemy
males. Rapes in wars are frequently gang rapes, which increases
the solidarity of the males involved. In the United States, gang
rapes or rapes by pairs of male buddies are usually planned be-
forehand and have little or nothing to do with being seduced or
"led on" by a woman. Here the idea of ownership of women by enemy males is transformed into the idea that all "unprotected"
women are fair game.

Not all women experience rape, but almost all women are aware of the possibility of rape and fear it. One of the few ways that middle-class parents directly control daughters more than sons is by showing a greater concern for girls' whereabouts and insisting on greater chaperonage for girls.[53] Mothers as well as fathers may restrict girls, but it is the male threat to girls that leads to these restrictions.

Rape has largely been defined, even by some feminists, as a problem women must cope with individually by staying at home or learning self-defense tactics or getting male "protection." A fairer solution for the long run would be to restrict men, not women. As Golda Meir suggested for Tel Aviv, "Why not a curfew for the men? They are the ones doing the raping."[54] A sign I saw recently on a van driven by a young woman said, "Sorry male hitchhikers, men rape, get your peers under control." I agree with the message.

Although the male-peer-group mentality supports rape, it is not necessarily rape by a group or rape by a single stranger that a woman need fear but also acquaintance rape in casual dating relationships, and beyond this of course, rape in committed relationships and the rape that occurs in marriage.[55] Several studies have indicated that male peers influence the likelihood of rape in these situations too. Christine Alder, in a study of young adult males who admitted to having engaged in physically forceful attempts at sexual activity, found that the circumstance most conducive to sexual aggression is having male friends who are also sexually aggressive. Alder reports that having friends who support sexual aggression is associated not with any one class level but is found in all classes. Sexual aggressors also were somewhat more likely to have been stationed in Vietnam and to tend to define women as "legitimate victims," that is, they acquiesced to statements such as "any woman who goes to a bar alone at night deserves whatever happens to her" and "most women enjoy being forced to have intercourse." Sexual aggressors' attitudes toward women on a liberal-to-traditional scale, however, were no different from those of men who had not used violence. Alder's findings, then, tend to confirm on a sample of males in the United States the view that rape or rape attempts are related to males being, or wanting to be, "one of the boys."[56]

In a study of "date rape," Eugene Kanin reports considerable evidence for the influence of male peers in explaining who rapes and who does not. Kanin compared seventy-one college undergraduates who defined themselves as "possible rapists" with two hundred other students of similar age and race (white) and found that a much larger percentage of "the rapists" had experienced pressure from their current friends to engage in sexual activity and had experienced even stronger pressure when they were in high school. In addition "the rapists" were more apt to have had a history of "collaborative sex" in which their sexual activities were directly supported by other males in "gang-bangs," or sequential sexual sharing of a female, or by having had "sexually congenial" women recommended to them by friends and being "fixed up" by a friend with a woman with whom to have first intercourse.[57]

Kanin undertook the study in part to examine the often-heard explanation for rape that men rape when legitimate sexual activity is unavailable to them for some reason. He found that "rapists" were not objectively deprived; in fact, they had had more sexual experience (excluding their rape experiences) and had experienced more orgasms per week than the controls. Thus if sexual deprivation was involved, it was felt deprivation relative to very high expectations for frequent sexual contact. According to Kanin, the "rapists" seemed to be constantly engaged in a more or less exploitative search for new sexual experiences. They were far more willing than the control subjects to use subterfuge to get a woman to acquiesce in intercourse—getting her drunk, falsely professing love, promising commitment, or threatening breakup. When subterfuge failed, or when deemed inappropriate, they used force. Although the cronies of "rapists" would not approve of using violence to get sex in general, they accepted the use of force if the females were in their view legitimate victims—bar pick-ups, known teasers, or economic exploiters. Thus, rape seems to be an extreme form of treating women as sex objects; this attitude was given strong backing by the male friends of Kanin's "rapists," especially in high school. Although all men do not rape, most men are aware of and share to varying degrees what I have been calling the male-peer-group mentality that makes rape at least "understandable."

There are laws against rape, which appear to provide women protection, but Catharine MacKinnon argues persuasively that rape law is not so much designed to prevent rape as to establish the rules by which the practice of rape is organized and legitimated. According to MacKinnon, rape law defines the circumstances under which forced sexual attacks on women constitute rape.[58] Women who have been raped but who do not conform to the male definition of what they should do and be in order not to be subject to rape are defined as not really having been raped. Thus, until recently, a husband who forced his wife to have intercourse with him could not be accused of raping her, because marriage made her a legitimate sex object. If any woman did not put up a terrific struggle, then a sexual attack on her was not rape, because she must have led him on. If a woman was loose or a prostitute, a sexual attack on her was not rape, because she asked for it. The rules then have to do with the circumstances under which women are legitimate sex objects, but all the rules are based on the idea that women are defined by their sexuality. This definition seems to fit especially well with the conception of women that often prevails when men are among males.

The incidence of rape is quite high in the United States, according to Diana Russell, who reports from a careful survey of 930 women of all ages over eighteen in San Francisco. Russell's women subjects were randomly selected in a probability sample of households and interviewed by trained interviewers for over an hour, using a detailed schedule of questions. The study used the legal definition of rape in California, which is "forced intercourse (i.e., penile-vaginal penetration), or intercourse obtained by threat of force, or intercourse completed when the woman was drugged, unconscious, asleep or otherwise totally helpless and hence unable to consent."[59] Russell found that 19 percent (175) of her sample of women had been raped, and this figure excludes attempted rape and marital rape. If one includes attempted rape, which official statistics do, the rate rises to 41 percent, and if marital rape is included, it rises to 44 percent. Only 8 percent of these rapes and attempted rapes were ever reported to the police. Moreover, when one compares the experience of different age groups—moving from older to younger—it becomes clear that rates of rape and attempted rape have "steadily and substantially increased at each age for the women reporting" (p. 53). There has been a very large increase in rape rates for the younger age groups—but not for child sexual abuse.

The increase of rape may be related to the increased participation of women in the wider society without a concomitant growth in respect for women as people. The image of a working woman or an emancipated woman as a sex object still prevails. A woman, competent as she may be, is still expected to play up to men and not refuse them. Women are still not seen as mothers, human beings, or people.

Male Bonding, Male Dominance, Heterosexuality, and Marriage

As we saw, there is a sense in which one can say that women's mothering is universal. Child care has universally been the province of women, not men. There is a similar sense in which the male peer group is universal. Although girls and boys self-segregate as children, girls are somewhat more adult-oriented than boys. Boys may elect to be (and adults encourage them to be) "on their own" with each other more than girls do. Marriage and the pursuit of husbands tend to break up female bonding (although the extent varies greatly cross-culturally).

Certainly the nature of male peer groups would be subject to considerable cross-cultural variation, just as the forms women's mothering takes varies greatly cross-culturally. I have speculated that males' bonding is connected to consolidating a gender identity that is other than female. Later on, this male bonding becomes a way of consolidating male privilege. Marriage can break up male bonding, but what can be described only as the male-peer-group mentality is there, in varying forms and degrees, to be activated under certain circumstances. There seem to be two general ways in which men resist women. One is by segregating themselves from women; the other is by establishing domestic authority and sexual dominance over women. In this society the trend is clearly and increasingly away from segregation of roles and tasks. As gender roles become less sharply differentiated and as women and men are in daily contact in the same contexts, the tendency to sexualize and hierarchicalize gender relationships may increase for a time. In this society sexual attraction has come to be seen as the defining characteristic of male-female relationships rather than any specific gender-based division of labor. As the emphasis on heterosexuality becomes stronger, the possibility for sexualizing cross-gender interaction becomes greater, and this in turn is related to both rape and sexual harassment of women on the job. As women become more assimilated, gender difference increasingly becomes reduced to sexual difference, and as things stand now heterosexual interaction is male-dominated.

In this society male dominance in heterosexual relationships is both expected and assumed; it becomes a metaphor for male dominance in general. The pornographic version of this male dominance in heterosexual relations might be that what ultimately makes a man a man is screwing women, and screwing women means keeping women in their place. The "romantic" version of this male dominance is that taking the sexual initiative in heterosexual encounters is a last bastion of male prerogative and even male duty. Men must make the first move even if women "make them make it." He puts his arm around her first, he leans toward her first, he sweeps her off her feet. Women are more likely to accept the romantic alternative, but both versions indicate, and are predicated on, male dominance.

Although specifically sexual heterosexual (i.e., cross-gender) interaction is a major case in point, virtually all interactions between males and females of the same class or race and generation are male-dominated. Studies indicate that adult males generally listen less and interrupt more than females and generally seem less inclined toward genuinely reciprocal give-and-take.[60] The general emphasis on heterosexual relationships in this society throws men and women together in more situations in which males dominate than might be the case if heterosexuality itself and the great emphasis on heterosexual couples had not become an organizing principle in the private sphere and to some extent in the workplace.

In this society, male peer groups generally offer strong reinforcement for heterosexuality, and heterosexuality for adult men has become a central symbol of masculinity, which in turn is clearly tied in with male dominance. As Joseph Pleck points out, "Our society uses the male heterosexual-homosexual dichotomy as a central symbol for all the rankings of masculinity, for the division on any grounds between males who are 'real men' and have power and males who are not. Any kind of powerlessness or refusal to compete becomes imbued with the imagery of homosexuality."[61] Thus the male homosexual is derided by other males because he is not a real man, and in male logic if one is not a real man, one is a woman.

Because gender has increasingly become defined in terms of sexuality, heterosexuality and male dominance in heterosexual relationships have become central to the definition of what masculinity *is*.[62]

Women develop the capacity to be intimately involved with another, truly open to and concerned with another, more strongly than men, and this capacity underlies female bonding. But even though women have the capacity to bond with one another to a greater extent than men, marriage and particularly the emphasis on the heterosexual couple as the primary social unit in this society breaks up relationships between women. Whereas men use their interest in women as objects as a basis for bonding together, women are less likely to bond together on the basis of their interest in men. Women may join together on the basis of kinship or friendship, but so much of middle-class women's lives in the twentieth century has rested on their being married and dependent on the fortunes of one particular male that the marriage relationship has taken precedence over bonds with females. Although a certain amount of mutual aid is undoubtedly exchanged between wives and women seeking husbands, until fairly recently the necessity of finding and keeping a husband constituted a very real structural constraint on mutual support between women.

When feminists, and perhaps especially radical feminists, cite the influence of other women in their lives, they are likely to specify an unmarried aunt, a widowed grandmother or a mother who saw herself more as a mother than as a wife. The consciousness-raising groups of the 1960s were deliberately created by middle-class white women to counteract the isolation they felt from other women. Women can and do continue to support one another, but the emphasis on marriage and the couple, and beyond this the tendency to sexualize all cross-gender relationships in this society, makes it structurally very difficult for women to act in unison on their own behalf.

Although male standards tend to prevail throughout society, men are not self-sufficient in their "homosocial" bonding, and their relationships with one another tend to be wary and distanced. The hope lies in males' early interactions with maternal figures counteracting, far more than causing, the male-peer-group's view that "male" is everything. Men know from their mothers, and from their fathers who act in a maternal way, that there are more egalitarian and mutual relational possibilities and that women are important as people and as friends. This need for women to be more than sex objects continues for most men throughout their lives. Both men and women tend to choose women for their confidants.[63] This tendency potentially gives women a measure of power if they choose to use it.

In spite of the lure of male camaraderie, men fall in love with women and become emotionally committed to them. After all, men did love their mothers. Such emotional involvement, however, is often viewed with distaste by men's male peers. Traditional Muslim societies go so far as to think of love as downgrading a man and robbing him of his masculinity. This may reflect a recognition of the truth that human commitment to a woman threatens male dominance. In the United States, rituals are still around that reflect the attitude of "the boys," that is, male peers, toward marriage. The stag party for the groom before the wedding is an occasion at which males commiserate with the poor prospective husband for having gotten himself "hooked." A wife was a free man's "ball and chain."

In *The Hearts of Men*, Barbara Ehrenreich describes the most recent manifestations of male resistance to marriage. She implies that the antimarriage stance of feminists has played directly into the hands of "the boys" who still do not want to commit themselves to a woman. Although the resistance that Ehrenreich describes is real enough, it must be seen in the context of marriage's continuing popularity with men; when their marriages break up, they remarry more frequently than women do—and usually marry younger women. The larger truth is that even though marriage may constrain men a bit, it empowers them a lot. Everybody needs a wife, but it is men who get them.

Summary and A Look Ahead

In this chapter I have suggested that analyses that connect women's responsibility for early child care to male dominance obscure the positive benefits for both females and males of women's mothering. In order to counterbalance the overemphasis on women's mothering as the cause of gender inequality, I discussed the debilitating features of marriage for women in Chapter 2 and the misogyny of the male peer group in this chapter. The relationship of the male peer group and marriage to male dominance presents a paradox. Marriage, by bringing women and men together in a relationship that is expected to be a lasting and serious commitment, can work against the male-peer-group mentality that tends to exclude and sex-objectify women. At the same time, however, marriages are male-dominant. In modern middle-class marriages, certainly, women's interests have been made to coincide with those of their husbands to a far greater extent than vice versa. So modern marriage, while offering women and men the chance for true person-to-person intimacy, still gives men the upper hand. The direction of solution to this paradox, toward which one hopes we may be moving as a society, involves neither an increase in male bonding nor a greater emphasis on marriage. Rather, the solution seems to be women and men coming together not as married couples but as people and friends who increasingly share similar problems and experiences. The latter types of relationships would help decrease misogynist tendencies in male peer groups and make for more egalitarian marriages.

In the next two chapters I will discuss the implications of men's fathering for gender inequality. This is especially important since shared parenting has been proposed as the solution to the male dominance presumed to result from women's mothering. In my view men's fathering in this society lies somewhere between the mothering and human mentality and the male-peer-group mentality; that is, fathering has aspects of a maternal orientation, but it also has aspects of an orientation derived from being a male-peer-group member. Men as fathers then are cross-pressured; moreover, their fathering now takes place in the context of marriage rules that reinforce male superiority.

Chapter Six

Fathers and Difference

Whereas Chodorow suggests that women's mothering lies behind women's being more relational than men, I stress the way in which fathers, not mothers, have influenced the specifically "sexual" differences between women and men. Fathers, I maintain, have more to do with how men and women relate to each other in heterosexual contexts than mothers do. In order to see how Chodorow's and my positions relate to each other, it helps to understand that Chodorow is focusing on what psychoanalytic theory calls the preoedipal period and the mother, and I am concerned with the oedipal period and the father.[1]

Chodorow argues that mothers differentiate between their male and female children. I argue that *fathers differentiate more than mothers* between their male and female children and in ways different from the mother's greater bonding with daughters. Fathers, I claim, influence the specifically heterosexual aspects of interaction more than mothers do, and these adult heterosexual interactions are characterized by male dominance. By heterosexual interaction, I mean all interaction that takes place between males and females, but, beyond "cross-gender interaction," I also imply that these relationships have a sexual or potentially sexual component and that they also tend to be male-dominated in adulthood. Heterosexual relations are not inherently male-dominated, but they tend to become so for psychological and structural reasons. Mothers may indeed be part of the reason for women's more relational personalities, but that does not determine in itself whether a woman would hold the power in any given relationship. Fathers, as family heads, I argue, are central to the genesis of male dominance in heterosexual relationships and to women's tendency to seek to marry males who are superior to them. That is, fathers train women to be wives whether they intend to or not.

My interest in the hypothesis that men have a tendency to stress sex differences (I use the term *sex* here to imply especially the heterosexual aspects of gender difference) arose in connection with my interest in the father-daughter relationship. At the time I was not "seeing" male dominance nor male bonding but rather was concerned with investigating parental influences on expressive and instrumental orientations in college women. To my surprise at the time, the differences I found among women had more to do with their relationships to their fathers than to their mothers. I then discovered by canvassing the literature concerning parental influences on gender-related phenomena that fathers seemed to *behave* more differently toward sons and daughters than mothers did and were responded to by sons and daughters more differently than were mothers. The facts had not been recognized nor emphasized by researchers, in part because there was no theory that could explain them or into which they could be assimilated.

In 1963, I wrote an article, "Sex Role Learning in the Nuclear Family," in which I attempted to make sense of the findings concerning fathers by using the reciprocal role interaction framework (see Chapter 5). My argument was that children of both genders first learned expressiveness in interaction with the mother in a reciprocal relationship whose main content was mutual "love." I then argued that fathers entered the child's purview somewhat later and introduced differentiation between boys and girls by further reinforcing an expressive orientation in the daughter and encouraging a less expressive (at the time I called it instrumental) orientation in the son. Although the daughter's interaction with her father is expressive, it also mimics the husband-wife relationship in which the daughter is the subordinate appreciator of the father. The son is also subordinate to the father, but in this relationship the son is being trained not so much to admire the father as to be like the father, in the sense of taking the attitude of the father toward projects, problems, and females themselves. I also pointed out that mothers' interaction with their sons is not the mirror image of the father-daughter relationship. A mother does not play wife to her son to the extent that the father plays husband to daughter.

In 1963, I described the above facts as the learning of "appropriate sex roles," but I now see that these same facts are intimately related to male dominance and learning one's place in a male-dominant society. From this point of view the father-daughter relationship becomes problematic for me as a feminist, because it reinforces male dominance. The mother-son relationship works against this dominance, however, because the mother is dominant when the son is a child. Thus in a male-dominant society, the male's learning to be masculine by interacting with his mother introduces a contradiction, since the mother-son relationship reverses the dominance situation that characterizes adult heterosexual relationships. Although mothers and sons may sometimes interact in a way that mimics an adult heterosexual relationship, the mother-son relationship is clearly not the prototype of such a relationship.[2]

The above observations have a parallel in mother-son incest being both less frequent and more tabooed than father-daughter incest. In fact, the social psychologist Serge Moscovici argues that because the mother-son relationship involves female dominance, the fundamental reason for the incest taboo attached to that relationship is to destroy the power of the mother and install male dominance. In essence, he says that if sons were allowed to marry their mothers, women, not men, would be the dominant group. Moscovici contends that the only true incest taboo is that between mother and son and that the fear of—and, I might add, fascination with—mother-son incest is inspired by the fear of female dominance.[3] From a developmental standpoint, male shows of dominance over women as wives is a method of minimizing males' incapacity to dominate women as mothers.

Father-daughter incest, in contrast, is the acting out of male dominance. Although daughters are not allowed to marry their fathers, they come much closer to it than sons come to marrying their mothers. Not only does father-daughter incest occur much more frequently than mother-son incest, but also the connotations of being a daddy's girl are far more socially acceptable than the connotations of being a mama's boy. A daddy's girl is likely to be considered cute and "feminine"; a mama's boy is seen as dependent, and definitely not masculine. These connections are basic to the argument that masculinity and femininity in contemporary society are defined in terms of dominance and nondominance in cross-gender relationships. Moreover, in the father-daughter relationship, the dominance aspects of adult heterosexual relationships are exaggerated, because the father is both male and a generation older than the daughter.

In sum, I am suggesting that adult heterosexual relationships are structured in terms of male dominance, if other contravening sources of power, such as social class, are not operating. This male dominance is fostered within nuclear families by the difference between the father-daughter relationship and the father-son relationship. Compared to the father-child relationship, the mother-child relationship is relatively undifferentiated by gender. Chodorow may be right about differing emotional ties between mothers and sons and mothers and daughters, but the evidence I present indicates that father-son and father-daughter ties differ much more. The description of research that follows will first simply document in various ways the general proposition that fathers are the focus of a certain type of differentiation. I will then show that the type of differentiation and male dominance that fathers foster has to do with the specifically sexual aspects of gender difference.

Examining the Father-Differentiating Hypothesis

The evidence has continued to accumulate since I brought it together in 1963 that fathers differentiate between sons and daughters more than mothers do. Although mothers clearly respond differently to their male and female children, the tendency to respond differently is more marked in fathers. Moreover, male and female children respond more differently to fathers than they do to mothers. The greater differentiation that fathers make between their sons and daughters and the greater differentiation sons and daughters make in their responses to fathers has been found in experimental and observational studies and in unconscious and conscious behavior and statements. These findings also seem to hold regardless of the age of the child. Although the associations are rarely strong and are not always found, the persistence of the trend in various types of studies suggests that they reflect an underlying phenomenon, namely, male dominance and male control over female sexuality.

This basic phenomenon is overlaid by other factors. First, in the middle class in the United States at least, there is a remarkable lack of differential treatment of children of either gender by either parent, and also few behavioral differences between males and females have been found.[4] Certainly compared to other societies, children in the United States are treated remarkably similarly and do not differ greatly from each other on the basis of gender, at least with respect to the variables ordinarily measured. Also in the larger picture, fathers not only have much less contact with children than mothers do, but also their style of interacting with children differs from that of mothers regardless of the child's gender. Fathers are more likely to engage in play activities than in routine caretaking, and they interact more briefly and intensely and physically with their children than do mothers. It is within these larger trends that the greater tendency for fathers to differentiate between genders occurs.

The greater differentiation on the part of fathers occurs even among parents who believe in "nonsexist" child-rearing and who conscientiously try to minimize gender-differentiating interactions. Moreover, this more-differentiating behavior of fathers cannot be explained by the fathers' lesser experience than mothers with early child care. Even when fathers are experienced primary caretakers, the differentiating behaviors continue.[5] These findings fit with the commonsense perception that men and women are different, and they suggest that there may be some unconscious basis for some of these tendencies.

Generally, the gender-differentiating behavior of fathers takes two forms: withdrawal from girls (or preference for boys) and a differentiated style of interaction with girls. Fathers explicitly state that they feel more responsibility toward a male child than toward a female child. Generally, fathers want to have male offspring, and in the event of divorce they are more likely to maintain frequent contact with their boys than with their girls.[6] Generally, fathers pay more attention to male children than to female children, both rewarding and punishing boys more than they do girls. For example, Margolin and Patterson, in a careful observational study of fourteen families with a boy and a girl, showed that although mothers did not differ in their responses to their sons and daughters, fathers provided almost twice as many positive responses to their sons as to their daughters.[7] Boys receive more punishment from both mothers and fathers than girls do, but fathers are more likely to physically punish boys than girls. Mothers tend to use indirect or more psychological methods on both genders.[8]

Studies concerning infants find that fathers touch and vocalize to their newborn sons more frequently and contingently than to their newborn daughters and that fathers' relative withdrawal from daughters becomes much more pronounced during the second year of life, when fathers become twice as active in interacting with their sons as with their daughters. Mothers do not withdraw from sons nor step up their interaction with daughters in a complementary fashion.[9]

A recent study of adult-child verbal interaction, using trained child confederates in order to control for the influence of children themselves, found that women did not respond differently on the basis of the child's gender in either an unstructured or a structured situation. Men, in contrast, made a substantial differentiation on the basis of gender; they spoke more often and longer with boys than with girls in the unstructured situation. In the structured situation men spoke more to both boys and girls than women did.[10] Here the father's actions might be interpreted as modeling for and being a fellow male with the boy and paying less heed to the girl.

Going beyond the question of amount of interaction, studies that have included both fathers and mothers and sons and daughters show that fathers both behave differently and reinforce gender-stereotypical behaviors more than mothers do. Fathers have more gender-stereotyped attitudes toward newborns than mothers do, and fathers are more likely to encourage gender-stereotyped toys and play behaviors.[11]

Fathers, more than mothers, interact in a different manner with boys and girls and "come across" to them differently. Alfred Heilbrun of Emory University found that brothers and sisters had differing reactions to the same father, with girls perceiving him as being more nurturant than boys saw him to be. Sons tended to describe their fathers in terms of adjectives depicting domination and control, such as *aggressive, assertive, autocratic, confident, dominant, forceful, outspoken,* and *strong.* Sons also use adjectives associating their fathers with goal attainment, such as *deliberate, enterprising, foresighted, industrious, inventive,* and *shrewd.* Daughters, by contrast, described their fathers as *forgiving, modest, praising, sensitive, talkative,* and *warm.* Brothers and sisters mostly agreed with each other in their perceptions of their mothers, though, and the disagreements that showed up had no consistent pattern.[12] Heilbrun's findings strongly suggest that boys associate fathers with dominance and instrumental qualities and that girls see fathers as expressive and nondemanding toward them.

Jeanne Block has reported that, in each of four separate studies of parents of children of four different age groups, greater paternal differentiation in child-rearing orientations is consistently found. Block has also showed that in teaching situations fathers interact differently with sons and daughters. With their sons, fathers set higher standards and place greater emphasis on solving the cognitive problem at hand; with their daughters, fathers are more likely to focus on the pleasures of interacting together. With daughters, fathers are less likely to explain principles and patterns or to show the way to solutions, and they are more likely to treat mistakes as nothing to worry about. A study on parents of toddler girls found that fathers like to have toddler girls around but are less likely than mothers to let them "help." Fathers are especially likely to comfort daughters and to try to protect them from experiencing failure.[13]

On the basis of findings such as these, it is not surprising that the factor of "paternal nurturance" has been found to be significantly associated with cognitive competence for boys but not for girls. Norma Radin, who reports this, suggests that perhaps the father's presence stimulates cognitive growth in girls only if the relationship is not too loving.[14] My feeling is that even if fathers were to emphasize the cognitive aspects of a learning situation with daughters, there would likely be some sort of metacommunication transmitted that refers to the father's perceptions of difference. I am thinking particularly of a scene in a film designed to encourage fathers to stimulate their daughters' intellectual capacities. In this scene the father is showing a leaf to his toddler daughter while he is holding her as if she were made of china and were likely to break. He was also speaking to her in a whispery voice that would seem quite strange if the child had been a toddler boy. At a somewhat later age the father may undercut cognitive learning with a flirtatious attitude toward the daughter. One of the earliest studies to discuss father differentiating phenomena noted that fathers of young girls were more likely to flirt with them than were mothers to flirt with young sons.[15]

The father is also likely to be giving messages about gender to his son, namely, that it is important for males to be cognitively competent and to compete effectively. A male student of mine once commented with some bitterness that his father was highly critical of his moves when he played chess with him, whereas he was very appreciative of his sister's least sign of intelligence. With the son, the father said in effect, "That will do for a start"; with the daughter, the father said, "You are so cute." It is in ways such as these that fathers encourage a kind of male-oriented "darling girl" orientation in daughters and a power-competence orientation in sons. Mothers with sons do not make differentiations symmetrical to fathers'.

In a systematic observational study of some seventy-eight parent-child dyads in Central Mexico, Phyllis Bronstein found that mothers did not differ in their behaviors toward girls and boys but that fathers did distinctly differentiate along the lines discussed above.[16] She suggests that this

may play an important role in the socialization of their children for traditional sex roles. Boys were listened to and shown how to do things, which would seem to convey the message that what they have to say is important and that they are capable of mastering new skills. Girls, on the other hand, were treated especially gently, and at the same time, with a lack of full attention and an imposing of opinions and values. The gentle treatment would seem to convey the message that they are fragile and docile. . . . The inattention and imposing of opinion would seem to communicate the view that what females have to say is less valuable than what males have to say, so that females need to be told more what to think and do, and can more readily be interrupted or ignored. Thus in this sample of Mexican families, very different messages were being transmitted to girls and boys—about their roles, their temperaments, their thinking, and their expected behavior—and fathers were the main transmittors of those messages.

(p. 1001)

These data are important in suggesting that at least in patriarchal cultures where fathers, as opposed to brothers or other male kin, head families, the behavior of fathers is similar.

Other evidence comes from a study by William McBroom of unmarried university women's acceptance of stereotyped expectations for the domestic role of married women. Using a scale containing such items as "a woman's place is in the home" and "a woman should yield to her husband regarding her own employment," McBroom found that women who rejected such items had poor childhood relationships with their fathers and that the women who endorsed such expectations had good relationships with their fathers. Good childhood relationships with mothers had no such traditionalizing effects.[17]

Fathers also seem to be less alarmed about aggression in sons than about their sons' not fitting in with their male peers. In a study of forty sets of middle-class parents of children of both genders, Margaret Bacon and Richard Ashmore report that mothers ranked hostile aggressive behaviors highest on a continuum of behaviors they would consider to be problems in both sons and daughters; fathers ranked poor peer adjustment as an even greater problem than aggression in boys. Fathers consider such hypothetical items as "being pushed around," "getting stomachaches before school," "being left out of games," and "just sitting around" to be more serious problems than being hostile and aggressive. The authors suggest that the fathers might have perceived poor peer relations as indicating "feminine" or "sissy" behavior in boys. Here again is some evidence that fathers are concerned about boys being masculine and that fathers mediate between boys and the male peer group.[18]

When one considers how many studies have been done on mother-child interaction and how few of these find differences in the way mothers interact with male and female children, and how few studies have been done on father- or adult male–child interactions and how many of these do find differences, one must suspect that fathers' differentiating attitudes will become increasingly apparent as more research on parenting includes both fathers and mothers.

A number of other studies seem to suggest in one way or another that girls who are close to their fathers are more, rather than less, "feminine" and that boys who are close to their fathers are more, rather than less, "masculine." In these studies, the measures of masculinity and femininity are highly problematic and often obscure the maternal heterosexual distinction that I am making. That is, one cannot tell whether the qualities being measured are those related to mothering or to being a dependent wife and a subordinate in heterosexual relations. Generally, the masculinity-femininity tests used were self-administered and consisted of questions describing behavioral preferences or attitudes that men and women tend to consistently answer differently, but the reasons for the differences are not always clear. Nevertheless, the studies are worth examining.

Perhaps the most frequently used masculinity-femininity test is the Gough Femininity Scale (Fe Scale) of the California Personality Inventory. This same inventory also has a Socialization Scale (So Scale), which differentiates to some extent between delinquents and nondelinquents and measures the degree to which individuals can view themselves from the point of view of the other. Jack Block, Anna Von der Lippe, and Jeanne Block examined the association between adult subjects' scores on these two scales and variables related to parents that were collected when the subjects were children. The results suggest that the mother plays a more prominent role in general socialization and that the father is more involved with "femininity," which on this test does not mean mothering but may mean being passive and attractive. In this study the prior variables that distinguished women who ranked high on the femininity scale from those who ranked low on the socialization scale were their own physical attractiveness, a rejecting mother who did not emphasize values of tenderness and love in relationships, and a seductive father. Since the mothers of the highly feminine girls were rejecting and inadequate, one might presume the girls' "femininity" did not come from them, but since the fathers were seductive, this seductiveness may have been the source of a passive, male-oriented (and nonmaternal) femininity. The other finding of interest was that girls who were ranked low on the femininity scale and high on the socialization scale were, first of all, the best adjusted group.[19] Femininity has been found in many other studies *not* to be related to adjustment. Less "feminine" women had affectionate fathers who were ranked high on marital adjustment, and who, presumably, were less inclined to play husband-wife games with their daughters. Fathers who play these games are powerfully reinforcing male dominance, because their own objective power position over the daughter is great.

There is considerable evidence that both boys and girls do use the relationship with their father, or with adult males, as a lever to help them out of their early dependency relationship with their mother. Father "identification" involving both imitation and attachment increases with age and intelligence for children of both genders.[20] Helene Deutsch uses clinical findings to make the same point in *The Psychology of Women*: "As the child with gradually increasing intensity turns away from the mother and childhood dependencies in favor of active adjustment to reality, this reality is represented more and more by the *father*—and this is true of both boys and girls" (vol. 1, p. 243). Significantly enough, Deutsch follows this by saying, "Contrary to our previous views, the girl's first turn toward the father has an active, not a passive character, and her passive attitude is only a secondary development" (p. 252). What seems to happen is that the girl turns to her father to help her out of her dependency on her mother, and within the father-daughter relationship the girl may indeed achieve a measure of independence from the mother, but she is at the same time likely to become dependent on the father and to overvalue men.

Whereas most fathers do seem to "traditionalize" daughters, there is considerable research support for the view that many, though by no means the majority of, female high achievers were close to their fathers and had their fathers' support and encouragement.[21] But this closeness and support may be a mixed blessing at best if it perpetuates women's achieving simply to please a man or to do credit to the judgment of a man. Being a daddy's girl can interfere with female autonomy. Susan Contratto writes of seeing many high-achieving middle-class women patients in therapy who in one way or another find it extremely difficult to be assertive with men.[22] Daddy's girls may be very assertive with men if the men approve of what they are being assertive about and back them up. Such women, however, have trouble asserting, or even knowing, their own needs. This lack of autonomy is the direct product of the nuclear family situation in which the father-daughter relationship can all too easily train the daughter, even though she may be highly "accomplished," in wifely deference.

Fathers and Differentiated
Sexual Interaction

In the research described so far, the nature of the gender differentiation that fathers seem to foster is not always clear. Generally, fathers seem to reinforce passivity, dependence, and attractiveness in girls. They do this with their more permissive and nurturant attitude toward girls and their more demanding stance toward boys. The lenience and nurturance toward daughters found to be characteristic of middle-class fathers may not be true, however, of working-class fathers. Several studies in the United States have found working-class fathers to be strict and punitive toward their daughters.[23] This contradiction may be more apparent than real, however.

If we take a sufficiently general perspective, class variations are not contradictory but reflect in different ways the father's awareness of the daughter's sexuality. Fathers may respond directly to their daughters' sexuality or they may suppress this response and focus on protecting the daughter from outsiders. Both responses, of course, can and do occur at once. The father may reward and reinforce the heterosexual aspects of his daughter's femininity both directly by interacting with her as an "interested" male and indirectly by protecting her from outside males.

Anne Parsons's description of the position of the daughter in a Southern Italian family reflects both these aspects.[24] "The most fully institutionalized masculine role in Southern Italy, one that is defined positively and not by rebellion, is that of the protection of the honor of the women who are tabooed" (p. 386). "Thus, the South Italian girl does not appear as inhibited or naive for precisely the reason that even though carefully kept away from outside men, she has in a great many indirect ways been treated as a sexual object by her father (and brothers or other male relatives) both at puberty and during the oedipal crisis" (p. 387).

The lack of symmetry between mother and son in these matters is so obvious that it is seldom pointed out. Mothers do not protect sons from outside women nor do they treat their sons as sexual objects—certainly not so clearly and not in the same way that men protect and sexualize their daughters. The insight that feminism brings to these findings is that they are very much related to male dominance and the sexual control of women by men. Thus paternal concern with gender differentiation, however benevolent it may seem, tends to reproduce and maintain the system in which men treat women as sex objects for themselves and protect them from outside men.

Data from the United States indicate that fathers are more likely than mothers to support a double standard of sexual behavior for their male and female children; fathers are more tolerant of pre-marital sexual activity for boys (sometimes positively enjoining it on them) than for girls. A large-scale study on a probability sample of parents in the Cleveland, Ohio, area, showed that fathers are more likely than mothers to want the son to receive one message about sexuality and the daughter another. Although many fathers were more liberal than mothers about what erotic practices, such as oral sex, might be considered desirable, they were more concerned about controlling or curtailing their daughter's sexual activity in general than mothers were.[25] In a study of occupational choices of high school students, a considerable number of girls answered the question, what would your father *not* want you to be, by saying their fathers would not want them to be a prostitute; few girls mentioned prostitution as an undesirable job their mother might think of.[26] The father's disapproval of his daughter being a prostitute reflects his control over her sexuality and his view that she should not make herself accessible to "outside" men.

In her book *Like Father, Like Daughter,* Suzanne Fields frequently speaks of fathers as being their daughter's "protectors." What these fathers largely seem to be protecting their daughters from is other men. They worry about their adolescent daughters and want to protect them because they know what their own male peers were like in adolescence. As fathers and husbands, men protect their domestic domain and their women from other men. They "understand" the male-peer-group mentality that makes women need protection from men. These facts are well known, but few seem to notice that "the problem" does not lie with the behavior of women but with the behavior of men.

Most fathers also protect themselves from any potential sexual temptation that their daughters might present. Fathers' withdrawal from girls, which I described at the beginning of this discussion, may well be a way of avoiding their sexuality. It is significant that the father's marked withdrawal, which Lamb and Lamb observed during the girl's second year of life, coincides with girls often beginning to show awareness of their genitalia and to masturbate in the second year. The father's avoidance of his daughter at older ages may also be related to his awareness of her sexuality. There is much evidence that males' overall style of caretaking consistently differs from females'. This difference exists even if the male is a primary caretaker. Generally, fathers "play" with children, and mothers "nurture" them. The context of play itself might act as a deterrent to sexualizing the relationship. Clearly there is much we do not know about the relationship between eroticism and child care and how or why it might differ between female and male caretakers. Patterns of sexual avoidance within the family is an important area for future research.

In this culture at least, outside the family nudity among males is a symbol of locker-room or peer group camaraderie, and nudity between males and females is seen by many (perhaps especially males) as being related to sexual contact, specifically intercourse. Kissing between males has generally been associated in this culture with homosexuality. Thus one may suppose that fathers' avoidance of kissing boys staves off homosexual threat with sons, and that fathers' avoidance of nudity with daughters defends against heterosexual threat with them. These findings fit with earlier research on touch that showed that men and women touch and are touched by their mothers and their friends of the other gender in equivalent degree but differ in their touching relationship to their fathers. A study on physical affection between parents and children finds that fathers display considerably more physical affection toward daughters than they do toward sons, while mothers express physical affection equally toward both boys and girls. Here fathers differentiate by denying physical affection to boys. This denial may contribute to males' tendency to distance themselves from nonsexual physical closeness. It may also contribute to the general tendency for males to be "distanced."[27]

In general, daughter-father sexual discomfort appears to be stronger than son-mother sexual discomfort. David Finkelhor found only one significant difference between boys and girls at the age of twelve with regard to what would cause them embarrassment with their mothers but several differences in what would cause embarrassment with their fathers. Girls report more often than boys that they would have been embarrassed to be seen naked or in their underwear by their father, to tell him a dirty joke, or to tell him about a sexual experience. Boys and girls did not differ from each other, however, with regard to the mother except that boys would have been more embarrassed than girls to be in the bathroom with her.[28]

In line with this, another study found that fathers are more likely to knock before entering their daughter's bedroom than their son's. Mothers knock less often than fathers and make little distinction between sons and daughters in whether or not they knock.[29]

With regard to "sex education," in the sense of explaining such things as intercourse and masturbation, middle-class fathers do not ordinarily give information to their children. The heart-to-heart talk a boy and his father are supposed to have about sex is indeed a myth. Certainly one major reason for a father's difficulties in talking to his son about sex may stem from the cross-pressures of his wanting his son to be a "real man" in terms of the standards of the male peer group and his wanting his son to be a "good person" in terms of more general humanistic and maternal standards. Does he tell his son to "get all he can" or that "women are human beings too"? He may say a little bit of both. Kanin, in his comparison of potential rapists with nonrapists, found that rapists' peers had encouraged sexual aggression more than their fathers, although rapists' fathers had discouraged it less than the fathers of the control group.[30]

All this suggests that fathers, more than mothers, see their daughters as potential sex objects for themselves or for other men. As fathers, they generally do not make their daughters into sex objects directly, but there are elements of flirtation and mock courtship in the relationship. One of the clearest expressions of this comes from an early study of upper-status parents of nursery school children. Fathers reacted with pleasure to their daughters being "little flirts" and knowing how to flatter them.[31]

The tendency in men to fall into a romantic relationship with their daughters gains specific support from a recent study by Diane Ehrensaft of five families in which the father was actively involved in child care along with the mother. Ehrensaft tells us that the fathers seem to be "in love with" their child and the mothers merely to "love" their child. Moreover, these heavily involved fathers prefer girls. Ehrensaft is careful to point out that these fathers do not sexualize the relationship, but clearly they do romanticize it. For example, she quotes one father as saying about his daughter, "I'm absolutely in love with her. Just passionately in love with her. On occasion that's almost frightening."[32]

Ehrensaft reports that one father admitted to using the child as a wife substitute in saying "I still have a lot of passion in me that I enjoy having Renee (daughter) available to share with me. And who Joan (mother) is, at times that's not available to me. That kind of romance. Renee and I have the metaphor of what it means to have a cozy place" (p. 330). Their outings seem like dates. "I go out with Renee. Go dancing together. Renee and I get all dressed up and go out for dinner" (p. 333). Ehrensaft does not find that mothers feel the same about their sons as fathers feel about their daughters. She reports that a mother "would talk about her attachment, her endearing feelings, her sense of closeness to her child, but never in the discourse of a love affair" (pp. 326–27). The mothers tend to think of parenting in terms of responsibility and display a certain ambivalent distaste for having too much responsibility. These women deliberately sought a man who would share the responsibility of child care, but the men did not turn out to be second mothers; instead, they became their children's lovers, albeit without overt sexual activity. The fathers, Ehrensaft found, took less responsibility than the mothers. For example, the fathers were more willing to take the child out to be cared for when sick than to stay home from work to take care of the child themselves. They were less concerned about diapers that were long overdue for a change or making sure the child was dressed appropriately for the occasion or the weather.

Ehrensaft's findings graphically support exactly what I mean when I say that the father-daughter relationship is more nearly a paradigm for adult heterosexual relationships than the mother-son relationship. A mother could not take her son out dancing without somehow threatening his masculinity, but a father finds it pleasurable and not at all anomalous to go out dancing with his daughter. From the father's standpoint, the father-daughter relationship offers a nice resolution to whatever fears he may have of being taken over by women as mothers. He is clearly in the superior position in this intimate relationship, and all threats of being overpowered by a dominant female are removed. Father-daughter intimacy does not pose the same threat to male power that mother-son intimacy does. In the father-daughter relationship, the father is in control; in the mother-son relationship, the mother is in control.

In line with Ehrensaft's observations, Dorothy Burlingham reported earlier that when fantasizing about a daughter, expectant fathers focused on her romantic love life, with the objects of her love clearly representing themselves. The fathers wanted their daughters to respond to their loving feelings. Burlingham noted that fathers' fantasies about sons, however, focused on the boy learning from the father and being strong, capable, and competent like the father's self-ideal.[33]

The fathers whom Ehrensaft studied had been nontraditional males when they were growing up, not tied in closely with a male peer group. Being nontraditional perhaps made it possible for them to take on the role of mothering in the first place, but the kinds of gratification they obtained were not those of mothers but of lovers. Having a lover instead of a mother as a young child could be a threat to the daughter's development as an adult woman and gives one pause about the "equal parenting" solution to male dominance. Mothers simply do not seem to see children as lovers in the way these fathers did. Mothers love their children without the romance.

Fathers and Male-Dominated Heterosexuality

Typically in this society one does not inquire about the "causes" of heterosexuality, because heterosexuality is assumed to be "normal" or "given." One asks instead about the cause of homosexuality. But many liberals concerned with human rights consider it reactionary to make inquiries into the causes of homosexuality because they feel it implies that homosexuality is a disease to be cured or a type of deviance to be prevented. This creates a situation in which it becomes impossible to subject either heterosexuality or homosexuality to investigation. The liberal view holds that homosexuals and heterosexuals do not differ much from each other and that sexual preference is a private matter. Discussion of the causes of homosexual preference, the liberal contends, simply serves to perpetuate discrimination. Another facet of this position is that investigation of the causes of sexual preference, especially those guided by a psychoanalytic perspective, tend unfairly to blame parents for their children's "deviance" and thus cause misery not only among homosexuals themselves but among their parents. It is this sensibility that caused the National Institute of Mental Health Task Force on Homosexuality in 1972 to list questions of "etiology" as its lowest priority.

Although I sympathize with this general stance, I nevertheless believe that sexual preference is an important area to investigate both because of the scientific "need to know" and because such knowledge can inform a feminist analysis, since heterosexuality and homosexuality are connected with male dominance. I am primarily interested in parental relationships and sexual preference because they relate to my general project of showing the extent to which the nuclear family with father as head perpetuates male dominance. My concern is not to punish or change individuals' sexual orientation or to lay responsibility for either homosexuality or heterosexuality at the feet of parents but rather to consider the implications of the findings about parents for my hypothesis concerning the father's involvement and the mother's lack of involvement in the specifically sexual aspects of gender differentiation.

The largest, best-designed, and one of the least heterosexist investigations of how sexual preference develops in both genders was conducted in the early 1970s by Bell, Weinberg, and Hammersmith but was not published until 1981. The subjects consisted of 979 homosexual and 477 heterosexual men and women living in the San Francisco Bay Area. The homosexuals were recruited from diverse settings to insure their being more representative of gays in the general population than had been the case in previous studies.[34] The only possible bias is that, because of the San Francisco location and the nature of the study itself, it is overweighted with activist, as opposed to closeted, homosexuals. If anything, this bias would probably work against finding support for any hypotheses concerning parental influences, because activist homosexuals have ordinarily been opposed to psychoanalytic speculations about parental involvements.

In fact the likelihood of disconfirming psychoanalytically based hypotheses concerning parental influences on sexual preference was increased by the authors' policy concerning "knowledge." They asked all of their homosexual respondents whether they had read any books or articles or had attended lectures on the causes of homosexuality. They then tested each homosexual-heterosexual difference that was found to see if the difference could be accounted for by exposure to these theories. If the difference could be accounted for by exposure to "theories," the authors did not report the difference. When findings appeared that applied equally to homosexuals who had and had not been exposed to the literature on homosexuality, only the figures for the unexposed homosexuals were used. These were unusual and perhaps unprecedented precautions to rule out the impact of theories and previous research findings about the causes of homosexuality on the subjects' responses. But again, the effect of these precautions is to make associations with parental relationships all the more credible if they are found.

Much of the earlier research on sexual preference was based on percentage differences between homosexuals' and heterosexuals' answers to questions concerning parental influences, gender nonconformity, peer relations, first sexual experiences, and so forth. Bell, Weinberg, and Hammersmith went beyond this and used "path analysis" to develop a model that included fifteen variables associated with these and other factors arranged in a temporal sequence leading up to adult sexual preference. (In path analysis the temporal sequence is supplied by the investigator on the basis of logic. The sequence may be varied to some extent to see which way explains the most variance.) As a statistical technique, path analysis cannot tell one whether the temporal sequence is correct, but it can show whether the influence of a certain variable on adult sexual preference is direct or indirect. It can also show how much influence a particular variable would have if the influence of all the other variables were controlled. Path analysis provides a considerably more stringent test of influence than simply comparing homosexual-heterosexual differences on one variable at a time because the latter procedure cannot tell us whether the association is due to the action of another related variable or to the variable in question.

The results of the analysis indicate that "gender nonconformity in childhood," especially for boys, is the major influence on sexual preference, but even here the connection is far from overwhelming. Thus males who described themselves as being different from other boys as children, as not possessing stereotypical masculine traits or as not enjoying masculine games and activities, are more likely to become homosexuals. Gender nonconformity is somewhat more salient for males than for females, whereas family relationships are more salient for females than for males.[35]

Joseph Harry, in a study largely focused on gay culture, also reports an association between gender nonconformity in childhood and adult homosexuality from a large survey of Chicago area gay and nongay males. In fact, a major thesis of Harry's book, *Gay Children Grown Up*, is that while gender-role preference is "neither necessary nor sufficient" to determine sexual orientation, it does make it "more likely than not" that the person who felt himself to be a gender nonconformist or "different" earlier will be gay later (pp. 12 and 15).

The finding of an empirical connection between gender role nonconformity and homosexuality in males may lead one to question the distinction I am trying to preserve between gender and sexual orientation. I do not claim the two are unrelated—certainly they have been thought to be related, especially in male thinking— only that they should be kept analytically or conceptually distinct. Whereas Bell, Weinberg, and Hammersmith tend to interpret this connection between gender nonconformity and homosexual preference as suggesting a biological basis for both, Harry suggests instead that a primitive gender identity is formed very early during the period of childhood amnesia, and therefore the presumably social interactional events that caused the identity (as opposed to biological causes) are inaccessible to consciousness and cannot be uncovered. Harry's findings suggest that male homosexuals are likely to be conscious of a preference for the female gender role between the ages of two and six. After this, many males consciously try to "defeminize" in order to conform more to male gender-typed standards. They do this, Harry says, under pressure from the male peer group and to avoid their father's disapproval (p. 23).

Overall, the Bell, Weinberg, and Hammersmith study disconfirms far more than it confirms about background factors in homosexuality. The authors show that almost all the alleged causes of adult sexual orientation are either nonexistent or highly exaggerated. The two positive findings they do note, however, are the aforementioned link between gender nonconformity and the development of homosexuality and that "poor relationships with *fathers* seemed more important than whatever relationships men and women may have had with their mothers."[36] Thus while hypotheses concerning mothers tended to be disconfirmed, "poor father relations" were not. "The homosexual men's generally negative relationships with their fathers and the lesbians' experiences of their fathers as detached, hostile, rejecting, and frightening displayed a very modest but direct connection to their gender-role nonconformity and to sexual elements of their development as well" (pp. 189–90). These findings support my own conclusions concerning the greater salience of fathers with respect to sexual orientation, based on my canvass of earlier studies.[37]

Gay Males

The most widely accepted psychoanalytic hypothesis guiding research about parental influences on male homosexuality has been that of a triangular system characterized by a close-binding (domineering-seductive) mother and a hostile or distant father. Within this triangular system, however, the mother relationship was generally considered to be the root cause. The importance of the mother was challenged in 1965 by Eva Bene, who, in a study of nonpatient heterosexuals and homosexuals using the Bene-Anthony Family Relations test, found that more than three times as many items showed significant differences in relation to the father than to the mother. According to Bene, "Far fewer homosexual than married men thought that their fathers had been cheerful, helpful, reliable, kind or understanding, while far more felt that their fathers had no time for them, had not loved them, and had made them feel unhappy. . . . Regarding the mother, the greatest difference between the two groups was that considerably more homosexual than married men thought that their mothers used to nag."[38] Many other researchers using nonpatient samples have also attested to the greater importance of the father relationship for men.[39]

Although the Bell, Weinberg, and Hammersmith study found that a larger percentage of homosexuals than heterosexuals are close to their mothers, this variable was the least important of those that were of enough significance to be entered into the path model. Moreover, they found no evidence whatsoever for the "seductive mother" hypothesis, and only a small fraction of respondents said their mothers had acted like girlfriends or lovers with them.[40] But their preliminary findings show that in a number of ways prehomosexual boys have less solidary relationships with their fathers than preheterosexual boys do. Rather than trying to isolate the various aspects of this negativity, the authors used a general measure—negative relationship with father—in the path analysis. These differences with respect to fathers contribute considerably more to the overall path analysis than do the differences with respect to mothers. Thus, the authors support the findings of Bene and others about the greater importance of the fathers. This negative relationship with father is somewhat positively correlated with homosexual arousal in childhood, childhood gender nonconformity, and feeling sexually different in childhood and is negatively correlated with identification with the father.[41]

Because homosexual subjects reported having worse relationships with their fathers when they were boys than heterosexual subjects did, the authors are unable to establish what is cause and what is effect. The data are as amenable to the interpretation that poor father relationships dispose to homosexuality as to the view that the child's being different or feeling different in the first place makes it difficult for him to maintain a good relationship with his father (p. 190). For my purposes this is not as critical a question as it may seem. The influence is likely to go both ways. The key point for now is that the father-son relationship is more associated with sexual preference than is the mother-son relationship. The data are certainly consonant with the hypothesis that fathers are more concerned about their boys being "properly masculine" than mothers are and therefore respond more negatively to a son's gender nonconformity.

There is some evidence in Joseph Harry's work to support the possibility that gay males share more basic gender characteristics with straight males than with females. Many of Harry's male subjects who rejected "masculinity" were nevertheless aggressive and competitive (nonrelational?) in acting out their version of femaleness, which involved being glamorous and seductive. He called this response "actorization." Another group of gay males, more akin to transsexuals, were nurturant and domestic. Both groups had rather stereotyped views of what women were like. It seems to me that there was still something very male and nonrelational about the femaleness of these gay males—perhaps especially among those who were actorized. The quasi-transsexuals, by contrast, had come nearer to adopting a maternal mother identification. Even with transsexuals, however, the maternal identification is not complete. Stoller notes that when one gets to know transsexuals outside of research questionnaires and evaluation interviews, one does not find mothering impulses in the femaleness of these transsexuals or the capacity to remain in extended relationships with males.[42] These observations suggest that the more basic aspect of gender difference is women's mothering and greater relational capacities.

Lesbians

Many theorists, especially the psychoanalytically oriented ones, attribute lesbianism to a reversed triangular system consisting of a hostile or distant mother and a close-binding father.[43] Other analysts, most notably Charlotte Wolff, argue that the quality of the mother relationship alone is central in the development of lesbianism. Eva Bene and others, however, again find evidence for the greater significance of the father relationship in differentiating heterosexual women and lesbians.[44]

Bell, Weinberg, and Hammersmith's research suggests the latter findings. Although they report that lesbians have more negative relationships with mothers than heterosexuals do, they conclude that the mother-daughter relationship is not basic to the development of sexual preference among females. Although they warn that the importance of the father relationship must not be overrated either, variables connected with the father are more prominent than variables connected with the mother. Variables labeled "detached, hostile father," "weak father," "mother-dominated father," "father uninvolved in family decisions" all appear in the path analysis as being somewhat connected with adult lesbianism.[45] (Lesbians did not rate their mothers as personally more domineering than heterosexuals rated theirs, but lesbians were more likely to describe their fathers as being dominated by their mothers. This tendency reflects an unusually nondominant father rather than an unusually dominating mother.) The effects of the four variables mentioned, however, are all indirect and sometimes contradictory. For example, there is a negative correlation between "detached, hostile father" and "mother-dominated father," but both are associated with childhood gender nonconformity and through that with homosexual arousal in childhood or adolescence.

A larger proportion of lesbians described themselves as being "masculine" when they were growing up than heterosexual women did. Feeling masculine, however, had no connection for these women with feeling dominant. In the path analysis no connection existed between the degree to which respondents said they had been dominant (or submissive) as children and their adult sexual preference. This lack of connection suggests that lesbians do not seek dominance any more than heterosexual women, although lesbians did describe themselves as being masculine in other ways. I am suggesting that lesbians may share with heterosexual women a more egalitarian orientation.

The researchers found that the majority of female respondents, whether homosexual or heterosexual, identified with their mothers and, more important, that lesbians (to the surprise of the researchers) identified less with their fathers than heterosexual women did. More homosexual women said that while they were growing up, they did not want to be like their fathers and felt very little or not at all similar to their fathers (p. 133). Although identification with the father turns out to have no importance for the development of sexual orientation among females, it is an important difference to note because it supports other evidence that more-"feminine" women may be more (not less) "father-identified" than other women.[46]

Whereas the parents' relationship to each other had little or no effect on sexual preference in males, "negative relationship between the parents" is a factor, albeit not a very strong one in female sexual orientation. Although a majority of both homosexuals and heterosexuals had described their parents' relationship "quite positively," more homosexual than heterosexual women thought their mothers had felt little or no affection for their fathers and vice versa.[47] This finding would fit with Bene's finding that the statements about mothers that differentiated lesbians from nonlesbians are not about the mother's attitudes toward the child but about the mother's attitudes toward her husband. Charlotte Wolff, who speaks of the great importance of the mother in lesbianism, relates the girl's lesbianism ultimately to the mother's attitude toward men. In her version the girl realizes that the mother values males more than females, so the girl becomes insecure about her own value.[48] The findings that lesbians are more likely to report negative interaction between their parents suggests that they may be reacting against marriage and being a wife rather than rejecting or feeling rejected by their mothers qua mothers.

There is considerable anecdotal evidence among lesbians having to do with "coming out" to their parents that suggests mothers are less "devastated" than fathers. The stories relate that mothers, after a certain amount of reacting and overreacting, usually come around to the position that as long as the daughter is a good person, functioning effectively in the world, and happy, her sexual orientation does not really matter. Mothers often say, however, "But it will kill your father" or even "Don't tell your father."[49] Mothers as mothers feel sexual orientation is not important. Mothers as wives, however, say, "You are going to disappoint your father because you are 'rejecting' men." Mothers qua mothers can understand "rejecting men."

The Social Meaning of Sexual Preference

In their summary, Bell, Weinberg, and Hammersmith comment that one of the major contributions of their study is "the lack of support it gives to many of the traditional notions about the causes and development of homosexuality."[50] Indeed, they found nothing to be very important in accounting for homosexuality except gender nonconformity and homosexual ideation and experience, all of which are at least partially connected by definition and are therefore tautological. In the end, the authors suggest that perhaps biological factors are involved, but their study was not designed to provide any direct evidence concerning how such factors might operate. They presume that if sexual preference is a biological phenomenon, no one can be blamed. These conclusions tend to fit well with the liberal stance I outlined at the beginning of this section.

Reviews of this research in the popular press have emphasized the probable biological basis of sexual preference and have emphasized the degree to which parental factors were found not to be critical. In a sense this emphasis is all to the good. Of course, parents do not cause homosexuality; to say they do simply reflects the nuclear family ideology (which psychoanalytic thinking has supported), which makes the family, and no one else, including the child, responsible for how children "turn out." Because the nuclear family has until very recently been central to a majority of children's upbringing, however, it stands to reason that parents would in fact be important mediators of societal expectations. Parents themselves are representatives of basic family roles in this society: mothers, fathers, wives, and husbands. It would be highly unlikely that parents and parental relations would have no connection whatsoever to their children's orientations given the salience of the nuclear family as "ideal" in this society and given the child's almost total material and emotional dependence on parents.

What neither Bell, Weinberg, and Hammersmith nor the popular press were able to deal with, and did not even attempt to deal with, were the findings concerning fathers. The authors argue that their findings disconfirm those psychoanalytic explanations of homosexuality that trace it back to unresolved oedipal feelings. But this is only half true. They note that "the connection between boys' relationships with their mothers and whether they become homosexual or heterosexual is hardly worth mentioning" and that they found "no evidence that prehomosexual girls are 'Oedipal victors'—having apparently usurped their mothers' place in their fathers' affections" (p. 184). This much may indeed be true, but they do not deal with the evidence that prehomosexual boys and girls have negative relationships with their fathers.

It is impossible from this kind of data to speculate in any detail about the causes of sexual preference, either biological or psychological, but the findings concerning both male and female homosexuals are compatible with Freud's version of the Oedipus complex, which makes the father the central character for both girls and boys. In effect, "feminine," that is, heterosexual and passive-submissive, girls (Freud's normal outcome) never really give up their fathers, and masculine, that is heterosexual and active-dominant, boys (Freud's normal outcome) internalize the father's rules. I will discuss the significance of Freud's ideas for the transmission of "patriarchy" in the next chapter. The differing perceptions of the father held by homosexuals and by heterosexuals certainly suggest that the system of male dominance is somehow involved.

Heterosexuals, both male and female, are accepting male dominance or are at least coming to terms with it, whereas homosexuals are refusing to play the male game, which in this society has come to mean male-dominated heterosexuality. The reasons or more proximate causes for this refusal may be varied and have by no means been sorted out. But many lesbian feminists and some gay male feminists have increasingly come to see being homosexual as a statement of resistance to the male dominance attaching to heterosexual institutions, including male-dominated heterosexual intercourse.[51] The negativity toward fathers found among gay males may represent a rejection of the male peer group's insistence on both heterosexuality and doing male-typed things. Joseph Harry suggests that gay males' tendency to have been loners in childhood and adolescence was a defense against the pressures they knew they would get from their male peers to do male things and be heterosexual.[52]

In 1963 I reported data that supported the hypothesis that "feminine" women are male-"identified," in terms of "felt identification," "assumed identification," or "solidarity" with the father.[53] In other words, girls who understood, sympathized with, and were close to their fathers were likely to be "feminine" and, not surprisingly, well adjusted in our culture. They were not well adjusted because they were like their father, but they were well adjusted because they liked and understood their father. The reverse with men and their mothers did not hold. "Courtship progress" is a case in point. The sociologist Robert Winch showed long ago that whereas males who were attached to their mothers made slow progress in courtship, females who were most attached to their fathers were most advanced in courtship,[54] and by that measure presumably well adjusted.

Nowadays, feminists sometimes refer to a lesbian as a "woman-identified woman," meaning a woman who likes and respects women. Would a gay male ever be referred to as a "man-identified man"? I think not. As far as I know, the phrase is never used and seems meaningless. Certainly, heterosexual males are not likely to call male homosexuals "male-identified." The unspoken understandings involved in this asymmetrical usage reveal that heterosexual women and heterosexual men are both seen as being identified with men in the sense of liking and respecting men. In a male-dominant culture, the assumption is made that a real woman (as opposed to a lesbian) needs a man, while a real man may use a woman for sex but is essentially self-sufficient with his male peers. Real women "identify" with men, and real men "identify" with men.[55] The data I have presented is consonant with this picture—a disturbing testimony to how gender difference has become defined in terms of male dominance.

Summary: Mothers versus Fathers

All of the data presented in this chapter support, or at least are not incompatible with, the idea that the initial identification of children of both genders is with the mother and that both girls and boys develop their generically human qualities in connection with a maternal figure. The maternal aspect of women may be seen as generic and as symbolizing the common humanity of both males and females. Males to some extent are constrained to establish their own identity in partial conflict with this maternal principle and, as a countermeasure, to stress the "difference," "dominance," and a perception of women as sex objects for men. The father in the nuclear family is partly a representative of the male peer group and partly a protector of his wife and children from the male peer group. Either way, the father seems to be the focus of a second differentiation that occurs, a differentiation that turns the tables on girls and makes boys superior. Girls add another identification to their maternal identification and become "male-identified" in the sense of learning to please and play up to males, whereas boys abandon their mothers in order to identify as males and join their male peers. Fathers may indeed reinforce what we may think of as "femininity" in women, but that father-oriented "femininity" is an overlay that may not be in a woman's best interests because it is a stance that makes a woman dependent and childlike.

To the extent that women's attitudes as mothers rather than male peer group attitudes prevail in the society, it is likely that the society will move away from a focus on gender conformity, compulsory heterosexuality, and male-dominated heterosexual relationships. My emphasis on the mother, however, does not mean that I consider lesbianism or male homosexuality as solutions to male dominance. Certainly, heterosexuality as it is institutionalized in marriage implies dominance for the husband and secondary status for the wife. Taken alone, this argument might imply that heterosexuality must go if male dominance is to go, and some feminists have taken this position. Although marriage today clearly does involve expectations of male dominance, the relations between women and men in marriage are at least potentially equalitarian, however, and they are already more equalitarian than the relations between women and men as defined by the male peer group. As we have seen, it is within male peer groups that women tend to be sex-objectified and that male dominance finds its most exaggerated expression. Male attitudes toward females in the context of the male peer group, whether homosexual or heterosexual in orientation, often embody male dominance to its greatest extent. The attitudes of males as "fathers" toward daughters may be less sexist than their attitudes as "one of the boys."

Thus, even though marriage still involves secondary status for the woman, marriage or heterosexual relationships in the context of commitment can work against male dominance by mitigating the views of women fostered in the male peer group. Since marriage constrains and limits women more than it does men, however, it may not be so salubrious for the individual woman who participates in it. In short, those of us committed to more equal gender relations may applaud some of the consequences of long-term heterosexual commitments for men, but until marriage itself becomes more genuinely a coalition of equals, heterosexuality for women seeking equality must remain problematic.

Chapter Seven

Freud, the Oedipus Complex, and Feminism

Whereas Chodorow and Dinnerstein have emphasized mothers in the development of male dominance, Freud emphasized fathers. I believe that his emphasis on fathers can tell us more about how male and female children "learn" male dominance than a focus on women's mothering can. Not that Freud knew he was describing the institutionalization of male dominance, but in fact he was. Freud's theory of the Oedipus complex in male and female children can be taken as a description of the psyches of children and adults within a family structure in which fathers are men and mothers are wives. Male-dominated marriage is the context in which women's mothering takes place and is still for many people the ideal, if not the actual, context in which children in this society grow up. The "husband superiority" expected in the husband-wife relationship tends to reproduce in female offspring the feelings of psychological dependence on men that can prove incapacitating to women as adults. The expected superiority of the husband over the wife also reproduces in sons a feeling of superiority to women. Freud's account supports this view as does the empirical data I presented in Chapter 6.

For Freud, "femininity" is only tangentially related to women's capacity to bear children and is defined largely in terms of men's capacity to impregnate women. The social structural parallel to his biological emphasis on impregnation as opposed to childbearing is his own assumption, reflecting general societal views, that women's mothering is subsumed under marriage and a woman's sense of self is based more on being a wife than on being a mother. The Oedipus complex as Freud describes it can be read as the critical point at which girls move toward being passive wives and boys move toward being active and dominant husbands.

I first examine Freud's description of the boy's Oedipus complex and suggest several levels of meaning this might have. I then examine Freud's account of the female Oedipus complex in light of the recent criticism that his Oedipal theory was an elaborate cover-up for his original theory that neurosis was caused by real sexual trauma brought on by real sexual attacks on girls by fathers and other male relatives. I argue that the theory of the girl's Oedipus complex and the theory of real sexual trauma are compatible and can be linked in such a way as to provide further insights into women's situation as daughters.

The linkage has to do with the idea of an incest continuum in which many women who would not ordinarily be considered incest victims participate. The "normal" state is for girls to interact with their fathers as heterosexual partners, even though the interaction usually stops short of direct sexual contact. I argue that this father-daughter relationship is what romance novels celebrate and that these fantasies reinforce the idea of male superiority and at the same time they encourage female achievement and assertiveness in women so long as they are male-controlled. Finally, I suggest that if Freud is interpreted as describing the process of becoming masculine and feminine in a "patriarchy," then homosexuality, particularly lesbianism, can be regarded as a type of protest, albeit often unconscious, against patriarchy.

The Oedipus Complex and Father Dominance

My thinking about the matters I discuss in this chapter has been especially influenced by Juliet Mitchell's reading of Freud.[1] Writing in the mid-seventies, Mitchell takes the position that Freud is not a biological determinist and that his work, with all its devaluation of women, can be taken as an accurate description of (not a prescription for) the social construction of psychological masculinity and femininity in a patriarchy. By *patriarchy*, Mitchell does not mean a particular kind of kinship structure in which the eldest male in a patrilineal line holds the power of life and death over a large extended family. Rather, Mitchell uses the term loosely to refer to the role the father image plays in the acquisition of masculinity in males and femininity in females during the oedipal period in a nuclear family setting.[2] Mitchell links her understanding of Freud to Lévi-Strauss's ideas about the exchange of women by men in marriage. These ideas imply that male dominance is located in marriage institutions that often give fathers their power.[3]

The egalitarian, or symmetrical, version of the Oedipus complex purveyed by some psychology texts has it that boys love their mothers and become jealous of their fathers and that girls love their fathers and become jealous of their mothers. Then, somehow, boys give up their mothers and identify with their fathers, and girls give up their fathers and identify with their mothers. If one reads Freud, however, it is clear that he does not say this. Instead he makes fathers the central figure in the Oedipus complex for both girls and boys. Boys end their Oedipus complex, that is, loving their mother, by giving her up "in-the-name-of-the-father," and girls never really get out of their Oedipus complex, that is, loving their father, "in-the-name-of-the-father."[4] Whereas a boy smashes his Oedipus complex to pieces, a girl, in Freud's scenario, enters and remains in the Oedipus complex as she comes to love her father "as a little woman." In Freud's account the girl never totally abandons her mother (there is some hope here), but she also continues to be tied to and dependent on her father until he passes her on to another man.

Mitchell's emphasis on the father in her symbolic-cultural account parallels my account in the last chapter in which I drew on the research findings from psychology. Although Mitchell overgeneralizes to all societies (as does Freud), reading Mitchell's analysis helps my own thinking about how the Oedipus complex relates to issues of power in the nuclear family. In recognizing my indebtedness to Mitchell, I do not accept her uncritical attitude toward Freud. As I will show later, there are deep flaws in his thinking that Mitchell does not recognize and that lead her to advocate doing away with gender in order to do away with male dominance—a "solution" I find utopian and uncompelling. What follows is my own analysis of Freud's account.

For Freud, becoming feminine for a girl means giving up her active (phallic) strivings for the mother and becoming passive toward the father. For a boy, becoming masculine means giving up his active striving for the mother out of fear of the father and waiting until he can have a woman of his own someday. Thus Freud can be read as saying that the father-child relationship is the pivotal relationship in effecting the dominance of males over females in heterosexual relationships. Freud spun this description out into a universal psychological and cultural truth and equated the beginning of human society with the installation of the rule of the father. Actually, his description is most apt for middle-class families since industrialization in which the husband-wife relationship takes precedence over other kinship relationships.

For Freud, heterosexuality was not problematic, because he assumed that masculinity meant being sexually desirous of females and that femininity meant being sexually desirous of males. That is, he tied heterosexuality by definition to masculinity for men and to femininity for women (I will reserve a discussion of just how problematic this link is for the next chapter). He thought, however, that a man's becoming entirely "masculine" or a woman's becoming entirely "feminine" was highly problematic and was especially difficult for women to achieve. The oedipal period was the point at which masculinity in males and femininity in females was established, precisely because becoming "feminine" represented a defeat for women. In the oedipal period the boy comes up against the father's prohibition on mother-son incest. It is this taboo on mother-son incest that interested Freud so much, and this mother-son taboo in turn relates to the internalization of male dominance.

The Boy's Oedipus Complex

In Freud's terms, the father threatens the son's masculinity (i.e., threatens to castrate him) if he continues his heterosexual attachment to his mother. But why, since Freud never doubted that this attachment was heterosexual,[5] does that attachment, in terms of Freud's own analysis, not ensure the son's masculinity? My answer is that the boy's love of the mother, this heterosexual love that Freud saw as essential to masculinity, is not the heterosexuality that a male-dominant society expects of the adult male. In the mother-son relationship the mother is clearly the more powerful individual by virtue of the generational difference and the relative helplessness and dependence of the child. Masculinity in this society and for Freud means not only heterosexuality but also dominance in heterosexual relations; this dominance would be threatened if the mother-son relationship were not radically rejected by the son. In my view the basic reason Freud stresses the boy's giving up the mother to retain his masculinity has to do with his assumption that one cannot be a proper male unless one is the dominant partner in a heterosexual relationship. A boy must therefore relinquish his mother or be a failure as a male.

This, of course, is not the way Freud looks at the situation, because in his initial analysis he overcame women's dominance by interpreting motherhood as just a roundabout way of getting a penis. Freud assumes "male dominance" in his unexamined statement that girls are castrated because they have no penis. Freud rarely allows himself to see mothers as powerful in their own right but instead makes them into relatively powerless wives. Thus in Freud's oedipal scenario, the boy is threatened with the loss of his masculinity not by the dominance of his mother but by the dominance of her husband. The mother, as wife of the boy's father, belongs to the father, who in turn lets the son know that if he gives up his mother (his father's wife, that is), he can have a wife of his own later on.

Thus Freud has the son repress his mother attachment until it can be transferred to a woman who is not his mother, in a context where the son can be the dominant partner. A husband, unlike the male child, can receive the benefits of his wife's mothering on his own terms because she is his wife. In Freud's account the boy resolves his Oedipus complex by repressing his love for his mother and identifying with or internalizing the authority of the father. I read this as the point at which the generational difference between parent and child comes to be represented by the father, not the mother, and the point at which male dominance is installed.

The boy resolves his Oedipus complex by giving up his desire for his mother and identifying with the patriarchal power of the father over his wife and children. He acquires a superego that embodies the patriarchal rules. In *Totem and Taboo*, Freud imagines that in the beginning or perhaps in separate instances, sons banded together, killed their father, and took his women, but their guilt was so great over the deed that they incorporated the father, made him a totem, and agreed to live by the law of the father. Notice that Freud in his formal anthropological speculations locates desire and hostility in the minds of the sons, not of the fathers. The sons desire their mother and sisters and hate the father, but in the end they accede to the law of the father that allows them manhood only if they give up the mother.

Freud named the Oedipus complex for Oedipus, who killed his father and married his mother, but, as many critics have noted, Freud chose to ignore the part of the Oedipus legend in which Oedipus's own father, Laius, crippled Oedipus as a child and exposed him in the wilderness to die. Leon Sheleff argues in favor of the sons and contends that it is the fathers who harbor murderous and jealous motives and whatever of these motives sons have, they develop in response to their fathers.[6]

The psychoanalyst Gregory Zilboorg long ago argued that the boy's fear of the father may be an accurate perception of unconscious hostility on the father's part. Zilboorg maintains that fathers have narcissistic and sadistic motives for establishing sexual control over women and are jealous of the mother-child bond that diminished their own primacy. Zilboorg claimed that "unconscious hostility against one's own children is a well nigh universal clinical finding among men" and suggests that "only after the children grow up and become more articulate human beings does the psychological attitude of the father change to increasing affection."[7] Thus the early ambivalence of fathers toward small babies so commonly reported may be a defense against the father's own aggressive impulses engendered by their jealousy of the mother's attention to the child.

Freud generally depicted the father as a terrifying person threatening castration if the sons did not give up the mother. At one point in his later work he says, however, "I cannot think of any need in childhood as strong as the need for a father's protection."[8] This was in the context of a child's feeling "helpless" without it. Freud could have implied by this that the father may help the boy fight helplessness by supporting him in his efforts to enter the world of adult males. In the contemporary nuclear family this may involve the father's forming a kind of coalition with the boy against the mother in support of male dominance. Practically speaking, however, a father could help his son join the world of males not by denigrating women but by making men seem less formidable and hostile by his own attitude toward his son. In terms of Freud's fable, the father does not castrate the boy (he controls his own aggression?), and the boy gives up the mother and prepares to join the world of males. Thus Little Hans's father attempted in his own interactions with his son to assuage his young son's fears of aggression from males. At times Freud implies that "real" fathers do not embody male dominance so much as they mediate between their sons and the threats posed by fearsome images of masculinity.

In fact, the Oedipus complex can be interpreted as "true" at several different levels. It can be taken as a "true" symbolic fable about patriarchy in which children come to take over the patriarchal law of the father in the name of the father. This is Mitchell's version, which stresses the symbolic power of the father. In addition (especially in Freud's case histories), the Oedipus complex can be read as a story about the attitudes and motivations of real fathers in the modern, relatively egalitarian but husband-dominant nuclear family. The implication of the latter approach is that real fathers by their attitudes can exacerbate or mitigate a fear of men or overvaluation of men on the part of women and men. Finally, the Oedipus complex can also be understood as a description of the working out of the interplay between gender and generation in which the father comes to represent the generational difference and the establishment of heterosexuality and male dominance. This is the social structural meaning of the Oedipus complex and the interpretation I have mainly spelled out above and will develop further.

In my view the most important "truth" in Freud's stages of development lies in their reliance on family structure for an explanation of personality. Talcott Parsons sees this clearly, especially with regard to gender differentiation. Parsons interprets the Oedipus complex as representing the stage at which the child perceives the nuclear family as an organized unit.[9] It is the point at which the male child learns that he is a male like his father but a child unlike his father, who is an adult. Similarly, the child learns that he is a male like his brother and also a child like his brother, whereas he is unlike his sister because he is a male but like his sister in being a child. At this level of generality the process is presumed to be the same for the female child. In learning these cross-cutting categorizations, the child is also learning to conceive of the family in its totality as a system of social relationships. The meaning of the resolution of the Oedipus complex then centers around the child's "internalizing" not only age and gender roles but also the idea of the family as an entire interactive system.

Parsons's analysis, however, does not sufficiently take into account the power differential between husband and wife. Parsons's way of taking male dominance into account is to say that in the oedipal period the father comes to represent the family as a whole and the pressures for growth that the mother had represented earlier. Although Parsons was more aware than most of structural differences in the situation of males and females, he tended not to see these differences in terms of power and authority, and thus did not stress the extent to which the male-headed nuclear family tends to juvenilize females more than males.

On a more concrete level, Kurt Fischer and Malcolm Watson have suggested that both the creation and the ending of the oedipal conflict can be explained by the child's developing cognitive understanding of the social relationships characterizing the nuclear family. They suggest that developmentally children at first cannot understand how husband and wife as categories are related. They can understand only another single role in relationship to themselves. But when children understand how husband and wife are related, they can then imagine being the husband or wife of the parent. The resolution of the conflicted feelings generated by the desire to marry the adult parent are resolved when the child realizes that the parent is in another generation and will age along with the child.[10] I believe that this is certainly a part of what goes on as the child matures cognitively. My point is that the Oedipus complex involves more than this, however. It also involves the child's cognitive awareness that fathers have more power and importance than mothers, and fathers come to stand for adulthood for both boys and girls.

Fischer and Watson imply that boys and girls experience the Oedipus complex identically, whereas Freud's account was distinctly asymmetrical. My intention is to show that Freud's account can be fit into a more social structural perspective, but I also argue that Freud's emphasis on the asymmetry of the Oedipus complex is correct. Male dominance lends a different meaning to the father-daughter relationship than to the mother-son relationship.

In the next section I discuss how the recent "discovery" of "real incest" relates to the foregoing discussion of Freud's description of the Oedipus complex and here again show how male-dominant nuclear family structure is involved.

Oedipus Versus the Reality of Father-Daughter Incest

Although Freud makes much of the taboo on incest between mother and son, he does not stress the taboo on incest between father and daughter. The problem for the girl, according to Freud, is not to give up her father but rather to transform her "active masculinity" vis-à-vis the mother to "passive femininity" vis-à-vis the father. She cannot become "feminine" until she detaches herself from her mother and attaches herself to the father, who is of course dominant in the relationship and remains so. For the girl in a male-dominant society, the father-daughter relationship remains the paradigm for her adult relationships with men, and in a male-dominant society, this relationship would not need to be radically repressed. Indeed, it was the perfect training ground for "femininity."

While Juliet Mitchell interprets Freud's account of the differing outcomes of the Oedipus complex for males and females as a description of women's oppressive situation within patriarchy, other feminists have criticized Freud for having obscured women's real oppression with his oedipal theory. The real problem, they say, is the reality of father-daughter incest. Florence Rush, in her book on incest, described how Freud suppressed his knowledge of real father-daughter incest initiated by the father and replaced it with his theory of the universal Oedipus complex in the mind of the child. Jeffrey Masson further substantiated Freud's suppression by examining previously unpublished letters written by Freud in which he expands his view that neurosis is caused by real sexual assaults.[11] Some feminists hail Masson's revelations as another blow to psychoanalytic theory, but I argue that one does not have to choose between the real sexual trauma theory and the oedipal theory; rather, I argue that both are "true" and are connected to each other. In so doing I explain the prevalence of father-daughter incest and the relative absence of mother-son incest in this society.

The tale Masson tells is fascinating in the manner of a good detective story. Masson unearthed in the Freud archives in London many more letters that Freud had written to his friend Wilhelm Fliess, a nose and throat specialist, during the late 1800s, around the time Freud arrived at his theory about the universal Oedipus complex. In these letters, Freud speaks of his belief that hysterical symptoms (usually paralyses of various kinds) in women were produced by their having been sexually molested by their fathers or close male relatives in childhood. Freud posed this theory against the prevailing view that hysteria was caused by an inherited defect.

Masson suggests that Freud abandoned his theory because he could not take the flak it produced among his colleagues and the public. Freud, says Masson, was an ambitious man; he wanted to be famous and clearly this theory was going to cause him to be ostracized instead of lionized. It is also possible that Freud's own father had been a sexual molester of family members and had perhaps molested Freud himself, a fact Freud simply could not face. To make matters worse for Freud, Masson chronicles a number of instances where individual women were placed in impossible and even dangerous situations by Freud's insistence that their troubles resulted from their own repressed desires for their fathers. Masson now sees himself as a feminist and is seeking allies against the psychoanalytic establishment among feminists.[12]

Freud's abandoning his real sexual trauma theory is not in itself news. Freud himself refers to having abandoned it in his later work. Freud did, however, deliberately disguise the extent to which he believed fathers were the abusers. Florence Rush uses Freud's letter to Fliess published earlier to show this disguise, and now Masson has found letters that had not been published and has added more detail, including a questioning of Freud's motives.[13]

Freud's de-emphasizing or abandoning his ideas about the sins of fathers is not new; the new event is society's concern about these sins. Although Freud's dropping his theory about actual sexual trauma and its consequences certainly contributed to our nonrecognition of it, Freud was also reflecting the general official blindness that prevailed in society and that has continued to prevail until recently. It was not until the 1970s that incest was "discovered" and a campaign launched against it.

It is very difficult to get good information on the prevalence of incest. Diana Russell reports from her San Francisco survey on sexual assault (described in Chapter 5) that 42 women or 4.5 percent of the women in her sample had been sexually abused by their fathers. This is considerably higher than the 1.3 percent reported by David Finkelhor from a survey of 530 college women. The difference between the figures is probably because Finkelhor's results were obtained by means of a paper-and-pencil questionnaire and Russell's results were obtained after good rapport had been established. Incest is such an emotional matter that even though the paper-and-pencil test is anonymous and affords privacy, one may not want to make such a disclosure, even to oneself. Both surveys are probably underestimations of the true rate, however, because of the reluctance to tell. The Russell survey had a very high initial refusal rate, and undoubtedly some incest victims refused because they did not want to be asked about it. It is also likely that many more women have been sexually molested by their fathers and have totally repressed the memory. As this possibility is spoken of more often in public and as therapists give serious credence to incest as fact not fantasy, women are likely to allow themselves to remember real incestuous events.[14]

Both surveys used a very broad definition of sexual abuse and included stepfathers and other father substitutes with biological fathers. Stepfathers are more likely to abuse than biological fathers and their inclusion inflates the rate. In Russell's survey if we exclude the "least serious sexual abuse" category—that is, complete and attempted acts of intentional sexual touching of buttocks, thigh, leg, or other body part or clothed breast or genitals and forced kissing—and if we exclude all fathers except biological fathers, the rate drops from 44 to 16 or from 4.5 percent to 1.7 percent.[15] There is little consolation in this exercise, however, since stepfathers are fathers in function and because sexual intent has a psychological impact.

There is little question that father-daughter incest is harmful to the psychological well-being of women. Finkelhor's study showed that it is the most traumatic kind of sexual experience that can occur, and various researchers have shown that incest victims have problems with intimacy and sexual response. It is also true that incest victims are often far more alienated from their mothers than they are from their fathers.[16] The reason for this has to do with father power, as we shall see. First, it is important to put the incest issue in historical context.

The Incest Continuum—From Patriarchal Incest to Daddy's Girl

It is possible that there has been fairly prevalent in the past in the United States a kind of father-daughter incest that was considered more or less the legitimate right of the patriarch. The father simply saw himself as the owner of the children—not their caretaker but their owner. Both mother and father might agree that for a child "to service the old man" sexually was not all that out of line with his rights. Social workers are familiar with this view.[17] A social worker once described to me how a female client had become quite exasperated with her for saying that the client's husband was "guilty of incest" with his daughter. The client said somewhat defensively, "Well, so what? He's had sex with his daughter; she's his'n, ain't she?"

These attitudes are more likely to prevail in isolated rural areas than in urban areas because they reflect an earlier definition of the parent-child relationship and the meaning of family life in general. After industrialization the family became a smaller and more emotionally intense unit. This process of making the family into a sentimental unit, responsible for molding personalities rather than training workers, was well on its way in Freud's time. Although modern families may be somewhat less authoritarian than the families Freud's patients came from, the basic family type was similar. Within a family of this type, sexual relations between parents and children would distinctly not be acceptable because of the idea that children are innocents and definitely different from (not just smaller and less competent than) adults. The emotional closeness that is enjoined in the unit might, however, increase the potential for sexualizing relationships within the family. Thus the "modern family" makes sexual relations between parents and children more abhorrent and at the same time more tempting.

At the time Freud was writing, there was a great deal of sexual repression in general and especially with regard to adult-child relationships. This was undoubtedly related to the new definition of children as precious individuals whose innocence must be protected. At the same time, however, there was a great deal of sexual preoccupation, as Foucault has shown.[18] Freud's theories, of course, which made sex and sexuality central, were both the result of and a reinforcement to that preoccupation. In this atmosphere of repression, fathers indeed may have used children as sexual objects furtively and with great guilt. In this atmosphere it is also likely that fathers may have responded to their children sexually but communicated their desires to their children covertly, subliminally, stimulating the child and also forbidding the child.

Although Freud's suppression of overt father-daughter incest is culpable, it need not mean that feminists can now ignore the Oedipus complex. Both the real sexual trauma theory and the theory of the Oedipus complex can be "true" if we view the oedipal situation as revealing the underlying structure of the nuclear family that makes father-daughter incest more likely than mother-son incest. In Freud's most general account of the Oedipus complex, all families are potentially incestuous, and, as I argued earlier, his implicit belief in male dominance lies behind his emphasis on the mother-son prohibition. Significantly enough, when Freud stopped emphasizing real father-daughter incest, he started emphasizing the prohibition on incest between mothers and sons.

As we have seen, in Freud's scenario the father enforces the mother-son incest taboo on the son. But who enforces the father-daughter taboo? There is no avenging father to prevent father-daughter incest and there is no avenging mother to enforce it either, because mother as wife to father does not have power equal to that of her husband. In Freud's account, the daughter turns away from the mother in resentment over not having a penis and turns toward her father. Freud leaves the girl in a semi-sexualized relationship with her father. The daughter never quite gives up the father and the father never gives her up until he "gives her away" in marriage to another man.

If all this sounds abstract, consider who it is that traditionally gives the bride away at marriage. Also consider the following story told me by an incest victim. She married a man to escape her in-

cestuous father and found herself to be totally sexually unresponsive with him. When she finally told her husband about the incest,
he confronted the father, whose response was to apologize to the
husband for having spoiled his pleasure ("I didn't mean to ruin her
for you, ol' buddy"). He was not disturbed by the harm he had
done to his daughter but by the harm he had done to his fellow male.

Freud's account, then, in which the girl does not give up the father but instead turns her active strivings into passive femininity
toward him is a fairly accurate description of the way things are
with daughters. Freud did not think active mothering had much to
do with being feminine; what made a woman feminine was being
her father's daughter, or in the modern, less authoritarian context,
her "daddy's girl." These women are not exactly incest victims, but
father-daughter incest is less prohibited than mother-son incest,
and being daddy's girl is considered cute and "feminine." No male
was ever considered masculine because he was a "mama's boy."

Daddy's girls generally interact with men in a very "feminine"
way. Mama's boys do not interact with women in a very masculine
way, almost by definition. Playing up to men is easy for Daddy's
girls and is rewarded by men and by the society, but it works
against gender equality and women's autonomy. Just as incest is not
good for the daughter, if she is to see herself as an equal to men,
neither is being a daddy's girl, to the extent that it means looking
up to men and depending on "feminine" wiles to influence them.

This may well be the situation that lies behind "hysteria," which
Juliet Mitchell has called "the daughter's neurosis."[19] Although
women are less subject today than they were in Freud's time to literal paralyses with no organic cause, women are still evincing conflict between being seduced by fathers and resisting that seduction
because it means being "taken over" by a powerful male. Whether
hysteria is manifested in the directly sexual dysfunctions often
characterizing incest victims or in the approach-avoidance dance of
women who behave seductively and then run, or in any number of
other ways, hysteria can be interpreted as conflict concerning fathers and male dominance.

Judith Herman suggests the idea of an incest continuum, saying
that "incest represents a common pattern of traditional female socialization carried to a pathological extreme."[20] Victims of overt in-

cest are described by Herman as often growing up "to become archetypally feminine women: very male-oriented, sexy without enjoying sex, repeatedly victimized yet repeatedly seeking to lose themselves in the love of an overpowering man, contemptuous of themselves and other women, hard-working, giving and self-sacrificing." Herman sees these women as being extreme cases of loss of autonomy and of seeking fulfillment through males (p. 108). Most of those working with incest victims corroborate that female incest victims are often far less upset with their fathers than with their mothers.

In addition to studying women from overtly incestuous families, Herman also studied women from what she called "seductive families" (pp. 109–125). In these families, father-daughter relationships stop short of overt sexual interaction and therefore do not require secrecy, but the relationships have highly sexual overtones. For example, the fathers might have spied on their daughters, interrogated them about sexual matters or their boyfriends, or acted out a romantic relationship with them. Herman found the daughters in seductive families to be psychologically better off than victims of overt incest, but they were caught in a dilemma. "They could remain their Daddy's good little girls, bound in a flirtatious relationship whose sexual aspect was ever present but never acknowledged, or they could attempt to become independent women, usually without any assistance from their mothers, and in the process risk their fathers' anger or rejection" (p. 118). Herman is quite clear about differentiating achievement from autonomy. The daughters of seductive fathers had little autonomy in the sense of self-respect and self-direction but might achieve in order to please their fathers.

In discussing the self-attitudes of incest victims, Denise Gelinas notes that at least those who seek treatment have no psychotic tendencies or basic gender confusion, but they are likely to be chronically depressed and possibly experience moments of dissociation and confusion. They are likely to feel they have no rights or even needs of their own and assume their mission is to meet the needs of those who demand that their needs be met.[21] This, in my view, is not so much "mothering" as it is "wifing." Mothers help define what others' needs are and to sort out legitimate and illegitimate needs. Incest victims as mothers do not do this but instead become slaves to the needs of others as those others define them. This description is related to the picture of "normal" women: pleasing daddy and keeping the world going for him.

From a psychosocial point of view, the consequence of the parent-child incest taboo within the isolated nuclear family is that it allows children to grow up into autonomous human beings. The limits set by the incest taboo on eroticism within the nuclear family protect the child from being overwhelmed by the eroticism of the parent. The phrase "owning one's own sexuality" is a way of expressing the individual's need for erotic autonomy so that he or she may be psychologically free to establish erotic bonds with others outside the family he or she grew up in. As mentioned earlier, relationships between parents and children in middle-class families are often characterized by emotional intensity, which could increase the likelihood of eroticizing those relationships. Two psychiatrists describe such families as being "emotional hothouses which constitute a high-temperature incubator of eroticized interactions" in which

The father may become so enamored of his little daughter's flirtation that he finds himself, a grown man, feeling pridefully puffed up by the daughter's attentiveness to him, to his genitals, to his body. He may imagine more than is actually there and see her very kiss or proposal of marriage as a seductive move. In short, he is narcissistic; he is also exhibitionistic, calling it natural nudity; he is seductive, calling it freedom; he is using projective identification—attributing 'evil' adult motives to a three- or four-year-old girl. With all these rationalizations and distortions, he may take the step to outright molestation of his daughter.[22]

These types of families were found among middle-class families in Vienna in Freud's day but are hardly confined to this setting. Incest that occurs within this hothouse situation may be more psychologically dangerous to children than patriarchal incest in that the parent (and hence the child) is more emotionally involved and when emotional involvement is coupled with sexuality and the parent's own guilt, it produces a combination that is emotionally overwhelming to the child. Even in so-called normal families, the father-daughter relationship reinforces "femininity" of the pleasing- and looking-up-to-men variety. A daughter in an oedipal family may indeed "seduce" her father in the sense of wrapping him around her little finger, manipulating him to get what she wants, and so forth, but this sort of seduction, precisely because of the father's greater power by virtue of the generational difference, is the seduction of the stronger by the weaker and acts in the end to validate the fundamental inequality of the relationship.

I would suggest that oedipal families, that is, "normal" male-dominant families, constitute a third, and the largest, category on the incest continuum. The incest involved here is psychological, not overtly sexual. The father takes his daughter over. She looks up to him because he is her father. He is the king and she is the princess. It is all OK because the male is dominant in "normal" adult heterosexual relations.

Whereas the father helps the son escape from the mother, who helps the daughter escape from the father? It could be the mother. The logic of my argument is that the more egalitarian the relationship between mother and father is and the more autonomous or less financially and otherwise dependent on the father the mother can feel, the better position the mother would be in not only to prevent actual incest but also to help her daughter free herself from childhood dependencies and grow into an autonomous adult.

Mothers are often blamed for letting incest happen, for letting it continue, or for doing something to cause it (such as not being a proper wife to the father). But the larger point is that so long as wives do in fact have less power than their husbands, then whatever weakens what power they do have may make it more difficult to prevent father-daughter incest. Actual father-daughter incest has been found to be more likely to occur if the mother is ill, dead, or has simply resigned. Linda Gordon and Paul O'Keefe, in a study of case records of incest in Boston families from 1880 to 1960, report that the one pattern most consistently associated with incest was father dominance by virtue of the weakness or absence of the mother, "her death, her illness, or disability."[23] Gordon and O'Keefe also report that male-headed single-parent households were overrepresented among incest cases (p. 30). Being the sole parent leaves the father in an even more powerful position vis-à-vis the daughter. Thus, it seems more reasonable to blame the husband dominance that the culture allows and expects than the mother's failings as an individual for both physical and psychological father-daughter incest. Fortunately, those who work with incest victims and their families now usually place the responsibility for incest on the father.

The therapeutic community's earlier tendency to blame the mother came after an initial tendency to blame the child. Blaming the child seems to have been caused by a literal interpretation of Freud's having placed the oedipal initiative in the mind of the child rather than in the mind of the parent. It also may have come from incest victims often feeling "guilty" that the incest was somehow their fault.[24] From a practical standpoint, however, no matter how seductively a child might behave or be perceived to behave, a child is "incapable of giving consent," given the obviously greater power that parents have over children.[25] This father power is not so much the authoritarian power of the Biblical patriarch as the psychological power that results from the isolation of the nuclear family and its having become almost totally an emotional enclave as opposed to a work unit. In other words, parents, especially in the middle class, have a great deal of psychological power and seem to carry an overload of psychological meaning for their children. In this context, perhaps even more than in a context of formal authority, the child is at least relatively powerless vis-à-vis the father because of his emotional significance for her.

One reason that Freud places the oedipal initiative in the mind of the child instead of in the mind of the parent is related to his view that "civilization," represented by the parents, imposed renunciations on the biological organism, represented by the child. That is, Freud sees each stage of development as involving the child's giving up certain biological impulses for the sake of "civilization" or society. From this societal perspective parents do in most cases impose the taboo on the child. So then why is mother-son incest more taboo than father-daughter incest?

If we focus on the taboo rather than on the taboo breaker, we see that because of male dominance the real taboo is on mother-son incest. If one reads Freud as a socialization theorist, the renunciation is imposed on the male child, who must renounce his tie to the mother. The daughter does not have to renounce the father so clearly; since after all she is to become a wife and accept her husband's control, the taboo is less strong. Freud assumes the father-daughter taboo is less strong and so deals with it less. The father-daughter taboo is also broken far more frequently than the mother-son taboo, and this itself partially reflects the weakness of the taboo.

Marrying Daddy: The Romance Novel

Suzanne Fields, in *Like Father, Like Daughter,* her book about the father-daughter relationship, describes how as a child she staged a make-believe marriage ceremony with her father. Readers who tend to think this is cute might be somewhat less charmed if her brother described acting out marrying his mother. I believe women continue to "marry daddy" in romance novels, not the rule-giving patriarch but the protecting, supporting daddy. A surprisingly large number of women consume several romance novels per week in this country. The Harlequin novel now has many competitors, but each new line can be viewed as selling a fantasy about the perfect father.[26] The heroes who win the girl in these novels are more like fathers as fantasied by the child than the real live males to whom the readers are married or the real live males who are available to be marriage partners. But we know the hero is a father because, in the first place, in romance novels he is usually considerably older than the heroine. In real life husbands are older than their wives, but usually only a year or so. The hero is also much taller and much stronger physically than the heroine. Descriptions of the two together often make much of the contrast between her vulnerability and his power. The hero appears at first to be hard and even cruel, but in the end, at least with the heroine, he becomes sensitive and gentle. All of this is close to the paradigm of the father-daughter relationship. In the middle class especially, daughters describe their fathers as being more nurturant and sensitive than their brothers describe the fathers to be.[27] And of course, when the daughter was a child, the physical contrast between her and her father was, in fact, quite marked.

The hero/father finds the heroine/daughter attractive because of her youth, her sexual innocence, and her naivete about the world. But at the same time this girl is not passive. She is a spirited girl who wants to engage the world. She has plans and enterprises, and she seeks to be the equal of men. These qualities are important to women readers, but as things turn out, the heroine needs to be rescued in the end.[28] No matter how smart and successful the heroine may be on her own, she cannot cope alone and needs saving. In the older novels the predicament from which she was saved often has to do with money owed. She must pay for the operation that will save her mother's life, or she must pay her irresponsible sister's gambling debts, or she must pay the back taxes on the farm. In more contemporary versions, the hero/father may rescue the daughter from her own business problems, which are no fault of her own. For example, in one story, the heroine sold computer security systems, and the hero saved a big sale for her at the last minute by discovering exactly how a competitor had been sabotaging the heroine's software. Thus the fantasy of a high-level job can readily be taken into account so long as in the end the woman requires rescue.

Modern heroines are also more sexy and sexually desirous than the older ones, but the hero is in control and runs the sexual show. He is in control of his own sexuality and keeps a strong hold on his passion and prevents things from getting out of hand. If it is the right time for the heroine's seduction, however, he makes the decision and gives her permission to be sexual.

If there is "another woman" in these novels, she is usually older than the heroine, more sophisticated, and more experienced sexually. She is also likely to be wise to the hero's tricks and not as overawed as the heroine. This could easily be the mother in the oedipal triangle, and the beauty of it for the heroine is that the man chooses the child. Janice Radway found that her romance readers did not like stories that included another woman; only the two romantics were needed. The absence of the third figure in the oedipal triangle could mean that the mother/other woman was already dead (and heroines are often orphans). This takes away any guilt regarding the usurpation of the mother.

Daddy's girl, then, can be sexual and accomplished, but the hero/daddy is the one with the power to choose whom he will love and on whom he will bestow his munificence. Even though the heroine protests that she can take care of herself and that her independence is critical to her self-esteem, she inevitably gives over responsibility for herself to the hero. It is the hero, older, taller, stronger, richer, wiser, who gives her her identity.

Radway, in her analysis of romance novels, argues that they fulfill women's desire to experience themselves in relationship and that the hero is a mother figure, not a father figure. The male becomes transformed by the women's more relational self and becomes like a mother. Radway is probably correct in saying that the fantasy involves wanting a real "relationship," an "intimate" relationship with a man; thus real men have to be transformed by fantasy. This aspect does not make romance novels so dangerous for women. The problem with romance novels is that they tend to put the woman in a childlike relationship to the man. Her relational needs are met not by an equal partner but rather by a man who is her superior and her caretaker. The fantasy of the superior male who is nevertheless "relational" has the advantage of keeping the woman from having to be "the mother" in the relationship, but it does so at the cost of making her the child. Because of this, the romance novel does not let the woman grow up but keeps her a daddy's girl. The romance novel ministers to women's relational needs but at a deeper level compromises women's need for equality and for connection with "real" women.

Rescuing Daddy's Girls

I have argued that there is psychological incest as well as physical incest in the case of daddy's girls. Fathers, especially in the "isolated" middle-class family, seem to carry an overload of psychological meaning for their children. What to do about it? Florence Rush answers harshly when she says, "Has anyone thought of the fantastic notion of getting rid of the father?"[29] I do not go this far. Yet, equal parenting is hardly the solution either. In my view the first step might be for women to rethink their relationship with their own mothers. Until women can understand and respect themselves as women without men, bringing men in, still unreconstructed, can hardly be of help. The question of women's own self-definition seems logically prior to the further inclusion of men.

A big part of being a daddy's girl often has involved not liking mother very much. Many women in this society seem bound and determined not to be like their mothers; they repudiate their mothers' lives and their mothers' weaknesses and sometimes their failure to protect them from father. Sometimes daughters collude with fathers about what is wrong with mother, about her deficiencies. This in itself contributes greatly to male dominance, sustains it, and reinforces it.

Practically speaking, covert and overt incest victims get over male dominance by rediscovering their mother either directly or indirectly through other women outside of the family. Therapy for physical incest victims often consists of a very deliberate effort to heal the wounds between mother and daughter and to get them to work together to stand up to the father. Women's consciousness-raising and support groups work to the same end. Daddy's girls of all sorts might begin to rediscover or create anew their mothers. Here I mean their mothers not as father's wife but as mother and person.

In actuality, we all know that many women find it very hard to think of their mothers without thinking of them in relation to their being the wives of their fathers and in relation to their dependency on men. It is quite true that many mothers believe that catching and holding a man is the be-all and end-all in life. Indeed, many mothers believe that the best thing they can do for their daughters is to teach them how to be a man's ideal wife. Thus finding one's own mother is easier said than done. As we witness a real decline in wives' dependency on husbands, however, it becomes easier to envision one's mother in a new and different light, and for mothers to envision new and better possibilities for their daughters.

The mother who is no longer herself dominated is most likely to be able to help daughters gain their freedom. In this connection, Jessica Benjamin points out that the basic flaw in Christopher Lasch's lament for the deterioration of paternal authority is "his failure to recognize that the mother who is no longer dominated provides the first opportunity in history for the freedom of *daughters*."[30] If the mother does not have to provide for her daughter through her husband, she is in a far better position to gain her daughter's respect. But even the daughters of "unliberated" mothers can find their mothers by the experience of mothering. Many women report that they discovered their own mothers for the first time when they had their own children. The experience of being a mother (a real mother or a mother in a relationship) can connect a woman with her own mother as mother, not as her husband's wife.

While feminists are well advised to reject many aspects of women's lives, rejecting women and their connections with each other and with their own mothers seems to offer no solution. The male-identified woman, who is the same as Freud's "feminine" woman, plays directly into the system of male dominance as it is organized by marriage in this society.

Homosexuality and Male Dominance

In the last chapter I argued that self-identified homosexuals differed from heterosexuals more in their attitudes toward their fathers than toward their mothers. If one interprets the Oedipus complex as the point at which the child first recognizes male dominance, then it would be possible to interpret homosexuality as a response that is related to male dominance. Sometimes this response may have misogynist outcomes but, following Freud's logic, it is also possible to associate it with resistance to male dominance. This association is especially true for lesbians, who are often quite conscious of their opposition to male dominance, but possibly also with regard to gay males.

Gay Males

Irving Bieber has an analysis concerning male homosexuality that is offensive and heterosexist on the face of it but that nevertheless fits with an interpretation of Freud as accurately describing unconscious psychic development in a male-dominant society. According to Bieber, all males would be heterosexual (presumably because of their first love for the mother) if they were not blocked from it. Male homosexuals, says Bieber, have rejected heterosexuality out of fear not of women but of men. Bieber's basic idea is that homosexuals unconsciously fear that they will be in some way punished for heterosexuality by aggressive males who are women's keepers. A boy might be blocked from heterosexuality then if this unconscious fear of dominant males who "own" women is not mitigated.[31]

This idea can also be found in some of Freud's observations. Freud describes male twins who were both apparently heterosexual until one twin "retired" in his brother's favor and gave up women as sexual partners. He did not like the idea of trespassing on his brother's territory. Freud also discusses treating a young male artist who found himself fleeing from both women and work simultaneously. Freud says, "The analysis which was able to bring him back to both, showed that *the fear of the father* was the most powerful psychic motive for both the disturbances, which were really renunciations. In his imagination all women belonged to the father, and he sought refuge in men out of submission, so as to 'retire from' the conflict in favor of the father" (italics added).[32] Certainly this reaction is understandable and could be interpreted as a protest, whether conscious or not, against male dominance seen ultimately as men's control over female sexuality. The choice then of males as sexual partners is simply what one must do if one is to have a sexual outlet at all, and other homosexual males seem safer than females, all of whom are seen as being owned by males.

Homosexuality in males could also be interpreted as seeking the loving protecting father one felt one never had. Bieber argues that gay males do like and love women, noting that they often choose female analysts, which suggests underlying heterosexuality, and that they genuinely grieve at the death of their mother but react in ways suggesting underlying hostility at the death of their father. Bieber's analysis implies that if heterosexuality continues to be considered a desirable societal goal, then it can most readily be fostered in males not by males who embody the system of male dominance but by males who are warmly supportive of their sons and who have a minimum of unconscious hostility toward them and who thus mitigate the image of the powerful, threatening, women-possessing male.

The idea that it is men not women who are feared can be interpreted as blaming the system of male dominance in heterosexual relationships itself (not mothers or even fathers) for creating the homosexual protest. This protest against male dominance does not mean that gay males' own fathers were necessarily themselves unusually dominant. Although some male homosexuals had fathers who were violent and terrifying, many others perceived their fathers to be weak, disinterested in them, and vaguely hostile.[33] In the first case the father directly represents theatening males to the boy; in the second instance, the father is no support to the boy in dealing with the threatening aspects of the male peer group.

C. A. Tripp has suggested that male homosexuality is related to an overevaluation of males and masculinity.[34] This suggestion is compatible with the Bieber position that stresses fear of males. In both cases, male power is at issue. The Tripp analysis suggests that gay males may have an exaggerated interest in and desire for masculine power. Unfortunately, in practical terms this may lead to the development of a kind of cult of supermasculinity that rejects women and glorifies the most problematic aspects of male bonding.

Joseph Harry points out that men who were effeminate as boys in terms of gender role expectations (some of whom are and some of whom are not gay) reject the competitiveness, violence, and dominance that characterizes masculine culture. Men who reported that they were effeminate as children became less so in their later years but continued to reject highly competitive pursuits and tended to pursue artistic and nurturant occupations.[35] Harry's work could be taken as pointing toward a gay critique of male dominance that in some ways parallels the lesbian critique.

Lesbianism as Protest

In Chapter 6 I noted that lesbians tell anecdotes about fathers' deeply negative reactions to lesbianism. Freud observed the same thing. Speaking of a father, Freud said:

When he first came to know of his daughter's homosexual tendencies he flared up in rage and tried to suppress them by threatening her; at that time perhaps he hesitated between different, though equally painful, views—regarding her either as vicious, as degenerated, or as mentally afflicted. . . . There was something about his daughter's homosexuality that aroused the deepest bitterness in him, and he was determined to combat it with all the means in his power.[36]

As for the mother Freud said:

The mother's attitude towards the girl was not so easy to grasp. . . . All that was clear was that she did not take her daughter's passion so tragically as did the father, nor was she so incensed at it. She had even for a long time enjoyed her daughter's confidence concerning the love-affair, and her opposition to it seemed to have been aroused mainly by the harmful publicity with which the girl displayed her feelings.

(pp. 135–36)

The logic of using Freud's account as a description of the acquiescence in heterosexuality and male dominance would lead to the conclusion that lesbianism represents resistance to that dominance. In *Love Between Women*, Charlotte Wolff, a clinician, makes these comments:[37]

Women who do not rebel against the status of object have declared themselves defeated as persons in their own right.

(p. 65)

The lesbian girl is the one who, by all means at her disposal, will try to find a place of safety inside and outside the family, through her fight for equality with the male. She will not, like other women, play up to him: indeed, she despises the very idea of it.

(p. 59)

The lesbian was and is unquestionably in the avant-garde of the fight for equality of the sexes, and for the psychical liberation of women.

(p. 66)

As noted earlier, Wolff sees mothers as the main force in the development of lesbianism. In Wolff's view, lesbianism arises from the girl taking a masculine competitive strategy to deal with the insufficiency of her mother's love. Thus she tends to see lesbians as "masculine." I see this as evidence of Wolff's tendency to conflate gender identity with sexual orientation, which of course Freud also does. Wolff's argument is that lesbian girls feel their mothers prefer males to them. This could be interpreted as saying that their mothers responded to men rather than women—as wives are supposed to do. In perceiving this, the girl is still responding to male dominance—by resenting her mother's acceptance of it. As a result of the structure of marriage in this society, many daughters do resent their mother's preoccupation with the father.

In Freud's account, girls do not ever entirely give up their mothers but remain in a bisexual triangle, vacillating between mother and father. Thus for Freud, females are more bisexual than males and more likely to be homosexuals than males are. Freud is probably right about women's greater bisexuality, and if lesbianism becomes increasingly associated with a protest against male dominance, more women may begin to express sexual feelings for women and more of those who are already lesbian in actions may come to accept "lesbian" as a self-definition. In this sense "lesbian" could be considered the ultimate in "politically correct" feminism.

It has often been pointed out that surely lesbians do not escape male dominance by refusing heterosexuality and relationships with men. Of course they do not; for example, lesbians, like heterosexual women, suffer pay inequities. Indeed many lesbians suffer the possibility of no income at all, that is no job at all, if their lesbianism becomes known. The point is that choice in a society is never free, and the costs of being a lesbian are made to be higher than the costs of being a heterosexual because of the strength of the heterosexual norm. This fact constrains women to take the heterosexual route, but it does not negate the lesbian argument that male dominance inheres "in the last instance," as it were, in heterosexual relations.

While interpreting homosexuality as a protest against male dominance makes sense in terms of Freud's assumptions, it becomes problematic as a political strategy because of the widespread view of homosexuality as deviance. The "deviance" label attaching to homosexuality serves as a control on any kind of protest against the male-dominant structure of heterosexual relationships. It reinforces the exclusive and absolute legitimacy of the male-dominated heterosexual couple. Although Freud was extremely liberal on the subject of homosexuality and by no means saw it as a crime against humanity, Freud's metatheory and psychoanalytic views, which connect masculinity and femininity with sexual preference, make "being heterosexual" a matter of extreme importance to those committed to the male-dominant status quo. Thus any kind of resistance to male dominance tends to be labeled as "deviant" and beyond the pale of social respectability.[38]

The feminist answer to the problem posed by the deviant status of homosexuality has been to broaden and transform the meaning of the term *lesbian* to include far more than (and not necessarily even including) "sleeping with women." Thus, as the authors of *The Powers of Desire* have commented, an identity that had been all sex became totally unsexed within a short period.[39] Whether this strategy can overcome the stigma of "lesbianism" remains to be seen. While lesbian separatism as a concrete strategy poses far more problems than it solves, it is important not to discount the logic of the argument.

In my view the contribution of radical lesbian analyses to feminism in general has been to clearly delineate the degree to which adult heterosexual relations in and out of bed are predicated on male dominance. At least in the United States, it is becoming less and less possible to discount this truth by labeling it "lesbian." It must be recognized that the most important impediment to developing a woman-centered approach is the overweening importance of heterosexual relationships that are male-centered and male-dominated.

Summary: Fathers Versus Mothers

Chodorow attempts to redress Freud's focus on fathers by emphasizing the overwhelming importance of mothers to women emotionally. This is an important step, but my treatment of Freud in this chapter reminds us that it is fathers who usurp the mother's power in Freud's account. Freud's account needs to be taken seriously lest we forget precisely who or what the villain in the piece really is. I do not mean by this statement that men as individual fathers are the villains but rather that men acting as members of male peer groups reinforce male dominance. Real fathers can work against male dominance by being more like mothers.

In both this chapter and the preceding one, I have argued from different empirical bases that fathers "feminize" girls and "masculinize" boys more than mothers do. By *feminize* I refer to training girls specifically in male-dominated heterosexual interaction. I do not believe this has to be what femaleness is (because femaleness is ultimately what we say it is), but for Freud femininity meant being male-oriented and passive. This is a male view of femininity. In this chapter I have interpreted father-daughter incest broadly and argued that the father-daughter relationship tends to reproduce in daughters a disposition to please men in a relationship in which the male dominates. The society and fathers themselves work against this disposition in sons toward mothers but accept it in daughters toward fathers as "the way things should be." If we preserve the mother-wife distinction, one might look at daddy's girls as in training to be wives. I argued that if daddy's girls are to gain their independence, they need to learn to construct an identity as the daughters of strong mothers as well.

The lesbianism-as-protest argument makes resistance center on male-dominated heterosexual relations in their widest construction. Chodorow's analysis minimizes these relationships by saying that most girls become genitally heterosexual but retain their strong mother ties. In developmental terms this may be true, but in terms of social structure this analysis misses the extent to which all heterosexual interaction (not specifically sexual-genital) between adults tend to be male-dominated. Marriage and the couple relationship is stressed in this society. Women are separated from one another as wives of men. Next then, it is important to understand the extent to which Freud's scheme assumes a definition of woman as wife, the lesser in any heterosexual context.

Chapter Eight

Psychoanalysis and the Making of Mothers into Wives

In previous chapters I discussed several senses in which one could interpret Freud's work, which generally focused on fathers, as "true," and showed that this same truth could be found in the data of academic psychology. In this chapter, I move to a discussion of the sense in which psychoanalysis as applied to gender development has obscured truth. Feminists have criticized psychoanalytic theory on many counts, but I believe the core problem with the psychoanalytic theory of gender development is its implicit definition of masculinity as being sexually attracted to females and acting as "subject" in heterosexual relationships, and its implicit definition of femininity as being sexually attracted to males and being an object in heterosexual relationships. These definitions equate what we now call gender with heterosexuality and dominance in heterosexual relationships if one is "masculine" and with submission in heterosexual relationships if one is "feminine." In short, psychoanalysis defines gender in terms of sexuality, and a male-defined sexuality at that.

Failure to be critical of the connections made within psychoanalysis between sexuality and gender led both Juliet Mitchell and Gayle Rubin (who have since changed their positions) to the discouraging conclusion that we must end gender differentiation in order to end male dominance and to "free" sexuality.[1] In my view, what we now refer to as gender identity, the gut conviction of feeling female or male, would be difficult to eradicate in any culture. It

would be much more possible to disassociate culturally a basic
sense of gendered self from issues of dominance and submission
and sexual preference. This process of separation is well on its way
outside psychoanalysis, but psychoanalysis itself and those who use
its approach have not yet come to terms with it. I argue that the
effect of the recent tendency to use the term *gender* instead of *sex*
will be to emphasize that sexuality is not definitive of gender, certainly at least not in the minds of women. Gender and sexuality
need to be analytically separated and each defined in terms that
take female perspectives into account.

Freud's Conception of Gender Difference

Chodorow's main concern in *The Reproduction of Mothering* is to
explain differences between men and women in relational capacities on the basis of women's mothering. She explicitly states that
she is not primarily concerned with the differential evaluation of
males and females or with gender identity or heterosexuality. In
contrast, Juliet Mitchell and Gayle Rubin have been concerned
with precisely these phenomena. But, as I said, both Mitchell's and
Rubin's analyses run into problems because they do not sufficiently
question the way in which psychoanalytic thinkers merge questions of sexuality with questions of gender.[2]

As both Mitchell and Rubin make clear, Freud, to his great
credit, does not take masculinity in males and femininity in females
for granted as being given at birth. Although there may be dis-
agreement about how large a weight Freud gives to biological factors (Mitchell and Rubin probably underestimate Freud's biologism), there can be no doubt that becoming "masculine" for males
and becoming "feminine" for females is something that is at least in
part "accomplished" rather than given. Freud sees each "sex" as
possessing elements of both masculinity and femininity and refers
to this as bisexuality. These elements are both physiological and
psychological in nature. For Freud, the psychic manifestations of
bisexuality include a wide range of behaviors from overt homosexuality to cross-gender nonerotic behavior. He makes it quite clear
that "normal" individuals are never totally masculine or feminine
in their behavior.[3]

The problem with Freud arises not with regard to any insensitivity on his part to the bisexual nature of both males and females. There is a problem, however, with the strong linkage he makes between sexual orientation and gender. In his scheme a female can deviate from femininity by being active or by choosing a female love object, and a male can deviate from masculinity by being passive or by choosing a male object. But what one cannot do within the scheme is deny the centrality of heterosexuality and dominance to masculinity and heterosexuality and passivity to femininity.

Many of Freud's other propositions depend on and perhaps derive from this basic assumption. In the first place, he concludes that a girl's femininity is less secure than a boy's masculinity because her first love relationship is with a female, thus "homosexual." The little boy, by contrast, has a head start on masculinity because of his early relationship with his mother, which, as Robert Stoller noted, Freud never doubted was "fundamentally heterosexual" (pp. 356–57). Even though Freud did make a few statements concerning the possibilities of an affectionate identification with the parent of the same gender, he generally thought of same-sex relationships as threatening gender identity and heterosexual relationships affirming it.[4] For example, in discussing the case of little Hans, Freud observes that the child's father was often the one who helped him urinate ("widdle") and in the process of helping him take out his "widdler," Hans was given "an opportunity for the fixation of homosexual inclinations upon him."[5]

Although Freud saw both males and females as being bisexual, the basic sexual orientation of both genders in his view was predominantly masculine defined as a phallic (by definition active) orientation toward the mother.[6] Thus Freud argued that a female first loved her mother as a little man. Her orientation to her mother was active and clitoral. To become "feminine" she must transform this orientation to being passive and vaginal. This tying of male to active and female to passive can also be seen in his idea that each gender experiences a positive and negative Oedipus complex. In the negative Oedipus complex, the boy loves his father passively; in the positive Oedipus complex, he loves his mother actively. The girl's negative Oedipus complex involves loving the mother actively, "like a little man," and in the positive Oedipus complex, she loves the father passively, "like a woman."

Although being actively mothered and perhaps seeing siblings being mothered is a first social experience of children of both genders, Freud maintains that mothering is not a primary wish in females, much less in males. As late as 1933, he explicitly states that the doll play of a young girl is "not in fact an expression of her femininity." He explains this by saying it could not be feminine because "it served as an identification with her mother with the intention of substituting activity for passivity."[7] Here Freud makes it clear that in his view femininity does not relate to motherhood, because motherhood is active, nor is femininity acquired by identifying with the mother. Femininity is acquired only when the doll becomes "a baby from the girl's father, and thereafter the aim of the most powerful feminine wish" (p. 87). This wish is to have a penis from the father.

In Freud's terms what is important in the child's mind is not the baby but who gave the mother the baby. Freud admits that in general it is hard to imagine the nature of the girl's active phallic wishes toward the mother, that is, "whether the child attaches a sexual aim to the idea, and what that aim is," but when a sibling is born, he tells us, "The little girl wants to believe that she has given her mother the new baby, just as the boy wants to, and her reaction to this event and her behavior to the baby is exactly the same as his."[8] Here Freud emphasizes the baby as a gift from a man but ignores the wishes often expressed by both males and females to be the mother, to own a baby.

In Freud's work there is no independent status for mothering; it is merely a roundabout way of getting a penis, which he claims is what women really want. The ultimate and true feminine wish is to have a male child, and this child becomes a substitute for the coveted penis. Motherhood is subsumed under penis envy and women are defined as failed men, with motherhood being their consolation prize. Thus Freud's theory provides a magnificently overdeveloped rationale in support of defining women primarily as wives, secondarily as mothers. For Freud getting a child from a man is the "feminine" wish, but getting a child, period, is not. The latter might imply more female independence and activity than Freud could countenance.

Yet Freud was more aware than most of the inadequacy of the terms *active* and *passive* to characterize masculinity and femininity, and he understood that on one level motherhood is a very active enterprise. He tries to solve the problem in part by suggesting that "one might consider characterizing femininity psychologically as giving preference to passive aims," explaining that "this is not, of course, the same thing as passivity: to achieve a passive aim may call for a large amount of activity."[9] Even so, the idea of passive aim gets us right back to the fit between Freud's scheme and the passive aim of being a wife, a state a woman might indeed actively pursue, since it has been "the only game in town."

Freud claims that "activity" versus "passivity" is relevant to masculinity and femininity when one thinks of the active sperm joining the passive egg and of the active male and passive female in intercourse. His discussion here provides us with a good example of how what appears to be a biological "fact" is stated and distorted in terms of essentially social meanings. Freud says, "The male sex-cell is actively mobile and searches out the female one, and the latter, the ovum, is immobile, and waits passively. This behavior of the elementary sexual organisms is indeed a model for the conduct of sexual individuals during intercourse. The male pursues the female for the purpose of sexual union, seizes hold of her and penetrates into her" (p. 117 fn.). Although the sperm does move toward the egg, dead sperm and inert particles of India ink reach the egg at about the same speed as live sperm, suggesting that the active-passive conceptualization is socially imposed even here.[10] Certainly too Freud's conceptualization of the act of intercourse is patently social. Thus in his hands "femininity" is rendered passive.

Roy Schafer maintains that Freud gives a prominent place to genital heterosexuality because it fits in with the general evolutionary emphasis on the propagation of the species.[11] But why did he not emphasize instead the survival of the progeny and note that among humans, survival depends heavily on postnatal care. It appears to be a peculiarly masculine bias to assume that sexual intercourse is the major event related to the evolution of the human species. For women, motherhood may be the major event related to the next generation, and men can relate to this only indirectly.

Freud's Gynecentric Opposition

Freud's emphasis on the Oedipal period and de-emphasis on women's mothering has been challenged from the very beginning even from within the psychoanalytic movement itself. Karen Horney argued long ago that Freud's view of women as defective males was patent male bias, and as Nancy Chodorow notes, of all the explanations of penis envy that have ever been put forth, only Freud's is inconceivable.[12] Freud claimed that the instant a girl sees a boy's penis she knows she has been shortchanged. Freud does not even seek an explanation for penis envy because for him the explanation was obvious: any girl in her right mind would want one.

The reason that Mitchell in contrast to so many feminists accepts Freud's attribution of primary penis envy to girls has to do with her Lacanian-influenced view of Freud as a purveyor of cultural symbolism. She would say that the human psyche is phallocentric and is recreated in each generation, in "masculine civilization." As she puts it, "there is nothing neither true nor false but thinking makes it so, and if patriarchal thought is dominant then femininity will reflect that system: 'nature' is not exempt from its representation in mental life."[13] Mitchell contrasts her symbolic approach to the biologism of Horney, Klein, Jones, and others who argued against Freud and the primacy of penis envy (pp. 125–31).

I am not concerned with countering either Mitchell's totally symbolic approach or the biologism of those she criticizes. Neither will I focus on the long-standing battle over penis envy, which now seems well on the way to being won by those who deny its primacy in the development of "femininity." I am concerned instead with the more serious problem that pervades both sides of the phallocentric-gynecentric debate within psychoanalysis. Neither Freud, who epitomizes the phallocentric emphasis, nor the gynecentric theorists who challenge this emphasis have a conception of pre-oedipal gender that is not closely tied to heterosexuality. Even those psychoanalytic thinkers who have stressed womb and breast envy in boys and who see penis envy in girls as a secondary development maintain in one way or another the connections between femininity, heterosexuality, and passivity. Karen Horney, for example, who was one of the first to argue against Freud's ideas concerning females' initial penis envy, did so only to conclude that penis envy was a secondary development in females, which acted as a defense against girls' innate heterosexual desires for the father![14] Even though Freud's phallocentric conclusions were related to his merger of male dominance, heterosexuality, and masculinity, those gynecentric theorists who stress women's mothering do not question the assumption that the basic elements of gender are heterosexuality and dominance-passivity. Fully as much as Freud, the gynecentric opposition sees passivity and heterosexuality as being the "normal" developmental result for females even though they posit differing starting points than did Freud and his followers.

Karen Horney, Ernest Jones, Melanie Klein, and more recently Janine Chassequet-Smirgel and Bela Grunberger all explain the girl's turn to the father as being related to an innate heterosexual desire.[15] They claim the girl does not want a penis because she feels shortchanged without one, but rather she wants a man because she is heterosexual. These authors do not see heterosexuality as being created in culture or interaction but as being given in nature. In a way this draws the connections between sexuality and gender even closer by treating them as purely biological. Freud, at least as Juliet Mitchell interprets him, can be seen as assuming women have to learn heterosexuality-femininity and at some cost to themselves at that. These gynecentric analysts, however, break the linkage Freud makes between reproduction and sexuality by treating sexuality, albeit heterosexuality, as intrinsically gratifying to women and not as a means to procreation, which Freud always interpreted it to be. Freud always assumed women wanted "sex" in order to have a baby, which was a penis substitute.

Freud increasingly came to understand that there were other relationships besides the Oedipus complex that established gender difference and lay behind the Oedipus complex. For example, in a paper written in 1921 entitled "Group Psychology and the Analysis of the Ego," he says: "A little boy will exhibit a special interest in his father; he would like to grow like him and be like him, and take his place everywhere. We may say simply that he takes his father as his ideal. . . . It fits very well with the Oedipus complex, for which it helps to prepare the way."[16] Here he suggests that he does have a conception of gender identity that rests on a simple identification with the father as a mentor and ideal. Finally, in the later years of his life Freud began to make statements about the importance of the preoedipal mother attachment in girls and commented to the effect that there were depths to mental life that psychoanalysis had not explored. He compares the early preoedipal period in girls to the discovery in anthropology of the Minoan-

Mycenaean civilization that preceded the civilization of Greece.[17] But even in recognizing the importance of this period, he does not relate it to female gender identification. For him girls are "masculine" until they become feminized by the father.

Even though Chodorow is aware of these connections within psychoanalytic theory, she does not directly challenge them.[18] As we saw earlier, she explicitly states that she assumes the heterosexuality of the mother. Rather, her contribution is to describe the relational context (the girl's experience of self in relationship, the boy's less relational self) in which "heterosexuality and these identifications get constituted" (p. 113). She does discuss how heterosexuality differs for men and women because of the primacy of the mother in the early lives of both genders. In so doing she makes a beginning toward decreasing the importance of heterosexuality to females as she discusses the daughter's emotional tie to her mother and her merely erotic tie to the father. She speaks of the daughter as being at least genitally heterosexual and implies that this erotic tie is not as deep as the female-to-female emotional tie. Chodorow's hedging suggests to me that she recognizes that if one gives up the tie that exists by definition between heterosexuality and gender, one comes dangerously close to giving up psychoanalytic accounts of gender development.

In sum, both phallocentric and gynecentric psychoanalytic conceptualizations conflate dominance and being sexually attracted to females with masculinity, and submissiveness and being sexually attracted to males with femininity. This has the effect of justifying inequality by making it appear that heterosexuality and deference to the male partner are central components of female gender identity. The alternatives open to women within this scheme appear to be to give up dominance and be feminine, to be asexual, which presumably makes one a neuter, or a nonperson, or to be homosexual, which of course Freud associated with being masculine. (This creates problems for those lesbians who attempt to use Freud, since many lesbians do not see themselves as masculine.) Gayle Rubin suggests that if fathers also mothered, primary object choice might be bisexual.[19] The bisexual solution does not challenge the fundamental categories, however; it merely makes an amalgam of them. Thus "bisexual" would be a mixture of masculine and feminine, which in terms of psychoanalytic assumptions would mean heterosexual and homosexual, dominant and submissive. Just as with the "androgyny" scales, putting two wrongs together does not make a right. Mitchell and Rubin, in accepting Freud uncritically as describing the way things are in the human psyche, can find no way out. For them the only way out would be to somehow do away with gender, which they assume must be defined in terms of sexuality. As noted earlier, both have now repudiated this formulation.

In her more recent work, Mitchell takes a very different tack and argues that by no means do we give up gender, since "human subjectivity cannot ultimately exist outside a division between the sexes—one cannot be no sex." But she then goes on to claim that the castration complex organizes what that difference is. This difference, she says, is not the presence of the penis in males and its absence in females and thus the difference between symbolic power and its absence, but is rather a problem in not being whole for both males and females. Thus she says, "The castration complex is not about women, nor men, but a danger, a horror to both—a gap that has to be filled in differently by each. In the fictional ideal type this will be [filled in] for the boy by the illusion that a future regaining of phallic potency will replace his totality; for the girl this will be achieved by something psychically the same: a baby. Phallic potency and maternity—for men and women—come to stand for wholeness."[20] Here Mitchell appears to have forgotten all about male dominance in the sense of the normativeness of "masculinity." In her earlier reading of Freud she gave full play to his view that it was harder for women to become feminine than it was for men to become masculine because femininity meant accepting phallocentric culture. At the very end of her article she begins to speculate that femininity is not the same as motherhood, because mothers are symbolically about plenitude, fullness, completeness. This may or may not lead her in the direction I have been taking.

Writing in the 1970s, Gayle Rubin declared that to end inequality, gender differentiation and the Oedipus complex must be destroyed. This followed from the assumption that gender was created in the oedipal period. In 1984 she argues we must distinguish between gender and erotic desire and points out that the "semantic merging [of sex and gender] reflects a cultural assumption that sexuality is reducible to sexual intercourse and that it is a function of the relations between women and men."[21] Her "solution" now is that we need to develop a theory of sexuality less tied to gender. I shall return to this later.

To some extent the French feminists, too, who are attempting to redefine femininity while remaining within the Freud-Lacan tradition have been caught up in a problem that psychoanalytic accounts of gender development have created. In my view these efforts fail to the extent that they fail to critique the conflation I have been discussing. At its best psychoanalysis can be seen as an attempt to describe the social construction of gender in the nuclear family, but at the same time it reinforces a construction that makes sex-object choice and the active-passive distinction the central problematic.

In sum, then, the psychoanalytic conceptualization of masculinity and femininity has conflated dominance and sexual attraction to females with masculinity, and submissiveness and sexual attraction to males with femininity. Then, in a manner somewhat analogous to the way in which androgyny scales were constructed, the assumption is made that biological males and females generally possess a mixture of both masculinity and femininity. Freud envisioned children as being bisexual and at other times both boys and girls as being masculine. In either case, the "normal" outcome was for masculinity to predominate in anatomical males (anatomy becomes destiny) and for femininity to predominate in anatomical females, although this was more difficult. Freud sees this transformation as occurring during the oedipal period with its final solidification taking place at adolescence, after a period of sexual latency.

While this conceptualization is "liberal" in the sense that femininity appears to be not at all a foregone conclusion but instead a defeat for women, the problem lies in the assumptions that Freud makes about the nature of masculinity and femininity in the first place. By tying heterosexuality to gender identity itself, Freud makes it impossible to see that what oppresses women is the way in which heterosexual relationships themselves are structured.

Reconstructing Gender

Today traditional psychoanalytic interpretations of gender have been challenged by research on adult transsexuals and on children whose gender identity is for some reason problematic. John Money and Anke Ehrhardt have concluded on the basis of their work with children with ambiguous genitalia that gender identity, the gut level conviction that one is a male or female, is formed early, before eighteen months, and therefore probably prior to the oedipal period when Freud thought gender differentiation occurred.[22] Money also explicitly states, contrary to Freud's implication, that "gender identity," the public expression of which is "gender role," does not rest on heterosexuality or male dominance.[23]

The finding that gender identity is established before the oedipal phase implies that gender identity per se does not have to be eliminated to eliminate sexism. In order to "free" sexuality, one does not have to give up gender identity. In my view the important step is to see that each individual's basic sense of gendered self can be separable from heterosexuality as a way of life and from expectations of male dominance in heterosexual relationships.

In his 1974 article in which he first articulated his concept of "core gender identity," Robert Stoller appeared to point the way toward a reconceptualization within psychoanalysis of gender development. In this article (which I described in Chapter 4) he argues that the boy's first interaction with the mother is not heterosexual but involves a merging with the mother's femininity, just as the girl merges with her femininity. Much hinges, of course, on what Stoller means by *femininity*, and he does not define it, but in 1974 he clearly seemed to be referring to a maternal impulse as opposed to a heterosexual impulse. Stoller argues that Freud misinterpreted the famous Schreber case (Schreber was a prominent judge) in calling Shreber's fantasies "homosexual," because these fantasies were actually about his body changing to female and procreating a new race. Schreber was thinking in terms of maternal creativity and power, and not of sexual relations.[24] Thus Schreber wanted to be a mother, not to have a man. Stoller's discussion appears to offer a basis for defining core femininity as being maternal rather than heterosexual.

In a later article, however, it is clear that Stoller remains an unreconstructed Freudian who has merely added on the idea of "core gender identity." He defines "core gender identity" as one's sense of being male or female, and "gender identity" as "the algebraic sum of the mix of masculinity and femininity found in an individual." He says he has nothing to add to Freud concerning femininity but wants to talk about primary femininity, which is established be-fore penis envy and the Oedipus complex. Quite remarkably, at this point he says primary femininity will consist in whatever the parents, especially the mother, encourages. "If one wants the ap-pearance of femininity in a baby, all one need do is encourage and encourage and encourage."[25] It is clear in this article that he does not mean maternal orientation by primary femininity—apparently, he means a kind of seductiveness. In his example of a woman who had not gotten beyond primary femininity he describes a woman whose core "femininity" seems to consist in being "lovely," a moth-er's doll on display. He sees this woman as basically a case of hys-teria because she was seductive toward him in therapy and implies that this is her primary femininity produced by her mother! Here, clearly, Stoller's primary femininity is of no help to feminists (in spite of his saying primary femininity can consist of anything) and reproduces (at an even earlier level) the idea that femininity relates to being sexy with men. As far as I can see, male and female chil-dren are absolutely dedicated to smiling at and being charming (sexy?) to anyone of any gender who smiles back. In their interac-tions, all parents and all children are engaged in "seduction" in its broadest sense.

John Munder Ross, who is not a psychoanalyst but who works within the psychoanalytic tradition, is beginning to move toward a different conception of early childhood desires—a conception that gives what he calls "generativity" a more important place in the self-conceptions of both males and females. He assumes children of both genders first take on a maternal identification, but he says a boy's wishes to have a baby are soon interrupted by his "developing perception of sexual differences." He argues that the boy needs an awareness of the man's part in reproduction through his sexual rela-tionship to a woman but also an appreciation of a man being able to take an active care-taking role. Thus the boy could imagine himself as a creative nurturant daddy who shares in both making and tend-ing babies. Ross also suggests that the role of the father is to be not the fearsome father that Freud depicts in *Totem and Taboo* but the mothering father who can conteract that fearsome image.[26]

This paternal identity is very different from the paternal identity Freud outlines and is more like the relational identity Chodorow outlines for women. Thus at least among the less classical theorists there does seem to be a movement toward recognizing gender differentiation occurring at an initial earlier stage of development, prior to the oedipal period. They suggest that this earliest identity is based on the development of a parenting motive as opposed to a heterosexual motive in both genders. Nancy Chodorow points out that in psychoanalytic theory "a girl identifies with her mother in their common feminine inferiority and in her heterosexual stance."[27] It seems to me that if we take the view that neither girls nor boys know their mother is inferior (or heterosexual) in their earliest relationship to her, it is quite possible to imagine that at first a child does not identify with her inferiority but with her active caretaking. An observational study of young children's fantasy play found that both boys and girls depicted "the wife" as a helpless individual. Girls depicted "mothers," however, as nurturant and efficient, but boys perceived males to be leaders both as fathers and husbands.[28]

It is likely that heterosexuality is so important to gender identity only in the male psyche. Whereas the preoedipal girl can identify with her mother directly in her maternal activities of nurturing children, the boy may tend to define himself more in terms of being husband to mother. Another way of putting this is that the girl seems first to attempt to enact a maternal identity, whereas the boy avoids this by enacting a heterosexual identity.[29] I believe these reorientations are very much on the right track, but they do not represent mainstream psychoanalytic opinion.

I have suggested at various points that women's basic sense of gender is likely to be related to a sense of mothering or relational capacities. This view is clearly implied in Chodorow's work. Dora Ullian comes to the same conclusion from what she calls a "constructivist" perspective.[30] She thinks that the main organizing factor by which girls construct a sense of gender identity may well be the association of femaleness with having babies. In support of this view, she cites Bernstein and Cowan's study of children's concepts of the origin of babies, which indicates that girls believe that they already have some form of baby inside them regardless of the accuracy or inaccuracy of their ideas about birth and conception (p. 249). She reviews other evidence relating to the young girl's identification with nurturance, including the study that showed the persistence of girl's doll play even when the "doll corner" was removed and Eleanor Maccoby's conclusion that girls and women are more responsive to infants than men and boys are and are more nurturant toward younger children who still need help and care (p. 244). Ullian concludes that "a feature of identity as salient as the capacity to bear children may represent a stable organizer of the child's identity and a significant determinant of her behavior. The preoccupation of girls with babies, dolls, various household items, friendships, and feelings bears testimony to the invariability of this female pattern" (p. 250).

One may ask how all this squares with the evidence that many, perhaps a majority of, girls declare that they were tomboys when they were growing up, which often meant having nothing to do with dolls.[31] Since this tomboyishness usually occurs after early childhood, it could develop on top of an identification with mothering at least partially as a response to the girl's growing awareness that the world thinks "boys are better." On another level tomboyishness may mean that American girls, happily, do not see active engagement of the world as a gender-differentiated trait.

Ullian points out that her account differs from Chodorow's in that she does not posit a lack of differentiation between young girls and their mothers but instead "links female 'connectedness' to the young girl's tendency to view herself as the mother of a real or imagined child."[32] The two positions are compatible. Chodorow is concerned with the nature of the relationship between mother and daughter and emphasizes the mother's identification with the daughter; Ullian focuses on the female child's perception that she is "connected, either metaphorically or physically" to another. Chodorow stresses the socioemotional (and unconscious) aspects primarily; Ullian, the cognitive aspects. In either case they tie female gender identity to mothering, although Chodorow is not specifically concerned with gender "identity" in the way Ullian is.

It is also important to understand that both Chodorow and Ullian would disagree with Freud and with Lawrence Kohlberg's version of Freud that the girl's sense of self develops as a result of an attempt to compensate for a lack of perceived male power. From any number of standpoints, and most basically from the structural fact that women mother, girls are likely to have a primary, noncompensatory gender identity that is tied in with responsible caretaking. Just what concrete shape this takes in the child's mind is another question, as is the salience of gender to a child, especially the female child. The primacy of girls' identification with mothering would fit with females having a more stable gender identity than males, even in the face of culturally based "male superiority."[33] This view is, of course, contrary to Freud, who thought boys had the more clear-cut gender identity.

The idea that girls see themselves first as female because of associating femaleness and mothering may be more plausible to the adult mind than to the child's mind, however. While female is connected to mothering and is "true" at some level, it is difficult to state this truth in such a way as to avoid the "adultomorphizing" of gender, that is, attributing to children adult ways of categorizing the world. We obviously do not know what preverbal infants think, and even when they can talk, we cannot know what they "know" at some level they cannot articulate. I am sometimes persuaded by arguments of nonpsychoanalytic thinkers that gender is something that is sustained in interaction and is, in a sense, created and recreated in daily life. Transsexuals challenge this view, however, in that they are aware of playing an "as if" game. They feel that they "really" are a female, and the interactions they participate in "as a male" do not "feel right." This suggests that there are some very early impressions that are crucial. We do not know what they are, but on balance I suspect that mothering is important.

Ullian attributes girls' tendency to be less aggressive than boys to perceptions by girls that they are physically more delicate than boys, particularly the perception that adult men are hairy and have tough skin and deep voices and that women have smoother, softer skin and higher voices. Ullian explains why "girls are good" and "fear being bad" on the basis of their perception of themselves as not being tough but, rather, small, fragile, and easily hurt. In my view Ullian exaggerates female perceptions of "delicacy" vis-à-vis boys since both boys and girls may feel delicate and vulnerable compared to adults, especially adult males. The idea that adult women are delicate is culturally variable, certainly more variable than the greater aggressiveness of males. Although we are far from a complete understanding of women's lesser tendency to aggress, there is little reason to believe that feeling fragile will figure prominently in the explanation.

In an unpublished paper, Ullian reports on a study of the ways in which females of different ages perceive themselves in relation to males.[34] Six- to ten-year-old girls tended to see boys as "show-offs" who were "not very nice." They were people who thought they were wonderful for no good reason. As one six-year-old put it, "When boys do something like fishing, they want to catch something real big but then they don't come home with anything. But girls, they don't say they are going to do this or to do that. They see how it is going to be and if they catch something, they catch something" (p. 7).

Girls in the ten- to fourteen-year-old group were aware of a conflict between women's autonomy and conventional standards for marital relations. In other words, they were ambivalent about wives who were dominant, feeling that it was both OK—"she has just as much right as the man"—but also not so OK—"it is very weird that she had a better job than he does. I guess they would probably get into a couple of arguments" (quote from a twelve-year-old; p. 11).

In contrast, middle-class high school and college women resolved the conflict in favor of the male. In spite of being opposed to male dominance in principle, these late adolescents personally wanted their particular male to be more successful and dominant than they and expressed emotional discomfort at the prospect of being superior to their mate. They often coupled this with the idea that women were emotionally stronger than men and did not need the ego enhancement that males did. One girl suggested that the reason for wanting the male to be superior was in order not to have to feel like a mother toward him. Both these rationales are based on a recognition of the superiority of women as mothers. The first reaction suggests a belief in women's ability to empower others and women's superior emotional strength, and the second reaction recognizes that a mother-son relationship would reverse the power situation. But surely the alternative to being the superior mother does not have to be that of inferior wife. Equality needs to rest on being lovers and friends.

Ullian comments that even the most highly educated and economically privileged women who were interviewed, women who aspired to demanding professional careers, nevertheless wanted a man they could "look up to." Thus the idea was that the successful marital relationship required male dominance. These findings suggest that male dominance is located in our notions of the good mar-

riage, but it is not the primary basis of women's gender identity.
This psychic position is not arrived at by women till adolescence. It
is a position that is intimately connected with the ideology of the
nuclear family, the structure of the economic world, and the link-
ages between the nuclear family and that world. Simply put, even
as the male provider role declines, a woman's life chances still depend on the man she marries far more than a man's life chances
depend on the woman he marries—a powerful reason for a woman
to look for a superior man. It was Freud's questionable contribution
to help define this as an ultimate psychic reality, to define deference to the male as what "femininity" is. This is not what women
are but rather reflects expectations for women as wives. The effect
of emphasizing the heterosexual couple in this society to the exclusion of others has been to emphasize the very relationship in which
men are defined as superior.

Separating Gender from Sex

Freud defines gender in terms of sexuality, and sexuality in terms
of a phallic or male model. This process involves two confusions:
defining gender in terms of sexuality and defining sexuality from a
male perspective. I discuss each issue in turn. In doing so I depart
from Freud and psychoanalytic theory and turn to language usage
and to changes that have occurred in that usage. These changes reflect changes in our thinking about sex and gender.

Throughout this book I have used the term *gender* where ten
years ago I would have used the term *sex*. Indeed, here I use *gender* where many people would still use the word *sex*. There is a
lack of agreement both among feminists and among the general
public concerning the usage of these terms. Clearly, however, the
word *sex* has been overloaded with disparate meanings and other
terms are needed. The merging of what we now call gender with
sex and male-oriented definitions of sexuality is endemic in the language and in Western (masculine) thinking. I use the term *gender*
largely to make a distinction between gender and the narrowly
sexual.

One confusion relates to *sex* being used to refer to one's civil
status as a female or male versus the use of sex to refer to genital erotic activity (sex in bed). Ambiguities such as the following

abound: Does "sexual emancipation" refer to what we usually mean by the "sexual revolution," which freed women for more sexual activity, or does "sexual emancipation" refer to progress toward equality between females and males? What is a television documentary entitled "A Matter of Sex" about? It is in fact about inequities in pay and promotion of female bank tellers, but one suspects that the title in 1982 was meant to mislead the audience into thinking it was about sexual activity. Then there are the tired old jokes familiar to academic feminists, "Hello, how are you, are you still interested in sex?" and "How's the sex business?" Heh. Heh. It was not too long ago that women were referred to as "the sex." So men "had sex" with "the sex." All these examples offer linguistic testament to the sexualization and heterosexualization of gender. Freud did not invent this, since these ideas are probably at least as old as patriarchy, but Freud related them to a privatized psychic reality, fundamental to the subjective sense of self.[35]

Thirty years ago, *gender* was strictly a grammatical term. In 1955, however, John Money, "the sexologist," used the term *gender role* in a paper on hermaphroditism. Money needed a word that meant physical role in sexual intercourse, but *sex role* had come to mean a "nongenitoerotic [a nonsexual] social sex role," and it therefore could not be used for this purpose. To solve his problem, Money used the term *gender role* to replace *sex role* as the latter had come to be used, that is, to refer to a nongenitoerotic social sex role. In sum, Money replaced *sex role* with *gender role* in order to reinstate *sex role* to mean specific physical role in sexual intercourse. He defined *gender role* broadly as "all those things that a person says or does to disclose himself or herself as having the status of boy or man, girl or woman, respectively. It includes, but is not restricted to, sexuality in the sense of eroticism."[36] Later on Evelyn Hooker began using the term *gender identity*, and Money took the position that gender role and gender identity were different sides of the same coin. Gender role was the public expression of the private conviction of having a male or female gender identity. According to Money in his recent reminiscence on the subject, it was Robert Stoller's book *Sex and Gender* published in 1968 that brought on the tendency (which Money considers unfortunate) to relegate sex to the biologists (body) and gender to the social scientists (mind).

For various reasons, the world was waiting for the term *gender.* *Gender* has been readily taken up not only in English but in translation, and has come to replace *sex* in certain contexts.[37] Feminist sociologists first began participating in this shift by taking up the idea that the term sex should be used to refer to biological or anatomical sex and *gender* should be used when speaking of socially defined masculinity and femininity. That is, *sex* was to be used to refer to the relatively dichotomous distinction between female and male based on genital difference, and *gender* was to be used to refer to the psychological and cultural definitions of the dimensions masculine and feminine.[38] Many psychologists tended to adopt this usage because it allowed them to speak of a woman's sex as being female and her gender as feminine, masculine, or androgynous. It fit in nicely with the thinking behind androgyny scales.

Others who argued that women are made in culture and not born in nature used the term *gender* to refer to the learned aspects of women's behavior and orientations. Those who stressed the importance of nurture over nature, of the social over the biological, often did so as a means of explaining women's alleged deficiencies. In my view these approaches often unwittingly played into the idea that women could gain equality if they could be "socialized" to be more like men. The underlying assumption behind this made "masculinity" the norm. I criticized this view in Chapter 2.

Suzanne Kessler and Wendy McKenna, who take what they call an ethnomethodological approach to gender, have criticized the tendency to make the distinction between sex and gender coterminus with a distinction between biological and social. They use *gender,* instead of *sex* as I do, even when referring to those aspects of being a woman or a man that are ordinarily viewed as biological. They do this in order to emphasize that there is an important element of social construction in all aspects of defining female versus male.[39] I believe they are quite correct in this. The last thing we need is a revival of the nineteenth-century dichotomy between nature and nurture. Biology is involved, but it is always socially constructed.

More recently *gender* has come to be used in the context of separating it from sex, which in turn is coming to be called *sexuality* to distinguish it from sexual activity. Throughout this book I have made much of the distinction between gender and what I have been calling the heterosexual aspects of gender differentiation. The use of the term *gender* makes it easier to talk about the degree to which psychoanalysis conflated gender with sexual orientation (another distinction) and dominance. I believe that Catharine Mac-Kinnon is making a similar distinction when she says that gender is defined by sexuality.[40] MacKinnon also rejects the distinction between *gender* and *sex* as indicating the social versus the biological or the learned versus the unlearned. In a footnote, she says she uses the terms relatively interchangeably because she is not really interested in the distinction the two terms are supposed to make.[41] Although MacKinnon does not discuss the term *gender* specifically, she generally uses the term to mean civil status and then goes on to argue that women as people have been defined (by men) in terms of their "sexuality." What she means by this is that men have defined women as beings whose sexuality is the most important thing about them and that women's sexuality belongs to men who make rules about its accessibility. In this sense she says "sexuality is the linchpin of gender inequality."[42] MacKinnon puts it this way: "Socially, femaleness means femininity, which means attractiveness to men, which means sexual attractiveness, which means sexual availability on male terms. . . . Sex as gender and sex as sexuality are thus defined in terms of each other, *but it is sexuality that determines gender, not the other way around*" (italics added; pp. 530–31). MacKinnon is emphasizing, in a somewhat different way than I have, the degree to which men have defined femininity as being a heterosexual object. I have shown how psychoanalysis does this too.

MacKinnon is saying that men make a definitional fusion between gender and sex and that this leads to sex discrimination. (It might be best to call this gender discrimination, but she cannot, because *sex discrimination* is in the legal language.) MacKinnon was helped toward her insight concerning sexuality defining gender by now being able to use the word *gender* to describe females as total people. The ultimate importance of using the word *gender* instead of *sex* in contexts where *sex* could imply sexuality can be to emphasize that sexuality as definitive of gender will no longer be tolerated. What MacKinnon does not make clear, however, is that the sexuality in terms of which women are defined is a male-defined sexuality; it is women's sexuality from a male point of view.

As noted earlier Gayle Rubin now explicitly repudiates her earlier implication that gender was defined by sexual orientation and
power, saying that she "did not distinguish between lust and gender, treating both as modalities of the same underlying social process."[43] In contrast to her perspective in "The Traffic in Women,"
she now argues that "it is essential to separate gender and sexuality
analytically to more accurately reflect their separate social existence" (p. 307). Rubin's aim in making this distinction is quite different from MacKinnon's. MacKinnon objects to the extent to which
women have been made into sex objects by men and campaigns
against pornography and sexual harassment as forms of discrimination against women. Rubin, in contrast, has recently been concerned about the repression of sexuality, which she sees as being a
separate issue from the oppression of women.[44] She points out that
lesbians who have joined ranks with heterosexual feminists and define themselves primarily as oppressed women need to remember
that they are also oppressed as sexual deviants, along with gay
males, prostitutes, transvestites, and fetishists. Rubin wants to
make a beginning toward developing an autonomous theory and
politics that is specific to sexuality. This theory and politics would
be different from, but could inform, a theory and politics of gender,
which has been the concern of feminists.

The personal political agendas of MacKinnon and Rubin are
poles apart. MacKinnon wants to save women from predatory males
and Rubin wants to save "sexuality" itself from public scrutiny and
control. They represent another set of divergent currents within
the feminist movement. Both of these thinkers, now, however, find
it important to make an analytical distinction between gender and
sexuality.

The potential conflict between pro-women politics and defense
of sexual freedom politics is apparent in the responses of lesbians to
the AIDS epidemic. While lesbians might well take the position
that they are the least likely group to contract the disease sexually
and to view AIDS as yet another threat to women caused by men,
many lesbians quite clearly identify politically with gay males.
Some lesbians take the position that the labeling and surveillance
of gay men, which is part of some proposed health policies, threatens lesbians too. Many lesbians are in the forefront of supporting
AIDS victims and attempting to formulate humane health policies

that protect sexual freedom. These two stances were discussed at a roundtable, "The Politics of AIDS and the Feminist Sex Debates," led by Beth Schneider at a session of the annual meetings of Sociologists for Women in Society in 1987. Although it was generally agreed that gay men would probably not rush to the defense of gay women if AIDS had begun among the latter, the immediacy of sexual oppression versus the historical continuity of male privilege seems to give the edge to concerns with the dangers of sexual as opposed to gender oppression among gay women.[45]

John Money claims that the term *gender* has been "neutered" and that at the same time sex has become "criminalized."[46] He means by this that feminists among others have taken "the sex" out of gender and have become antisex in a wave of Puritanism. He also means that his field of "sexology" has been taken over by the study of "victimology." (Here Money is making the same point that Gayle Rubin is making from a very different standpoint.) I do not believe that most feminists are becoming antisexual, although it is clear that feminists diverge on sexual issues. Those feminists who appear to be antisex are largely objecting to having female sexuality defined in terms of the type of male perspective that conceives of women as sexual objects to be preyed upon.

Reconstructing Sexuality

Sexuality—bodily desire, lust, eroticism—which may or may not be focused on the genitals, may or may not be connected to reproduction, and may or may not be heterosexual, is the subject of concern here.

The Sexual Revolution

In the nineteenth century, women, at least "nice" women, were defined as being asexual. It is quite possible that Victorian women themselves supported this definition as a way of limiting the number of children they had. There is some evidence that fertility was largely controlled in the nineteenth century by limiting the amount of intercourse within marriage.[47] Although most women, including feminists, were against contraception, they wanted to limit childbearing. Wives may have used "disinterest" in sexual activity as a mechanism to control their husband's "lust." This strategy could succeed in a context in which emotional intimacy between husbands and wives was coming more and more to be expected. That is, in a love relationship, a woman's "lack of desire" would likely be taken as a legitimate deterrent by her husband and intercourse would be less frequent. The aim of limiting the number of children was related to the emerging definition of children as valued personalities, not as workers. Thus, controlling the number of births fit in with the nineteenth century's sentimentalizing of motherhood. Whether mothers allowed themselves erotic pleasure from nursing and caring for their children is not known, but I am suggesting that being asexual vis-à-vis men may have had its advantages for women seeking to limit childbearing.

Freud, and the psychoanalytic movement he founded, served as an intellectual bridge to bring female sexuality out of Victorian repression to greater freedom of expression. At the same time, as we have seen, Freud's views also contributed to a view of women as "failed men" and made sexual orientation (heterosexual-homosexual) and mode (active-passive) the basis of definitions of gender difference. Now, after the sexual revolution of the 1960s, for which psychoanalysis of the 1920s set the stage, women are expected to be sexual too. This has been another step in the process of inclusion, in assimilating men and women to the same world. As we shall see, however, this newly legitimated sexuality for women has continued to be defined from a perspective that accords sexual agency to males.

In the early days of the most recent women's movement, feminists set about trying to increase their sexual gratification and express their own sexual needs by using the work of Kinsey and especially of Masters and Johnson regarding women's physiological sexual capacities. It was good to have "science" confirm that women are capable of multiple orgasms and can climax quickly and repeatedly given adequate stimulation. It was good to hear that orgasms do not originate in the vagina.[48] Feminists used these data to point out the extent to which the physical aspects of traditional sexual intercourse have worked against women's gratification. More attention to the clitoris was called for.[49] At the same time other feminists began to talk about foreplay as being "the play." Heterosexual and lesbian women alike agreed that the penis did not hold the same significance for women as it seemed to for men.

While Masters and Johnson's findings and their concept of "mutual pleasuring" are potentially liberating and democratic, more often than not they have been interpreted in ways that do not challenge male agency. Sexual activity that takes place between a male and female somehow still gets defined as his show. If a woman does take initiative, it is because he wanted her to; if she "responds" more powerfully than he, he feels powerful for "making it happen." Fellatio is more likely to be defined as "servicing" and cunnilingus looked upon as "controlling." A woman whose behavior cannot be squeezed into a male control paradigm is not considered healthily sexual at all, but instead "crazy," that is, "out of control." Thus females are expected by most males to be "responsive" and "responsible," else they cause alarm. Women usually take pity when men become anxious and help them out, by not posing a threat, by being "pleased."

It is convenient in preserving dominance for men to consider women as hyposexual—a little sexual but not as sexual as men. As noted earlier, male identity and self-esteem seem to rest more on being sexual than does female identity and self-esteem. Being potent and virile is tied in with male self-respect. In part because of this, male sexuality often has a driven quality about it that stems more from power anxiety than from lust. From this standpoint, as Ethel Person has pointed out, it might be appropriate for women to call men hypersexual.[50]

Female Resistance

The degree to which female sexuality continues to be defined from a perspective that accords sexual agency to males can be seen most clearly in language usage. There is no comparable word for male potency that can be applied to a female. Women are not seen as sexual agents, rather they are expected to "respond" to male agency. Male potency is complemented by female "receptivity." A good woman nowadays is "sexually responsive"; one never asks if a male is sexually responsive. If a woman does not respond, she is called "frigid," and women have put a great deal of energy into not being, or appearing not to be, unresponsive. There is no positive word for female sexual initiative and neither is there a positive word for "reluctance to respond" to male initiative. As Dale Spender points out, refusal to respond (as a way of expressing dissatisfaction with the

way things are) "has been underrated by the dominant group."[51]
From the standpoint of power, the Victorian wife at least had the
power that disinterest or refusal could confer. This power is less
available to women today.

Another way to resist the confines of male-controlled sexuality
besides "nonresponsiveness" is to be "bad." There is evidence that
prostitutes take some pleasure in the power that illicit trade in sex
provides. There is a certain pleasure to be had in exercising control
over the customer in a sexual encounter. It is true that the prostitute "serves" the customer and that she is ultimately very vulnerable not only to him but also to pimps and police, but on another
level she is "being bad" and is temporarily running the show. She is
in business, she has experience, the customer is in her hands, she
can think of herself as manipulating him for her own profit.[52] It is
probably no accident that many prostitutes have been incest victims, who suffer early from male sexual control. One psychological
meaning of prostitution for these women could be that it is a way of
redressing the sexual power situation that they encountered in
their childhoods.

There are other ways of being bad. In another context, I have
already discussed lesbianism as protest. Being a lesbian can also be
thought of as a way of being "bad." There is danger and excitement
in the "badness" of being attracted to a person of the "wrong" gender. Finally, seducing a male is "bad." Seductiveness is a kind of
female power that, like motherhood, is kept under male control.

On Seduction

Perhaps no issue has been more problematic for feminists, and for
women in general for that matter, than the power of seduction.
Let's face it, women can be very seductive to men and to women.
They were known to be seductive in the Middle Ages; it was an
accepted power. But women's seductiveness has been subjected
to extensive patterning in this and every other society. It is expected to be directed toward men and is for the purpose of pleasing
men. In this society we are told that women's seductiveness is
flaunted, but this is not the exact truth. Women are in fact made to
seem, or are thought to be or are told to be, seductive in contexts
where they are rendered harmless. In being seductive they are at

the same time denied sexual agency. I believe that this is the meaning of being made into a sex object. (Being seductive is not the same as being a sex object. To be sex objectified is to be thought of not as a sexual agent but as a sexual object.)

Rape is a male sexual control mechanism par excellence, and the rapist tries to justify his actions by blaming them on the power of women's seductiveness. She made him do it, she wanted it, she asked for it! Things are turned around. If a woman wanted it, she would not have called it rape. Muriel Schulz has written about *rape* not being a word that brings up horror. It is, instead, a rather neutral word that is used in polite conversation and apparently does not make people uncomfortable. Yet *rape* means something very bad indeed to females. A name is needed that communicates the sense of powerlessness and being used that rape involves.[53] This need to see rape as a violation of self may help explain why some feminists have wanted to call rape an act of violence rather than a sexual act.

Because of sexual violence and male dominance in general, feminists have been very wary of female seductiveness. It gets used against women, just as motherhood in a different way is used against women. Ultimately, both motherhood and seduction can be sources of power, and it is a measure of the power of the particular structuring of male dominance in this society that these have been seen as women's "problem." Marabel Morgan, the founder of the Total Woman Movement, recommends that women try the power of seduction but recommends it in the context of their total submission to their husbands.[54] This is another reason for feminist distrust of seduction; it can be a sexual service—a way for the weak to get their way. Mutual seduction in a context of equality, however, can be empowering for both males and females. In this sense the sexual revolution opens up possibilities for real equality but much needs to be worked out. Women and men sharing sexual pleasure is an important and necessary step in the process of inclusion, but female sexual expression in itself does not bring on the millenium.

Gender and Sexuality

As Foucault has argued so convincingly, sexuality has been both repressed and brought into existence as an area appropriate to scientific specification and scrutiny. Creating a discourse about sex is the exercise of power; defining and describing what is normative and what is deviant is itself a powerful means of control. "Normal" sexual behavior has been defined, and deviations from it have been endlessly proliferated and ranked. It occurs to me that women qua women are less likely than men to accord sexuality such overarching importance. This is not because women are hyposexual, but because women are less inclined to tie identity to sexuality. Also, the various distinctions and subdivisions to which sexuality has been subjected do not make good sense. Somehow the whole idea of categorizing sexual orientations flies in the face of a much more complex erotic reality. Freud himself was aware of these complexities, more so perhaps than some present day "sexologists."

In the process of categorizing sexual behavior, sexuality itself has come to be thought of as a relatively constant and highly salient attribute of the individual. The "nature of one's sexuality" has almost come to mean who one is. In other times and places there were proscribed acts but not proscribed people.[55] And as a part of this same process, as we have seen, psychoanalysis defined masculinity and femininity in terms of "sex object choice" and sexual mode. Now more heterosexual women are questioning "heterosexuality," not in the sense of choosing homosexuality, but questioning the salience and the rigidity of the heterosexual-homosexual distinction.

Although there is considerable agreement that sex and sexuality have been very much in the province of male prerogative and definition, there is considerably less agreement among feminists about what general stance to take with respect to sexuality. It is one thing to say that definitions concerning sexuality have a male bias and that women have been denied sexual agency, but what do women want? Women have been very reluctant to talk about sex among themselves except within certain rather narrowly defined parameters. But now feminist questioning is becoming more wide-ranging and is beginning to extend to examining the significance of sexuality itself. Is it the secret door to power that men have preempted for themselves, or is it a weapon against women that men use? Some feminists suspect that sexuality may be the place to look for the keys to power and feel that its potentialities should be explored more fully by women. Other feminists see "sex" as at the heart of the way in which women have been victimized.[56]

There is also the issue of how sexuality might fit in with a discussion of women's greater orientation to relationships. Certainly, many women feel that their erotic feelings differ from those of men, but in saying how, we place ourselves in the midst of the dangers that recognizing "difference" can lead us into. How much difference is there? What kind of difference is it? How does the relational-nonrelational difference between women and men affect the way one is sexual?

Difference and Sexuality

The old cliché that women are interested in love and men are interested in sex must be revised in the light of the post–sexual revolution era. Many women no longer expect to be "in love" to enjoy sex and many women have participated in one-night stands with great pleasure. It still seems true, however, that women prefer sex and understand sex in a relational context. Studies of college students continue to report that males find it easier than females to participate in sexual intercourse without an emotional commitment and that females want more psychological involvement.[57] Lillian Rubin argues that among the married people she interviewed, emotional attachment calls up the sexual for women, whereas for men the sexual allows there to be attachment.[58] She also maintains that women who seem to feel as men do about sex really do not, because even short-term encounters have some interpersonal meaning for them (pp. 113–14). The women she interviewed also spoke of half-consciously withholding orgasm with a man they did not trust, whereas many of the men she interviewed continued to have sexual trouble with women to whom they were emotionally close.

The most striking research confirmation to date that gender difference should not be confused with heterosexuality or dominance submission comes from Blumstein and Schwartz's large-scale study of married, cohabiting, gay, and lesbian couples. Examining these four couple types provides a unique opportunity to study the relationship between gender and sexuality. The authors report that their strongest overall finding is the continuity of male behavior, whether that of husbands, cohabitors, or gays, and the continuity of female behavior, whether that of wives, cohabitors, or lesbians.[59] Blumstein and Schwartz found a need for dominance in men, but they did not find a need for submission in women. What they found was a reluctance to dominate in women, which is not the same as passivity, acquiescence, or submission. Rather, it represents a different principle, which I have been calling relationality.

In the area of sexuality, Blumstein and Schwartz find that lesbians have sex far less frequently than any other type of couple, and they do not have a compensating rate outside the relationship (p. 195). These data could be interpreted as indicating the hyposexuality of females but they could also be interpreted as indicating that other forms of eroticism are more prized. Blumstein and Schwartz explain the finding in part by reminding us that "having sex" means genital sex. They report that the lesbians they interviewed are much more likely to consider foreplay as an end in itself. But such activities do not count as "having sex" as it is ordinarily defined. Another possible explanation for the low rates is that women want neither to dominate nor to be dominated. Thus, taking the initiative becomes problematic for lesbians. Neither wants to initiate sex.

Interestingly enough, Blumstein and Schwartz found that among heterosexual couples, intercourse, as opposed to other forms of genital contact, is more prized by women than by men. Even though intercourse is not as genitally stimulating for women as for men, it can be satisfying because of its intimacy and mutuality. Blumstein and Schwartz suggest that "intercourse requires the equal participation of both partners more than any other sexual act. Neither partner only 'gives' or only 'receives.' Hence women feel a shared intimacy during intercourse they may not feel during other sexual acts" (p. 227). Kissing is also popular with women. It is most frequent among lesbians and least frequent among gay males (p. 226). Again, kissing is a mutual activity and it is also personal in the sense of engaging the face.

Other evidence for women's relationality affecting their sexual life comes from the striking differences between lesbian relationships and gay male relationships. Public bath-houses, a common recreational site for gay males before the threat of AIDS, are not similarly attractive to lesbians, and sexual encounters in public restrooms are virtually unheard of among lesbians. Gay male bars are places to pick up "tricks" for men, but lesbian bars are places where lesbian women gather socially in couples and individually. What

Blumstein and Schwartz speak of as the "tricking mentality" among gay males is far less present among most lesbians. The word *trick*, derived from the world of prostitutes, means that the encounter is entirely sexual and highly impersonal. This is not to say there is no love between gay men, but love relationships can and often are separated from sex for sex's sake (pp. 295–98).

Blumstein and Schwartz's findings regarding gender differences in sexuality lend considerable support to the description of gender difference given by Donald Symons in *The Evolution of Human Sexuality*. Symons makes it quite clear that differences in male and female sexuality should not be construed as a matter of hyposexuality in women or hypersexuality in men. He is well aware of the studies showing that females as well as males are sexually aroused by depictions of explicitly sexual activity. His argument is, however, that female and male sexual responses are equally intense but occur for different reasons, with males' initial arousal being more impersonal than that of females, who put themselves into the situation rather than depicting males as objects. Symons notes that males' interest in pornography is clearly greater than females'; this does not necessarily mean more sexual interest but a kind of impersonal sexual interest that pornography can satisfy. He goes on to argue that "men and women differ far less in their potential physiological and psychological responses during sexual activities per se than they do in how they negotiate sexual activities and in the kinds of sexual relationships and interactions they are motivated to seek."[60] I agree. I disagree with his sociobiological explanation, however, which seems simplistic. Blumstein and Schwartz note the compatibility of their findings to Symons's analysis but attribute them to "socialization", whatever this catchall term may mean, rather than to biology.

A note of caution is important here. One cannot assume that somehow lesbians represent "pure" femaleness and that male gays represent "pure" maleness, even if one says the "pure" femaleness and maleness result from "socialization" rather than biology. Lesbians and gay men may represent female and male behavior under conditions of stigma. For the female there is the stigma of the cultural definition of what a female is and the stigma of sexual "deviance." For the male there is the stigma of "deviance" but the freedom and power that being male makes possible. These facts complicate the picture in ways that need to be more fully understood. For example, the reason lesbians may be less involved in genital sex could be related to not wanting to be like men, yet the stigma of the "bull dyke" says lesbians are like men. To the extent that lesbians are protesting male dominance, one might expect even more ambivalence about initiating than might be found among heterosexual women.

Finally, Blumstein and Schwartz report that having children in the home disturbs husbands far more than wives. In their interviews, husbands complained about the effect children had on their sex lives, whereas mothers accepted the disruptions caused by children more readily. In summary, they say, "Women do not feel less satisfied sexually when they have children. This makes them very different from their husbands and can introduce a serious marital issue."[61] All of these findings and observations suggest that gender differences in relationality (women's more relational orientation) may cause males and females to differ in the meanings they confer on sexual activity and sexuality.

Eroticism is more of a female word than a male word because it implies diffuse bodily pleasure more than genitally focused bodily pleasure. It is hard to think of eroticism as being "driven," and it fits in well with mutuality and a more relational orientation. I take it as a good sign that the word *erotic* is being increasingly substituted for the word *sexual*. Perhaps its use is a way of bringing men more into the orbit of women. Men have tended to deny diffuse eroticism as they deny relationality in general and connect sex with aggression and degrading the object.[62] In moving toward a society where heterosexual relations can be mutually pleasurable and empowering, it is all to the good to enlist the human capacity for eroticism as a counter to an exclusively genital focus.

Similarity and Sexuality

Findings of the sort reported by Blumstein and Schwartz showing gender difference must not be allowed to obscure the larger truth that men and women are very similar sexually. Masters and Johnson have showed that on a physiological level female and male sexual responses are very similar, and they have also showed no differences between homosexuals' and heterosexuals' physiological responses.[63] Genital pleasure is genital pleasure and orgasm is orgasm and both women and men can feel empowered by it. One might conclude from Blumstein and Schwartz that genital stimulation is what men want and generalized body eroticism is what women want. This is precisely the conclusion that feminists who want to explore sexuality more thoroughly are resisting. It is important for women to use sexuality as a power, and this sexuality may not fit into the neat categories currently available, including domination and submission, and heterosexual-homosexual, or even relational-nonrelational. In terms of gender difference, I repeat, women can be relational and at the same time they are also instrumental, sexual, agentic.

Motherhood and Sexuality

One of the major problems I encounter in emphasizing mothering as important to women is that it is immediately and automatically construed as taking sexuality away from women.[64] To many moderns—feminist and nonfeminist—to speak of mothering conjures up images of the Virgin Mary. But as I tried to make clear in the previous section, sexuality is something both males and females possess and enjoy. To point out that women are maternal does not mean that they are not also sexual. In this society we make a split between the sexual and the maternal;[65] I would argue, however, that this split has more to do with male thinking (by which we are all influenced) than with female thinking.

The Greeks, too, had a penchant for segregating the maternal from the erotic as can be seen in Greek myths. Paul Friedrich points out that Aphrodite, whom he sees as uniquely synthesizing the maternal and the erotic, has been relatively obscure in the pantheon of goddesses for this very reason.[66] Only Sappho, the female poet who lived on the isle of Lesbos and from whom the term *lesbian* derives, celebrated Aphrodite and emphasized the close harmony between maternal and erotic love. Thus it took a lesbian sensibility to appreciate the erotic in the maternal and to connect it with love for women. Generally in Greek myths, erotic, sensuous female figures tend to be somewhat immature and are segregated from the "mature" and asexual motherly ones. Both in this society and in Greece, childlike women are eroticized; this could well be explained as a defense against and way of coping with the psychological threat to male dominance posed by strong maternal women.[67] De-eroticizing women's mothering is a way of disempowering women's mothering.

As Jessica Benjamin points out, under current conditions the father is the symbol of desire for both females and males. Benjamin worries that we seem unable to produce a female image or symbol that could counterbalance the phallus and the father as a symbol of desire.[68] I agree that in this culture the mother image cannot function as a symbol of desire, not because it is a passive image but because it is clearly not syntonic with Western culture to imagine mothers qua mothers as lustful or sexually desiring creatures, certainly not toward their children. But it hardly works for fathers to serve as a symbol of erotic desire either! The father's turning the daughter into an object of desire has been a problem symbolically and in reality. My argument is again that women and men are sexual, have desire, are lustful, are erotic. Sexuality is not a point of gender differentiation, although gender and a maternal identification may affect the meaning of desire and how it is expressed by women.

Benjamin makes a good effort to define this gender-influenced desire and suggests that it can come from the mother. She notes that the girl must identify with the mother not only in her maternal aspects but as a sexual subject, not as a sexual object. I agree. The problem then becomes one of finding not just a symbol of desire to replace the phallus but another "psychic mode"—beyond the father. Benjamin suggests an intersubjective mode that does not distinguish between subject and object. This mode "where two subjects meet, where both woman and man can be subject, may point to a locus for woman's independent desire, a relationship to desire that is not represented by the phallus" (pp. 92–93). Here Benjamin takes a step forward, I believe, in better defining relationality and interdependence in which the desire to be known for oneself and to know the other coalesce: "The desire for the heightened sense of self, 'really being there,' is the central meaning of getting pleasure *with* the other" (p. 93). As a clinician, Benjamin finds that women have a hard time finding their own inner desire because of the fear of impingement, intrusion, and violation. Ideally, this "other" is experienced not as an intruder but as a holding other, making a safe place to experience both self and other and to experience one's own desire freely. "It is not a different desire, but a different relation of self to other that is at stake" (p. 97).

Benjamin concludes that women "are seeking to find a relationship to desire in *freedom to:* freedom to be both with and distinct from the other. This relationship can be grasped in terms of intersubjective reality, where subject meets subject. . . . The discovery of our own desire will proceed, I believe, through the mode of thought that can suspend and reconcile such opposition, the dimension of recognition between self and other" (p. 98).

It is important for women not to let their fear of dependence create suspicion of interdependence. Perhaps there is a female way of expressing sexuality—one that grants the other their own self-space, leaves integrity intact, does not require domination or submission. It would be good if sex could involve a merging with the other in mutual recognition, letting one be fully oneself while at the same time being totally unself-conscious in the sense of wanting to be the self one thinks the other wants. It would be good for both partners to be "present," neither resenting the "presence" of the other. This stance is akin to what Marilyn Frye calls "the loving eye" as opposed to "the arrogant eye." The "loving eye" (in or out of erotic contexts) grants space to others and simultaneously preserves one's own space—appreciating and loving but not feeling dominated or invaded, feeling one's own power but not denying the power or "presence" of the other.[69]

Benjamin is assuming heterosexual "sex," Frye is assuming lesbian "sex," but the two views seem similar and both in a way transcend narrow "sex" in that they are talking about a far more generalized stance. It is just possible that both men and women could see advantages to this stance—in bed and out. The erotic, however, precisely because it involves both body and mind, is an especially important sphere for really "feeling" how mutual empowerment could be.

Summary

I have argued in this chapter that the psychoanalytic account of gender development has contributed to the general societal tendency to conflate masculinity and femininity with dominance and submission. It cannot be easily rectified, because it is built into the most basic assumptions of the scheme. The confusion is not done away with by those theorists who oppose Freud's phallocentrism, either. Gynecentric theorists carry over the assumption that masculinity is active and heterosexual and that femininity is passive and heterosexual. The task of undoing this conflation, then, involves separating both gender from sexuality and sexuality from its male-biased definition.

Using the word *sex* to describe sexual activity and the difference between males and females attests to the degree to which gender has been conflated with sex. In truth both men and women are sexual and their sexuality is not what distinguishes them from each other. Gender difference is not primarily one of sexual difference but rather a difference that from both biological and developmental standpoints may have more to do with females' capacity to bear children and women's greater relationality. Whereas developmental psychology has taken for granted the primacy of mothers in the lives of children, psychoanalysis constructs a theory that gives primacy to fathers and construes gender difference as one of active subject versus passive object in sexual intercourse. Separating gender from sex linguistically helps break up this assumption. To some extent male and female sexuality does differ, but the difference reflects gender difference in the sense of women's more relational stance and men's greater aggression and impersonality. It is not a difference between submission and dominance, lesser and greater, object and subject. These differences have tended to be part of a definition of sexual difference in a male paradigm.

The so-called sexual revolution in the last analysis must be considered all to the good, because allowing women to be actively sexual makes it possible for sexuality to be redefined on female, human terms rather than male terms. There is no inherent reason why sexuality could not be a meeting ground for males and females on terms of equality even in the presence of difference. The sexual revolution clearly did not liberate women in any ultimate sense, but perhaps sexual expression can be empowering for women if it ceases to be male-defined and -controlled.

Chapter Nine

Women as Wives: Cultural and Historical Variations

If it is true from the standpoint of human development that a maternal orientation works against gender hierarchy, it might be conceptually neat if societies that stress women's mothering were characterized by greater gender equality than those in which women were defined primarily as wives. But such neatness is obviously not to be found in cross-cultural studies, and attempts to generalize about the degree of gender equality in various societies are rife with empirical and conceptual problems. Although I have neither the expertise nor the temerity to attempt a cross-cultural overview, it is possible to make certain limited generalizations relevant to the mother-wife distinction and gender equality. I begin this chapter, then, by describing findings concerning greater gender equality in those simple societies that are characterized by matrilineal descent rules and matrilocal residence rules. These societies are more likely to have less gender hierarchy than patrilineal-patrilocal societies. I also examine the different but related cases of so-called matrifocal enclaves found occasionally in class societies. These also seem to be characterized by less gender hierarchy. Matrifocal societies have in common with matrilineal-matrilocal societies a tendency to de-emphasize the wife role, and this seems to be related to greater gender equality.

Although these cross-cultural examples of relatively egalitarian arrangements are instructive in thinking about alternatives to the present situation, any attempt to implement them would have to take into account the larger modern context. The major part of this chapter is devoted to describing the historical development of this modern context, beginning with a description of the agrarian patriarchal societies that preceded modern industrial societies.

It is generally agreed that the patriarchal societies that arose along with the state and social classes were more oppressive to women than either modern industrial societies or most preclass societies.[1] Although modern women's situation in the industrial societies that succeeded the agricultural era derives from the situation of women under Western versions of patriarchy, it differs from it in important respects. In modern industrial Western societies and perhaps especially in the United States, patriarchy has been much moderated by the influence of Protestantism, with its doctrines of individualism, and the nuclear family ideal.

But the nuclear family system, although different from classic patriarchy, creates its own problems for women in an individualistic society. I trace the vicissitudes of the definitions of women in the "modern family" that arose in the nineteenth century. These definitions moved, within the context of individualism, from a stress on women as mothers in the nineteenth century to an emphasis on women as wives in the twentieth. Finally, I return to the concerns with which I began the chapter and present a theory concerning what I will call "middle-class matrifocality" and its connection to the rise of the Women's Movement in the late 1960s.

Matrilineal Horticultural Societies

Some of the most widely studied cases of societies in which females enjoy relatively high prestige and power are matrilineal-matrilocal horticultural societies. These societies count descent mainly through the mother's line, and husbands live on lands owned by the matrilineage. Matriliny does not eliminate male authority, because the mother's brother is likely to exercise some authority over his sister's son, but matriliny does tend to weaken the husband's authority over wife and children. When descent is matrilineal and the residence of the married couple is matrilocal, there is at least the potential both for breaking up the solidarity of brothers and for weakening the authority of husbands, since brothers leave their own territory when they marry to become husbands of wives who own the land. Among the Iroquois, unrelated men lived in a long-house with wives who were each other's sisters. Thus, as brothers men have less chance to exercise authority over their sisters' sons, and as husbands they also have less authority over their own wives and children.

Indeed, one of Lévi-Strauss's arguments for his view that marriage constitutes "an exchange of women by men" is the relative rarity of matrilineal-matrilocal arrangements. The reason for this is that matriliny coupled with matrilocality weakens the position of men as husbands and threatens "sexual asymmetry," that is, "male dominance." Lévi-Strauss notes that such societies generally have some compensating features that counteract the disadvantages to husbands that the matrilineal, matrilocal situation entails.[2] These compensatory mechanisms suggest that husband's authority over wife may be, from the male's standpoint, something very important to preserve in all kinship arrangements.

Evidence for the importance of matrilineal kinship in enhancing women's status comes from a study designed to test a hypothesis proposed by the sociologist Randall Collins about causes of variation among societies in male sexual dominance. Collins suggested that the degree of male "sexual" dominance ("sexual" in the narrow sense, resting ultimately, he claims, on males' physical desire and greater strength) would vary more in relation to economic and political factors than in terms of kinship variables. A study designed to test Collins's hypothesis on a cross-cultural sample found to the contrary that marital residence and descent rules of the society (i.e., kinship variables) were the better predictors of degree of sexual inequality. Specifically, the researchers found that male sexual dominance and control over sexuality was less developed in matrilineal descent groups and that whatever the residence rules, matriliny weakened the concentration of male power.[3]

More recent support comes from the family sociologist Ira Reiss, who, using the Standard Cross-Cultural sample, finds, not surprisingly, greater male sexual rights in patrilineal than in matrilineal societies. Moreover, Reiss finds that in those patrilineal societies where males also lived together in the same community, there was a "greater likelihood of a low evaluation of the female gender."[4]

Significantly enough, matrilineal-matrilocal societies often seem to be characterized by what can be described only as a "maternal" ideology. For example, the Navaho culture has been described as making all one's kin "into differentiated kinds of mothers."[5] The major deity in Navaho religion is Changing Woman and she is referred to as "Mother." She is associated not with heterosexual relationships but with fertility, creativity, growth, renewal, and change. Changing Woman was created by the sexual union of First Man and First Woman. She is then a mother who is the product of the coming together of both maleness and femaleness. Femaleness is not seen as deviance from maleness as it is in Western culture, but rather Changing Woman encompasses both maleness and femaleness as a mother, and males and females in turn are expected to relate to each other as her equal children.[6]

The Hopis are similar in belief to the Navaho; indeed the Navaho beliefs were likely derived from the Hopi. Navahos conceive of female roles and male roles as different but equal and complementary. It is true that women are associated with the domestic sphere and men with the wider community, but in another sense the wider community itself is conceptualized metaphorically as a house—the center of domesticity. It is the household and the clan, which is centered in the female-governed household, that shelters the individuals who compose the community. In a sense the private is the public, and the domestic is the community. Among the Hopi there are both male and female ceremonies; the women's ceremonies express and celebrate the interdependence of male and female.[7] Nevertheless, as with the matrilineal, matrilocal Iroquois and Navaho, men hold the formal positions of authority in the community, even though that authority may be of little "real" significance.

In matrilineal societies in the Pacific, men bring personal renown to themselves in their own ceremonies, but this is counterbalanced by women symbolizing both women and men and thus the community as a whole in theirs. In the Trobriands, another matrilineal society, women have value not so much because they reproduce biologically but because they are seen as social and cultural reproducers. Women are charged with regenerating the *dala* (the unnamed ancestral beings through which Trobrianders trace their descent). It is through them that the entire community, both women and men, gain their being.[8]

Thus in matrilineal societies, women are more likely to connect both women and men as equals, a connection related ultimately to the early dependency of both female and male infants on women.

This is very different from the modern Western emphasis on women as the "wives" of men and as the mothers of their husband's children.

Scott Coltrane, also using the Standard Cross-Cultural Sample of preindustrial societies, finds that societies having a patrilineal kinship system and a male-dominant residence pattern were negatively correlated with public status of women. Coltrane also finds that one can predict women's public status even more accurately if one adds paternal participation in early child care to the regression equation. (Adding other variables, however, such as women's contribution to subsistence, does not help explain the variance in women's public status.)[9] Thus, while arrangements other than patrilineal and male-centered residence patterns may or may not enhance the likelihood of women's public status, patrilineal and male-centered residence patterns are associated with lesser public status for women.

Although the mechanisms that produce these correlations are not clear, it may be significant that the highest correlation Coltrane obtained between paternal nurturance and various facets of female public status was with "female origin symbolism." This correlation was higher than the correlations between paternal nurturance and female access to positions of authority or between paternal nurturance and female public participation. The strong connection between paternal nurturance and female origin symbolism suggests that societies governed by a maternal paradigm would tend to justify and encourage males to participate in maternal activities.

I am not suggesting that women's cause in modern society would be served by reestablishing the rigid gender division of labor characterizing many matrilineal horticultural societies or by duplicating any other nonpatrilineal form found in preindustrial societies. It is nevertheless instructive to examine the world views of such societies to see how they contrast with the more typically male constructions of our own society. I would especially stress the sense in which the maternal represents the common humanity of both males and females and that often this is associated with males' participating along with females in early child care.

Matrifocal Enclaves in Class Societies

Modern class societies are far removed from horticultural societies and thus it is perhaps even more relevant to examine the matrifocal (as opposed to matrilineal-matrilocal) systems that are found under various circumstances within class societies. Such matrifocal societies also tend to have greater gender equality because of the power of a maternal paradigm. In these societies, regardless of the particular type of kinship system, women play roles of cultural and social significance and define themselves less as wives than as mothers. Raymond Smith, who coined the term *matrifocality* and who studied matrifocality in the Caribbean, describes it as involving "priority of emphasis (being) placed upon the mother-child and sibling relationship, while the conjugal relationship is expected to be less solidary and less affectively intense." According to Smith, the weak intensity of the conjugal relationship "is crucial in producing matrifocal family structure."[10]

Matrifocality, however, does not refer to domestic maternal dominance so much as it does to the relative cultural prestige of the image of mother, a role that is culturally elaborated and valued. Mothers are also structurally central in that mother as a status "has some degree of control over the kin unit's economic resources and is critically involved in kin-related decision making processes" (p. 131). It is not the absence of males (males may be quite present) but the centrality of women as mothers and sisters that makes a society matrifocal, and this matrifocal emphasis is accompanied by a minimum of differentiation between women and men.

Nancy Tanner uses three Indonesian societies, the Igbo of West Africa, and black Americans as examples of societies in which the culturally defined role of mother is made central. This is not always the genealogical mother, but sometimes the senior woman in a kinship unit. In all of these societies, relationships between women and men are relatively egalitarian and there is a minimum of differentiation between genders. Tanner notes that in Java there is "little difference between women and men with regard to initiative, assertiveness, autonomy, decisiveness" (p. 155). Overall, women in matrifocal societies find their identity not as appendages to husbands or brothers but rather as relatively independent and active women and mothers.

Tanner notes that the image of the strong, active mother, with which black women are more identified than middle-class white women are, has made middle-class black women less ambivalent than their white counterparts about combining careers with marriage. The image of black mothering is the most accessible image middle-class white women have that can counter the tendency to assimilate "mother" to "wife," that is, counter the tendency to attribute to mothering the dependency and side-kick status that attaches to "wife."

Black women often have little respect for white women because of the degree to which their identity derives from being a dependent, infantilized wife. Toni Morrison explains: "Black women have no abiding admiration of white women as competent complete people; whether vying with them for the few professional slots available to women in general, or moving their dirt from one place to another, they regarded them as willful children, pretty children, mean children, but never as real adults capable of handling the real problems of the world."[11]

Alice Walker's novel *The Color Purple* is perhaps the most widely read example of what could properly be called a matrifocal spirit although it takes place in an early twentieth-century black patriarchal setting. Walker chronicles the resilience, power, and strength of women and the closeness of sisters, and in the end the patriarchs in her vision are transformed into friends, lovers, and brothers. Sexuality is not always seen as heterosexual, nor are heterosexual relations ideally envisioned as female "surrender" and male domination.

Walker does not depict men as personages so powerful that "separatism" can be the only "solution" for women. I suspect that separatist views are more typical of a middle-class white women's response to perceptions of sexism than of black women's. From black women's standpoint, separatism would mean abandoning their loyalty to the men of their community as their mothers and sisters. In this connection I was struck by the comment made to me by a young black lesbian, in an informal discussion of lesbian separatism, that she would never want to join any woman's organization that would exclude her brother. Her vision of equality involved women and men as sisters and brothers. This is both African and also very much a part of Protestant imagery, adopted in this country more fully by blacks than by whites, that expresses equality and solidarity through the terms "sister" and "brother."[12]

Diane K. Lewis offers further evidence of more egalitarian relations between black husbands and wives, which she too attributes to an African cultural heritage. She notes that in black families both husband and wife have power and make tacit agreements based on individual preferences about areas in which each will be dominant. In addition, black women are more likely than white women to be sexually assertive: "While in Euro-American culture the male is the aggressor and the female the passive receptor, in Afro-American culture, the woman is expected to take an active role in the male's attempt to establish a sexual encounter." Lewis also points out that males as well as females take a "mothering" attitude toward infants and young children.[13]

Clearly there are some complex problems in analyzing the situation of blacks in the United States, and it would be racist to deny that economic problems among non-middle-class blacks are increasing. Female-headed households are also increasing rapidly today, and this is probably less a manifestation of matrifocality as an ideal than of joblessness among lower-class black males. In spite of the complexities involved, I believe that matrifocality should be examined more seriously by middle-class white feminists for clues as to how greater gender equality might look. That matrifocality is often found in situations in which some type of internal or external colonial exploitation is occurring should not in itself discredit matrifocality. It simply reflects the links between capitalist exploitation and male dominance.

Both matrilineal-matrilocal societies and matrifocal societies provide examples of structural arrangements that de-emphasize a definition of women as wives and thereby tend to enhance the status of women in the public sphere. We have also seen that these societies are characterized—in different ways—by what might be called a maternal paradigm that includes both men and women as equals. Before examining what I will call middle-class white matrifocality and its role in the emergence of modern feminism, we need first to examine patriarchy itself. Patriarchal societies involve a very different kind of organization with very different implications for the status of women. Patriarchy is important to look at because the historical roots of modern industrial societies are patriarchal.

Agricultural Societies, the Rise of the State, and Patriarchy

Engels declared long ago that the patriarchy that arose with the great agrarian states represented "the world defeat of women."

Feminists of various camps—especially radical and Marxist feminists—have used the term *patriarchy* as the name for the overall system that has oppressed women. Heidi Hartman emphasizes the male peer group by defining patriarchy as "a set of social relations which has a material base and in which there are hierarchical relations between men and solidarity among them which enables them to dominate women." She goes on to say that "The material base is men's control over women's labor power."[14] This definition implies that the ultimate mechanism of enforcement is male solidarity and I agree, but I would specifically emphasize that under patriarchy this control is exercised by fathers as heads of households. Patriarchy literally means "father rule." Moreover, I restrict the use of *patriarchy* as a system to the great agrarian states where fathers of adult sons headed extended "families."

Today, most anthropologists would agree, regardless of their stance on issues such as the universality of male dominance, that an entirely different order of male dominance became associated with the rise of the large and populous agricultural states organized in terms of classes. The patriarchal systems that emerged brought women for the first time under the direct control of fathers and husbands with few cross-cutting sources of support. Women as wives under this system were not social adults, and women's lives were defined in terms of being a wife. Women's mothering and women's sexuality came to be seen as requiring protection by fathers and husbands. Protecting unmarried women's virginity appears to go along with the idea of the domestication of women and an emphasis on a radical dichtomy between the public and the private sphere. The private sphere is watched over and protected by men, and women are excluded from the public domain. These agrarian societies that give power over women and sons to fathers should properly be called "patriarchal."

Agrarian patriarchies vary greatly from one another and are rationalized and guided by differing religions and religious teachings. Patriarchal societies include the classical Chinese and the Islamic and Hindu societies in which brides are likely to be brought into the patriarchal household. Wives belong completely to the husband's family and their sexuality is strictly controlled, their marriages are arranged by parents, and virginity is a symbol of value.

Not all societies that can be called patriarchal are patrilineal, however. Bilateral systems have tended to characterize kinship in most of the Western world for a long time. In these systems a woman's dowry and her husband's inheritance are pooled to form a conjugal fund or estate, which has the effect of minimizing lineage and emphasizing the conjugal unit. But here too, marriages are arranged and virginity is prized.

Although, at least to the modern mind, there can be no doubt that women's status worsened under these restrictive patriarchal systems, some features of patriarchy can be interpreted as advantageous for women. Sherry Ortner points out that one meaning of patriarchy is that men took more responsibility for families. Ortner argues that the development of patriarchal family structure can best be understood not as just the domestication of women but also as the domestication of men, since men as fathers became responsible for families. With the rise of the state, "the husband/father was no longer simply responsible *to* his family, but also *for* his family in the larger system."[15] Fathers were economically, legally, and politically responsible for the family and its "proper functioning." The system makes sons dependent on fathers, and sons under the father's authority are juvenilized for a much longer period. Ortner sees this domestication of men as part of an evolutionary trend that will lead to fathers participating increasingly in family life.

The domestication of men theme is developed considerably more fully and explicitly by David Bakan with respect to Western Christianity. Bakan interprets the Bible as a chronicle of the transformation of "wild males" into responsible fathers who nurture and protect their families in the manner of mothers. Patriarchy, Bakan argues, "maternalizes" males by forcing them to care about and be responsible for "families." But, at the same time, fathers "juvenilize" those adults under their "protection."[16]

Although there is some truth to the idea of the juvenilization of males by maternal fathers, it is important not to lose sight of the other side of this picture: the permanent juvenilization of women. Men may attain some semblance of adult status sooner or later by becoming husbands and fathers of fathers, but women pass from the control of father to husband. Wives become in this system perennial children, and patriarchy can rightly be interpreted as the juvenilization of women by men.

From Patriarchy to the Male-Headed
Nuclear Family

With industrialization the patriarchal family underwent radical change. It became smaller and more egalitarian but remained father-dominant. The Protestant idea of "family" as constituting a little spiritual commonwealth, a "little church" carrying out the divine will, predated industrialization. It was modeled originally on the economically productive households of yeoman farmers under feudalism and later those of landowning peasants and craftsmen. The small producing unit under the headship of the father was ready and waiting to be the "ideal" family for capitalist industrialization—except that industrialization led to a redesigning of husband and wife "roles."[17]

Protestantism gave a new interpretation to patriarchal ideology that on balance represented a gain for women. The progressive aspect of this new definition was that it considered husbands and wives to be equal, even beyond the spiritual realm. Husband and wife were to be friends and lovers to each other; marriages were civil contracts and could be broken by either party. The view gave women a new dignity and more equality. But equality was contradicted by wives also being told to be meek and mild and above all obedient to their husbands, who in turn were obedient to God. Loving companion and obedient wife is a contradiction. Protestant ministers must have been aware of this because of the rhetorical effort they put into denying it.

Protestant ideas of equality and individual accountability ultimately lie behind the feminist push for equality, but at the same time, these ideas increased the significance of husbands in the lives of women and increased the extent to which women's "life chances" (Max Weber's felicitous term) depended on whom they married. This dependence was exacerbated by marriages no longer being arranged by parents; a woman was on her own in choosing a partner. If she chose badly, she "had no one to blame but herself." Women's dependence was to become even greater when their livelihood came to depend solely on their husbands' earnings. This had not been true when the Protestant idea of family was developed—a time when the family was a joint agricultural enterprise.

Each country's story is different in detail, and I now begin to speak mainly about the United States. By the nineteenth century, as production was increasingly removed from the home, a recognizable "modern" family ideology began to be touted in middle-class periodicals and from the pulpit. The family no longer farmed, it was no longer an enterprise, but a haven—no longer the world in microcosm, but a refuge from the world. The home was often depicted as a vine-covered cottage with a picket fence, but unsullied by cows or chickens or crops. Husbands were to go out from the haven to work in the world and wives were to stay at home and cheerfully perfect it, to re-create the male worker. Wives were also to be mothers, cherishing children and preparing them spiritually and psychologically (though the word was not used then) to leave home to make their mark in the world. Although this ideology was centered in the rising middle class, in time it came to affect all of the society. Men wanted their wives not to have to work, and black women's having to work became a racial stigma.

The history of capitalism and of industrialization in the West is associated with the rise of "individualism" as an overarching ideology. Individualism has gained an especially strong hold in the United States because as a new territory, it lacked a feudal or aristocratic tradition. At first, individualism applied mainly to men. Blackstone's dictum that "husband and wife are one, and that one is the husband" reflects the idea that husbands are the individuals, beholden to no one, and their wives live through them.

But individualism also opened up the possibility that women might be individuals too. Throughout the nineteenth century, married women increasingly gained rights as individuals, beginning with the passage by states of Married Women's Property Rights Acts. Finally in 1920, women gained the right to vote as individuals at all levels of government. And now, the egalitarian and individualistic ideology that grew out of Protestantism provides part of the impetus for women's present-day push for equality in the job world.

The husband-wife relationship is not one of equality, however. In the "modern family," middle-class white women in the United States were increasingly defined as wives and in fact their life chances increasingly depended on whom they married. Women's fortunes depended on getting and keeping a man who was better off than they were, to "provide" for them and their children. This phenomenon accounts for the persistence of the "marriage gradient," well known to family sociologists, in which unmarried women tend to be high status in terms of their own family background and personal accomplishments, that is, "the cream of the crop," whereas unmarried men tend to be at the bottom of the status hierarchy, that is, "the bottom of the barrel." Although most men and women marry within their social class, the system as a whole tends toward "hypergamy," that is, women marrying up.[18]

Nineteenth-Century Mothering in the United States

Freud did not invent the idea of the critical importance of the childhood years for the individual character; it began much earlier, as part of nineteenth-century religious teachings. For example, in 1843, in a widely read book, the Reverend Horace Bushnell wrote, "Let every Christian father and mother understand, when the child is three years old, that they have done more than half of what they will ever do for his character."[19] Because so much was thought to depend on the early years, mothers were seen as especially appropriate for the task of this early molding because of their association with early child care.[20] In the nineteenth century, religion also came to be less associated with men and more associated with women and concomitantly with personal morality. Husbands, although they clearly retained the formal headship of the household and acted as the court of last resort, were expected to consult their wives on matters of morality and child-rearing.

As noted earlier, women used their newfound hegemony in the home over mothering and morality as an opening wedge to gain access outside the home to education and political influence in order to attack directly problems related to community morality and human welfare. Women claimed they needed education to be proper mothers and wives, and by the latter part of the nineteenth century and early twentieth century, women's organizations had pressured state legislatures and Congress, not to mention innumerable local governing bodies, into enacting a host of laws concerning child labor, social hygiene, and women's equity.[21] Married women's "outside" activities in the name of motherhood did not challenge their central role as wife, however. Indeed, later, the wife role was to become even more prominent.

Unmarried Women versus the Heterosexual Imperative

By the late 1800s and early 1900s more women were choosing not to marry and were supporting themselves. These women were the early professionals and had usually graduated from one of the excellent women's colleges that had been established in the late 1800s. They rejected their mothers' primary identification as wives and sought to achieve a sense of personal accomplishment for themselves. Although valuing the "manly" qualities of health, strength, and brains, these women were definitely "woman-identified" in the sense of living and working with and for women in women's colleges, in settlement houses, and in reform organizations.[22]

But these New Women and their humanistic (I would say, motherly) enterprises were cruelly treated by what historian Mary Ryan has called the "heterosexual imperative." The cultural emphasis placed on the heterosexual couple and the denigration of nonmarriage for women arose along with corporate capitalism, mass advertising, and consumerism. The dominant images of the 1920s, just after women had obtained the vote, were those of youth and romance, marrying a prince charming, and at the same time being his equal and pal. Whatever else the "emancipated" flapper image might connote, one thing was certain: the flapper was not a mother figure and she was very, very interested in men and sex. Jane Addams, the nonmarried and maternal founder of Hull House, was aghast at the new emphasis on sex and the couple and deplored the way the world was changing.

The flapper promised women fun and sexual titillation in return for forgetting about their mothers' "silly old power." The dream was to meet and marry a rich man, rise in the social scale, and live happily and nonpolitically ever after. This dream was purveyed to ever-widening audiences through the movies and defined the hopes of working girls from rural or immigrant backgrounds. The emphasis on being attractive to men, catching a man, and so forth had of course been present in the nineteenth century and before, but adding a more overt sexuality to the image and setting the hetero-sexual couple in center stage of subjective existence called into question the affectional ties between middle-class women that had been taken for granted in the nineteenth century.

At this time, the newly minted term *lesbian* began to be used to punish female autonomy. According to Carroll Smith-Rosenberg, male sex reformers, psychologists, and physicians redefined the issue of female autonomy in sexual terms, so that women who competed with men for economic independence and political power were labeled Mannish Lesbians. While the Mannish Lesbian threatened men, the sexually repressed, man-fearing Lady in Lavender lesbian image threatened the flapper, who was expected to be quite the opposite (pp. 265, 282–83).[23] Both images were used to discredit child and maternal welfare programs by characterizing them as the work of "unnatural celibates." By the 1920s accusations of lesbianism had become the way to discredit women professionals, reformers, and educators. Overall, the hegemony of "the heterosexual couple" made women more male-oriented and at the same time kept women out of public affairs.

Women in the Mid-Twentieth Century

Whereas women's association with nurturance in the nineteenth century became for many an avenue of entry into the public sphere, women's mothering by the mid-twentieth century had been thoroughly privatized. Yet women as mothers remained very much responsible for how their children turned out. They were expected to devote themselves to their children, but not in such a way as to "castrate" their male children. Nobody much worried about female children. The Freudians in the 1940s and 1950s ignored Freud's emphasis on fathers and worried about "seductive" mothers and "castrating" mothers instead. In effect the idea was that such mothers would juvenilize males. At that time it was not possible to see that the "wife role" allowed, even demanded, that ordinary men juvenilize females as a matter of course.

Lundberg and Farnham, in a chapter melodramatically entitled "The Slaughter of the Innocents" in their 1947 book, *Modern Woman, The Lost Sex,* described various ways in which mothers could ruin children. These authors also assured us that the "femi-

nine woman" left her man to his projects in the world and knew she
was dependent on him and "the phallus." Thus, women were ad-
monished not to "castrate" their husbands by in any way competing with them. They were to keep out of men's business and at the
same time not overinvest in children.

Women's clubs, which had dealt with serious and even radical
issues at the turn of the century, were now more likely to be depicted as laughable. The professionalization of many of the activities in which women had engaged in the nineteenth century had
made volunteer work vulnerable to being seen as the meddling of
amateurs. In 1942, Philip Wylie, in his best-selling book, *Generation of Vipers*, coined the term *momism* and criticized the middle-
aged woman during World War II for building "clubhouses for the
entertainment of soldiers where she succeeds in persuading thou-
sands of them that they are momsick and would rather talk to her
than take Betty into the shrubs" (p. 193). Here Wylie manages in
one sentence to blame the middle-class woman for her two-pronged
predicament. He ridicules her for attempts to find meaningful projects outside the home and he accuses her of being a bad mother by
interfering with her adult children's heterosexual pursuits. Moms
for Wylie were ugly and useless. Women were to be sexy wives.

In a distorted way, Lundberg and Farnham (a journalist and a
psychiatrist) recognized that mid-twentieth-century middle-class
women were not in a good situation. They felt that women were
dissatisfied, that middle-class woman's sphere was narrowing to the
point of extinction, and that mothering and glamour were not
enough for "the healthy ego." Yet these authors explicitly and un-
remittingly attacked feminism as they understood the term. For
them feminism from a psychological standpoint had a single objective: "the achievement of maleness by the female, or the nearest
possible approach to it."[24]

If feminism was nothing but masculinism and hence no solution,
how could women's situation be improved? Lundberg and Farnham's solution, not very thoroughly worked out, was for married
women to take over the jobs of spinsters! "All public teaching posts
now filled by women would be reserved not only for married women
but for those with at least one child" (pp. 364–65). The progressive
aspect of this proposal was that it protested the practice of barring
married women from teaching and many other professions. But

only wives could take on such roles, and wives were definitely expected to be dependent physically, psychologically and financially on men. Thus Lundberg and Farnham were unable to break out of their overriding commitment to the male-dominated heterosexual couple. Indeed, they strongly reinforced this commitment and stigmatized nonmarriage.

During the 1950s, more and more people in the middle class were marrying at younger and younger ages. These young couples were buying single-family homes in the suburbs and contributing to the "baby boom." Here the consolidation of the isolated nuclear family as ideology and, to a lesser extent, reality reached its height. Women's mothering had become privatized, women's extrafamilial maternal activities were ridiculed, and women's lives were expected to revolve around their husband's "career." By 1950, servants, boarders, and unattached kin in the household had generally become a thing of the past.[25] Wives had become more equal to their husbands as their friends and sex partners, but at the same time wives were expected to feel successful only vicariously through their husband's accomplishments. Wives were in each other's physical presence in the suburbs, but their fate was too bound up with their husbands' occupations to allow most of them to bond in more than superficial ways. There was little sharing of child care with other women, in part because these women usually were not employed outside the home and because each mother had her own views of child-rearing and a certain competitiveness. Each little nuclear unit had its separate agenda that revolved around the husband's career.

Parsons's Analysis

Talcott Parsons, later to become a target of feminist criticism, began writing on the family during the same period as Philip Wylie and Lundberg and Farnham. While most other sociologists were devising scales to measure the personal compatibility of prospective marriage partners, Parsons was engaged in a genuinely analytical attempt to understand how family structure and its mode of articulation with the "occupational sphere" affected both genders. For Parsons the mid-twentieth century situation for middle-class women looked like this: They had been educated similarly to men at least through college and were taught to value occupational achievement but were then married and were faced with a husband who was totally immersed in a career away from home, a shrinking domestic role, and, most important, a lack of a clear-cut definition of just what women's "role" was.[26]

Parsons did not consider either strict domesticity or a full-fledged career as a viable solution. He also saw problems with what he called "the glamour role" and with "the good companion role" as compromises. The glamour role emphasized women's specific sexuality, while the good companion role stressed cultural and humanistic interests that wife and husband had in common. But glamour and exaggerated sexual differentiation could not last forever, and "the good companion role" was not something that husbands had time to share (pp. 95–98).

In historical perspective, the glamour role was a precipitate of the heterosexual imperative and the "emancipation" of women in the 1920s. The good companion role was essentially an updated version of the cultural interests, charity work, and moral activity that occupied nineteenth-century wives. Neither updated version provided any real solution to inequality. Parsons concluded that "in the adult feminine role there is quite sufficient strain and insecurity so that widespread manifestations are to be expected in the form of neurotic behavior" (p. 99). Although Parsons failed to predict the reemergence of feminism, he was keenly aware that the "feminine role," as he called it, was a crucial point of "strain" in the nuclear family system.

Parsons was also well aware that some middle-class married women worked outside the home. His own wife worked as a secretary on the Harvard campus while he was teaching there. He did not stress the positive advantages of working for women, however, but focused instead on the destabilizing consequences of women's competing occupationally with their husbands. He pointed out that the jobs middle-class women held were usually not full-fledged careers and hence were not a threat to the solidarity of the couple.

Understandably, Parsons's hypothesis that marital solidarity would be threatened by wives' having jobs comparable to their husbands struck liberal feminists of the 1960s and 1970s as highly reactionary. He appeared to be opposing equal job opportunities for women by saying that occupational equality was incompatible with stable marriage.[27] But he can also be interpreted as saying middle-class women's jobs were far from equal and were therefore not comparable to their husbands. From a more radical feminist standpoint, as we shall see later, Parsons was correct about there being a negative association between marital stability and occupational equality. Parsons, however, did not understand the degree to which financial dependency rather than "role differentiation" may have been accounting for the "marital stability" associated with the non-employment and low-paying jobs of wives.

The Women's Movement

The feminism that emerged in the sixties focused on the increasingly felt contradiction between equality and individualism and on women's exclusion from the world of work outside the home. It also for the first time named and challenged the "sexism" that was apparent in male-female interactions. The former was first articulated by professional women, and the latter by younger women radicals. But as I have argued, this conflict between individualism and being a wife is a long-standing one in this society. The question remains, why did it serve as the basis for a movement at this point? The issue of when feminist perspectives are embraced by large numbers of the population can ultimately be accounted for by economic, demographic, and ideological changes in complex interaction.

Certainly a major role in the reemergence of feminism was played by the steady increase in women's working outside the home. By 1955 almost 50 percent of American women were working outside the home.[28] Women wanted to work, service sector jobs were available, and younger families especially needed women's wages. As middle-class women began to work, they surely changed their view of themselves and became more responsive to feminist concerns. Seminaries, law schools, and medical schools were experiencing declining enrollments, and women students who could afford the tuition became very welcome. These women needed the supporting ideology of feminism.

It is also possible that feminist perspectives became especially persuasive when they did because the ratio of marriageable males to marriageable females (if males must be older) had become "less favorable" to females.[29] "Suitable" husbands were in short supply, so for some portion of the female population being one's own person became a necessity.

In addition to middle-class women's increased labor force participation and the "marriage squeeze," however, a change in consciousness among middle-class youth also coincided with these events. The more androgynous sensibilities, or less gender-differentiated personalities, that characterized the youth of the late sixties may have stemmed from what I will call middle-class matrifocality.

Middle-Class White Mothers
and Matrifocality

In my view de facto and only partially culturally legitimated matrifocality among upper middle-class professionals has been very much connected with the role crossovers that occurred among their offspring and with the rise of feminism itself in the late 1960s. In the white middle class, mothers have been central in the home, whereas fathers have tended to be psychologically, and often literally, absent. Fathers played neither a patriarchal role nor a nurturant role. Middle-class mothers did not work regularly outside the home, or if they did, it was in relatively low-level jobs. Thus, women did not make an important direct economic contribution to the family, which would rule out calling the white middle class matrifocal by Tanner's definition. Yet these mothers who were so central in their children's lives often had a comparable kind and level of education to that of their husbands and were likely to have come from a higher class than their husbands.

Although marriages tend toward hypergamy (women marrying up), the probability that a considerable number of college-educated wives will come from a higher class than their husbands is due to the tendency since World War II for the women to be of higher status than the men in educational institutions, where many marriages are contracted. This tendency results from the following process. In any family able to consider a college education for their children, sons are likely to be favored over daughters so that (other things being equal) the son will be sent to a better school than the daughter if funds are limited. Thus, the brother of a woman at a state university is likely to attend a more highly ranked school than she is, whereas the sister of a man at a state university is likely to be at a less highly ranked school than he is. It is clear from my colleagues' and my research on social science undergraduates at the University of Oregon that the women come from families of higher socioeconomic status than do the men.[30]

It is my impression, although I have no formal documentation, that the parents of the young middle-aged today often consist of a lower-class man who went to college on the GI bill after World War II and a middle-class woman whose parents paid for her college education. In this sense, these wives are their husbands' equals by virtue of their class "superiority" even though they do not have an occupational role comparable to that of their husband. Families with these characteristics are especially likely to be found in professional segments of the middle class and are closer to realizing matrifocality by Tanner's definition than one might think. These families do not represent the hypergamous marriages that characterize the overall marriage gradient. They constitute an exception to it. It is almost as if the "feminine mystique," with its emphasis on the male-oriented woman, was designed to overcome middle-class mothers' not being in many vital respects inferior to or beholden to their husbands and being understood by their husbands (albeit ambivalently) not to be.

It is certainly not out of the question that the adolescents of the sixties, with their challenges to traditional definitions of masculinity and male-serving femininity, are in part a product of the kind of matrifocality found in middle-class professional families. Here mother dominance, in the sense of a maternal orientation in the context of factors equalizing the relationship between husband and wife, may have fostered less gender-typed attitudes in the children. Rather than producing compulsive masculinity, these mothers seem to have reared a generation of males who are, as Richard Flacks describes them, "likely to be less motivated for dominance, less physically aggressive and tough, less physically competitive, and more emotionally expressive and aesthetically inclined."[31] Some of these same characteristics in males were described less favorably earlier by Kenneth Keniston in *The Uncommitted: Alienated Youth in American Society.* Flacks goes on to speculate that "many girls raised in these ways are likely to be less submissive, more assertive and more self-assured and independent" (p. 32). As more and more middle-class mothers work outside the home, the

trend toward role crossovers should continue—and on a less ambivalent basis—because mothers can act directly as role models for
their daughters.

Sexism, Classism, and Racism

The women whose history I have been describing in this section
have generally been privileged in terms of both class and race. Perhaps it fell to privileged middle-class white women to focus on
"sexism" precisely because of their economic privilege. From the
vantage point of class and race privilege, it was possible to focus
directly on the dominance men took for granted as men. Although
less-privileged women had been coping with male dominance for
years, and very often virulent forms of it from white males, middle-
class women were in a better position to label male dominance in
general as "oppression" and put it front and center in their analyses. The white middle class has been the central locus of the ideology of individualism and achievement, and it is this ideology that
conflicts with middle-class women's situation as wives.

Understandably, radical "feminism," which focused on male oppression within the middle class, may have seemed ridiculous in
the larger scheme of things to poor women and women of color,
who had more immediate problems associated with class and race
oppression. Often for these women the solidarity of the family has
been a means of surviving this class and race oppression. Both
blacks and Hispanics in this country have used the solidarity of the
family and kin as their primary source of support in a hostile world.
Thus for them it would seem counterproductive to condemn the
masculine privilege within the family that is exercised by oppressed men.

Twentieth-century feminism is the first social theory that has
used gender as a fundamental category of social analysis.[32] Before
this, gender (and male dominance) has been rendered invisible by
other cross-cutting categories. Only when the unit of analysis becomes the individual can one think in terms of "pure" gender and
see systematic discrimination against women. Oppressed minori-
ties might be the last to see this because their unit of analysis is
more likely to be the family. The middle class, with its individualistic ideology, would likely be the first to think in terms of "sex"
oppression.

Although it is not particularly helpful to argue that the "original" oppression was sex oppression, as some radical feminists do, I believe that it is legitimate for certain purposes to use sex inequality in the sense of male dominance in heterosexual relations as a central focus, simply because men and women "marry" in every class and race group. In this sense it is not being insensitive to class and race to focus directly on this relationship.

It is also important to remember that "sexism" does provide an opportunity for male bonding across class lines. A male restaurant owner and a male employee can form a solidarity against the female "help" on the basis of pure gender prejudice. Unless of course the woman is a wife. Then a middle-class husband is able to "protect" her.

The Aftermath

Feminism is no longer "popular," as the gains for middle-class women in the work force it helped to garner have come to be taken for granted. Some say feminism is no longer needed. From the standpoint of gender equality, however, the millennium is hardly here. Women's working has not brought on a "symmetrical" family in which husband and wife work equal time for equal wages and share equally in child care. Women's wages are still far below those of men; men whose wives work for wages do not help in the home or share child care significantly more than men whose wives do not work for wages.[33] Many "working mothers" are clearly overworked.

Indeed, more prominent than any trend toward equality within families brought about by women's working outside has been the trend toward family breakup. As married women began to work outside the home in increasing numbers, the divorce rate burgeoned, doubling between 1965 and 1975, and high divorce rates, though leveling off, are still very much with us. The rate began its precipitous rise well before no-fault divorce laws were passed, and it is associated with the great increase in young married women's working—the age group in which divorces are most likely to occur.[34]

The most general explanation for the connection between the rising divorce rate and the rising employment of women outside the home is simply that having a job allows a woman to realistically "choose" divorce, that is, having a job increases her alternatives. Even a poorly paying job might give a woman an opportunity to survive financially outside a marriage that she found oppressive.

Beyond this, longitudinal studies indicate that the likelihood of divorce increases as a wife's actual or potential earnings approach those of her husband (p. 54). Here one might speculate that the wife's earnings posed a threat to the husband's marital hegemony but also that her earnings made her marriage less essential for her financially. Generally, however, wives' earnings are well below those of husbands. Thus, in the large majority of families, wives' working for wages does not alter or threaten to alter the power structure.

Parsons's argument that women's working at jobs commensurate with their husbands' was associated with unstable marriages turns out to be partially right. Parsons himself suggested in a footnote that the higher divorce rate that characterized working-class marriages at the time might have resulted from wives in the working class holding jobs comparable in status to those of their husbands.[35] It is becoming clearer, however, that it is the earnings or potential earnings of the wife, not the status of her job, that is related to divorce.

Moreover, the decision to divorce is more often made by wives than by husbands. Several recent studies that have obtained information from both husbands and wives on the causes of the decision to divorce find that women are clearly more likely to seek the breakup than men. Wallerstein and Kelly found in their California study that in 75 percent of the couples they interviewed it was the wife who wanted the divorce.[36] These findings suggest that the exodus from marriage which we have been witnessing has been led by women.[37] A study comparing the complaints of husbands and the complaints of wives found that wives, not husbands, are dissatisfied with their marriages. Husbands often said in answer to a question about why the marriage broke up that they were "not sure what happened."[38] The wives' complaints are now less likely to be about the husband's failure to "provide" (and characteristics related to this) and are more likely to be complaints about the husband's affective or emotional failings (pp. 103–15).[39]

In spite of ritualized male complaints about the shackles of marriage, the evidence on divorce suggests women are more dissatisfied with marriage than men are—dissatisfied at least with marriage as it is presently constituted. Women who can be employed are now more able to express their dissatisfaction by seeking divorce. More-

over, women are less likely than men to remarry. Surely, not re-
marrying is a deliberate choice on the part of some women and is not
just because they were not asked, as many seem to assume. Again,
I do not see nonmarriage as a large scale "solution" for women.
Rather, I look forward to a rethinking of marriage and a transformation in the nature of the implicit marriage contract.

Summary

In this chapter I have attempted to put the situation of middle-class
women into a larger social context. I have suggested that individualism has provided the ideological basis for the feminist protest and
that middle-class matrifocality, among other factors, has helped
produce children who are less gender differentiated and more sensitive to gender inequality.

Chapter Ten

Mothers as Wives in an Individualistic Society

I begin this chapter with a discussion of some of the unintended consequences for women that can result from "gender-blind" stances. Although the belief that people should be judged on the basis of their performance and not on their gender has served as a spur to modern feminism, efforts to implement this belief by "ignoring" gender have not been entirely successful. I argue that gender-blind policies superimposed on an underlying structure that works against women—specifically, the implicit rules of the marriage contract—may temporarily exacerbate rather than counteract women's disadvantage. I discuss this in connection with Blood and Wolfe's study of power in the family and with no-fault divorce laws.

From a psychological standpoint the cultural emphasis on sexuality coupled with individualism helps explain the obsessive concern with sexual orientation as a quality of the whole person. The cultural emphasis on the individual also explains the creation of the concepts of "masculinity" and "femininity" themselves—concepts that have little meaning in other cultures. "Femininity" requires women to render themselves harmless and to enhance the male ego by means of deference displays that must never become crudely obvious. This "femininity" is seen as a pervasive quality of the person and becomes a built-in handicap for women in competition with men, whereas at the same time, failure to be "feminine" keeps women from being let into the game at all. The concept of "femininity" is the generalized personality cognate of "wife" and is a necessary prerequisite to being "chosen" to be a "wife."

Within the context of individualism, movement toward greater gender equality seems to be taking the form of a decreasing salience of the wife "role" for women and a new definition of what being married may mean. The "new love ethic" and the high divorce rate are connected with greater independence for women. Increasing age at marriage, female longevity, and nonmarriage also mean less dependency on husbands for women and offer women opportunities for greater connectedness with other women.

Overall, I argue that "the maternal values," which in some respects contradict "individualistic values," may ultimately become more prominent in the society as a whole as women become increasingly active as citizens and gain a stronger foothold in the public sphere. As maternal values themselves are given more credence in the society, they will reinforce the trend for fathers to participate in child care in a way that is less reinforcing of the debilitating aspects of "femininity." At the same time, maternal values can lead to an increasing insistence that the welfare of children should depend not on individual parents alone but become instead the responsibility of the nation as a whole.

Individualism and Sexism

In contrast to previous periods in which the division of labor between women and men was relatively clear-cut and each gender depended on the other for survival, the modern doctrine of individualism, coupled with the idea of economic rationality as the guide to behavior, has rendered women "unequal" in a new way.[1]

"Sexism" in the Economy

Modern individualism in my view grew out of patriarchy and narrowed "father rule" to the nuclear family unit. Patriarchy was made to fit individualism by making the relevant individuals husbands and fathers. The idea is simple: women are linked to the economy through the men they marry; men are free to be individuals so long as they provide; women are to live vicariously through their husbands. The male provider became rational "economic man," and his wife and children became his economic dependents. Thus the economy took care of the "welfare issue" posed by "nonworkers"— that is, women and children not earning in the market economy—

by assigning them to husband-fathers. It has been only since married women began to work in the market economy and to become divorced that we have been able to understand the extent to which the marriage contract has rendered women economic dependents, a form of juvenilization.

Marxists have showed the myriad ways in which these dependent women are in fact doing "work." Housework is necessary work that is unpaid. They have also showed how housewives (whether in the paid labor force or not) as consumers increasingly have had to take on, without pay, tasks that capitalist enterprises and "professionals" themselves could be doing. Christine Delphy, a Marxist, points out, however, that there is not much point in discussing the value of women's work so long as it is not theirs to exchange. She argues convincingly that it is not the nature of women's work that causes it to be unpaid, but rather women's work is not paid for because it is performed within marriage. The nature of women's tasks has no connection to their relations of production because all married women, no matter what they do or do not do, have the same relations of production. Women's work is paid for in goods and upkeep by their husbands. Women's "relations of production," that is, the way they make their living, are very different from those of men. Men are paid in the market; women as wives are paid in goods by men.[2]

Delphy may overstate her case, especially in times when marriage is decreasing in importance, but I believe she is correct to stress the marriage contract itself rather than the more often used "family," or "wife-mother" or "patriarchy." As I have argued throughout, it is not what women do, including women's mothering, that puts women at a disadvantage; it is the way the implicit marriage contract sidelines wives and mainstreams men. Delphy goes on to argue that "the position of women in the labor market and the discrimination that they suffer are the result (and not the cause) of the marriage contract."[3]

In my view, marriage continues to define women's secondary position in the wider society. In a very direct and often explicit way, the expectation that women are married, will be married, or have been married accounts for their disadvantage in the occupational world. In answering the question, why female workers in this country earn considerably less than male workers earn, some employers may still explicitly state that a woman does not need to be highly paid because it is her husband's job to provide for her. Wives' work is seen as supplementing the husband's income. The extensive job segregation, which acts to defeat the "equal pay for equal work" principle, is also directly related to women as wives. Jobs held predominantly by females are seen as requiring less commitment (and therefore less pay) than men's jobs, because a woman is expected to put her major effort into her marriage.[4] Whereas most analyses of women's secondary status in contemporary society have focused in one way or another on women's work, I am arguing that ultimately in this society women's secondary status is related to the definition of women as wives.

As married women increasingly enter the labor force, however, the older assumption of women's dependency on men is forgotten and the liberal rule of gender blindness prevails. This is important, necessary, and good under some circumstances, but gender blindness can cover over the handicaps under which women operate. Because marriage organizes gender roles and even defines gender difference in terms of women being dependent wives and men being providers, the system is rigged against women at work outside. Assumptions of genderlessness give the appearance that men have won out in the job market in some sort of fair competition, a naturally satisfying view for winners.

An example of what I mean by this last statement is provided by Blood and Wolfe's now-classic study of power in the family.[5] The authors fairly burst with liberal pride when they announce that gender no longer determines who holds the power in the family. Patriarchy is dead because power now belongs to the person who brings home the most resources and "sometimes" that person may be a woman. They find that family power is based on economic power, income, education, occupation, and organizational membership, but they assume that gender no longer determines who does what, and so it is possible for women to "earn" family power in free competition. The implication is, then, that if women do not "choose" to go out and earn as much money as their husbands, then they have no right to resent his power.

In 1971, Dair Gillespie subjected Blood and Wolfe's "personal resource theory" (which I describe above) to a scathing critique.[6] She argues that, in addition to "socialization," the marriage contract itself determines who brings home the bacon. It is not a matter of personal choice; it is a matter of the implicit marriage contract that assumes that men are the breadwinners and are expected to support their wives, who are in turn supposed to care for home and children. Thus, sexism takes over when gender-blind individualism fails to see how marriage rules define gender roles and how these rules handicap women by not taking motherhood into account.

More recently, Lenore Weitzman has reported, from a fifteen-year study of the results of no-fault divorce laws, that the assumption that men and women are individuals whose individual circumstances must be taken into account in making decisions about who gets what in divorce settlements has so far worked to the detriment of women. According to Weitzman, men experience a 42 percent improvement in their post-divorce standard of living, and women experience a 73 percent decline. This disparity results from the inadequacy of court awards, the expanded demands on the wife's resources because she is likely to have the children with her, and the husband's greater earning power.[7] Overall, it is a testament to wives' and children's economic dependence on husbands. Court awards are likely to be inadequate because judges often assume that the divorced wife has the same market opportunities as the divorced husband. She does not, of course, because she has been a wife and has never had the help of a wife, and because the jobs available to women generally pay less than the jobs available to men. Beyond this, husbands tend not to pay the child support assigned to them, and judges and attorneys seem reluctant to enforce the rules on their fellow males.

Gender-blind rules do not work if they are simply written over and above a structure that still disadvantages women in terms of the old "rules," which assume male-headed nuclear families. But the solution is certainly not to do away with no-fault divorce and return to the status quo ante, as Phyllis Schlafly suggests.[8] The old laws assume that women require economic support; the new laws assume women can support themselves. The older view assumes that women are nothing but wives and mothers; the newer view forgets that women are wives—dependent on men for their and their children's livelihood—and gives women responsibility as persons under assumptions of an equality which does not exist.

Certainly, liberal individualism must not be destroyed. As I have noted before, individualism provided the ideological impetus for the feminist protest in the first place. Women, like men, want to be treated as persons. Women cannot have equal opportunity, however, if the implicit marriage contract that makes women into wives and subsumes women's mothering under husband-fathers remains in place. There are no easy solutions. My suggestion is that we become more aware of the unequalizing effect of the wife role as it is currently defined. And beyond the marriage contract, we cannot ignore the sexism that characterizes heterosexual relations in general.

"Sexism" in the Psychology of the Heterosexual Couple

The structure of the heterosexual couple relationship has a psychological aspect as well as an economic aspect. Both aspects work toward making women into wives who are secondary to men. In Chapter 8, I discussed the idea that for women marriage means finding a man who they feel is superior to them. This seeking the superior ultimately might be explained entirely by women's economic dependence on men, but certainly it is also embedded in our psychological concepts and our ideas about love and romance and may, as I have suggested, have to do with men's fathering. Seeking a husband who is one's superior is the adult echo of being a daddy's girl.

In heterosexual contexts that are not cross-cut by class or age, male gender serves as a marker for dominance in the psyches of both men and women. As the specific and elaborate differences in men's and women's societal roles decrease and as women are included more in men's world, this tendency may become more rather than less apparent. In other words, the difference does become one of dominance, when nonmaternal, economistic individualistic assumptions reign supreme.

The idea that it is the essence of femininity to be associated with a male whom one genuinely believes to be one's superior is the core assumption behind Freud's definition of femininity and remains alive and well in the social structure and in many men's and women's psyches. Thus heterosexuality itself is often identified with the "psychological necessity for the male to be superior." Psychoanalysis did not invent this view, but it did contribute to the general emphasis on subjective states rather than political action,[9] and it provided women with a subjective sense of self in which femininity meant seeking a male partner whom one felt was superior enough to justify one's subordination.

It can be no accident that psychoanalytic theory that swept the field in the early part of the century coincided with an emphasis on the heterosexual couple. As we have seen, what psychoanalysis ultimately does is to define gender in terms of sexual aim and sexual object. Its core assumptions mystify the nature of gender difference, at least from the standpoint of many women's perceptions of it. As I argued earlier, women and certainly feminists do not necessarily see the difference between women and men as being that women are more dependent on men than men are on women and so forth. This mystification then becomes the psychological legitimation for making mothers into wives and for making male-dominated heterosexuality the single most important organizer of the self.

Homosexuality as Antithesis

The reason for our culture's preoccupation with homosexuality as deviance is undoubtedly related to the contemporary emphasis on the male-dominated heterosexual couple as the central social relationship in the society. The Japanese psychiatrist, Takeo Doi, makes this connection explicit:

I was astonished to discover the special emphasis laid in American, unlike traditional Japanese, custom, on the ties between the sexes, not only after marriage but before it as well. . . . For members of the same sex always to act together, or to show excessive familiarity, is to lay them open immediately to suspicion of homosexuality, and people are particularly sensitive on this score. Japan, on the other hand, is the ideal place for enjoying friendship with members of the same sex openly and unashamedly.[10]

(Doi's observations on tolerance may become increasingly less true as emphasis on the heterosexual couple and the isolated nuclear family gains ascendancy in Japan.)

Foucault's writings have led to the recognition that the terms *heterosexual* and *homosexual* applied to individuals as total persons are themselves social products of relatively recent times. In other times and places what might be labeled "homosexual" now in the United States would have been considered a part of the normal spectrum of human eroticism and might or might not have been considered deviant. Certainly, in other places the distinction would not have been so overwhelmingly salient nor so totally encompassing of an individual's personality. But before homosexuality could be labeled deviant, or so totally damning, it had to be seen as totally characterizing who a person was.[11] Homosexual subcultures designed by homosexuals to counteract the pathological label given to homosexuality have unfortunately strengthened rather than weakened the conception of homosexuality as being an absolutely fundamental quality of the total person.

In Lévi-Strauss's analysis, men and women were induced to marry each other because the gender-based division of labor in a society in effect constituted a "taboo" against men doing women's "work" and vice versa. This meant that certain activities essential for both genders could be performed only by one gender, which according to Lévi-Strauss, made marriage necessary for both to survive. The degree of structural differentiation characterizing modern industrial societies would make basing gender on occupational assignment, as it was in simple societies, out of the question.[12] Now, in a highly differentiated, individualistic, achievement-oriented society, the emphasis on heterosexual attraction seems to serve as a mechanism for sustaining the usefulness of women and men to each other. The conception of "vive la différence" does not refer to differentiated roles in society so much as it celebrates heterosexuality itself. The problem with this, however, is that the structure of adult heterosexual relationships takes power away from women.

Individualism and the Concept of Femininity

In contrast to the term *wife*, which implies a lesser status or role in a marital or quasi-marital relationship, the term *femininity* is used to describe an all-encompassing "quality" characterizing the total person. The concept "wife" can be talked about cross-culturally since it is a universal status vis-à-vis superior husband that assumes different shapes depending on the wider social organizational context and depending especially on how it is embedded in wider kinship systems. "Femininity" is a more culture- and class-bound concept that fits in with individualism and its focus on the overall qualities of individuals rather than on disparate social roles. "Femininity," as well as "wife," is related to female subordination.

"Femininity" might be defined as an ever-present readiness to be "the lesser." Femininity connotes being little, vulnerable, indecisive, in need of protection, soft, delicate, frivolous, and in every way, a nonthreat. Femininity is an attitude, a stance of playing "weak" to his "strength" in a way that both emphasizes and disguises inequality. "Femininity" also connotes the happy, light, fun things, and can be a kind of denial of weighty, noisy, self-absorbed masculinity. But when women embrace this "femininity" with all its temptations, they abdicate power and the right to be taken seriously.

"Femininity" did not disappear when women became workers. It is alive and well in the workplace. Susan Brownmiller describes how women use "femininity" as a competitive maneuver in getting and keeping jobs.[13] Women try to succeed in the occupational world by being "feminine"; this is supposed to give them the competitive edge, because it pleases men who are the gatekeepers. In a sense "femininity" allows the wife role to move into the marketplace and to become glamorized in the process.

Brownmiller's definition of femininity correctly focuses on making oneself harmless. Her definition tends to merge exactly those qualities that I keep separate, however. This merging of course is understandable since the concept of femininity does merge concern for others with dependence. Brownmiller defines the masculine principle as "a driving ethos of superiority designed to inspire straightforward, confident success, while the feminine principle is composed of vulnerability, the need for protection, the formalities of compliance and the avoidance of conflict—in short, an appeal of dependence and good will that gives the masculine principle its romantic validity and its admiring applause" (p. 25). Thus, she, like so many others, merges "weakness" with conflict-avoidance and good will. This buys into the more typically masculine way of looking at the world. Conflict-avoidance and good will represent not weakness but an alternative to the "dominate or be dominated" principle that threatens to destroy the world.

If women's more relational orientation is to prevail, however, and shift all relationships to a less adversarial mode, then women must have power. "Femininity" in the sense of weak and dependent must give way to "female," and "female" must emphasize the humanity that women in their maternal aspect have fostered. Brownmiller barely mentions women as maternal, and when she does, it is to say that motherhood makes women vulnerable and in need of protection, or alternatively that maternity makes women less "feminine" by causing unattractive stretch marks (p. 137)!

Women in patriarchal societies, although clearly oppressed by modern standards, are not oppressed by the concept of "femininity." Women are able to view their lives as a series of unfolding and interlocking family roles rather than identifying as a total person with "femininity," or the role of woman viewed as a single entity, as in modern society. Women in patriarchal societies do not perceive gender as a psychological category connected with a generalized orientation; rather, being a woman involves a number of dissimilar roles. Manisha Roy, in explaining the situation of the traditional Indian woman, argues that such a woman does not think of herself as "feminine" in the sense of possessing a set of traits for all time, but rather she thinks of herself as filling "roles" that change throughout the life cycle. In India a woman is not thought of as more or less feminine; she is feminine by virtue of being a woman, presumably meaning her ability to have children. Her "femininity" does not depend on her ability to attract and appeal to males. Rather, what is expected of women and the power they wield depends on their age and stage in the life cycle.[14] Roy suggests, for example, that aggressiveness is quite acceptable in a Bengali woman if she is a forty-year-old matron mother. Significantly enough, the low point comes with marriage itself, and suicide is all too frequent among young brides in India, and formerly in China. In classic patriarchal societies a woman's power tends to increase with age, but this is less true in the United States where aging is considered a threat to maintaining that all-important "femininity," that is, nonthreatening youthfulness. In a sense "femininity" permanently "juvenilizes" women as it "sexualizes" them.

Generally, as agrarian patriarchies modernize, it is not as difficult as one might suppose for women to hold jobs in the public sphere alongside men or to act in positions of authority over men. In these situations women are not regarded by men as sex objects, nor do they try to relate to or appeal to men sexually. Instead, men and women relate to each other in terms of the idioms of kinship. Thus Roy notes that a woman in India may treat her male office colleagues as she would her male cousins. Even in modern China, kinship terms still predominate, and strangers may be assimilated by making them into elder or younger siblings. This has the effect of removing heterosexual connotations from the interactions. In South America, a woman running for public office would likely play on the image of mother and grandmother as a means of gaining respect.[15] Indira Gandhi and Golda Meir adopted images of powerful mothers of adult children.

These ways of compromising with the system should not allow us to forget, however, that in an overall sense women were characterized in patriarchal societies as naturally weak and dependent creatures requiring protection from father, husband, and sons. African societies, by contrast, although highly variable with respect to the degree of male dominance, are likely to allow for, even to expect, female initiative and assertion.[16] Individualism, in one sense, is the key to modern women's equality, but, paradoxically, individualism works against equality to the extent that women are defined with reference to heterosexual contexts and interaction, because in these, women are expected to be "the lesser" in the couple.

Summary

One way of dealing with "difference" in an individualistic society is to declare that gender should not make a difference and to make rules that are gender-blind. Gender-blind rules create the impression that women's relative lack of power is a result of their own actions, their own individual choices. Gender-blind assumptions ignore the way gender relations are organized by the implicit marriage contract, which specifies the rights and duties of each gender, and these rights and duties in turn profoundly affect individual choices. The stigma of homosexuality acts as a psychological reinforcement to marriage and male dominance, and the economic dependence of wives serves as the economic reinforcement to marriage and male dominance.

Just as liberal individualism has its virtues, so does marriage. Marriage for women can be a defense against far more exploitative sexual and economic arrangements with men. Marriage is also potentially egalitarian and offers women an opportunity to "socialize" men. My point is, however, that we must be aware of the degree to which two potentially good things—individualism and marriage—are in conflict and the extent to which the implicit marriage contract and the psychological definition of femininity place women at a disadvantage.

What Is Happening to the Nuclear Family?

The last several decades represent a critical period of economic and ideological transition affecting marriage, and the amount of dislocation is great. Poverty among women and children is increasing. Men are coming to resent the male provider role, and women seek to be less economically dependent on men. Until very recently the penalties for nonmarriage for white women have been greater than the inequities embodied in the implicit marriage contract. Now many middle-class white women are postponing marriage, and some have children without marriage. Black women, partially because of discrimination against black men, have often had less to gain from marriage, and the nonmarriage rate among blacks too is increasing. As all females' work participation becomes more continuous, the discrepancy between women's and men's earnings remains. As marriages break up, women still overwhelmingly seek custody of children and have primary and often sole responsibility for them without adequate financial resources. Lesbian mothers are likely to be denied custody of their children. Working mothers with husbands are overworked. Moreover, things may get worse for women and children before they get better.[17]

Even though the economic problems involved, from one standpoint, are paramount, they do not in themselves effect changes in gender relations. Even in countries that have made far greater progress than the United States has with respect to pay equity and child care, gender relations themselves remain remarkably unreconstructed.[18] In some ways, the United States has moved farther toward gender equality than other industrialized societies. The process of reconstructing marriage on a more egalitarian basis is well advanced and involves both feminists and those who do not identify as feminists. In one sense this is but a continuation of a long-term trend toward greater inclusion and equality that has to do with American individualism.

Since the 1960s, the trend toward increasing individualism as applied to women has led to a decline in the isolation and the salience of the nuclear family. It is not so much that we are moving to a new family type as that the lines between the nuclear family and other relationships are becoming blurred and the nuclear family itself is becoming less stable as married couples break up. The family can be seen as consisting in the less stable couple relationship and the more stable mother-child relationship. Because of these changes, we are able to understand and be more critical of the assumptions underlying nuclear family living. It is always difficult to predict, however, where we are going and where feminist movement will take us.

In the following sections I discuss three main areas in transition: the marriage relationship, parenting, and women in the public sphere.

Trends in Marriage

College texts give a strong egalitarian gloss to their descriptions of marriage. They deplore sexism, tout equality, and in so doing reinforce the view held by many students that the struggle for equality is over, feminism has won and is no longer needed. Actually, we have a long way to go and outcomes are increasingly uncertain. Inequality is so much a part of the fabric of marriage that it is not perceived.

To ask how we can make marriage more of an equal proposition is, in the last analysis, to ask how we can have marriage without "wives." Making marriage equal in this society means breaking up the connection between primary identity as a female and being a wife, that is, secondary. It requires redefining both the term *wife* and the term *femininity*. How to be loved and loving, committed and the object of commitment, and not be defined as a wife?

Both increasing individualism and the push for more equality in marriage have fed into the development of a "new love ethic," which potentially decreases the centrality of marriage to the individual's "identity" and hence the salience of "wife."[19] It also redefines the relationship between spouses. Although the new love ethic continues to embody expectations of diffuse involvement and solidarity, the relationship need not necessarily last a lifetime to be considered successful, nor is it expected to be absolutely exclusive. Thus the new love ethic is a compromise between romantic-love approaches to marriage and more contractual approaches. Marriage is seen as an ongoing negotiable and renegotiable love relationship that needs attention to make it go well. It challenges the notion that marriage fixes one's identity for life and defines marital love as something that changes and grows. Whereas the older love was characterized as "true and deep," the newer love is more likely to be seen as "vital and alive." The older emphasis on self-sacrifice gives way to an emphasis on self-realization. At the same time it implies a new legitimacy for marital breakup.

The new love ethic fosters egalitarian relations by its emphasis on honest communication, sharing, and negotiation between partners. In the new ethic a wife is expected to be assertive and to have her "own" work. She is not locked into her husband's world so tightly. Thus the new love ideology is compatible with egalitarian relations and more individualism for women.

Men in modern times have never defined themselves as husbands as totally as women have defined themselves as wives, so these changes will affect women more than men. Although I do not expect to see the centrality of the couple relationship end in this society,[20] there are many indications that it has become less salient in the lives of middle-class women and it was never as salient for women in classes where extended kin and quasi-kin relationships assume more importance.

As women gain power as people, they gain power within marriage itself. Increased female labor force participation, increased divorce and hence remarriage, increased singleness among women, increasing age at marriage, and increased female life expectancy all provide opportunities for women to expand their horizons and their relationships with others, especially with other women. Women gain more opportunity to see themselves in other relationships and in other capacities than that of "wife."

All of the liaisons and connections a woman may develop outside marriage decrease her dependence on her husband and give her a basis of equality with him. As more and more women are employed, they form friendships at work, friendships that are not connected to being a wife. Indeed, one objection husbands have had to their wives working is that it threatens their centrality in their wives' lives. Women may also gain a sense of efficacy by working for wages even when the work itself is not pleasant.

Although the nuclear family "ideal" remains very much with us, the nuclear household exists for only some women and for only part of women's lifetime. In the middle class, women are marrying later and divorcing more frequently, thus the period they are married is shorter. Even though most divorced people eventually remarry, older women remarry less than older men. But even remarriage can weaken the centrality of "wife" by extending the ties that married women have with others.

Another factor likely to produce more egalitarian attitudes within marriage is the increasing age at marriage. The consequence for young adults of leaving home earlier and marrying later as they are now doing is that they spend a longer time living independently and gain more experience in forming relationships alternative to family living. Longitudinal surveys of young adults show that young women who had lived independently are more likely to expect to be employed, to want fewer children, and in other respects to hold less traditional views than those who lived with their parents. Young men were affected in the same direction but less so. Moreover, college education and nonfamily living both appear to reinforce each other in creating less traditional attitudes and more egalitarian expectations in marriage.[21]

In addition, women are more likely to be widowed than men because women live longer than men do. Not to be married can mean loneliness in this coupled society, but it also creates the possibility of forming ties with other women as non-wives. Indeed, one of the most important (and unprecedented) demographic changes that will affect gender relations and reduce the salience of "wife" is the aging of the population. Since most older people are female, a population of single women is rapidly growing. These older women are potentially in a position to lead a movement toward less "husband-oriented" relationships.[22] As the periods of nonmarriage lengthen in women's lives, women gain opportunities for forging ties that expand their identity beyond that of "wife." Moreover, not being married forces a change of consciousness on women as they learn to do things on their own and thereby gain confidence in their abilities.

Essentially, the move toward more egalitarian marriages that I have outlined is being bought at the cost of less stable marriages and a decreased salience for marriage itself. It is possible that marital relationships could become more stable as women become partners rather than wives.

In my view, for a loving egalitarian relationship to "work," it would need to be patterned more like women's relationships to women than "normal" heterosexual relationships. What most women seek is not power but the absence of domination. Also, as we have seen, most lesbians and heterosexual women are relationship-centered, but the words we use to describe this, such as *caring* and *nurturant*, sound vaguely insipid. Our language itself is predicated on the individual, isolated from relationships, so that one is at a loss for ways to talk about that "something else" that binds us together. Women are in a better position than men to move us toward a new language of love that can somehow overcome the sharpness of the distinction between self and other without domination or self-abnegation.

Married couples as "loving partners" would be more than sexual partners or business partners or friends, although they would be these too. Loving partners would be tied together by love made increasingly stable by the experiences, both the good and the bad times, they have shared together. Women as loving partners to men would act neither as men's mothers nor men's daughters nor men's wives. They would be loving adult female partners of loving adult males. Moreover, there should be nothing in the concept of "loving partners" to prevent people of the same gender from formally and freely joining together in a love relationship. Ending the definition of women as wives would allow homosexual relationships and heterosexual relationships to exist as "marriages" without dominant partners.

Fathers, Mothers, and Trends in Parenting

Precisely because of the progress toward legal equality that women have made, we are now at a point where we can begin for the first time to examine gender differentiation and the significance of parental influences more dispassionately and with a keener sense of the implications of such study for gender equality. Ignoring gender does not make it go away. It will not disappear because we stop investigating it. To the contrary, the considerations discussed in the last section suggest that we must take the opposite tack and examine gender in order to effectively create more equal relationships between women and men.

Almost all feminists, with the exception of some radical feminists, have advocated that fathers share child care equally with mothers. Equal parenting viewed as a "solution" to the problem of child care has great appeal especially for middle-class women accustomed to the isolated nuclear family, because it preserves the husband-wife relationship and the integrity and isolation of the nuclear unit. As I have suggested throughout this book, however, there may be problems with equal parenting because of gender differences and because "husbands" and "wives" are not equal. Equal parenting may be more of a utopian vision that attempts to preserve the integrity of the nuclear unit than a realistic aim. Moreover, the focus on male parenting deflects attention away from alternative forms of child care and societal responsibility for child care.

Fathers. While equal parenting may be utopian, I applaud the idea of finding ways to include men more constructively in parenting. One important reason for including fathers as child-carers is that if males are nurturant, the male child would find it easier to identity with being male and would not have to deny femaleness so compulsively. Beyond this, if fathers or other male caretakers included nurturance in their views of appropriate male behavior, boys and men might be able to nurture themselves more adequately.

As things stand now, men depend too much on women for nurturance and then, fearing that the nurturance they receive is infantilizing, they may deny their dependence by shows of power. As we saw in Chapter 7 men who cannot nurture others or themselves may also tend to resent the nurturance they see their wives give their children. This resentment and hostility may show up in their relationship with their children in the form of direct violence or in the form of hostile withdrawal. Violent or hostile fathers cannot counteract the fear of males in children and deter their sons' ability to identify comfortably as "male."

Beyond urging less distancing and more warmth, there are few clearly agreed upon guidelines for fathering. Supporters of equal parenting suggest that if fathers were more involved in their children's day-to-day care, it would decrease the possibility of their becoming sexually involved with them. On a very general cognitive level it is likely true that the more one is committed to being a parent and the more one defines oneself as a parent responsible for a child's well-being, the less likely one would be to sexually abuse one's child.[23] A conscientious father who finds himself sexually aroused by his child would try to put himself into another gear by reminding himself that he is a parent, not a lover. Incest's greater frequency among stepfathers than among natural fathers is compatible with the argument that the more one feels oneself to be a parent, the more one is committed to the parental role and the less likely one is to sexually abuse.[24] Stepfathers can tell themselves that they are not the child's "real" father and thus are not required to behave in a parental way.

Increasingly there are fathers who are able to be genuinely loving—neither sexually threatening nor rejecting toward their children. We need to know more about how this balance is achieved and what other attitudes on the part of the fathers themselves and what structural arrangements might contribute to this good outcome. The question of structural arrangements is complex. For example, less isolation of the family and less emotional intensity within the family might decrease the likelihood of incest (see my discussion in Chapter 7). Family breakup and the increasing presence of stepfathers may increase the likelihood of incest. Either possibility makes the empowering of mothers as people especially important.

Certainly one basic deterrent to incest would be greater equality in the husband-wife relationship. As I noted in Chapter 7, an important aspect of ending father-child incest is to strengthen mothers to support the child when they need protection from the father. All too often, mothers now give their primary allegiance to incestuous fathers rather than to their children because of their own and their children's financial and social dependence on him.

In my view, the issue should be less that of attempting to get fathers to participate equally in child care than of helping fathers learn to bring out their own maternal, human, empathetic feelings toward their children. In so doing they can come to represent a new definition of "manhood," not the definition purveyed by their male peers but a definition that rests on a maternal base. Ideologically, we have been slowly moving toward a definition of fathers as mothers for several generations, perhaps even longer, and the current generation of fathers seems to embody this definition to a greater extent than any previous one.[25] Sons are amazing their own fathers with their new attitudes. The factors encouraging these new attitudes I believe are increasing individualism for women and matrifocality.

Mothers.   In Chapter 9, I suggested that de facto matrifocality in the professional segment of the middle class may have had some important effects on the psyches of the children in these families. Even though they were criticized for it, many mothers in the 1950s were not totally appendages of men, and emphasized mothering instead. They were well-educated, ambitious and likely to be their upwardly mobile husbands' superiors or equals in class background. They encouraged achievement in both girls and boys, even though they themselves were not able to directly model it. I argued that these mothers may have had a distinct influence on the role crossovers that occurred in the 1960s and early 1970s, which culminated in the antiwar movement and feminism.

Now mothers themselves have joined the labor force, and in the middle class we are moving toward a more genuine matrifocality in which women have gained more public respect as people outside of the family. Beyond this, women's maternal attitudes are coming even more to prevail over paternal authoritarianism within the family. That is, fathers are increasingly moving toward a more maternal stance. This should discourage strong gender-typing in children and lead to more egalitarian marriages.

When wives were not employed outside the home, fathers were the only representatives of the outside world that middle-class boys and girls had. Many adult women's attachment to their fathers rests on their fathers having served as a model for them. As more and more mothers work outside the home, women may more directly become models for their daughters and they will be perceived more as mothers and individuals than as wives. Moreover, mothers will be able to act more freely as a caring parent and less as persons constrained by being father's wife.

In a sense the fragility of marriage is changing the context of child-rearing, and middle-class mothers are no longer quite as involved with their children as they used to be. In the 1950s, a frequent media theme was that fathers were absolutely essential to save children from the clutches of their mothers. But as women become less totally psychologically invested in their children, the felt "need" for fathers to "rescue" children should also decline. Although male models are needed, households without "fathers" are not necessarily pathological. Although single mothers are often poor and operate under extreme financial and time pressures, single mothering can be a positive experience for women to the extent that not being a "wife" allows them to act on their own—as an adult. Women without husbands learn to trust their own judgment in a way they may not have when they were wives. They must be themselves. Having a mother who is not a wife is bound to affect children's view of what women are like—they are real people who are also mothers, not wives.

Much of the psychoanalytic account of gender development rests on the assumption of a nuclear family, isolated from other relationships and offering a very distinctive and separate kind of emotional closeness. As individuals become integrated in a wider set of relationships outside of the nuclear unit, the power of this account to define the proper relations between women and men will decrease. Moreover, the psychoanalytic account, both the gynecentric and phallocentric versions, will simply have less relevance because the isolation of women and of the nuclear unit will have decreased. In short, there will be less compulsion to overcome women's psychological power as mothers and to solve it by making mothers into wives.

Supports for Parents.   As things stand now women are not paid equally to men and this is rationalized by the belief that women do not need equal pay because they are dependent wives. We are still rewarding male providers but not female providers. Employers justify paying men more than women on the grounds that they have a family to support, but when a woman is in fact supporting a family, she is not paid more; indeed, she may be considered a less good worker. The deeper truth is that our society rewards men who financially support families but not women who financially support families. Over half the families living below the poverty level are headed by women only.

The labor force participation rate of women with children is now over 60 percent. This represents an increase of more than 50 percent since 1970.[26] Working mothers with and without husbands need day care. Indeed, mothers, working outside the home or not, and their children need day care. Husbands and lovers as child-carers are no overall solution, any more than women being at home alone caring for children full-time is a solution. Out-of-home child care is not something one turns to when mothers "fail"; such care is at least potentially good for not only mothers and fathers but also, and especially, for children.

Sheila Kamerman calls child care an issue for gender equity and for women's solidarity. I agree, good child care arrangements beyond "the couple" are long overdue. The United States is woefully behind other industrialized nations, capitalist and socialist, in the provision of out of home care.[27] In the future, although the actual time a mother spends with her children may be lessened, the control women exercise over child care may be strengthened. This would include working toward equal economic opportunity and wage equity, control of fertility, various child care options, and custody rights in divorce. This would be a kind of matrifocality that is compatible with individualism.

Sylvia Hewlett has written an impassioned plea for recognizing the handicaps under which mothers are placed as they attempt to survive in a competitive economy. Hewlett tends to blame feminism for this. I disagree and have provided a different and more complex picture of feminism—one that shows its "maternal" facet. One must not let her critique of feminism, however, prevent us from taking her description of the desperate need to end the handicaps of working mothers very seriously.[28]

Women in the Public Sphere

Throughout this book I have attempted to justify women's "difference" in terms of an alternative, nonmarket or nonindustrial set of standards, that is, general humanistic standards that de-emphasize difference and hierarchy and emphasize interdependence between women and men. These are the standards that women as mothers have fostered, and if more typically maternal values predominated in the public sphere, idioms of kinship and friendship might begin to take precedence over male-dominated heterosexual relationships and over the male peer group. In the workplace mutual egalitarian respect could counteract the "old boys' network" and the expectations that women workers are merely displaced "wives." If this is to happen, "femininity" as it is currently defined, and the definition of women as wives, must go.

The overall impact women can make in the public sphere may be to introduce a way of interacting that cross-cuts "politics" to some extent and changes men's own approach. The overall result could be that women will be truly included in the category of "people" as opposed to "wives" and that instead of being assimilated to the category of men, women's presence can cause men to alter their own approach.

It is also possible that women can make a direct political difference, but so far the voting gaps between age, class, and race groups are far greater than the voting gap is between genders. The main impediment to women's solidarity with each other is their vested interest in marriage, which forces their economic "class" interests to coincide with their husbands', even as the unwritten rules of marriage penalize women. Exciting as the prospect may be, in view of marriage and the emphasis on couples in this society, it is not likely that women as a group are going to band together to vote as women, but the other side of the coin is that men are also in a position to be influenced by "their" women. As William Goode has pointed out men have been converted to feminism by witnessing discrimination against their "own" wives and daughters.[29] Although I view this proprietary attitude with some ambivalence, conversion by this means is better than no conversion at all.

I do not expect to see a mass movement led by women without men, because many men may join them. Part of feminist movement means supporting increasing individualism; the other aspect is bringing maternal values into the public sphere. Because of men's orientation to economic "rationalism," they may be most likely to join women with regard to issues supporting increasing individualism.

For example, there was little "gender gap" between women and men with regard to the ERA proposal, which was based on minimalist and individualistic assumptions. In spite of earlier reports to the contrary, Ronald Reagan's 1980 anti-ERA stand lost him votes from about equal proportions of male and female supporters of the ERA. Women did indeed vote against Reagan because of the ERA, but so did men.[30] In fact a greater percentage of men than women reported supporting the ERA. Men who favored the ERA were likely to have wives who worked, whereas men who opposed the ERA were married to housewives. Women who were housewives were *not* less supportive of the ERA, however, than were working women. This is probably because many housewives see themselves as potential workers and can identify with employed women.[31] In sum, men are more likely to support measures that fit with individualism for women if their wives work.

With regard to maternal values, the issue on which almost all researchers agree there is a consistent and persistent gender gap is the use of force and violence. Women tend to differ from men in being against aggression, both domestic and foreign. Feminist and nonfeminist women alike were more likely than men to have opposed the Vietnam War, and women are more reluctant than men to prescribe the use of force in the event of urban unrest.[32] In view of the orientational differences between women and men I described earlier, these findings would certainly be expected. Women's more relational stance clearly involves a stance against aggression.

The next largest gender difference occurs with regard to women's tendency to favor policies that regulate and protect consumers, citizens, and the environment. Women's interests in peace and environmental issues coalesce in their strong stands against nuclear power. Finally, there is some tendency for women to vote favorably on so called "compassion" issues, such as spending on social programs to improve social welfare, education and health, but this tendency is cross-cut by voting that shows that women are still more traditional and conservative than men.[33]

In sum, although the differences between the voting and opinion patterns of men and women are relatively small, the differences that do show up reflect women's association with nonaggression and preservation—the maternal or humanizing values. It is likely that child welfare issues, including good day care, will prove to be another cause around which women as a group can rally. Women in executive positions are already concentrated in the human services, and political support for these services (the liberal agenda) should increase their power.

In Conclusion

There is often an implicit assumption among "minimalists" that equality depends on assuming identity of capacities and equal sharing of tasks. I have argued instead that within the larger trend toward role-sharing and role crossovers which I applaud, it is naive to believe that denying all difference will make difference disappear. I have also argued that difference in itself need not produce inequality; it is what we make of gender difference and what we do about it that produces inequality. In my view we must take into account that women bear children and are likely to continue doing so and that women will generally be more involved in early child care than men. If this minimal division of labor is not to penalize women in the public sphere, public supports for child care are necessary.

In the past, women's childbearing has been taken into account by making individual mothers into "wives," dependent on husbands for support. I have deliberately focused on the inequalities of the marriage relationship that juvenilizes women as a counter to the reigning assumption that women's childbearing and child-rearing inevitably causes women's inequality. It is the male-dominated context of women's childbearing and child-rearing that underlies inequality. Women are strong as mothers but made weak by being wives.

Throughout the book I have tried to show how the concrete fact of women's childbearing is related to orientational differences between women and men. Women's greater ability to sustain relationships is not a defect but a virtue. At the same time these orientational differences between men and women are relatively small and they in no way justify confining women to domesticity or to jobs that can somehow be defined as maternal.

Assumptions that women will work outside the home and are both different from men and equal to men are impacting change even as the term *feminism* is less used. Young people today have mothers who work outside the home and who have divorced. These young people have had a different set of experiences and are ready for new definitions and new forms. They are still family-oriented but family does not mean the same thing that it used to.

Neither women nor men are complete rationalists, saying one could live without solidarity with others, but the personal solidarities are more shifting and the individual as community citizen becomes more prominent.

It is probably true that one needs to go through a period of emphasizing the notions of equality, similarity, and individualism before it is possible to study gender difference without playing into the tendency to render women "the lesser." I have tried to specify the nature of difference in a new way—one that does not act as a rationalization for inequality but that locates sources of inequality.

The dialectic within feminist movement between similarity and difference has been with us a long time and will continue. Both emphases are necessary and correct. I have tried to spell out a contemporary relationship between a focus on similarity and difference that I hope will prove healing among us.

Notes

Chapter One

1. Geng, "Requiem for the Women's Movement."
2. See especially Frye, *Politics of Reality,* and more recently, MacKinnon, *Feminism Unmodified.*
3. Chodorow, *Reproduction of Mothering;* and Dinnerstein, *Mermaid and Minotaur.* See also Chodorow, "Feminism and Difference."
4. "Missing Feminist Revolution." See also Harding, "Analytical Categories of Feminist Theory" and *Science Question in Feminism.*
5. Lorde, *Sister Outsider,* p. 110.
6. The concept of role has been criticized by many feminists, most notably Barrie Thorne (see "Gender," and Stacey and Thorne, "Missing Feminist Revolution"). Among other things, Thorne points out that the term *role* masks power differences, but I use the distinction between mother role and wife role precisely to emphasize the differential power the two roles carry. I agree, however, that the term *gender role* as a unitary concept is not useful. I also agree that *role* is not a particularly useful term in describing informal spontaneous interactions, such as children's play, but even at this level *role* is useful because children often act out their perceptions of adult roles, especially those of mother and father, wife and husband.
7. Marxist feminists have analyzed women's situation in terms of the work they do, especially housework. While wives often do housework, I will maintain that inequality does not so much inhere in what women do, as in the nature of the relationship defined by the terms *husband* and *wife.*
8. Gayle Rubin ("Traffic in Women") and Juliet Mitchell (*Psychoanalysis and Feminism*) are feminists who have also analyzed male domi-

nance. They do so from a more phallocentric psychoanalytic perspective. Interestingly enough, they also concluded that the solution to male dominance is shared child care, which they argued would render children bisexual. They have both since changed their views.

9. See Parsons, *Social Structure and Personality*, especially the essays in Part 1. See also Parsons, "The Position of Identity in the General Theory of Action," and Parsons and Bales, *Family Socialization*.

10. I am adopting the idea of using "feminist movement" instead of "*the* feminist movement" from Bell Hooks (see *Feminist Theory*). I hope this usage comes to be widely accepted, because it suggests process and progress rather than a state, and it implies an ongoing stream of feminist thought that includes diversity and contradictions.

Chapter Two

1. Lorber, "Minimalist and Maximalist Feminist Ideologies," cites a lecture given by Stimpson in 1980, entitled "The New Scholarship about Women: The State of the Art," at the City University of New York Graduate Center, New York City, October 6. Stimpson has continued to use this distinction in her lectures up to the present.

2. See Gordon, "Feminism, Reproduction, and the Family."

3. For an excellent description of the vicissitudes of the tension between similarity and difference in gender roles and gender symbolism that goes back to the beginnings of the modern world in the sixteenth century, see Bloch, "Untangling the Roots."

4. Ehrenreich and English, Introduction to *For Her Own Good*.

5. For summaries see Degler, *At Odds;* Ryan, *Womanhood in America*; Rothman, *Woman's Proper Place*.

6. For a good sampling of differing perspectives among feminist historians on the tension between women's rights versus women's culture in the nineteenth century see Walkowitz et al., "Politics and Culture in Women's History."

7. In 1985 the median full-time earnings for women were 65 percent of men's earnings, and 56 percent of women working in the civilian labor force were married.

8. Friedan, *Feminine Mystique;* Rossi, "An Immodest Proposal"; Firestone, *Dialectic of Sex*.

9. See, for example, Bunch, "Lesbians in Revolt." Myron and Bunch, *Lesbianism and the Women's Movement* contains a number of other early lesbian feminist analyses.

10. See "Institution of Sexual Intercourse."

11. For a more recent version of the radical feminist argument against

difference, see Ringelheim, "Women and the Holocaust." Ringelheim describes how she now rejects her emphasis on women's special virtues in caring for one another in a way men did not while imprisoned during the holocaust. She became convinced (apparently by Ti Grace Atkinson) that her focus on difference detracted from a focus on women's oppression and a willingness to fight that oppression. The argument is that if difference exists in the context of oppression (no theory here about causation), to emphasize or point to difference is to valorize oppression. The terms of her argument are so general that it is difficult for me to see its logic. In this book I try to break down difference into two aspects and argue that their relationship to oppression needs to be analyzed separately.

12. Kanter, "Women and the Structure of Organizations."

13. Kessler and McKenna, *Gender*.

14. Weisstein, "'Kinder, Küche, Kirche.'" Lipman-Blumen, *Gender Roles and Power*, pp. 69–98. Unger, *Female and Male;* see especially Chapter 1.

15. Goldberg, *Inevitability of Patriarchy*.

16. In later interviews, de Beauvoir continued to associate femininity with being "secondary," "modest," and "powerless." Asked how we might break out of this vicious circle of "femininity," de Beauvoir acknowledged that there are problems with women's "joining the rat race with men" but that it is necessary to gain power. De Beauvoir never approved of much of anything about women, including motherhood, which she described in *The Second Sex* as passive and debilitating. She also continued to be irritated when she was accused of saying this or that *because* she was a woman (Schwarzer, *After the Second Sex*, especially pp. 115–18). To me this suggests a reluctance to identify with women.

17. Barrett, *Women's Oppression Today*.

18. See especially *Gyn/Ecology*.

19. Rossi, "Biosocial Perspective on Parenting." Smith-Rosenberg, "Female World of Love and Ritual." Bernard, *Female World*. Smith, "Women's Perspective." See also Smith, "Sociology for Women," and Daniels, "Feminist Perspectives."

20. On mothering as a basis for gender difference, see Ruddick, "Maternal Thinking," and Rich, *Of Woman Born*. On mothering as a cause of gender difference, Chodorow, *Reproduction of Mothering;* Keller, "Gender and Science"; Benjamin, "Bonds of Love."

21. Gilligan, *In a Different Voice*.

22. For an excellent discussion of some of the dangers and excesses involved in the difference position, especially with regard to the family, see Stacey, "New Conservative Feminism."

23. Chodorow, "Feminism and Difference."

24. Elshtain seems to come close to this position at times, but I believe her intent is to critique the public sphere by citing the virtues that are now realized only in the private sphere. See "Antigone's Daughters."

25. Wives of course may "mother" their husbands, but when they do, it is in a context of dependency on them.

26. Tiger and Fox, *Imperial Animal*, p. 110.

27. Sacks, *Sisters and Wives*.

28. Rossi makes the point that in this society women's mothering has been subordinated to men's sexuality. She argues that while children are of importance to women in and of themselves, men tend to view children as consequences of or appendages to mating. See "Biosocial Perspective on Parenting."

29. See O'Brien, *Politics of Reproduction*, and "Dialectics of Reproduction."

30. M. O'Brien, *Politics of Reproduction*, p. 50.

31. M. O'Brien, "Dialectics of Reproduction," p. 236.

32. Lévi-Strauss, *Elementary Structures of Kinship*. K. Paige and J. Paige, *Politics of Reproductive Ritual*.

33. M. O'Brien, "Dialectics of Reproduction," p. 235.

34. M. O'Brien, *Politics of Reproduction*, p. 91.

35. Holter, "The Reorganized Patriarchy."

36. Ruddick, "Maternal Thinking."

37. Most notably, Friday, *My Mother/My Self*.

38. Barry, *Female Sexual Slavery*. MacKinnon, *Sexual Harassment*.

39. See, for example, the critique of Rich made by Ferguson, "Patriarchy, Sexual Identity."

40. Ti Grace Atkinson, "Institution of Sexual Intercourse."

41. Wittig, *Les Guerillères*, and especially "One Is Not Born a Woman."

42. Shaktini makes this clear in "Displacing the Phallic Subject."

43. Allen, "Motherhood."

44. Pogrebin, *Growing Up Free*, p. 40.

45. Ryan, *Womanhood in America*, pp. 337–39.

46. Lamphere, "Review Essay," p. 622.

47. Lloyd, "Yoruba of Nigeria."

48. D. O'Brien, "Female Husbands." For instance, over forty African populations have the status of "female husbands." While woman-woman marriages are often a mechanism for a wealthy patriarch to hold on to valuable resources in the absence of male heirs, in those cases where a woman moves into an extradomestic status of high prestige on her own, such as political leader or diviner, she must take on the social role of "husband" and head of a household. Even though most female husbands are not powerful in their own right, it would be anomalous for those who have power to be in the role of "wife."

49. About five out of six men and about three out of four women remarry after a divorce (Cherlin, *Marriage, Divorce, Remarriage*). Men typically spend less time separated and divorced than women. White males spend more time married than any other group, and black females the least. (Espenshade, "Marriage Trends in America," especially pp. 210–12.)

50. Between 1940 and 1980 the proportion of births outside marriage increased from less than 4 percent to over 18 percent and continues to rise. This increase in births to never-married women is not the result of an increased rate of childbearing by unmarried women, however, but mainly the result of an increase in the number of unmarried women "at risk" of bearing a child. Between 1970 and 1979 the number of nonmarital births increased by roughly 50 percent, while the nonmarital fertility rate went up by only 5.3 percent. (Espenshade, "Marriage Trends in America.")

Chapter Three

1. *Ms.* magazine named Gilligan "Woman of the Year" in January 1984.

2. Linda K. Kerber, "Some Cautionary Words for Historians," in "On *In a Different Voice:* An Interdisciplinary Forum," *Signs* 11 (1986): 304–33 (pp. 304–10).

3. Catherine G. Greeno and Eleanor E. Maccoby, "How Different Is the 'Different Voice,'" in ibid., pp. 310–16; and Zella Luria, "A Methodological Critique," in ibid., pp. 316–21. Several suggest that the differences Gilligan is talking about may relate to class, not gender. Others maintain that in studies of actual behaviors, as opposed to stated orientations, the differences do not show up so clearly. It depends on the measure. In my view the differences are blatantly apparent if one considers gender differences in violent crime and sexual assault, to take an extreme example.

4. Stack, "The Culture of Gender: Men and Women of Color," in ibid., pp. 321–24.

5. See "Reply by Carol Gilligan," in ibid., pp. 324–33, especially p. 328. Philosophical and methodological critiques of Gilligan may be found in the entire issue of *Social Research*, 50, no. 3 (1983).

6. For a fuller discussion of the various stages and transitions in women's moral development, see Gilligan's article, "In a Different Voice."

7. Belenky et al., *Women's Ways of Knowing*. Significantly enough the authors report that mothers were very often the empowering persons in the lives of the women they interviewed.

8. Gutmann, "Female Ego Styles." Bakan, *Quality of Human Existence*. The instrumental-expressive distinction was first explicitly formulated by Parsons, *Social System*, and by Parsons and Shils, *General Theory*, pt. 2. Partially because of the development of his four-dimensional conception of action space, the definitions of instrumental and expressive

were somewhat altered in Parsons, Bales, and Shils, *Working Papers*. Throughout all these works the terms were never defined clearly, and Parsons tackled the definitional problem only indirectly by trying to link the concepts with other elements in the scheme. Later he dropped these terms almost entirely as analytical variables as he developed further his fourfold conception of action space: adaptation, goal attainment, integration, and latent pattern maintenance.

9. Carlson, "Sex Differences in Ego Functioning," and "Understanding Women."

10. Bakan, *Quality of Human Existence*, p. 15.

11. Carlson, "Understanding Women."

12. Carlson, "Sex Differences in Ego Functioning."

13. Jeanne Block, "Conceptions of Sex Role."

14. Finigan, "Effects of Token Representation."

15. The term *expressive* is something of a misnomer but not entirely. Perhaps a better term for what its definition describes would be *relational*. Nevertheless, I will continue to use *expressive* along with *relational* because I do not want to lose entirely the connotation of "feeling" that expressiveness carries. Relationships themselves cannot be encompassed or thought about without taking feeling into account. Expressive symbolism and expressive patterns are used to define relationships when they are the primary focus of interest.

16. When Parsons applies the terms *expressive* and *instrumental* to family roles, he explicitly does not see them as carrying differential power. Rather, he treats the difference between instrumental and expressive as descriptive of the gender axis in the family; he treats the generational difference between parents and children as the power axis. In spite of this apparent symmetry, however, Parsons makes clear that the female role is a major locus of strain within the family, in part because the culture itself has such a strong instrumental bias.

17. Lewin, in "Psychological Measures," claims that *instrumental* and *expressive* are simply "euphemisms for 'dominant' and 'subordinate'" (p. 195). This distorts Parsons's position, as I will try to show in the discussion to follow. (See also note 16.) In the rush to discover and repudiate sexism in all past "scientific" conceptualizations, we may find ourselves prematurely abandoning exactly that which requires examination. The problem is not to start from scratch but to examine in new ways what "is known."

18. Hochschild, *Managed Heart*, pp. 164–65.

19. Gough and Heilbrun, *Joint Manual*.

20. The word *obliging* and perhaps others may seem to some to connote a yielding acquiescence, but perhaps only from an instrumental

point of view. Being helpful does not necessarily make one a doormat. When one looks at intercorrelations, men are more likely than women to see relational or expressive traits as being associated with passivity and dependence.

21. Bennett and Cohen, "Men and Women," p. 125.

22. For the detailed report of this study, see M. Johnson et al., "Expressiveness Re-evaluated."

23. In these analyses we excluded the items chosen to represent the negative versions of each of the three dimensions under investigation.

24. This is only one of several ways that our analysis differs from the analysis Alice Echols attributes to what she calls "cultural feminists." See "New Feminism of Yin and Yang."

25. On the multidimensionality of masculinity and femininity, see E. Lewis, *Developing Woman's Potential*, pp. 69–71. For an excellent summary of earlier scales, see Constantinople, "Masculinity-Femininity."

26. Bem, "Measurement of Psychological Androgyny."

27. Spence and Helmreich, *Masculinity and Femininity.*

28. Jones, Chernhovetz, and Hansson, "Enigma of Androgyny"; K. Morgan, "Androgyny"; Pedhazur and Tetenbaum, "Bem Sex Role Inventory"; Locksley and Cotten, "Psychological Androgyny." ·

29. Mary Daly, "Qualitative Leap Beyond Patriarchal Religion," expressed this idea many years ago in her comment that androgyny seems to mean combining John Wayne and Brigitte Bardot. The particular personalities used in the analogy need to be constantly updated, but the idea remains the same: a "man's man" and a "man's toy" combined in the same person can hardly solve the problem of the devaluation of women.

30. Bem, "Sex Role Adaptability."

31. For a discussion of these other studies, see Gill et al., "Measuring Gender Differences."

32. The prevalence of the belief that "male equals human" was documented early on by Broverman et al., "Sex Role Stereotypes."

33. Bem, "Gender Schema Theory."

34. See also Eichenbaum with Orbach, *What Do Women Want?*

35. For the annals of not-so-trivial trivia, I must note that Bardwick and Douvan, "Ambivalence," attribute this quote to Talcott Parsons in a 1942 article. This is an error of course. This statement in no way reflects Parsons's thinking in the article cited or in any other article of his.

36. L. Rubin, *Women of a Certain Age*, especially the chapter "Who Am I, The Elusive Self."

37. Gottfried, "Feminism and College Educated Women."

38. J. Miller, *New Psychology of Women*, especially p. 89.

39. See Stockard and Wood, "Myth of Female Underachievement."

40. Vanek, "Household Work."

41. I am indebted to Hanne Haavind of the University of Oslo for this illustration.

42. Gove and Hughes, "Sex Differences in Physical Health."

43. Maccoby and Jacklin, *Psychology of Sex Differences.*

44. Martin, "Maternal and Paternal Abuse."

45. Frodi, Macauley, and Thome, "Are Women Always Less Aggressive?"

46. Maccoby and Jacklin, "Sex Differences in Aggression." See also Maccoby, *Social Development*, p. 216. Here she reiterates that "the tendency in males to be more aggressive than females is perhaps the most firmly established gender difference and is a characteristic that transcends culture." For a review of gender and aggression studies, see White, "Sex and Gender Issues." White emphasizes the role of learning and the variability of aggression depending on the definition of the situation. White suggests that women and men do not "really" differ much in aggression, perhaps because she also accepts the view that male "aggression" somehow explains male dominance.

47. Newton, *Maternal Emotions.*

48. Barbara Ehrenreich suggests that this new emphasis may be associated with preserving class boundaries and consumerism. See "Feminist's View."

49. M. Goodwin and C. Goodwin, "Children's Arguing."

Chapter Four

1. For other summaries and critiques, see the articles in part 2 of Trebilcot, ed., *Mothering.* See also Gottlieb, "Mothering and Reproduction of Power."

2. Although Chodorow uses the argument relating male dominance to women's mothering in *Reproduction of Mothering*, it is not the central theme of her book. The hypothesis was, however, an important theme in Chodorow's earlier work, and she developed a slightly different version of it in "Feminism and Difference."

3. See Mitchell, *Psychoanalysis and Feminism*, p. 120.

4. Klein, *Psychoanalysis of Children*, p. 338. See also "Early Stages of Oedipus Conflict."

5. Horney, "Dread of Woman," especially pp. 145–46.

6. Karen Horney, "Flight from Womanhood," especially pp. 176–77.

7. Mead, "Freud's View of Female Psychology," especially p. 97.

8. Before Dinnerstein's book, the best popular work that clearly attempted to relate human institutional arrangements, including the exclu-

sion of women from male affairs, to men's fear and envy of women was *The Dangerous Sex* by H. R. Hays, first published in 1964. Hays argues that social institutions in societies from the most primitive to the most modern have been designed to defend men against their fears of women by circumscribing, regulating, and containing women. He ends with a plea not for equal parenting but for men to abandon their magical approach to women, to accept their existential anguish, and to realize that the menace of the female lies within themselves (p. 283, 1972 ed.).

9. Dinnerstein, *Mermaid and Minotaur,* p. 95.

10. In their article, "Fantasy of the Perfect Mother," Chodorow and Contratto contend that many feminists display primary process thinking with regard to mothers. Feminists have tended to talk either about the malevolence of mothers or they have overidealized motherhood. In either case, "the fantasy of the perfect mother" underlies these responses.

11. W. Miller, "Lower Class Culture," especially p. 270.

12. Rohrer and Edmonson, *Eighth Generation,* pp. 162–63.

13. Parsons, "Certain Primary Sources and Patterns of Aggression in the Social Structure of the Western World," in his *Essays in Sociological Theory,* pp. 298–322.

14. Fiedler, *Return of Vanishing American.*

15. J. Whiting, Kluckhohn, and Anthony, "Male Initiation Rites," and Burton and J. Whiting, "Absent Father."

16. Bacon, Child, and Barry, "Cross-Cultural Study."

17. B. Whiting, "Sex Identity Conflict."

18. Hartley, "Sex-role Pressures."

19. David and Brannon, eds., *Forty-nine Percent Majority.*

20. Chodorow's earlier article, "Being and Doing," discusses male misogyny more from the standpoint of the fear and envy hypothesis than from the tenuous gender identity standpoint.

21. Stockard and Johnson, "Social Origins of Male Dominance."

22. Money and Ehrhardt, *Man and Woman.*

23. Stoller, "Freud's Concept of Bisexuality."

24. B. Whiting, "Sex Identity Conflict."

25. For a more detailed discussion and critique of Pleck, see my review in *American Journal of Sociology.*

26. See especially Chodorow, "Feminism and Difference," pp. 13–14.

27. See especially M. Johnson, "Fathers, Mothers, and Sex Typing."

28. Tooley, "Johnny, I Hardly Knew Ye."

29. See chapter "The Critique of Masculinity," in Eisenstein, *Contemporary Feminist Thought,* pp. 96–101, especially p. 101.

30. Keller, "Gender and Science" and "Feminism and Science"; see also *Reflections on Gender and Science.*

31. Benjamin, "Oedipal Riddle," p. 209.
32. Keller, "Gender and Science."
33. Benjamin, "Bonds of Love."
34. Benjamin, "Bonds of Love," p. 167.
35. Benjamin suggests that mothers may be making differentiation harder for their children because their lack of autonomous roles outside of the family gives them little else in which to invest except their children. Mothers' lack of autonomous roles may make it difficult for mothers to tolerate and encourage their children's differentiation. Benjamin's idea has been developed slightly differently by Philipson in "Narcissism and Mothering." She argues that the narcissistic personality of today is a result of the situation in which women mothered in the 1950s. These mothers were so frustrated by their isolation and the heavy expectations placed on them that they were unable to be sensitive to the child's need for autonomy and could not empathize with the child, but responded instead to the child in terms of their own needs. How women's isolation in the home might have affected the quality of their mothering is a complex issue and one that must be kept analytically separate from that of how the mother is perceived by the child. Benjamin's brief remarks tend to confuse the two.
36. Benjamin, "Oedipal Riddle," p. 220.
37. Peterfreund, "Psychoanalytic Conceptualizations of Infancy." See also Greenberg and S. Mitchell, *Object Relations in Psychoanalytic Theory,* and Horner, "Psychic Life of the Young Infant."
38. Stern, *Interpersonal World of the Infant,* especially p. 10.
39. For a discussion of various developmental approaches to the emergence of self during infancy, see Harter, "Developmental Perspectives."
40. Chodorow discusses some of these issues in "Feminism and Difference."

Chapter Five

1. To say that women have been primarily responsible for mothering in all societies does not mean that women have regularly mothered their own biological children or that all women have mothered. For example, in the early days of capitalism and urban industrialization in France and other countries, mothers in the middle and working classes gave their babies over to the care of wet nurses in the country (see Badinter, *Mother Love*).
2. For a discussion of the degree to which the kibbutz experiment did not begin with similar roles for women and men, see Blasi, review of *Gender and Culture* by Spiro.
3. Chodorow, *Reproduction of Mothering.*

4. Rossi, "Biosocial Perspective on Parenting." Others who agree with Rossi's point of view include Dan and Newton, comments in "Considering a Biosocial Perspective on Parenting."

5. Janet Sayers does this in *Biological Politics*.

6. See Rossi, "Gender and Parenthood," especially p. 15. See also Dan and Newton, comments in "Considering a Biosocial Perspective on Parenting."

7. See for example, Fausto-Sterling, *Myths of Gender;* Bleier, *Science and Gender;* Lowe and Hubbard, eds., *Woman's Nature;* and Sayers, *Biological Politics.* These books differ in perspective, but they all basically argue against biological determinism while they at the same time carefully examine biological factors. Sayers argues for a middle position within feminism between "biological essentialism" and what she calls "social constructionism." The other three books are more suspicious of biological influence but move us toward a more complex view of the interactions between body, mind, and culture. Bleier, for example, in her chapter on the brain points to the remarkable flexibility of the human brain and argues that culture constrains the brain far more than the brain sets limits to culture.

8. See the group of articles by radical feminists in Trebilcot, ed., *Mothering.* These include Allen, "Motherhood"; Valeska, "If All Else Fails"; and Polatnick, "Why Men Don't Rear Children." Something of this same position is also taken by the Marxist-feminist Gimenez in "Feminism, Pronatalism, and Motherhood."

9. Firestone, *Dialectic of Sex.*

10. Rossi, "Transition to Parenthood."

11. Bane, *Here To Stay;* Cherlin, *Marriage, Divorce, Remarriage.*

12. See Fairbairn, *Object-Relations Theory of Personality,* and Guntrip, *Personality Structure and Human Interaction.* See also, Greenberg and Mitchell, *Object Relations in Psychoanalytic Theory.*

13. See Parsons with White, "The Link Between Character and Society," in Parsons, *Social Structure and Personality,* pp. 183–235; and Horkheimer, "Authority and the Family."

14. Cf. Eisenstein, *Contemporary Feminist Thought,* p. 91. Eisenstein appears to misunderstand Freud on this point.

15. Person takes a similar view in "Sexuality as Mainstay of Identity." As I will show in Chapter 8, psychoanalytic theory tends to define what we now call gender in terms of sexuality. This conflation was very basic in Freud's thinking and ultimately renders psychoanalysis a "dangerous doctrine" even in the hands of those with benign intentions.

16. Chodorow, "Feminism and Difference."

17. Flax, "Mother-Daughter Relationships," emphasizes the problematic aspects of mothers' ties to daughters. In another view, L. Hoffman, "Early Childhood Experiences," claims that "girls need a little maternal rejection if they are to become independently competent and self-confident."

18. Chodorow stresses heterosexuality even more than my account of her work might suggest. She argues that women's heterosexuality is triangular and requires a third person—a child—for its structural and emotional completion, whereas for men the heterosexual bond alone is sufficient. My account will question all of this.

19. Rossi, "Biosocial Perspective on Parenting."

20. Sayers, *Biological Politics*, pp. 149, 161.

21. "Reply by Nancy Chodorow," especially p. 507.

22. See Chodorow, "Being and Doing," especially pp. 270–86; and "Family Structure and Feminine Personality."

23. See Lamphere, "Review Essay: Anthropology," especially p. 622.

24. Young, "Male Gender Identity," argues that Chodorow does collapse these categories. I take the view that Chodorow in making the relational-nonrelational distinction between women and men does not imply that women are by definition inferior. She suggests that their relationality connects them with domesticity. This does not necessarily mean "inferiority," although it certainly means that in middle-class white culture. See Strathern, "Domesticity and the Denigration of Women."

25. Chodorow, *Reproduction of Mothering*, p. 10.

26. Parsons, "Social Structure and the Development of Personality," *Social Structure and Personality*, pp. 78–111, especially p. 91.

27. For an excellent discussion of the drive-focused theories of Marcuse and Brown (utilized by Dinnerstein) versus the object relations approach Chodorow favors, see Chodorow, "Beyond Drive Theory." Parsons's work is at a higher level of abstraction and encompasses both the "drive" and the "object relations" aspects of Freud's thinking.

28. Rossi discusses this permissiveness in "Maternalism, Sexuality, and New Feminism."

29. Maccoby and Jacklin, *Psychology of Sex Differences*, pp. 313, 201.

30. For the association of maternal warmth with conscience in children, see Yarrow, Campbell, and Burton, *Child Rearing*, p. 103. For the lack of differentiation by gender, see, for example, Stayton, Hogan, and Ainsworth, "Infant Obedience and Maternal Behavior," especially p. 1058.

31. Maccoby and Jacklin, "Gender Segregation in Childhood."

32. Fagot, "Beyond the Reinforcement Principle."

33. Maccoby, "Social Groupings in Childhood."

34. Lever, "Sex Differences in Games."

35. Maltz and Borker, "Male-Female Miscommunication."

36. M. Goodwin, "Directive-Response Speech Sequences."

37. Fagot, "Beyond the Reinforcement Principle."

38. Fagot and Leinbach, "Play Styles in Early Childhood," especially p. 113.

39. Fagot and Hagan, "Aggression in Toddlers."

40. Best, *We've All Got Scars*, pp. 71–87.

41. Eisenhart and Holland, "Learning Gender from Peers," especially p. 322.

42. Carter and McCloskey, "Peers and Sex-Typed Behavior."

43. Thorne, "Girls and Boys Together."

44. J. Whalen and M. Whalen, "'Doing Gender.'" For "rules" of conversational turn-taking, see West and Zimmerman, "Small Insults." For a discussion of the conversation-sustaining work that women do, see Fishman, "Interaction: The Work Women Do."

45. Esposito, "Sex Differences in Children's Conversation."

46. M. Goodwin, "Directive-Response Speech Sequences," especially pp. 170–72. M. Goodwin and C. Goodwin, "Children's Arguing."

47. Ullian, "Regression in Service of Male Ego."

48. M. Goodwin, "Directive-Response Speech Sequences," pp. 170–72.

49. Kinsey, Pomeroy, and Martin, *Sexual Behavior in Human Male*, p. 168.

50. Finkelhor, *Sexually Victimized Children*, p. 91.

51. See Pleck's discussion of this in "Men's Power," p. 424.

52. Brownmiller, *Against Our Will*. See also Griffin, "Rape."

53. J. Newson and E. Newson, *Four Years Old*.

54. Quoted in Unger, *Female and Male*, p. 427. When I tell this story in class, it often evokes the response from males that this surely shows me to be a man-hater. I believe it indicates that men have not yet realized that the fear of rape confines and restricts women as do "the rules" that blame rape on women failing to protect themselves rather than on the men doing the raping.

55. For acquaintance rape, see Kanin and Parcell, "Sexual Aggression." See also Kanin, "Date Rape." For rape in marriage, see Russell, *Rape in Marriage;* and Finkelhor and Yllo, *License to Rape*.

56. Alder, "Self-Reported Sexual Aggression."

57. Kanin, "Date Rapists."

58. MacKinnon, "Toward Feminist Jurisprudence." See also "An Agenda for Theory."

59. Russell, *Sexual Exploitation*, especially p. 35.
60. See especially West and Zimmerman, "Small Insults," and Fishman, "Interaction: The Work Women Do."
61. Pleck, "Men's Power," p. 424. See also Lehne, "Homophobia Among Men."
62. Herek, "On Heterosexual Masculinity."
63. L. Rubin, *Just Friends*. See especially pp. 63–64.

Chapter Six

1. As more research is done on fathers and infants and as theories concerning "stages" in general become more questionable (see Chapter 4), this distinction may become less meaningful. But those who employ psychoanalytic categories assume that the oedipal period initiates the significance of father for children of both sexes. In truth the father's salience in matters pertaining to sexuality seems to occur over and over from infancy to maturity and beyond. I have brought together the research on this in the following articles: M. Johnson, "Sex Role Learning in Nuclear Family," "Fathers, Mothers, and Sex Typing," "Heterosexuality, Male Dominance, and Father Image," and "Fathers and 'Femininity' in Daughters."

2. Without explicitly mentioning male dominance, Maccoby and Jacklin observe that the mother-son relationship is not the prototype of adult male-female relations (note the shift in which gender comes first), commenting that "clearly there are instances in which the role demands of parenthood (especially motherhood) are not consistent with habitual male-female interaction patterns" (*Psychology of Sex Differences*, p. 306).

3. Moscovici, *Society Against Nature*.

4. For a summary, see Deaux, "A Decade's Research on Gender."

5. Radin, "Childrearing Fathers in Intact Families," part 1.

6. For fathers feeling more responsibility toward male children, see Gilbert, Hanson, and Davis, "Parental Role Responsibilities," and Fagot, "Influence of Sex of Child." For fathers' preference for male offspring, see Hoffman, "Changes in Family Roles." For divorced fathers' greater tendency to maintain contact with sons, see Hetherington, "Divorce: A Child's Perspective."

7. Margolin and Patterson, "Differential Consequences."

8. For differences in punishment, see Finkelhor, "Sexual Climate in Families." For mothers' punishment styles, see Bronfenbrenner, "Familial Antecedents."

9. For a summary of the father-infant research, see Parke and Tinsley, "Father's Role in Infancy"; Pedersen, ed., *Father-Infant Relationship;*

Parke, *Fathers;* and Ricks, "Father-Infant Interactions." Specifically, for the tendency of fathers, in contrast to mothers, to withdraw from daughters, see M. Lamb and J. Lamb, "Father-Infant Relationship."

10. C. Hoffman et al., "Comparison of Interactions."

11. For a comparison of gender-stereotyped attitudes, see J. Rubin, Provenzano, and Luria, "Eye of Beholder." For a comparison of encouragement of gender-stereotyped toys and play, see Fagot, "Influence of Sex of Child." See also Langlois and Downs, "Mothers, Fathers, and Peers."

A study designed to determine whether or not fathers treated infants differentially found they did so with regard to physical closeness and discipline and control with twelve-month-old infants (Snow, Jacklin, and Maccoby, "Sex-of-Child Differences").

While most of the studies I am describing refer to the father's behavior, I do not mean to imply that fathers cause differentiation. Male and female infants may in fact be different and their differences in preferences may be able to be reinforced positively or negatively. What psychologists are trying to measure in individuals are often pale reflections of social structural phenomena relating to gender and generation, which cannot be captured when one uses gender-neutral measures.

12. A. Heilbrun, *Human Sex Role Behavior,* pp. 161–62.

13. For studies showing greater paternal differentiation, see Jeanne Block, "Conceptions of Sex Role." For differentiation in teaching situations, see Jeanne Block, "Socialization Influences on Personality Development," and "The Pinks and the Blues." For study on parents of toddler children, see Fagot, "Influence of Sex of Child." For fathers' tendency to comfort daughters, see Rothbart and Maccoby, "Parents' Differential Reactions." For fathers' tendency to protect daughters from failure, see Osofsky and O'Connell, "Parent-Child Interaction."

14. Radin, "Role of the Father."

15. Goodenough, "Interest in Persons."

16. Bronstein, "Mothers' and Fathers' Behaviors."

17. McBroom, "Parental Relationships."

18. Bacon and Ashmore, "Mothers and Fathers Categorize Descriptions."

19. Jack Block, Von der Lippe, and Jeanne Block, "Sex Role and Socialization Patterns."

20. Kohlberg and Zigler, "Impact of Cognitive Maturity."

21. Kundsin, ed., *Women and Success.*

22. Contratto, "Father's Presence."

23. Droppleman and Schaefer, "Boys' and Girls' Reports," and Elder and Bowerman, "Family Structure and Child-Rearing Patterns."

24. A. Parsons, "Oedipus Complex."

25. Roberts, Kline, and Gagnon, *Family Life and Sexual Learning*, Vol. 1. See also Kaats and Davis, "Sexual Behavior of College Students."

26. I thank Benton Johnson for making the questionnaires available to me for this analysis. The original research is described in Langford, "Religion and Occupational Choice."

27. For research on touch, see Jourard and Robin, "Self-Disclosure and Touching." For the study on physical affection between parents and children, see Barber and Thomas, "Fathers' and Mothers' Supportive Behavior."

28. Finkelhor, "Sexual Climate in Families."

29. Parke and Sawin, "Children's Privacy."

30. Kanin, "Date Rapists," especially p. 227.

31. Goodenough, "Interest in Persons."

32. Ehrensaft, "Dual Parenting," p. 326.

33. Burlingham, "Preoedipal Infant-Father Relationship."

34. It is, of course, misleading to apply the terms *homosexual* and *heterosexual* to individuals, because it implies that there are two distinct types of people. Alan Bell, one of the authors of the book under discussion, in an earlier article, "Research in Homosexuality," discussed the myriad ways in which homosexuals differ from one another sexually, not to mention nonsexually. More recently Robert Stoller has affirmed this diversity even more strongly to the point of saying that there is no such thing as homosexuality: "There are *the* homosexualities and they are as varied in etiology, dynamics, and appearance as the heterosexualities." See the chapter "Psychoanalytic 'Research' on Homosexuality" in *Observing the Erotic Imagination*, especially pp. 171–72. For the purposes of this study, however, the researchers agreed on a procedure based on both feelings and behaviors, which divided the sample into clearly differentiated groups.

35. Bell, Weinberg, and Hammersmith, *Sexual Preference*, p. 190.

36. Bell, Weinberg, and Hammersmith, *Sexual Preference*, pp. 188 and 189.

37. M. Johnson, "Heterosexuality, Male Dominance, and Father Image."

38. Bene, "Genesis of Male Homosexuality," especially p. 812. Regarding Bene's distinction, although being married is no guarantee that the individual is heterosexual, it is reasonable to assume that he is heterosexual or bisexual.

39. Apperson and McAdoo, "Parental Factors in Childhood of Homosexuals"; Stephan, "Parental Relationships and Early Social Experiences";

Saghir and Robins, *Male and Female Homosexuality;* and Evans, "Childhood Parental Relationships."

40. Bell, Weinberg, and Hammersmith, *Sexual Preference,* p. 44.

41. Ibid.; see path diagram for white males in appendix.

42. Stoller, *Sex and Gender,* Vol. 2.

43. Kaye et al., "Homosexuality in Women." These researchers found, contrary to their expectations, that the mothers of the lesbians did not differ markedly from their counterparts in the control group. The authors report, however, "When we turn to the fathers . . . we find a significantly contrasting picture, for they seem to be an alien breed in contrast to the control fathers" (p. 629). See also Saghir and Robins, *Male and Female Homosexuality.*

44. Wolff, *Love Between Women.* Bene, "Genesis of Female Homosexuality." Loney, "Family Dynamics in Homosexual Women"; Thompson et al., "Parent-Child Relationships and Sexual Identity"; and M. Johnson et al., "Women's Perceptions of Parents."

45. Bell, Weinberg, and Hammersmith, *Sexual Preference.* See path analysis for white females in the Appendix. The data do not show that "inadequate" fathers cause lesbianism but may indicate instead that lesbians view their fathers as inadequate.

46. For further discussion of parental identification and girls, see M. Johnson, "Sex Role Learning in Nuclear Family," and A. Heilbrun, *Human Sex Role Behavior,* pp. 132–66.

47. Bell, Weinberg, and Hammersmith, *Sexual Preference,* pp. 136–37.

48. Bene, "Genesis of Female Homosexuality," especially p. 133. Wolff, *Love Between Women.*

49. Conversation with Marilyn Frye, 1985.

50. Bell, Weinberg, and Hammersmith, *Sexual Preference,* p. 183.

51. This is the stance taken in Chafetz, et al., *Who's Queer?*

52. Harry, *Gay Children Grown Up.*

53. M. Johnson, "Sex Role Learning in Nuclear Family."

54. Winch, "Oedipus Hypothesis."

55. Alfred Heilbrun, in *Human Sex Role Behavior,* reports that "within the nuclear family configuration, a daughter's primary identification with a stereotypically masculine father has been found to correlate positively with adjustment with femininity and curiously with depression in the daughter." Perhaps the depression is a response to being a well-adjusted girl in a male-dominant society.

Chapter Seven

1. See Mitchell, *Psychoanalysis and Feminism*, and "On Freud and the Sexes." For a similar version of this section set in a somewhat different context, see M. Johnson, "Reproducing Male Dominance."

2. Mitchell, "On Freud and the Sexes," p. 36.

3. G. Rubin ("Traffic in Women") provides a more anthropologically sophisticated discussion of "the exchange of women."

4. Mitchell, "On Freud and the Sexes," p. 36.

5. Stoller, "Freud's Concept of Bisexuality."

6. Sheleff, *Generations Apart*.

7. Zilboorg, "Masculine and Feminine," especially p. 288.

8. Freud, *Civilization and Its Discontents*, p. 19. This statement is made in a context that makes one expect him to say "a mother's protection," but he does not. Real life for Freud begins with father.

9. Parsons, "Family Structure and the Socialization of the Child" in Parsons and Bales, *Family Socialization*, pp. 35–131. See also Parsons, "Social Structure and the Development of Personality" in his *Social Structure and Personality*, pp. 78–111.

10. Fischer and Watson, "Explaining the Oedipus Conflict."

11. Rush, "Freudian Cover-Up." Masson, *Assault on Truth*.

12. On this see Masson, "Persecution and Expulsion of Jeffrey Masson."

13. Bonaparte, Freud, and Kris, eds., *Letters of Wilhelm Fliess*.

14. Russell, *Sexual Exploitation*, pp. 177–214, especially p. 186. Finkelhor, *Sexually Victimized Children*, p. 88.

15. Russell, *Sexual Exploitation*, p. 189.

16. Finkelhor, *Sexually Victimized Children*, p. 101. For research on problems with intimacy, see Meiselman, *Incest*; Herman, *Father-Daughter Incest*. For alienation of incest victims from mothers, see Herman, *Father-Daughter Incest*.

17. Armstrong, *Kiss Daddy Goodnight*.

18. Foucault, *History of Sexuality*.

19. Mitchell, *Women, The Longest Revolution*, pp. 295–313, especially p. 308.

20. Herman, *Father-Daughter Incest*, p. 125.

21. Gelinas, "Negative Effects of Incest."

22. Adams-Tucker and Adams, "Role of Father," p. 230.

23. Gordon and O'Keefe, "Incest as Family Violence," especially pp. 32–33.

24. Gelinas, "Negative Effects of Incest."

25. Finkelhor, *Sexually Victimized Children*, pp. 50–51.

26. For many of these thoughts on the romance novel, I am indebted

to an unpublished paper by Marcia Stille, a graduate student in Interdisciplinary Studies at the University of Oregon.

27. A. Heilbrun, *Human Sex Role Behavior*, pp. 161–62.

28. Radway, *Reading the Romance*, p. 125. Radway interviewed a sample of women readers of romance novels about what they got out of them.

29. Rush, "Sexual Abuse of Children," p. 71.

30. Benjamin, "End of Internalization," especially note on p. 60.

31. Bieber, "Clinical Aspects of Male Homosexuality."

32. Freud, "Psychogenesis of Homosexuality in a Woman," pp. 145–46nn.

33. For summaries of these studies see M. Johnson, "Heterosexuality, Male Dominance, and Father Image."

34. Tripp, *Homosexual Matrix*.

35. Harry, *Gay Children Grown Up*.

36. Freud, "Psychogenesis of Homosexuality in a Woman," p. 135.

37. Gayle Rubin quotes these statements in a footnote in "Traffic in Women," p. 202.

38. For a good discussion of the controlling function of the deviance label with respect to lesbians, see Zita, "Historical Amnesia and Lesbian Continuum." Zita's comment is one among several excellent commentaries on Adrienne Rich's ideas concerning a lesbian continuum contained in *Signs* 7 (1981). See Ferguson, Zita, and Addelson, "Compulsory Heterosexuality and Lesbian Existence."

39. Snitow, Stansell, and Thompson, eds., *Powers of Desire*, p. 34.

Chapter Eight

1. Mitchell, *Psychoanalysis and Feminism*; G. Rubin, "Traffic in Women." Rubin repudiates her position explicitly in "Thinking Sex," p. 307. Mitchell repudiates her position indirectly in the last essay in her *Women, The Longest Revolution*, p. 307.

2. The material in the remainder of this section (pp. 187–95) draws from my article "Reproducing Male Dominance."

3. For a good statement and partial critique of Freud's concept of bisexuality, see Stoller, "Freud's Concept of Bisexuality."

4. For several passages referring to parental identification, see Burlingham, "Preoedipal Infant-Father Relationship," especially pp. 26–27.

5. Quoted in Burlingham, "Preoedipal Infant-Father Relationship," p. 27.

6. For example, in "Female Sexuality" (p. 53), Freud says, "In this the complete identity of the pre-Oedipus phase in boys and girls is recog-

nized, and the girl's sexual (phallic) activity towards her mother is affirmed and substantiated by observations."

7. Freud, "Femininity," p. 87.

8. Freud, "Female Sexuality," p. 51.

9. Quoted by Mitchell from Freud's "Femininity" in her *Psychoanalysis and Feminism*, p. 117n.

10. Rossi cites this in "Biosocial Perspective on Parenting," especially p. 17.

11. Schafer, "Freud's Psychology of Women."

12. Chodorow, *Reproduction of Mothering*, p. 165.

13. Mitchell, *Psychoanalysis and Feminism*, p. 128.

14. Horney, "Flight from Womanhood."

15. Chodorow, *Reproduction of Mothering*, pp. 115–17.

16. Quoted by Burlingham, "Preoedipal Infant-Father Relationship," p. 27.

17. Mitchell, *Psychoanalysis and Feminism*, p. 56.

18. See Chodorow, *Reproduction of Mothering*. She says, for example, "A second assumpton is that sexual orientation and mode define gender. A little girl is a little man or boy because she loves a woman, and her sexuality is active and clitoral. 'Changing sex,' as Freud puts it means giving up her clitoris and her activity" (p. 147). And again in parentheses she says, "for psychoanalysts, femininity *means* genital heterosexuality" (p. 111).

19. G. Rubin, "Traffic in Women," p. 199.

20. Mitchell, *Women, The Longest Revolution*, p. 308.

21. G. Rubin, "Thinking Sex," p. 307.

22. Money and Ehrhardt, *Man and Woman*.

23. See chapter 7, "Minimizing Versus Maximizing Sex Differences," in Money, *Love and Love Sickness*. For Money, gender identity and gender role are two sides of the same coin, which he refers to as Gender-Identity/Role or G-I/R. In his terms, G-I/R definitely includes heterosexuality, and he speaks against those feminists who assume that gender identity is nothing but a matter of declaring oneself male or female (pp. 87–88). He excludes passivity or submission from the role, however. He has little conception of the rootedness of male dominance in social structure and simply pronounces it "obsolete."

24. Stoller, "Freud's Concept of Bisexuality," pp. 351–53.

25. Stoller, "Femininity," p. 132.

26. J. Ross, "Towards Fatherhood."

27. Chodorow, *Reproduction of Mothering*, p. 113.

28. Matthews, "Sex-Role Perception."

29. This point is similar to that made by Abelin, who speaks of a little girl enacting a maternal generational identity while the boy emulates a

male gender identity. Abelin tends to make the usual assumption, however, that gender means sexual, since he refers to the girl's generational identity as a "madonna asexual complex." (E. Abelin, Panel contribution, "The Role of the Father in the Preoedipal Years," *Proceedings of the Sixty-sixth Annual Meeting of the American Psychoanalytical Association*, April 1977, Quebec. See also J. Ross, "Fathering."

30. Ullian, "'Why Girls Are Good.'"

31. Unger, *Female and Male*, pp. 213–14.

32. Ullian, "'Why Girls Are Good,'" p. 250.

33. Kohlberg, "Children's Sex Role Concepts." See also Kohlberg and Zigler, "Impact of Cognitive Maturity."

34. Ullian, "Regression in Service of Male Ego."

35. Wickert, "Freud's Heritage."

36. Money, "Conceptual Neutering of Gender," p. 282.

37. Ibid.

38. When speaking of roles, a learned role was a gender role. Sex role then would refer to role in sexual intercourse. (See Tresemer, "Assumptions Made About Gender Roles.") This usage is confusing since surely learning is also involved in intercourse.

39. Kessler and McKenna, *Gender*.

40. MacKinnon, "An Agenda for Theory."

41. MacKinnon, "Toward Feminist Jurisprudence," especially p. 635.

42. MacKinnon, "An Agenda for Theory," p. 533.

43. G. Rubin, "Thinking Sex," p. 307.

44. Rubin sees MacKinnon as wanting "to subsume sexuality under feminist thought" and seems to think that MacKinnon is making a definitional fusion between gender and sex. My reading of MacKinnon indicates that this is not the case.

45. For more discussion of the politics of AIDS, see Fitzgerald, *Cities on a Hill*.

46. Money, "Conceptual Neutering of Gender."

47. Degler, "Women in Making of Demographic Transition" in his *At Odds*.

48. See Kinsey et al., *Sexual Behavior in Human Female*, and Masters and Johnson, *Human Sexual Response*.

49. See especially Koedt, "Myth of Vaginal Orgasm."

50. Person, "Sexuality as Mainstay of Identity."

51. The above comments were stimulated by and built on Spender, "The Politics of Naming," especially p. 177.

52. Goldman, "Prostitution."

53. Schulz, "Rape Is Four-Letter Word." See also discussion in Spender, "The Politics of Naming," especially pp. 179–80.

54. M. Morgan, *Total Woman*, especially pp. 106–7 and back cover.

55. Foucault, *History of Sexuality.*

56. Snitow, Stansell, and Thompson, eds., *Powers of Desire*, especially pp. 30–33.

57. For example, see Carroll, Volk, and Hyde, "Motives for Sexual Intercourse."

58. L. Rubin, *Intimate Strangers*, p. 104.

59. Blumstein and Schwartz, *American Couples.*

60. Symons, *Evolution of Human Sexuality*, pp. 170–184, especially p. 179.

61. Blumstein and Schwartz, *American Couples*, p. 205.

62. For the connection of sex and aggression, see Stoller, *Sexual Excitement.* For the connection with degrading the object, see Freud, "Degradation in Erotic Life."

63. Masters and Johnson, *Human Sexual Response*, and *Homosexuality in Perspective.*

64. Spender, "The Politics of Naming," pp. 172ff.

65. Contratto, "Maternal Sexuality."

66. Friedrich, *Meaning of Aphrodite*, p. 181.

67. For a more psychoanalytic version of this theory, see Slater, *Glory of Hera.*

68. Benjamin, "Desire of One's Own."

69. Frye, "Harm's Way," in *Politics of Reality.*

Chapter Nine

1. Whyte, *Status of Women*, see especially the concluding chapter. Whyte is very leery of making cross-cultural generalizations concerning *the* status of women because so many different variables are involved, but he does tend to argue that the agrarian societies were generally more oppressive than both simpler and more complex modern societies.

2. Lévi-Strauss, *Elementary Structures of Kinship*, pp. 116–18. For a classic discussion of the characteristics of matrilineal societies, see Schneider, "Matrilineal Descent Groups."

3. Collins, "Conflict Theory of Sexual Stratification." G. Johnson and Hendrix, "Test of Collins's Theory."

4. Reiss, "Sociological Journey into Sexuality," especially p. 236. See also *Journey into Sexuality.*

5. Witherspoon, *Navajo Kinship and Marriage.*

6. I am indebted to Estep, "Feminist Consciousness and Navajo World View," for this general picture.

7. Schlegel, "Male and Female in Hopi Thought."

8. Weiner, "Trobriand Descent."

9. Coltrane, "Father-Child Relationship."

10. Quoted in Tanner, "Matrifocality," p. 156.

11. Toni Morrison is quoted in Hooks, *Feminist Theory*, p. 50.

12. African kinship provides a sharp contrast to the husband/father-headed family with which we are familiar. In many African societies, bridewealth circulates around the society and represents the reciprocal obligations of one corporate kin group to another. Women work for their husbands but do not own the products of this work as a family member; their ties are to their own kin group. Women engage in joint work activities with other women, and a woman can pass on property to her children separately from her husband. In this system the idea of father as we know it does not exist. Although the degree of gender equality existing in African societies is complex and controversial, women are definitely not juvenilized as they are under patriarchal systems. See especially Sacks, *Sisters and Wives*.

13. D. Lewis, "The Black Family," p. 229 (quoted).

14. Hartmann, "Marxism and Feminism," p. 18.

15. Ortner, "Virgin and State," especially p. 29.

16. Bakan, *They Took Themselves Wives*, especially p. 14.

17. See especially Hamilton, *Liberation of Women*.

18. Bernard, *Future of Marriage*, p. 335.

19. Quoted in Demos, "Changing Faces of Fatherhood," especially p. 432.

20. Degler, *At Odds*, p. 74.

21. Ryan, *Womanhood in America*, p. 218.

22. Smith-Rosenberg, "New Woman as Androgyne," in *Disorderly Conduct*, especially pp. 253 and 256.

23. It is interesting that Betty Friedan in the early days of renewed feminism referred to the "lavender menace" as a threat to the Women's Movement. Fortunately, Friedan later changed her position and "accepted" diversity within the movement.

24. Lundberg and Farnham, *Modern Woman*, p. 167.

25. Laslett, "Family Membership."

26. Parsons, "Age and Sex in the Social Structure of the United States," in his *Essays in Sociological Theory*, pp. 89–103, especially p. 98.

27. Oppenheimer, "Women's Economic Role in Family," challenges this view with the argument that strain might not arise in a two-career family if there was no norm against wives' working.

28. Ryan, *Womanhood in America*, p. 255.

29. Heer and Grossbard-Shectman, "Female Marriage Squeeze." See also Guttentag and Secord, *Too Many Women?*

30. Surveys conducted in 1982 and 1987 on random samples of all non-foreign University of Oregon undergraduates twenty-three years old and under show that in both years the males were more likely than the females to have fathers with only a high school education or less. (Findings of the Sociology Department's graduate seminar in survey methods, taught by Patricia Gwartney-Gibbs.) See also B. Johnson, "Sex Differences in College Aspirations."

31. Flacks, *Youth and Social Change*, p. 32.

32. Gordon, "Feminism, Reproduction, and the Family," p. 41.

33. Pleck continues to be optimistic. He believes we are seeing an increase in fathers' time spent in the family, but only because he takes decreasing family size into account. Generally, however, even Pleck would have to agree that what little convergence there is in men's and women's family time is due far more to working women's decrease in time spent in the home than to men's increase in time spent working in the home. See his *Working Wives/Working Husbands*. A more recent study (Barnett and Baruch, "Fathers' Participation in Family Work") finds that maternal employment status does not directly predict father involvement but rather creates the conditions under which other variables emerge as significant predictors within the employed and unemployed groups.

34. Cherlin, *Marriage, Divorce, Remarriage*, pp. 49–50 and 54–55.

35. Parsons, "Age and Sex," p. 94, n. 4.

36. Wallerstein and Kelly, *Surviving the Breakup*. See also Kelly, "Divorce: The Adult Perspective."

37. It is true that there has been an increase in men who file for divorce since no-fault divorce laws were put into effect, but who files for divorce is a separate issue from who found the marriage the most unsatisfactory. See Dixon and Weitzman, "When Husbands File for Divorce."

38. Kitson and Sussman, "Marital Complaints," p. 93. This was the third most common response for men and the twenty-ninth most common for women.

39. See also Levinger, "Sources of Marital Dissatisfaction."

Chapter 10

1. Illich's book, *Gender*, published in 1982, is devoted to making this point. Illich argues, in what appears to me to be an unnecessarily cryptic way, that the market standard is a male standard and that therefore women in the market are paid less than men. He also recognizes that under "economistic" or utilitarian cost-benefit assumptions, it is hard to measure women's unpaid nonmarket work, that is, what women do—for children, for men, in the home and in the community. I argue that it is the work of women as wives that Illich is trying to conceptualize. This work is broader

than housework but includes it; it also includes women's mothering, but mothering that is strictly privatized and subordinated to the heterosexual couple. Wives' work, since it is not directly marketable in a market economy, gets defined as worthless.

2. Delphy, *Close to Home*, pp. 94–95. Joan Acker, in an influential early article ("Women and Stratification"), stressed that hierarchies based on gender create different conditions for women and men within the same family. Although this insight was an important first step in making women visible in stratification studies, it is also important to recognize that gender hierarchy is itself related to the extent to which married women's life chances depend on those of their husbands.

3. Delphy, 1984, *Close to Home*, p. 96.

4. See especially Coser and Rokoff, "Women in the Occupational World."

5. Blood and Wolfe, *Husbands and Wives*.

6. Gillespie, "Who Has the Power?"

7. Weitzman, *Divorce Revolution*, pp. 337–43. Other studies made on larger populations representing the nation as a whole come up with less dramatic percentages but they are still in the same direction: income up for men, down for women upon divorce. See especially Duncan and Hoffman, "Economic Consequences of Marital Dissolution." Duncan and Hoffman's main point is that most women do not remain in poverty because they remarry. Thus the solution to poverty for women is to again become dependent on a husband's income!

8. Debate between Phyllis Schlafly and Sara Weddington, February 27, 1986, University of Oregon.

9. Wickert, "Freud's Heritage."

10. Doi, *The Anatomy of Dependence*.

11. Altman, *Homosexualization of America*.

12. See Whitehead's discussion of the berdache in American Indian societies ("Bow and Burden Strap," p. 95). Whereas earlier interpreters of this status in which a man adopted a woman's activities focused on its "homosexual" implications, Whitehead maintains that homosexuality was "never mentioned as one of the indicators of the budding berdache." The berdache involved taking on female occupation and dress, with sexual orientation playing only a minor role.

13. Brownmiller, *Femininity*.

14. Roy, "Concepts of 'Femininity' and 'Liberation,'" p. 221.

15. Stevens, "Women's Liberation Movement in Latin America," p. 75.

16. D. Lewis, "Black Family."

17. For a good summary of trends with respect to women and the family, see Cherlin, "Women and the Family."

18. Holter, ed., *Patriarchy in Welfare Society*.

19. Swidler, "Love and Adulthood in American Culture." See also Bellah et al., *Habits of the Heart*, chapter 4.

20. The pollster Daniel Yankelovich reports that in 1970 and again in 1980, 96 percent of all Americans "declared themselves dedicated to the ideal of two people sharing a life and home together" (*New Rules*, p. 249). The couple, presumably any two people—not men's groups, not women's groups, not kin groups nor even friends—is the central locus of loyalty and commitment among adult citizens in the United States.

21. Waite, Goldscheider, and Witsberger, "Nonfamily Living." See also Marini, "Age and Sequencing Norms."

22. Roebuck, "Grandma as Revolutionary."

23. Gordon and O'Keefe, "Incest as Family Violence," report from a study of fifty incest cases in Boston from 1880 to 1960 that, although they could not measure the father's participation in child-rearing directly, they did find that the presence of the father in the household (which at least made it possible for him to have child care responsibilities) was more likely to be associated with nonsexual abuse than with incest. "Ninety-five percent of male nonsexual child-abuse assailants lived in the same household as their children, as compared with 68% of incest assailants. This is the more striking considering that sharing a house often provided more opportunity for an illicit sexual relationship" (p. 30). This at least suggests that overt incest is not necessarily encouraged in males by their living in the same household, at least if the mother is present. H. Parker and S. Parker ("Father-Daughter Sexual Abuse," especially p. 545) have reported research comparing a sample of incestuous fathers with age-matched nonincestuous fathers in penal and psychiatric facilities. The authors found that the abusing fathers were much less likely to have lived in the home during the first three years of the child's life. Their major conclusions were that the combination of a father's own early parental-attachment deficits and his low level of involvement in the socialization of his daughter increased considerably the probability of abuse.

24. On incest's being more common among stepfathers than among fathers, see Finkelhor, *Child Sexual Abuse*, p. 25.

25. See C. Lewis, *Becoming a Father*, for an explicit presentation of the following "beliefs" about fathers: "that fathers have only recently been discovered by family researchers, . . . that in previous generations fathers were not involved in childrearing, . . . and that recently men have started to become highly involved in and committed to child care."

26. Kamerman, "Child Care Services."

27. Ibid.

28. Hewlett, *A Lesser Life*.

29. Goode, "Why Men Resist," p. 139.

30. For clarification of this issue, see Mansbridge, "ERA and Gender Gap."

31. Gill, "Attitudes Toward Equal Rights Amendment."

32. Poole and Zeigler, *Women, Public Opinion, and Politics*, p. 6.

33. Shapiro and Mahajan, "Gender Differences in Policy Preferences."

References

Acker, Joan. "Women and Stratification: A Case of Intellectual Sexism." *American Journal of Sociology* 78 (1973): 936–45.

Adams-Tucker, Christine, and Paul L. Adams. "Role of the Father." In Martha Kirkpatrick, ed., *Women's Sexual Development: Explorations of Inner Space*. New York: Plenum, 1980.

Alder, Christine. "An Exploration of Self-Reported Sexual Aggression." Ph.D. dissertation, Department of Sociology, University of Oregon, 1982.

Allen, Jeffner. "Motherhood: The Annihilation of Women." In Joyce Trebilcot, ed., *Mothering*, pp. 315–30. Totowa, NJ: Rowman and Allanheld, 1983.

Altman, Dennis. *The Homosexualization of America*. Boston: Beacon, 1982.

Apperson, Louis Behrens, and W. George McAdoo, Jr. "Parental Factors in the Childhood of Homosexuals." *Journal of Abnormal Psychology* 73 (1968): 291–96.

Armstrong, Louise. *Kiss Daddy Goodnight: A Speak-Out on Incest*. New York: Hawthorn, 1978.

———. "The Cradle of Sexual Politics: Incest." In Martha Kirkpatrick, ed., *Women's Sexual Experience*. New York: Plenum Press, 1982.

Atkinson, Ti Grace. "The Institution of Sexual Intercourse." In *Amazon Odyssey*. New York: Links Books, 1974.

Bacon, Margaret K., and Richard D. Ashmore. "How Mothers and Fathers Categorize Descriptions of Social Behavior Attributed to Daughters and Sons." *Social Cognition* 3 (1985): 193–217.

Bacon, Margaret K., Irvin L. Child, and Herbert Barry III. "A Cross-Cultural Study of Correlates of Crime." *Journal of Abnormal and Social Psychology* 66 (1963): 291–300.

Badinter, Elisabeth. *Mother Love: Myth and Reality.* New York: Macmillan, 1981.

Bakan, David. *The Quality of Human Existence.* Chicago: Rand-McNally, 1966.

————. *And They Took Themselves Wives: The Emergence of Patriarchy in Western Civilization.* San Francisco: Harper and Row, 1979.

Balbus, Isaac D. *Marxism and Domination: A Neo-Hegelian, Feminist, Psychoanalytic Theory of Sexual, Political, and Technological Liberation.* Princeton, NJ: Princeton University Press, 1982.

Bales, Robert F. *Personality and Interpersonal Behavior.* New York: Holt, Rinehart, and Winston, 1970.

Bane, Mary Jo. *Here to Stay: American Families in the Twentieth Century.* New York: Basic Books, 1976.

Barber, Brian K., and Darwin L. Thomas. "Dimensions of Fathers' and Mothers' Supportive Behavior: The Case for Physical Affection." *Journal of Marriage and the Family* 48 (1986): 783–94.

Bardwick, Judith, and Elizabeth Douvan. "Ambivalence: The Socialization of Women." In Vivian Gornick and Barbara K. Moran, eds. *Woman in Sexist Society: Studies in Power and Powerlessness.* New York: Basic Books, 1971.

Barnett, Rosalind C., and Grace K. Baruch. "Determinants of Fathers' Participation in Family Work." *Journal of Marriage and the Family* 49 (1987): 29–40.

Barrett, Michele. *Women's Oppression Today: Problems in Marxist Feminist Analysis.* London: Verso; New York: Schocken, 1980.

Barry, Kathleen. *Female Sexual Slavery.* Englewood Cliffs, NJ: Prentice-Hall, 1979.

Bart, Pauline. "The Mermaid and the Minotaur: A Fishy Story That's Part Bull." *Contemporary Psychology* 22 (1977): 834–35.

Belenky, Mary Field, Blythe McVicker Clinchy, Nancy Rule Goldberger, and Jill Mattuck Tarule. *Women's Ways of Knowing.* New York: Basic Books, 1986.

Bell, Alan P. "Research in Homosexuality: Back to the Drawing Board." *Archives of Sexual Behavior* 4 (1975): 421–31.

Bell, Alan P., Martin S. Weinberg, and Sue Kiefer Hammersmith. *Sexual Preference: Its Development in Men and Women.* Bloomington: Indiana University Press, 1981.

Bellah, Robert N., Richard Madsen, William M. Sullivan, Ann Swidler, and Steven M. Tipton. *Habits of the Heart: Individualism and Commitment in American Life.* Berkeley and Los Angeles: University of California Press, 1985.

Bem, Sandra Lipsitz. "The Measurement of Psychological Androgyny." *Journal of Consulting and Clinical Psychology* 42 (1974): 155–62.

———. "Sex Role Adaptability: One Consequence of Psychological Androgyny." *Journal of Personality and Social Psychology* 31 (1975): 634–43.

———. "Gender Schema Theory and Its Implications for Child Development: Raising Gender-aschematic Children in a Gender-schematic Society." *Signs* 8 (1983): 598–616.

Bene, Eva. "On the Genesis of Female Homosexuality." *British Journal of Psychiatry* 111 (1965): 815–21.

———. "On the Genesis of Male Homosexuality." *British Journal of Psychiatry* 111 (1965): 803–13.

Benjamin, Jessica. "The End of Internalization: Adorno's Social Psychology." *Telos* 32 (1977): 42–46.

———. "The Bonds of Love: Rational Violence and Erotic Domination." *Feminist Studies* 6 (1980): 144–74. Reprinted in Hester Eisenstein and Alice Jardine, eds., *The Future of Difference*, pp. 41–70. Boston: G. K. Hall, 1980. Also reprinted in Ann Snitow, Christine Stansell, and Sharon Thompson, eds., *The Powers of Desire: The Politics of Sexuality*. New York: Monthly Review Press, 1983.

———. "The Oedipal Riddle." In John P. Diggins and Mark E. Kann, eds., *The Problem of Authority in America*. Philadelphia: Temple University Press, 1981.

———. "A Desire of One's Own: Psychoanalytic Feminism and Intersubjective Space." In Teresa de Lauretis, ed., *Feminist Studies: Critical Studies*. Bloomington: Indiana University Press, 1986.

Bennett, Edward M., and Larry R. Cohen. "Men and Women: Personality Patterns and Contrasts." *Genetic Psychology Monographs* 59 (1959): 101–55.

Bernard, Jessie. *The Female World*. New York: Free Press, 1981.

———. "The Good-Provider Role: Its Rise and Fall." *American Psychologist* 36 (1981): 1–12.

———. *The Future of Marriage*. 1972. Reprint. New Haven: Yale University Press, 1982.

Best, Raphaela. *We've All Got Scars: What Boys and Girls Learn in Elementary School*. Bloomington: University of Indiana Press, 1983.

Bieber, Irving. "Clinical Aspects of Male Homosexuality." In Judd Marmor, ed., *Sexual Inversion*. New York: Basic Books, 1965.

Blake, Judith. "Coercive Pronatalism and American Population Policy." In Ellen Peck and J. Senderowitz, eds., *Pronatalism: The Myth of Mom and Apple Pie* (pp. 44–50). New York: Thomas Y. Crowell, 1974.

Blasi, Joseph R. Review of *Gender and Culture: Kibbutz Women Revisited*, by Melford E. Spiro (1979). *Journal of Marriage and the Family* 43 (1981): 451–56.

Bleier, Ruth. *Science and Gender: A Critique of Biology and Its Theories on Women*. New York: Pergamon, 1984.

Bloch, Ruth H. "Untangling the Roots of Modern Sex Roles: A Survey of Four Centuries of Change." *Signs* 4 (1978): 237–52.

Block, Jack, Anna Von der Lippe, and Jeanne H. Block. "Sex Role and Socialization Patterns: Some Personality Concomitants and Environmental Antecedents." *Journal of Consulting and Clinical Psychology* 41 (1973): 321–41.

Block, Jeanne. "Conceptions of Sex Role: Some Cross-Cultural and Longitudinal Perspectives." *American Psychologist* 28 (1973): 512–26.

———. "Socialization Influences of Personality Development in Males and Females." In M. M. Parks, ed., APA Master Lecture Series on Issues of Sex and Gender in Psychology. Washington, D.C.: American Psychological Association, 1973.

———. *The Pinks and the Blues*. PBS program produced by NOVA, 1980.

Blood, Robert O., and Donald M. Wolfe. *Husbands and Wives: The Dynamics of Married Living*. New York: Free Press, 1960.

Blumstein, Philip W., and Pepper Schwartz. "Bisexuality: Some Social Psychological Issues." *Journal of Social Issues* 33 (1977): 30–45.

———. *American Couples: Money, Work, Sex*. New York: William Morrow, 1983.

Bonaparte, Marie, Anna Freud, and Ernst Kris, eds. *The Origins of Psychoanalysis: Letters of Wilhelm Fliess, Drafts and Notes, 1887–1902*. Trans. by Eric Mosbacker and James Strachey. New York: Basic Books, 1954.

Brim, Orville. "Family Structure and Sex Role Learning by Children." *Sociometry* 21 (1958): 1–16.

Bronfenbrenner, Urie. "Some Familial Antecedents of Responsibility and Leadership in Adolescents." In L. Petrullo and B. M. Bass, eds., *Leadership and Interpersonal Behavior*, pp. 239–71. New York: Holt, Rinehart and Winston, 1961.

Bronstein, Phyllis. "Differences in Mothers' and Fathers' Behaviors Toward Children: A Cross-Cultural Comparison." *Developmental Psychology* 20 (1984): 995–1003.

Broverman, Inge K., Susan R. Vogel, Donald M. Broverman, Frank E. Clarkson, and Paul S. Rosenkrantz. "Sex Role Stereotypes: A Current Appraisal." *Journal of Social Issues* 28 (1972): 59–78.

Brownmiller, Susan. *Against Our Will: Men, Women and Rape.* New York: Simon and Schuster, 1975.

———. *Femininity.* New York: Simon and Schuster, Linden Press, 1984.

Bunch, Charlotte. "Lesbians in Revolt." In Nancy Myron and Charlotte Bunch, eds., *Lesbianism and the Women's Movement.* Oakland, CA: Diana Press, 1975.

Burlingham, Dorothy T. "The Preoedipal Infant-Father Relationship." *Psychoanalytic Study of the Child* 28 (1973): 23–47.

Burton, Roger V., and John W. M. Whiting. "The Absent Father and Cross-sex Identity." *Merrill-Palmer Quarterly* 7 (1961): 85–95.

Carlson, Rae. "Sex Differences in Ego Functioning: Exploratory Studies of Agency and Communion." *Journal of Consulting and Clinical Psychology* 37 (1971): 270–71.

———. "Understanding Women: Implications for Personality Theory and Research." *Journal of Social Issues* 28 (1972): 17–32.

Carroll, Janell L., Kari Doray Volk, and Janet Shibley Hyde. "Differences Between Males and Females in Motives for Engaging in Sexual Intercourse." *Archives of Sexual Behavior* 14 (1985): 131—39.

Carter, Bruce D., and Laura McCloskey. "Peers and the Maintenance of Sex-Typed Behavior: The Development of Children's Conceptions of Cross-Gender Behavior in Their Peers." *Social Cognition* 2 (1983–84): 294–314.

Chafetz, Janet S., Paula Beck, Patricia Sampson, Joyce West, and Bonnye Jones. *Who's Queer?: A Study of Homo- and Heterosexual Women.* Sarasota, FL: Omni Press, 1976.

Cherlin, Andrew. *Marriage, Divorce, Remarriage.* Cambridge: Harvard University Press, 1981.

———. "Women and the Family." In Sara E. Rix, ed., *The American Woman 1987–88.* New York: W. W. Norton, 1987.

Chodorow, Nancy. "Being and Doing: A Cross-Cultural Examination of the Socialization of Males and Females." In Vivian Gornick and Barbara K. Moran, eds., *Woman in Sexist Society: Studies in Power and Powerlessness,* pp. 259–91. New York: Basic Books, 1971.

———. "Family Structure and Feminine Personality." In Michelle Rosaldo and Louise Lamphere, eds., *Woman, Culture and Society,* pp. 43–66. Stanford, CA: Stanford University Press, 1974.

———. *The Reproduction of Mothering.* Berkeley and Los Angeles: University of California Press, 1978.

———. "Feminism and Difference: Gender, Relation, and Difference in Psychoanalytic Perspective." *Socialist Review* 46 (1979): 51–69. Reprinted as "Gender, Relation, and Difference" in Hester Eisenstein and Alice Jardine, eds., *The Future of Difference*, pp. 3–18. New Brunswick, NJ: Rutgers University Press, 1980.

———. "Reply by Nancy Chodorow." *Signs* 6 (1981): 500–514.

———. "Beyond Drive Theory: Object Relations and the Limits of Radical Individualism." *Theory and Society* 14 (1985): 271–319.

Chodorow, Nancy, and Susan Contratto. "The Fantasy of the Perfect Mother." In Barrie Thorne with Marilyn Yalom, eds., *Rethinking the Family*. New York: Longman, 1982.

Collins, Randall. "A Conflict Theory of Sexual Stratification." *Social Problems* 19 (1971): 1–20.

Coltrane, Scott. "The Father-Child Relationship and the Status of Women." *American Journal of Sociology* 93 (1988): 1060–95.

Constantinople, Anne. "Masculinity-Femininity: An Exception to a Famous Dictum?" *Psychological Bulletin* 80 (1973): 389–407.

Contratto, Susan. "Maternal Sexuality and Asexual Motherhood." *Signs* 5 (1980): 766–82.

———. "Father's Presence in Women's Psychological Development." In Jerome Rabow, Gerald Platt, and Marion S. Goldman, eds., *Advances in Psychoanalytic Sociology*. Malabar, FL: Krieger, 1987.

Coser, Rose L., and Gerald Rokoff. "Women in the Occupational World: Social Disruption and Conflict." In Rose L. Coser, ed., *The Family: Its Structures and Functions*, 2d ed. New York: St. Martin's, 1974.

Daly, Mary. "The Qualitative Leap Beyond Patriarchal Religion." *Quest* 1 (1975): 20–40.

———. *Gyn/Ecology: The Metaethics of Radical Feminism*. Boston: Beacon, 1978.

Dan, Alice J., and Niles Newton. Comments in symposium, "Considering a Biosocial Perspective on Parenting." *Signs* 4 (1979): 698–700.

Daniels, Arlene Kaplan. "Feminist Perspectives in Sociological Research." In Marcia Milliman and Rosabeth Kanter, eds., *Another Voice*. Garden City, NY: Doubleday, 1975.

David, Deborah, and Robert Brannon, eds. *The Forty-Nine Percent Majority: The Male Sex Role*. Reading, MA: Addison-Wesley, 1976.

Deaux, Kay. "From Individual Differences to Social Categories: Analysis of a Decade's Research on Gender." *American Psychologist* 39 (February 1984): 105–16.

De Beauvoir, Simone. *The Second Sex*. Trans. by H. M. Parshley. New York: Knopf, 1953.

Degler, Carl N. *At Odds: Women and the Family in America from the Revolution to the Present*. New York: Oxford University Press, 1980.

Delphy, Christine. "Interview with Christine Delphy by Daniele Leger." *Feminist Issues* 1 (1980): 23–50.

——. "Women in Stratification Studies." In Helen Roberts, ed., *Doing Feminist Research*. Boston: Routledge and Kegan Paul, 1981.

——. *Close to Home: A Materialist Analysis of Women's Oppression*. Amherst: University of Massachusetts Press, 1984.

Demos, John. "The Changing Faces of Fatherhood: A New Exploration in American History." In Stanley H. Cath, Alan R. Gurwitt, and John Munder Ross, eds., *Father and Child: Developmental and Clinical Perspectives*, pp. 425–49. Boston: Little, Brown, 1982.

Deutsch, Helene. *The Psychology of Women: A Psychoanalytic Interpretation*. Vol. 1. New York: Bantam, 1944.

Dinnerstein, Dorothy. *The Mermaid and the Minotaur: Sexual Arrangements and Human Malaise*. New York: Harper and Row, 1976.

Dixon, Ruth B., and Lenore J. Weitzman. "When Husbands File for Divorce." *Journal of Marriage and the Family* 44 (1982): 103–15.

Doi, Takeo. *The Anatomy of Dependence*. Trans. by John Bester. New York: Kodansha International, 1973.

Dowling, Colette. *The Cinderella Complex: Women's Hidden Fear of Independence*. New York: Pocket Books, 1981.

Drake, C. T., and D. McDougall. "Effects of the Absence of a Father and Other Male Models on the Development of Boys' Sex Roles." *Developmental Psychology* 13 (1977): 537–38.

Droppleman, L. F., and E. S. Schaefer. "Boys' and Girls' Reports of Maternal and Paternal Behavior." *Journal of Abnormal and Social Psychology* 67 (1963): 648–54.

Duncan, Greg, and Saul D. Hoffman. "A Reconsideration of the Economic Consequences of Marital Dissolution." *Demography* 22 (1985): 485–97.

Echols, Alice. "The New Feminism of Yin and Yang." In Ann Snitow, Christine Stansell, and Sharon Thompson, eds., *Powers of Desire: The Politics of Sexuality*, pp. 439–59. New York: Monthly Review Press, 1983.

Ehrenreich, Barbara. *The Hearts of Men: American Dreams and the Flight From Commitment*. Garden City, NY: Doubleday, Anchor Press, 1984.

——. "A Feminist's View of the New Man." *The New York Times Magazine*. May 20, 1984.

Ehrenreich, Barbara, and Dierdre English. *For Her Own Good: 150 Years of the Experts' Advice to Women*. Garden City, NY: Doubleday, Anchor Press, 1978.

Ehrensaft, Diane. "Dual Parenting and the Duel of Intimacy." In Gerald Handel, ed., *The Psychosocial Interior of the Family*, 3d ed. New York: Aldine, 1985.

Eichenbaum, Luise, and Susie Orbach. *What Do Women Want?* New York: Coward, McCann and Geoghegan, 1983.

Eisenhart, Margaret A., and Dorothy C. Holland. "Learning Gender from Peers: The Role of Peer Groups in the Cultural Transmission of Gender." *Human Organization* 42 (1983): 321–32.

Eisenstein, Hester. *Contemporary Feminist Thought*. Boston: G. K. Hall, 1983.

Eisenstein, Hester, and Alice Jardine, eds. *The Future of Difference*. New Brunswick, NJ: Rutgers University Press, 1985.

Elder, Glenn, and Charles Bowerman. "Family Structure and Child-Rearing Patterns: The Effect of Family Size and Sex Composition." *American Sociological Review* 28 (1963): 891–905.

Elshtain, Jean Bethke. "Antigone's Daughters." *Democracy* 2 (April 1982): 46–59.

―――. "Feminist Discourse and Its Discontents: Language, Power, and Meaning." *Signs* 7 (1982): 603–21.

Esposito, Anita. "Sex Differences in Children's Conversation." *Language and Speech* 22 (1979): 213–20.

Erikson, Erik. *Childhood and Society*. New York: W. W. Norton, 1950.

Espenshade, Thomas J. "Marriage Trends in America: Estimates, Implications, and Underlying Causes." *Population and Development Review* 11 (1985): 193–245.

Estep, Susan. "Feminist Consciousness and the Navajo World View." Department of Sociology. University of Oregon. Typescript, 1984.

Evans, Ray B. "Childhood Parental Relationships of Homosexual Men." *Journal of Consulting and Clinical Psychology* 33, no. 2 (1969): 129–35.

Fagot, Beverly I. "The Influence of Sex of Child on Parental Reactions to Toddler Children." *Child Development* 49 (1978): 459–65.

―――. "Beyond the Reinforcement Principle: Another Step Toward Understanding Sex Role Development." *Developmental Psychology* 21 (1985): 1097–1104.

Fagot, Beverly I., and Richard Hagen. "Aggression in Toddlers: Responses to the Assertive Acts of Boys and Girls." *Sex Roles* 12 (1985): 341–51.

Fagot, Beverly I., and Mary D. Leinbach. "Play Styles in Early Childhood: Social Consequences for Boys and Girls." In Marsha Liss, ed., *Social and Cognitive Skills: Sex Roles and Children's Play*, pp. 93–116. Orlando, FL: Academic Press, 1983.

Fairbairn, Ronald. *An Object-Relations Theory of the Personality*. New York: Basic Books, 1952.

Fausto-Sterling, Anne. *Myths of Gender: Biological Theories About Women and Men*. New York: Basic Books, 1985.

Ferguson, Ann. "Patriarchy, Sexual Identity, and the Sexual Revolution: Heterosexual Ideology as a Coercive Force." In Alison M. Jaggar and Paula S. Rothenburg, eds., *Feminist Frameworks*, 2d ed., pp. 420–22. New York: McGraw-Hill, 1984.

Ferguson, Ann, Jacquelyn N. Zita, and Kathryn Pyne Addelson. "On Compulsory Heterosexuality and Lesbian Existence: Defining the Issues." *Signs* 7 (1981): 158–99.

Fiedler, Leslie. *The Return of the Vanishing American*. New York: Stein and Day, 1968.

Fields, Suzanne. *Like Father, Like Daughter: How Father Shapes the Woman His Daughter Becomes*. Boston: Little, Brown, 1983.

Finigan, Michael. "The Effects of Token Representation on Participation in Small Decision Making Groups." *Economic and Industrial Democracy* 3 (1982): 531–50.

Finkelhor, David. *Sexually Victimized Children*. New York: Macmillan, Free Press, 1979.

———. "The Sexual Climate in Families," May 1980. Mimeograph available from Family Violence Research Laboratory, University of New Hampshire, Durham, NH.

———. *Child Sexual Abuse: New Theory and Research*. New York: Free Press, 1984.

Finkelhor, David, and Kersti Yllo. *License to Rape: Sexual Abuse of Wives*. New York: Holt, Rinehart and Winston, 1985.

Firestone, Shulamith. *The Dialectic of Sex*. New York: Bantam, 1970.

Fischer, Kurt W., and Malcolm W. Watson. "Explaining the Oedipus Conflict." In Kurt W. Fischer, ed., *Cognitive Development in New Directions for Child Development*, No. 12. San Francisco: Jossey-Bass, 1981.

Fishman, Pamela. "Interaction: The Work Women Do." In Barrie Thorne, Cheris Kramarae, and Nancy Henley, eds., *Language, Gender and Society*. Rowley, MA: Newbury House, 1983.

FitzGerald, Frances. *Cities on a Hill*. New York: Harper and Row, 1986.

Flacks, Richard. *Youth and Social Change*. Chicago: Markham, 1971.

Flax, Jane. "Mother-Daughter Relationships: Psychodynamics, Politics and Philosophy." In Hester Eisenstein and Alice Jardine, eds., *The Future of Difference*. New Brunswick, NJ: Rutgers University Press, 1985.

Foucault, Michel. *The History of Sexuality.* Vol. 1, *An Introduction.* Trans. by Robert Hurley. New York: Vintage, Random House, 1980.

Freud, Sigmund. "The Most Prevalent Form of Degradation in Erotic Life." 1912. In Philip Rieff, ed., *Sexuality and the Psychology of Love.* New York: Collier, 1963.

———. *Totem and Taboo.* 1913. In vol. 13 of *The Complete Psychological Works: Standard Edition,* ed. and trans. James Strachey, pp. 1–161. New York: W. W. Norton, 1976.

———. "The Psychogenesis of a Case of Homosexuality in a Woman." 1920. In Philip Rieff, ed. *Freud: Sexuality and the Psychology of Love.* New York: Collier, 1963.

———. "Some Psychological Consequences of the Anatomical Distinction Between the Sexes." *International Journal of Psychoanalysis* 8 (1927): 133–142.

———. *Civilization and Its Discontents.* 1930. Trans. by James Strachey. New York: W. W. Norton, 1961.

———. "Female Sexuality." 1931. In Jean Strouse, ed., *Women and Analysis.* New York: Grossman, 1974.

———. "Femininity." 1933. In Jean Strouse, ed., *Women and Analysis.* New York: Grossman, 1974.

Friday, Nancy. *My Mother/My Self.* New York: Delacorte, 1977.

Friedan, Betty. *The Feminine Mystique.* New York: Dell, 1963.

———. *The Second Stage.* New York: Summit, 1981.

Friedrich, Paul. *The Meaning of Aphrodite.* Chicago: University of Chicago Press, 1978.

Frodi, Ann, Jacqueline Macauley, and Pauline R. Thome. "Are Women Always Less Aggressive Than Men? A Review of the Experimental Literature." *Psychological Bulletin* 84 (1977): 634–60.

Frye, Marilyn. *The Politics of Reality: Essays in Feminist Theory.* Trumansburg, NY: Crossing Press, 1983.

Fury, Kathleen. "The Title No Woman (In Her Right Mind) Wants." *Working Woman,* April 1984.

Geng, Veronica. "Requiem for the Women's Movement." *Harpers* 253 (November 1976): 49–68.

Gelinas, Denise J. "The Persisting Negative Effects of Incest." *Psychiatry* 46 (1983): 312–33.

Gilbert, Lucia A., Gary R. Hanson, and Beverly Davis. "Perceptions of Parental Role Responsibilities: Differences Between Mothers and Fathers." *Family Relations* 31 (1982): 261–69.

Gill, Sandra K. "Attitudes Toward the Equal Rights Amendment: Influence of Class and Status." *Sociological Perspectives* 28 (1985): 441–62.

Gill, Sandra, Jean Stockard, Miriam M. Johnson, and Suzanne Williams. "Measuring Gender Differences: The Expressive Dimension and Critique of Androgyny Scales." *Sex Roles* 17 (1987): 375–400.

Gillespie, Dair L. "Who Has the Power? The Marital Struggle." *Journal of Marriage and the Family* 33 (1971): 445–58.

Gilligan, Carol. "In a Different Voice: Women's Conception of Self and of Morality." *Harvard Educational Review* 47, no. 4 (1977): 481–517.

————. *In a Different Voice*. Cambridge: Harvard University Press, 1982.

Gimenez, Martha E. "Feminism, Pronatalism, and Motherhood." In Joyce Trebilcot, ed., *Mothering: Essays in Feminist Theory*. Totowa, NJ: Rowman and Allanheld, 1983.

Goldberg, Steven. *The Inevitability of Patriarchy*. New York: William Morrow, 1974.

Goldman, Marion S. "Prostitution, Economic Exchange and the Unconscious." In Jerome Rabow, Gerald Platt, and Marion S. Goldman, eds., *Advances in Psychoanalytic Sociology*. Malabar, FL: Krieger, 1987.

Goode, William. "Why Men Resist." In Barrie Thorne with Marilyn Yalom, eds., *Rethinking the Family: Some Feminist Questions*, pp. 131–50. New York: Longman, 1982.

Goodenough, Evelyn W. "Interest in Persons as an Aspect of Sex Difference in the Early Years." *Genetic Psychology Monographs* 55 (1957): 287–323.

Goodwin, Marjorie H. "Directive-Response Speech Sequences in Girls' and Boys' Task Activities." In Sally McConnell-Ginet, Ruth A. Borker, and Nelly Furman, eds., *Women and Language in Literature and Society*. New York: Praeger, 1980.

Goodwin, Marjorie Harness, and Charles Goodwin. "Children's Arguing." In Susan Philips, Susan Steele, and Christina Tanz, eds., *Language, Gender and Sex in Comparative Perspective*. New York: Cambridge University Press, forthcoming.

Gordon, Linda. "Feminism, Reproduction, and the Family." In Barrie Thorne with Marilyn Yalom, eds., *Rethinking the Family: Some Feminist Questions*, pp. 40–53. New York: Longman, 1982.

Gordon, Linda, and Paul O'Keefe. "Incest as a Form of Family Violence: Evidence from Historical Case Records." *Journal of Marriage and the Family* 46 (February 1984): 27–34.

Gornick, Vivian, and Barbara K. Moran, eds. *Woman in Sexist Society: Studies in Power and Powerlessness*. New York: Basic Books, 1971.

Gottfried, Rosalind. "Feminism and the Lives of College Educated

Women Born Between 1952 and 1955." Paper delivered at the spring meetings of the Pacific Sociological Association in Albuquerque, NM, 1985.

Gottlieb, Roger. "Mothering and the Reproduction of Power: Chodorow, Dinnerstein, and Social Theory." *Socialist Review* 14 (1984): 93–119.

Gough, Harrison G., and Alfred B. Heilbrun. *Joint Manual for the Adjective Check List and the Need Scales for the ACL.* Palo Alto, CA: Consulting Psychologists Press, 1965.

Gove, Walter, and Michael Hughes. "Possible Causes of the Apparent Sex Differences in Physical Health." *American Sociological Review* 44 (1979): 126–46.

Greenberg, Jay R., and Stephen A. Mitchell. *Object Relations in Psychoanalytic Theory.* Cambridge: Harvard University Press, 1983.

Greenson, Ralph. "Dis-identifying From Mother: Its Special Importance for the Boy." *International Journal of Psycho-Analysis* 49 (1968): 370–74.

Greenspan, Miriam. *A New Approach to Women and Therapy.* New York: McGraw-Hill, 1983.

Griffin, Susan. "Rape: The All-American Crime." In Jo Freeman, ed., *Women: A Feminist Perspective.* Palo Alto, CA: Mayfield, 1975.

Guntrip, Harry. *Personality Structure and Human Interaction: The Developing Synthesis of Psycho-dynamic Theory.* New York: International Universities Press, 1961.

Guttentag, Marcia, and Paul F. Secord. *Too Many Women? The Sex Ratio Question.* Beverly Hills, CA: Sage, 1983.

Gutmann, David. "Female Ego Styles and Generational Conflict." In Judith Bardwick, Elizabeth Douvan, Matina Horner, and David Gutmann, eds., *Feminine Personality and Conflict.* Belmont, CA: Brooks/Cole, 1970.

Hamilton, Roberta. *The Liberation of Women: A Study of Patriarchy and Capitalism.* London: George Allen and Unwin, 1978.

Harding, Sandra. "The Instability of the Analytical Categories of Feminist Theory." *Signs* 11 (1986): 645–64.

———. *The Science Question in Feminism.* Ithaca, NY: Cornell University Press, 1986.

Harry, Joseph. *Gay Children Grown Up: Gender Culture and Gender Deviance.* New York: Praeger, 1982.

Harter, Susan. "Developmental Perspectives on the Self System." In E. Mavis Hetherington, ed., *Socialization, Personality, and Social Development,* vol. 4 of *Handbook of Child Psychology* (Paul Mussen, ed.), 4th ed. New York: John Wiley, 1983.

Hartley, Ruth. "Sex-role Pressures and the Socialization of the Male Child." *Psychological Reports* 5 (1959): 457–68.

Hartmann, Heidi. "The Unhappy Marriage of Marxism and Feminism: Towards a More Progressive Union." In Lydia Sargent, ed., *Women and Revolution: A Discussion of the Unhappy Marriage of Marxism and Feminism.* Boston: South End Press, 1981.

Hays, H. R. *The Dangerous Sex: The Myth of Feminine Evil.* 1964. Reprint. New York: Pocket Books, 1972.

Heer, David M., and Amyra Grossbard-Shectman. "The Impact of the Female Marriage Squeeze and the Contraceptive Revolution on Sex Roles and the Women's Liberation Movement in the United States, 1960 to 1975." *Journal of Marriage and the Family* 43 (1981): 49–65.

Heilbrun, Alfred B., Jr. "Sex Role, Instrumental-Expressive Behavior and Psychopathology in Females." *Journal of Abnormal Psychology* 72 (1968): 131–36.

———. *Human Sex Role Behavior.* New York: Pergamon, 1981.

Heilbrun, Carolyn G. *Reinventing Womanhood.* New York: W. W. Norton, 1979.

Herek, Gregory M. "On Heterosexual Masculinity." *American Behavioral Scientist* 29 (1986): 563–77.

Herman, Judith. *Father-Daughter Incest.* Cambridge: Harvard University Press, 1981.

Hess, Beth B., and Myra Marx Ferree. *Controversy and Coalition: The New Feminist Movement.* Boston: Twayne, 1985.

Hetherington, E. Mavis. "Divorce: A Child's Perspective." *American Psychologist* 34, no. 10 (1979): 851–58.

Hewlett, Sylvia Ann. *A Lesser Life: The Myth of Women's Liberation in America.* New York: Warner, 1986.

Hochschild, Arlie. *The Managed Heart.* Berkeley and Los Angeles: University of California Press, 1983.

Hoffman, Charles D., Sandra Eido Tsuneyoshi, Marilyn Ebina, and Heather Fite. "A Comparison of Adult Males' and Females' Interactions with Girls and Boys." *Sex Roles* 11 (1984): 799–811.

Hoffman, Lois Wladis. "Early Childhood Experiences and Women's Achievement Motives." In Martha T. Mednick, Sandra S. Tangri and Lois W. Hoffman, eds. *Women and Achievement: Social and Motivational Analyses.* New York: Halsted Press, 1975.

———. "Changes in Family Roles, Socialization and Sex Differences." *American Psychologist* 32 (1977): 644–57.

Holter, Harriet. "The Reorganized Patriarchy: New Possibilities and Limitations for Women." Lecture at the University of Oregon sponsored by

the Center for the Study of Women in Society, April 17, 1984.
———, ed. *Patriarchy in Welfare Society.* New York: Columbia University Press, 1984.

Hooks, Bell. *Feminist Theory from Margin to Center.* Boston: South End Press, 1984.

Horkheimer, Max. "Authority and the Family." 1936. In *Critical Theory.* New York: Herder and Herder, 1972.

Horner, Thomas M. "The Psychic Life of the Young Infant: Review and Critique of the Psychoanalytic Concepts of Symbiosis and Infantile Omnipotence." *American Journal of Orthopsychiatry* 55 (1985): 324–43.

Horney, Karen. "The Flight From Womanhood: The Masculinity Complex in Women as Viewed by Men and by Women." 1926. In Jean Strouse, ed., *Women and Analysis*, pp. 171–86. New York: Grossman, 1974.

———. "The Dread of Women." In her *Feminine Psychology*, ed. Harold Kelman, pp. 133–46. New York: W. W. Norton, 1967.

Hrdy, Sarah Blaffer. *The Woman That Never Evolved.* Cambridge: Harvard University Press, 1981.

Huston, Aletha C. "Sex Typing." In E. Mavis Hetherington, ed., *Socialization, Personality, and Social Development*, vol. 4 of *Handbook of Child Psychology* (Paul Mussen, ed.), 4th ed. New York: John Wiley, 1983.

Illich, Ivan. *Gender.* New York: Pantheon, 1982.

Jaggar, Alison M., and Paula S. Rothenburg, eds. *Feminist Frameworks*, 2d ed. New York: McGraw-Hill, 1978.

Johnson, Bryce. "Sex Differences in College Aspirations." Master's thesis, Department of Sociology, University of Oregon, 1967.

Johnson, G. David, and Lewellyn Hendrix. "A Cross-Cultural Test of Collins' Theory of Sexual Stratification." *Journal of Marriage and the Family* 44 (1982): 675–84.

Johnson, Miriam M. "Instrumental and Expressive Components in the Personalities of Women." Ph.D. dissertation, Department of Social Relations, Harvard University, 1955.

———. "Sex Role Learning in the Nuclear Family." *Child Development* 34 (1963): 319–33.

———. "Fathers, Mothers and Sex Typing." *Sociological Inquiry* 45 (1975): 15–26.

———. "Androgyny and the Maternal Principle." *School Review* 86 (1977): 50–69.

———. Review of *The Reproduction of Mothering*, by Nancy Chodorow. *Harvard Educational Review* 50 (1980): 98–101.

———. "Heterosexuality, Male Dominance, and the Father Image." *Sociological Inquiry* 51 (1981): 129–39.

———. "Fathers and 'Femininity' in Daughters: A Review of the Research." *Sociology and Social Research* 67 (1982): 1–17.

———. Review of *The Myth of Masculinity*, by Joseph Pleck. *American Journal of Sociology* 88 (1983): 1336–38.

———. "Reproducing Male Dominance: Psychoanalysis and Social Structure." In Jerome Rabow, Gerald Platt, and Marion S. Goldman, eds., *Advances in Psychoanalytic Sociology.* Malabar, FL: Krieger, 1987.

Johnson, Miriam M., Jean Stockard, Joan Acker, and Claudeen Naffziger. "Expressiveness Re-evaluated." *School Review* 83 (1975): 617–44.

Johnson, Miriam M., Jean Stockard, Mary Rothbart, and Lisa Friedman. "Sexual Preference, Feminism, and Women's Perceptions of Their Parents." *Sex Roles* 6, no. 1 (1981): 1–18.

Johnston, Jill. *Lesbian Nation: The Feminist Solution.* New York: Simon and Schuster, 1973.

Jones, Warren H., M. E. Chernhovetz, and R. O. Hansson. "The Enigma of Androgyny: Differential Implications for Males and Females?" *Journal of Consulting and Clinical Psychology* 46 (1978): 298–313.

Jourard, Sidney M., and Jane E. Robin. "Self-Disclosure and Touching: A Study of Two Modes of Interpersonal Encounter and Their Interrelation." *Journal of Humanistic Psychology* 8 (1968): 39–48.

Kaats, Gilbert R., and Keith E. Davis. "The Dynamics of Sexual Behavior of College Students." *Journal of Marriage and the Family* 32 (1970): 390–99.

Kamerman, Sheila B. "Child Care Services: An Issue for Gender Equity and Women's Solidarity." *Child Welfare* 64 (1985): 259–71.

Kanin, Eugene J. "Date Rape: Differential Sexual Socialization and Relative Deprivation." *Victimology* 9 (1984): 95–108.

———. "Date Rapists: Differential Sexual Socialization and Relative Deprivation." *Archives of Sexual Behavior* 14 (1985): 219–31.

Kanin, Eugene J., and Stanley R. Parcell. "Sexual Aggression: A Second Look at the Offended Female." *Archives of Sexual Behavior* 6 (1977): 67–76.

Kanter, Rosabeth Moss. "Women and the Structure of Organizations: Explorations in Theory and Behavior." In Marcia Millman and Rosabeth M. Kanter, eds., *Another Voice*, pp. 34–74. Garden City, NY: Doubleday, 1975.

Kaplan, Alexandra G., and Joan P. Bean, eds. *Beyond Sex-Role Stereotypes: Readings Toward a Psychology of Androgyny.* Boston: Little, Brown, 1976.

Kaye, Harvey E., Soll Berl, Jack Clare, Mary R. Eleston, Benjamin S. Gershwin, Patricia Gershwin, Leonard S. Kogan, Clara Torda, and Cornelia B. Wilbur. "Homosexuality in Women." *Archives of General Psychiatry* 17 (1967): 626–34.

Keller, Evelyn Fox. "Gender and Science." *Psychoanalysis and Contemporary Thought* 1 (1978): 409–33.

———. "Feminism and Science." *Signs* 7 (1982): 589–602.

———. *Reflections on Gender and Science.* New Haven: Yale University Press, 1985.

Kelly, Joan B. "Divorce: The Adult Perspective." In Benjamin B. Wolman, ed., *Handbook of Developmental Psychology.* Englewood Cliffs, NJ: Prentice-Hall, 1982.

Keniston, Kenneth. *The Uncommitted: Alienated Youth in American Society.* New York: Harcourt, Brace and World, 1960.

Kessler, Suzanne J., and Wendy McKenna. *Gender: An Ethnomethodological Approach.* New York: John Wiley, 1978.

Kinsey, Alfred C., Wardell B. Pomeroy, and Clyde E. Martin. *Sexual Behavior in the Human Male.* Philadelphia: Saunders, 1948.

Kinsey, Alfred C., Wardell B. Pomeroy, Clyde E. Martin, and Paul H. Gebhard. *Sexual Behavior in the Human Female.* Philadelphia: Saunders, 1953.

Kitson, Gay C., and Marvin B. Sussman. "Marital Complaints, Demographic Characteristics, and Symptoms of Mental Distress in Divorce." *Journal of Marriage and the Family* 44 (1982): 87–101.

Kittay, Eva. "Womb Envy: An Explanatory Concept." In Joyce Trebilcot, ed., *Mothering: Essays in Feminist Theory.* Totowa, NJ: Rowman and Allanheld, 1984.

Klein, Melanie. "Early Stages of the Oedipus Conflict." *International Journal of Psycho-Analysis* (1928): 167–80.

———. *The Psychoanalysis of Children.* 1932. New York: Grove, 1960.

Koedt, Anne. "The Myth of the Vaginal Orgasm." In Anne Koedt, Ellen Levine, and Anita Rapone, eds., *Radical Feminism.* New York: The New York Times Book Co., Quadrangle, 1973.

Kohlberg, Lawrence. "A Cognitive-Developmental Analysis of Children's Sex Role Concepts and Attitudes." In Eleanor Maccoby, ed., *The Development of Sex Differences.* Stanford, CA: Stanford University Press, 1966.

Kohlberg, Lawrence, and E. Zigler. "The Impact of Cognitive Maturity on the Development of Sex Role Attitudes in the Years 4 to 8." *Genetic Psychology Monographs* 75 (1967): 89–165.

Kundsin, Ruth B., ed. *Women and Success: The Anatomy of Achievement.* New York: William Morrow, 1974.

Lamb, Michael E., and Jamie E. Lamb. "The Nature and Importance of the Father-Infant Relationship." *The Family Coordinator* 25 (1976): 379–87.

Lamphere, Louise. "Review Essay: Anthropology." *Signs* 2 (1977): 612–27.

Langford, Charles. "Religion and Occupational Choice: A Study of Pacific Northwest High School Seniors." Ph.D. dissertation, Department of Sociology, University of Oregon, 1971.

Langlois, Judith, and A. Chris Downs. "Mothers, Fathers and Peers as Socialization Agents of Sex-Typed Play Behaviors in Young Children." *Child Development* 51 (1980): 1217–47.

Laslett, Barbara. "Family Membership, Past and Present." *Social Problems* 25 (1978): 476–90.

Lehne, Gregory K. "Homophobia Among Men." In Deborah S. David and Robert Brannon, eds., *The Forty-Nine Percent Majority: The Male Sex Role*, Reading, MA: Addison-Wesley, 1976.

Leibowitz, Lila. *Females, Males, Families: A Biosocial Approach.* North Scituate, MA: Wadsworth, Duxbury Press, 1978.

Lever, Janet. "Sex Differences in the Games Children Play." *Social Problems* 23 (1976): 478–87.

Levinger, George. "Sources of Marital Dissatisfaction Among Applicants for Divorce." *American Journal of Orthopsychiatry* 36 (1966): 803–7.

Lévi-Strauss, Claude. *The Elementary Structures of Kinship.* Boston: Beacon, 1969.

Lewin, Miriam. "Psychological Measures of Femininity and Masculinity: From '13 Gay Men' to the Instrumental Expressive Distinction." In M. Lewin, ed., *In the Shadow of the Past: Psychology Portrays the Sexes.* New York: Columbia University Press, 1984.

Lewis, Charlie. *Becoming a Father.* Philadelphia: Open University Press, Milton Keynes, 1986.

Lewis, Diane K. "The Black Family: Socialization and Sex Roles." *Phylon* 36 (1975): 221–37.

Lewis, Edwin C. *Developing Woman's Potential.* Ames: Iowa State University Press, 1968.

Lipman-Blumen, Jean. *Gender Roles and Power.* Englewood Cliffs, NJ: Prentice-Hall, 1984.

Lloyd, Peter C. "The Yoruba of Nigeria." In James L. Gibbs, ed., *Peoples of Africa.* New York: Holt, Rinehart and Winston, 1965.

Locksley, Anne, and Mary Ellen Cotten. "Psychological Androgyny: A Case of Mistaken Identity." *Journal of Personality and Social Psychology* 37 (1979): 1017–31.

Loney, Jan. "Family Dynamics in Homosexual Women." *Archives of Sexual Behavior* 2 (1973): 343–50.

Lorber, Judith. "Minimalist and Maximalist Feminist Ideologies and Strategies for Change." *Quarterly Journal of Ideology* 5 (1981): 61–66.

Lorde, Audre. *Sister Outsider.* Trumansburg, NY: Crossing Press, 1984.

Lowe, Marian, and Ruth Hubbard, eds. *Woman's Nature: Rationalizations of Inequality.* New York: Pergamon, 1983.

Lundberg, Ferdinand, and Marynia F. Farnham. *Modern Woman, the Lost Sex.* New York: Harper, 1947.

Luttrell, Wendy. "Beyond the Politics of Victimization." *Socialist Review* 14 (1984): 42–47.

McBroom, William H. "Parental Relationships, Socioeconomic Status, and Sex-Role Expectations." *Sex Roles* 7 (1981): 1027–33.

Maccoby, Eleanor. *Social Development: Psychological Growth and the Parent-Child Relationship.* New York: Harcourt Brace Jovanovich, 1980.

———. "Social Groupings in Childhood: Their Relationship to Prosocial Behavior in Boys and Girls." In D. Olwens, Jack Block, and Marian Radke-Yarrow, eds., *Development of Antisocial and Prosocial Behavior.* Orlando, FL: Academic Press, 1985.

———, ed. *Development of Sex Differences.* Stanford, CA: Stanford University Press, 1966.

Maccoby, Eleanor, and Carol Nagy Jacklin. *The Psychology of Sex Differences.* Stanford, CA: Stanford University Press, 1974.

———. "Sex Differences in Aggression." *Child Development* 51 (1980): 964–80.

———. "Gender Segregation in Childhood." In Hayne W. Reese, ed., *Advances in Child Development and Behavior* 20. New York: Academic Press, 1987.

MacKinnon, Catharine. *Sexual Harassment of Working Women: A Case of Sex Discrimination.* New Haven: Yale University Press, 1979.

———. "Feminism, Marxism, Method, and the State: An Agenda for Theory." *Signs* 7 (1982): 515–44.

———. "Feminism, Marxism, Method, and the State: Toward Feminist Jurisprudence." *Signs* 8 (1983): 635–58.

———. *Feminism Unmodified.* Cambridge: Harvard University Press, 1987.

Maltz, D. N., and R. A. Borker. "A Cultural Approach to Male-Female Miscommunication." In J. J. Gumperz, ed., *Language and Social Identity.* New York: Cambridge University Press, 1982.

Mansbridge, Jane J. "Myth and Reality: The ERA and the Gender Gap in the 1980 Election." *Public Opinion Quarterly* 49 (1985): 164–78.

Marini, Margaret Mooney. "Age and Sequencing Norms in the Transition to Adulthood." *Social Forces* 63 (1984): 229–44.

Margolin, Gayla, and Gerald R. Patterson. "Differential Consequences Provided by Mothers and Fathers for Their Sons and Daughters." *Developmental Psychology* 11 (1975): 537–38.

Martin, Judith. "Maternal and Paternal Abuse of the Children: Theoretical and Research Perspectives." In David Finkelhor, Richard J. Gelles, Gerald T. Hotaling, and Murray A. Straus, eds., *The Dark Side of Families: Current Family Violence Research*. Beverly Hills, CA: Sage, 1983.

Masson, Jeffrey. *The Assault on Truth: Freud's Suppression of the Seduction Theory*. New York: Farrar, Straus and Giroux, 1984.

———. "The Persecution and Expulsion of Jeffrey Masson: As Performed by Members of the Freudian Establishment and Reported by Janet Malcolm of *The New Yorker*." *Mother Jones* (December 1984): 35–37, 42–47.

Masters, William, and Virginia Johnson. *Human Sexual Response*. Boston: Little, Brown, 1966.

———. *Human Sexual Inadequacy*. Boston: Little, Brown, 1970.

———. *Homosexuality in Perspective*. Boston: Little, Brown, 1979.

Matthews, Wendy. "Sex-Role Perception: Portrayal and Perception in the Fantasy Play of Young Children." *Sex Roles* 7 (1981): 979–87.

Mead, Margaret. "On Freud's View of Female Psychology." In Jean Strouse, ed., *Women and Analysis*. New York: Grossman, 1974.

Meiselman, Karin C. *Incest*. San Francisco: Jossey-Bass, 1978.

Miller, Jean Baker. *Toward a New Psychology of Women*. Boston: Beacon, 1976.

Miller, Walter D. "Lower Class Culture as a Generating Milieu of Gang Delinquency." 1958. In Marvin E. Wolfgang, Leonard Savitz, and Norman Johnston, eds., *The Sociology of Crime and Delinquency*. New York: John Wiley, 1962.

Mitchell, Juliet. "On Freud and the Distinction Between the Sexes." In Jean Strouse, ed., *Women and Analysis*. New York: Grossman, 1974.

———. *Psychoanalysis and Feminism*. New York: Vintage, 1974.

———. *Women, The Longest Revolution: Essays on Feminism, Literature, and Psychoanalysis*. London: Vintage, 1984.

Money, John. *Love and Love Sickness*. Baltimore: Johns Hopkins University Press, 1980.

———. "The Conceptual Neutering of Gender and the Criminalization of Sex." *Archives of Sexual Behavior* 14 (1985): 279–90.

Money, John, and Anke A. Ehrhardt. *Man and Woman, Boy and Girl*. Baltimore: Johns Hopkins University Press, 1972.

Morgan, Kathryn P. "Androgyny: A Conceptual Critique." *Social Theory and Practice* 8 (1982): 245–83.

Morgan, Marabel. *The Total Woman*. New York: Pocket Books, 1975.

Moscovici, Serge. *Society Against Nature*. 1972. Trans. by Sacha Rabinovitch. Atlantic Highlands, NJ: Humanities Press, 1976.

Myron, Nancy, and Charlotte Bunch, eds. *Lesbianism and the Women's Movement*. Oakland, CA: Diana Press, 1975.

Newson, John, and Elizabeth Newson. *Four Years Old in an Urban Community*. Harmondsworth, England: Pelican, 1968.

Newton, Niles. *Maternal Emotions*. New York: Paul B. Hoeber, 1955.

———. "Interrelationships between Sexual Responsiveness, Birth, and Breast Feeding." In Joseph Zubin and John Money, eds., *Contemporary Sexual Behavior: Critical Issues in the 1970s*. Baltimore: Johns Hopkins University Press, 1973.

O'Brien, Denise. "Female Husbands in Southern Bantu Societies." In Alice Schlegel, ed., *Sexual Stratification*. New York: Columbia University Press, 1977.

O'Brien, Mary. "The Dialectics of Reproduction." *Women's Studies International Quarterly* 1 (1978): 233–39.

———. *The Politics of Reproduction*. Boston: Routledge and Kegan Paul, 1981.

Oppenheimer, Valerie. "The Sociology of Women's Economic Role in the Family." *American Sociological Review* 42 (1977): 387–406.

Ortner, Sherry. "The Virgin and the State." *Feminist Studies* 4 (1978): 19–35.

Osofsky, J. D., and E. J. O'Connell. "Parent-Child Interaction: Daughters' Effects Upon Mothers' and Fathers' Behaviors." *Developmental Psychology* 7 (1972): 157–68.

Paige, Karen Ericksen, and Jeffery M. Paige. *The Politics of Reproductive Ritual*. Berkeley and Los Angeles: University of California Press, 1981.

Parke, Ross D. *Fathers*. Cambridge: Harvard University Press, 1981.

Parke, Ross D., and D. B. Sawin. "Children's Privacy in the Home: Developmental, Ecological and Child-Rearing Determinants." *Environment and Behavior* 11 (1979): 87–104.

Parke, Ross D., and Barbara R. Tinsley. "The Father's Role in Infancy: Determinants of Involvement in Caregiving and Play." In Michael E. Lamb, ed., *The Role of the Father in Child Development*, 2d ed. New York: John Wiley, 1981.

Parker, Hilda, and Seymour Parker. "Father-Daughter Sexual Abuse: An Emerging Perspective." *American Journal of Orthopsychiatry* 56 (1986): 531–49.

Parsons, Anne. "Is the Oedipus Complex Universal?" In Robert McVicker Hunt, ed. *Personalities and Cultures*. Garden City, NY: Natural History Press, 1967.

Parsons, Talcott. *The Social System*. Glencoe, IL: Free Press, 1951.

———. *Essays in Sociological Theory*. Rev. ed. Glencoe, IL: Free Press, 1954.

———. "The Position of Identity in the General Theory of Action." In Chad Gordon and Kenneth J. Gergen, eds., *The Self in Social Interaction*. New York: John Wiley, 1968.

———. *Social Structure and Personality*. New York: Macmillan, Free Press, 1970.

Parsons, Talcott, and Robert F. Bales. *Family Socialization and Interaction Process*. Glencoe, IL: Free Press, 1955.

Parsons, Talcott, Robert F. Bales, and Edward Shils. *Working Papers in the Theory of Action*. Glencoe, IL: Free Press, 1953.

Parsons, Talcott, and Edward Shils. *Toward a General Theory of Action*. Cambridge: Harvard University Press, 1952.

Pederson, Frank A., ed. *The Father-Infant Relationship: Observational Studies in the Family Setting*. New York: Praeger, 1980.

Pedhazur, Elazar, and Toby Tetenbaum. "Bem Sex Role Inventory: A Theoretical and Methodological Critique." *Journal of Personality and Social Psychology* 37 (1979): 996–1016.

Person, Ethel Spector. "Sexuality as the Mainstay of Identity: Psychoanalytic Perspectives." *Signs* 5 (1980): 605–30.

Peterfreund, Emanuel. "Some Critical Comments on Psycho-analytic Conceptualizations of Infancy." *International Journal of Psycho-Analysis* 59 (1978): 427–41.

Philipson, Ilene. "Narcissism and Mothering: The 1950s Reconsidered." *Women's Studies International Forum* 5 (1982): 29–40.

Pleck, Joseph. "Men's Power with Women, Other Men, and Society." In Elizabeth H. Pleck and Joseph H. Pleck, eds., *The American Man*. Englewood Cliffs, NJ: Prentice-Hall, 1980.

———. *The Myth of Masculinity*. Cambridge: MIT Press, 1981.

———. *Working Wives/Working Husbands*. Beverly Hills, CA: Sage, 1985.

Polatnick, M. Rivka. "Why Men Don't Rear Children: A Power Analysis." In Joyce Trebilcot, ed., *Mothering: Essays in Feminist Theory*. Totowa, NJ: Rowman and Allanheld, 1983.

Pogrebin, Letty. *Growing Up Free*. New York: McGraw-Hill, 1980.

Poole, Keith T., and L. Harmon Zeigler. *Women, Public Opinion, and Politics*. New York: Longman, 1985.

Radin, Norma. "Childrearing Fathers in Intact Families." I: "Some Antecedents and Consequences." *Merrill-Palmer Quarterly* 27 (1981): 489–514.

———. "The Role of the Father in Cognitive, Academic and Intellectual

Development." In Michael Lamb, ed., *The Role of the Father in Child Development*, 2d ed., New York: John Wiley, 1981.

Radway, Janice A. *Reading the Romance: Women, Patriarchy, and Popular Literature.* Chapel Hill: University of North Carolina Press, 1984.

Raymond, Janice G. *The Transsexual Empire: The Making of the She-Male.* Boston: Beacon, 1979.

Reage, Pauline. *The Story of O.* Trans. by S. D'Estree. New York: Ballantine, 1965.

Reiss, Ira L. *Journey Into Sexuality: An Exploratory Voyage.* Englewood Cliffs, NJ: Prentice-Hall, 1986.

————. "A Sociological Journey into Sexuality." *Journal of Marriage and the Family* 48 (1986): 233–42.

Rich, Adrienne. *Of Woman Born: Motherhood as Experience and Institution.* New York: W. W. Norton, 1976.

————. "Compulsory Heterosexuality and Lesbian Existence." *Signs* 5 (1980): 631–60.

Ricks, Shirley S. "Father-Infant Interactions: A Review of the Empirical Literature." *Family Relations* 34 (1985): 505–11.

Ringelheim, Joan. "Women and the Holocaust: A Reconsideration of Research." *Signs* 10 (1985): 741–61.

Roberts, Elizabeth J., David Kline, and John Gagnon. *Family Life and Sexual Learning.* Vol. 1, *Summary Report.* Prepared by Project on Human Sexual Development. Cambridge, MA: Population Education, 1978.

Robinson, Marie N. *The Power of Sexual Surrender.* New York: Doubleday, 1959.

Roebuck, Janet. "Grandma as Revolutionary: Elderly Women and Some Modern Patterns of Social Change." *International Journal of Aging and Human Development* 17 (1983): 249–66.

Rohrer, John H., and Munro Edmonson. *The Eighth Generation.* New York: Harper, 1960.

Rosaldo, M. Z. "The Use and Abuse of Anthropology: Reflections on Feminism and Cross-Cultural Understanding." *Signs* 5 (1980): 389–417.

Ross, Heather L., and Isabel V. Sawhill. *Time of Transition: The Growth of Families Headed by Women.* Washington, DC: Urban Institute, 1975.

Ross, John Munder. "Towards Fatherhood: The Epigenesis of Paternal Identity During a Boy's First Decade." *International Review of Psychoanalysis* 4 (1977): 327–47.

————. "Fathering: A Review of Some Psychoanalytic Contributions on Paternity." *International Journal of Psycho-Analysis* 60 (1979): 317–27.

Rossi, Alice. "Equality Between the Sexes: An Immodest Proposal." *Daedalus* 93 (1964): 607–52.

―――. "Transition to Parenthood." *Journal of Marriage and the Family* 30 (1968): 26–39.

―――. "Maternalism, Sexuality, and the New Feminism." In Joseph Zubin and John Money, eds., *Contemporary Sexual Behavior: Critical Issues in the 1970's*. Baltimore: Johns Hopkins University Press, 1973.

―――. "A Biosocial Perspective on Parenting." *Daedalus* 106 (1977): 1–31.

―――. "Gender and Parenthood." *American Sociological Review* 49 (1984): 1–19.

Rothbart, Mary K., and Eleanor E. Maccoby. "Parents' Differential Reactions to Sons and Daughters." *Journal of Personality and Social Psychology* 4 (1966): 237–43.

Rothman, Sheila M. *Woman's Proper Place: A History of Changing Ideals and Practices*. New York: Basic Books, 1978.

Roy, Manisha. "The Concepts of 'Femininity' and 'Liberation' in the Context of Changing Sex Roles: Women in Modern India and America." In Dana Raphael, ed., *Being Female: Reproduction, Power and Change*. Chicago: Aldine, 1975.

Rubin, Gayle. "The Traffic in Women: Notes on the Political Economy of Sex." In Rayna Rapp Reiter, ed., *Toward an Anthropology of Women*. New York: Monthly Review Press, 1975.

―――. "Thinking Sex: Notes for a Radical Theory of the Politics of Sexuality." In Carole S. Vance, ed., *Pleasure and Danger: Exploring Female Sexuality*. Boston: Routledge and Kegan Paul, 1984.

Rubin, Jeffrey Z., Frank J. Provenzano, and Zella Luria. "The Eye of the Beholder: Parents' Views on Sex of Newborns." In Alexandra G. Kaplan and Joan P. Bean, eds., *Beyond Sex-Role Stereotypes: Readings Toward a Psychology of Androgyny*. Boston: Little, Brown, 1976.

Rubin, Lillian B. "Blue Collar Marriage and the Sexual Revolution." In L. Rubin, *Worlds of Pain: Life in the Working Class Family*. New York: Basic Books, 1978.

―――. *Women of a Certain Age: The Midlife Search for Self*. New York: Harper and Row, 1979.

―――. *Intimate Strangers: Men and Women Together*. New York: Harper and Row, 1983.

―――. *Just Friends: The Role of Friendship in Our Lives*. New York: Harper and Row, 1985.

Ruddick, Sara. "Maternal Thinking." In Barrie Thorne with Marilyn Yalom, eds., *Rethinking the Family: Some Feminist Questions*, pp. 76–94. New York: Longman, 1982. Reprinted in Joyce Trebilcot, ed., *Mothering: Essays in Feminist Theory*. Totowa, NJ: Rowman and Allanheld, 1984.

―――. "Pacifying the Forces: Drafting Women in the Interests of Peace."

Signs 8 (1983): 471–89. Reprinted in Joyce Trebilcot, ed., *Mothering: Essays in Feminist Theory.* Totowa, NJ: Rowman and Allanheld, 1984.

Rush, Florence. "The Sexual Abuse of Children: A Feminist Point of View." In Noreen Connell and Cassandra Wilson, eds., *Rape: The First Sourcebook for Women.* New York: New American Library, 1974.

——. "A Freudian Cover-Up." In F. Rush, *The Best Kept Secret: Sexual Abuse of Children.* New York: McGraw-Hill, 1980.

Russell, Diana E. H. *Rape in Marriage.* New York: MacMillan, 1982.

——. *Sexual Exploitation: Rape, Child Sexual Abuse and Workplace Harassment.* Beverly Hills, CA: Sage, 1984.

Ryan, Mary P. *Womanhood in America: From Colonial Times to the Present,* 3d ed. New York: Franklin Watts, 1983.

Sacks, Karen. *Sisters and Wives: The Past and Future of Sexual Equality.* Westport, CT: Greenwood, 1979.

Safilios-Rothschild, Constantina. *Love, Sex and Sex Roles.* Englewood Cliffs, NJ: Prentice-Hall, 1977.

Saghir, Marcel T., and Eli Robins. *Male and Female Homosexuality: A Comprehensive Investigation.* Baltimore: Williams and Wilkins, 1973.

Sayers, Janet. *Biological Politics: Feminist and Anti-Feminist Perspectives.* New York: Tavistock, 1982.

Schafer, Roy. "Problems in Freud's Psychology of Women." *Journal of the American Psychoanalytic Association* 22 (1974): 459–85.

Schlegel, Alice. "Male and Female in Hopi Thought and Action." In A. Schlegel, ed., *Sexual Stratification.* New York: Columbia University Press, 1977.

Schneider, David M. "The Distinctive Features of Matrilineal Descent Groups." In David M. Schneider and Kathleen Gough, eds., *Matrilineal Kinship.* Berkeley and Los Angeles: University of California Press, 1961.

Schulz, Muriel. "Rape is a Four-Letter Word." *Etc: A Review of General Semantics* 32 (1975): 65–69.

Schwarzer, Alice. *After the Second Sex: Conversations with Simone de Beauvoir.* New York: Pantheon, 1984.

Scott, Joan W., and Louise A. Tilly. "Women's Work and the Family in Nineteenth-Century Europe." In Charles E. Rosenberg, ed., *The Family in History.* Philadelphia: University of Pennsylvania Press, 1975.

Shaktini, Namascar. "Displacing the Phallic Subject: Wittig's Lesbian Writing." *Signs* 8 (1982): 29–44.

Shapiro, Robert Y., and Harpreet Mahajan. "Gender Differences in Policy Preferences: A Summary of Trends from the 1960s to the 1980s." *Public Opinion Quarterly* 59 (1986): 42–61.

Sheleff, Leon. *Generations Apart.* New York: McGraw-Hill, 1981.

Shulman, Alix Kates. "The War in the Back Seat." In Peter J. Stein, Judith Richman, and Natalie Hannon, eds., *The Family: Functions, Conflicts, and Symbols.* Reading, MA: Addison-Wesley, 1977.

Slater, Philip. *The Glory of Hera: Greek Mythology and the Greek Family.* Boston: Beacon, 1968.

———. "Because She's There or Social Climbing Begins at Home." In P. Slater, *Earthwalk.* New York: Anchor, 1974.

Stayton, Donelda J., Robert Hogan, and Mary D. Salter Ainsworth. "Infant Obedience and Maternal Behavior: The Origins of Socialization Reconsidered." *Child Development* 42 (1971): 1057–69.

Smith, Dorothy. "Women's Perspective as a Radical Critique of Sociology." *Sociological Inquiry* 44 (1974): 7–13.

———. "A Sociology for Women." In Julia A. Sherman and Evelyn T. Beck, eds., *The Prism of Sex: Essays in the Sociology of Knowledge,* pp. 135–87. Madison: University of Wisconsin Press, 1979.

Smith-Rosenberg, Carroll. "The Female World of Love and Ritual: Relations between Women in Nineteenth-Century America." *Signs* 1 (1975): 1–29.

———. "The New Woman as Androgyne: Social Disorder and Gender Crisis, 1870–1936." In C. Smith-Rosenberg, *Disorderly Conduct: Visions of Gender in Victorian America.* New York: Knopf, 1985.

Snitow, Ann, Christine Stansell, and Sharon Thompson. Introduction to A. Snitow, C. Stansell, and S. Thompson, eds., *The Powers of Desire: The Politics of Sexuality.* New York: Monthly Review Press, 1983.

Snow, M., Carol Jacklin, and Eleanor Maccoby. "Sex-of-Child Differences in Father-Child Interaction at One Year of Age." *Child Development* 54 (1983): 227–32.

Spence, Janet T., and Robert L. Helmreich. *Masculinity and Femininity.* Austin: University of Texas Press, 1978.

Spender, Dale. "The Politics of Naming." In D. Spender, *Man Made Language.* Boston: Routledge and Kegan Paul, 1980.

Stacey, Judith. "The New Conservative Feminism." *Feminist Studies* 9 (1983): 559–83.

Stacey, Judith, and Barrie Thorne. "The Missing Feminist Revolution in Sociology." *Social Problems* 32 (1985): 301–16.

Stack, Carol B. *All Our Kin.* New York: Harper and Row, 1974.

Stephan, Walter G. "Parental Relationships and Early Social Experiences of Activist Male Homosexuals and Male Heterosexuals." *Journal of Abnormal Psychology* 82 (1973): 506–13.

Stern, Daniel. "The Early Development of Schemas of Self, of Other and of Various Experiences of Self with Other." In J. Lichtenberg and S.

Kaplan, eds., *Reflections on Self Psychology*. Hillsdale, NJ: Analytic Press, 1983.

———. *The Interpersonal World of the Infant: A View from Psycho-analysis and Developmental Psychology*. New York: Basic Books, 1985.

Stevens, Evelyn P. "The Prospects for a Women's Liberation Movement in Latin America." In Peter J. Stein, Judith Richman, and Natalie Hannon, eds., *The Family: Functions, Conflicts, and Symbols*. Reading, MA: Addison-Wesley, 1977.

Stille, Marcia L. "Marrying Daddy? The Appeal of the Contemporary Series Romance Novel." Unpublished paper, Interdisciplinary Masters Project at the University of Oregon, 1986.

Stockard, Jean, and Miriam M. Johnson. "The Social Origins of Male Dominance." *Sex Roles* 5 (1979): 199–218.

———. *Sex Roles: Sex Inequality and Sex Role Development*. Englewood Cliffs, NJ: Prentice-Hall, 1980.

Stockard, Jean, and J. Walter Wood. "The Myth of Female Underachievement: A Reexamination of Sex Differences in Academic Underachievement." *American Educational Research Journal* 21, no. 3 (1984): 825–38.

Stoller, Robert J. *Sex and Gender*. New York: Science House, 1968.

———. "Facts and Fancies: An Examination of Freud's Concept of Bisexuality." In Jean Strouse, ed., *Women and Analysis*. New York: Grossman, 1974.

———. *Sex and Gender*. Vol. 2. New York: Science House, 1976.

———. *Sexual Excitement: The Dynamics of Erotic Life*. New York: Pantheon, 1979.

———. "A Different View of Oedipal Conflict." In Stanley I. Greenspan and George H. Pollock, eds., *The Course of Life: Psychoanalytic Contributions Toward Understanding Personality Development*. Vol. 1, *Infancy and Early Childhood*. Washington, D.C. (U.S. Department of Health and Human Services): U.S. Government Printing Office, 1980.

———. "Femininity." In Martha Kirkpatrick, ed., *Women's Sexual Development*. New York: Plenum, 1980.

———. *Presentations of Gender*. New Haven: Yale University Press, 1985.

——— "Psychoanalytic 'Research' on Homosexuality: The Rules of the Game." In R. J. Stoller, *Observing the Erotic Imagination*. New Haven: Yale University Press, 1985.

Strathern, Marilyn. "Domesticity and the Denigration of Women." In Denise O'Brien and W. Tiffany, eds., *Rethinking Women's Roles*. Berkeley and Los Angeles: University of California Press, 1984.

Swidler, Ann. "Love and Adulthood in American Culture." In Neil J. Smelser and Erik H. Erikson, eds., *Themes of Work and Love in Adulthood.* Cambridge: Harvard University Press, 1980.

Symons, Donald. *The Evolution of Human Sexuality.* New York: Oxford University Press, 1979.

Tanner, Nancy. "Matrifocality in Indonesia and Africa and Among Black Americans," in Michelle Rosaldo and Louise Lamphere, eds., *Woman, Culture and Society.* Stanford, CA: Stanford University Press, 1974.

Thompson, Norman L., Jr., David M. Schwartz, Boyd R. McCandless, and David A. Edwards. "Parent-Child Relationships and Sexual Identity in Male and Female Homosexuals and Heterosexuals." *Journal of Consulting and Clinical Psychology* 41, no. 1 (1973): 120–27.

Thorne, Barrie. "Gender—How Is It Best Conceptualized?" In James Wirtenberg and Barbara Richardson, eds., *Methodological Issues In Sex Roles and Social Change.* New York: Praeger, 1980.

———. "Girls and Boys Together . . . But Mostly Apart: Gender Arrangements in Elementary Schools." In William W. Hartup and Zick Rubin, eds., *Relationships and Development.* Hillsdale, NJ: Erlbaum, 1985.

Tiger, Lionel. *Men in Groups.* New York: Random House, 1969.

Tiger, Lionel, and Robin Fox. *The Imperial Animal.* New York: Dell, 1974.

Tooley, Kay. "Johnny, I Hardly Knew Ye." *American Journal of Orthopsychiatry* 47 (1977): 184–91.

Trebilcot, Joyce, ed. *Mothering: Essays in Feminist Theory.* Totowa, NJ: Rowman and Allanheld, 1983.

Tresemer, David E. "Assumptions Made About Gender Roles." In Marcia Millman and Rosabeth Moss Kanter, eds., *Another Voice.* New York: Doubleday, 1975.

Tripp, C. A. *The Homosexual Matrix.* New York: New American Library, 1975.

Ullian, Dora. "'Why Girls Are Good': A Constructivist View." *Sex Roles* 11 (1974): 241–56.

———. "Regression in the Service of the Male Ego." Speech delivered at the Massachusetts Psychological Association convention at Wheelock College, 1979.

Unger, Rhoda K. *Female and Male: Psychological Perspectives.* New York: Harper and Row, 1979.

Valeska, Lucia. "If All Else Fails, I'm Still a Mother." In Joyce Trebilcot, ed., *Mothering: Essays in Feminist Theory.* Totowa, NJ: Rowman and Allanheld, 1983.

Vanek, Joann. "Household Work, Wage Work and Sexual Equality." In
  Sarah Fenstermaker Berk, ed., *Women and Household Labor*, pp. 275–
  91. Beverly Hills, CA: Sage, 1980.
Waite, Linda J., Frances K. Goldscheider, and Christina Witsberger.
  "Nonfamily Living and the Erosion of Traditional Family Orientations
  Among Young Adults." *American Sociological Review* 51 (1986):
  541–54.
Walker, Alice. *The Color Purple*. New York: Harcourt Brace Jovanovich,
  1982.
Walkowitz, Judith, Ellen Dubois, Mari Jo Buhle, Temma Kaplan, Gerda
  Lerner, Carroll Smith-Rosenberg. "Politics and Culture in Women's
  History: A Symposium" *Feminist Studies* 6 (1980): 26–64.
Wallerstein, Judith S., and Joan B. Kelly. *Surviving the Breakup: How
  Children and Parents Cope with Divorce*. New York: Basic Books,
  1980.
Walters, Margaret C. "The Rights and Wrongs of Women: Mary Woll-
  stonecraft, Harriet Martineau, Simone de Beauvoir." In Juliet Mitchell
  and Ann Oakley, eds., *The Rights and Wrongs of Women*, pp. 304–78.
  New York: Penguin, 1976.
Weiner, Annette B. "Trobriand Descent: Female Male Domains." *Ethos*
  5 (1977): 54–70.
Weisskopf, Susan (Contratto). "Maternal Sexuality and Asexual Mother-
  hood." *Signs* 5 (1980): 766–82.
Weisstein, Naomi. "'Kinder, Küche, Kirche' As Scientific Law: Psychol-
  ogy Constructs the Female." In Robin Morgan, ed., *Sisterhood is
  Powerful*. New York: Vintage, 1970.
Weitzman, Lenore J. *The Divorce Revolution: The Unexpected Social and
  Economic Consequences for Women and Children in America*. New
  York: Macmillan, Free Press, 1985.
West, Candice, and Don H. Zimmerman. "Small Insults: A Study of In-
  terruptions in Cross-Sex Conversations between Unacquainted Per-
  sons." In Barrie Thorne, Cheris Kramarae, and Nancy Henley, eds.,
  Language, Gender and Society. Rowley, MA: Newbury House, 1983.
Whalen, Jack, and Richard Flacks. *Echoes of Rebellion: The New Left
  Grows Up*. Philadelphia: Temple University Press, 1988.
Whalen, Jack, and Marilyn Whalen. "'Doing Gender' and Children's
  Natural Language Practices." Working Paper no. 23, Center for the
  Study of Women in Society, University of Oregon, 1986.
White, Jacquelyn W. "Sex and Gender Issues in Aggression Research." In
  Russell G. Geen and Edward I. Donnerstein, eds., *Aggression: Theo-
  retical and Empirical Reviews*, Vol. 2. New York: Academic Press,
  1983.

Whitehead, Harriet. "The Bow and the Burden Strap: A New Look at Institutionalized Homosexuality in Native North America." In Sherry B. Ortner and Harriet Whitehead, eds., *Sexual Meanings: The Cultural Construction of Gender and Sexuality.* New York: Cambridge University Press, 1981.

Whiting, Beatrice B. "Sex Identity Conflict and Physical Violence: A Comparative Study." *American Anthropologist* (Special Publication on the Ethnography of Law) 67, no. 6, part 2 (1965): 123–40.

Whiting, Beatrice B., and John W. M. Whiting. *Children of Six Cultures.* Cambridge: Harvard University Press, 1975.

Whiting, John W. M., Richard Kluckhohn, and Albert Anthony. "The Function of Male Initiation Rites at Puberty." In Eleanor E. Maccoby, T. M. Newcomb, and E. L. Hartley, eds., *Readings in Social Psychology.* New York: Holt, Rinehart and Winston, 1958.

Whyte, Martin K. *The Status of Women in Preindustrial Societies.* Princeton, NJ: Princeton University Press, 1978.

Wickert, Gabrielle. "Freud's Heritage: Fathers and Daughters in German Literature (1750–1850)." In Miriam Lewin, ed., *In The Shadow of the Past: Psychology Portrays the Sexes.* New York: Columbia University Press, 1984.

Winch, Robert F. "Further Data and Observations on the Oedipus Hypothesis." *American Sociological Review* 16 (1951): 784–95.

Winnicott, D. W. *Playing and Reality.* New York: Basic Books, 1971.

Witherspoon, Gary. *Navajo Kinship and Marriage.* Chicago: University of Chicago Press, 1975.

Wittig, Monique. *Les Guerillères.* 1971. Reprint. Boston: Beacon, 1985.

———. "One Is Not Born a Woman." *Feminist Issues* 2 (1981): 47–54.

Wolff, Charlotte. *Love Between Women.* London: Duckworth, 1971.

Wylie, Philip. *Generation of Vipers.* 1942. Reprint. New York: Giant Cardinal Pocketbooks, 1959.

Yankelovich, Daniel. *New Rules: Searching for Self-Fulfillment in a World Turned Upside Down.* New York: Bantam, 1982.

Yarrow, Marian Radke, John D. Campbell, and Roger V. Burton. *Child Rearing: An Inquiry into Research and Methods.* San Francisco: Jossey-Bass, 1968.

Young, Iris. "Is Male Gender Identity the Cause of Male Domination?" In Joyce Trebilcot, ed. *Mothering: Essays in Feminist Theory.* Totowa, NJ: Rowman and Allanheld, 1983.

Zilboorg, Gregory. "Masculine and Feminine: Some Biological and Cultural Aspects." *Psychiatry* 7, no. 3 (1944): 257–96.

Zita, Jacquelyn N. "Historical Amnesia and the Lesbian Continuum." *Signs* 7 (1981): 172–78.

Index

Compositor:	G & S Typesetters, Inc.
Text:	11/13 Caledonia
Display:	Caledonia
Printer:	Maple-Vail Book Mfg. Group
Binder:	Maple-Vail Book Mfg. Group